Praise fo

"Richard Borden played an important role in the Ecological Society of America by leading the establishment of a human ecology section that focuses on the relationship between humans and their environment. His book continues his life-long commitment to expand our understanding and appreciation of this relationship."

—KATHERINE MCCARTER, executive director of the Ecological Society of America (ESA)

"If we want to learn how to think of life on a limited planet this is the book to read and absorb. Borden's wide range of experience and thoughts about the beauty of the blend of humans and the natural world will help us develop our own thinking—and maybe make us all into human ecologists. As Borden says: We are surrounded by the deep experience of life everywhere we go. If we can discover ways to be in touch with it, and allow it to touch us, this world will be a better place."

—EVA EKEHORN, trustee, Commonwealth Human Ecology Council (CHEC), UK

"Borden takes us on an amazing journey across time, space, and even mind, which makes us realize the existence of a tacit but strong keynote of the earth—ecology."

—CHIHO WATANABE, professor and head, Department of Human Ecology, University of Tokyo

"If you are at all interested in human ecology, the intersection of mind, nature, and higher education, you must read this indispensable, accessible, wonderful book. Borden respects and understands the rigor of disciplinary research, but reaches beyond its findings and questions to ones that lurk beyond the stream of the analytic mind. In this intellectual tour-de-force, an ultimate magnum opus, Borden offers ways to think and feel the world and ourselves whole, anew."

—GENE MYERS, professor, Huxley College of the Environment, Western Washington University, author of *Children and Animals*, and coauthor of *Conservation Psychology*

"*Ecology and Experience* is a compelling, inviting, and wise book. Richard Borden seamlessly blends intellectual biography and memoir with the dynamic challenge of our time—how to lead an ecologically sound life in a world of daunting change. The book is a conceptual masterpiece, covering an extraordinary range of ideas and concepts, all ultimately connected to human ecology and educational leadership. Whether Borden describes his childhood experiences, his intellectual maturation and development, his pioneering work as an academic dean, or his tireless efforts on behalf of human ecology, his stories and explanations are riveting, insightful, and rewarding. By uncovering the connecting threads of his own life, he helps us understand what matters most to many of us—living a rich and meaningful intellectual life."

>—MITCHELL THOMASHOW, author of *Ecological Identity* and *Bringing the Biosphere Home*

"Professor Borden's book is human ecology. I don't mean it's about human ecology—it is human ecology. It is an essential read . . ."

>—DAVID HALES, president, Second Nature

"In *Ecology and Experience* Richard Borden addresses two fundamental and interlinked questions: "What makes life possible?" and "What makes life worth living?" The result is a unique inquiry, revealing both the development of Borden's quest to understand these questions and inviting the reader to reflect on his own learning experience and future pathways. Such challenges are necessary for us all if we are to collectively create humane, worthwhile, and sustainable futures within which we can flourish."

>—ROBERT DYBALL, convener, Human Ecology program, Fenner School of the Environment, Australian National University; president, Society for Human Ecology; and coauthor of *Understanding Human Ecology*

"This absorbing book is a multi-faceted gem that reveals a different aspect of life and humanity with the turning of every page. Fascinating, innovative, insightful, and inspiring, this book shows how important it is to think laterally about the ways we look at the world, the ways we convey our understanding of the world to others, and the way we teach and learn about ourselves, society, our relationships with others, with other living things, and with the landscapes and oceans of this blue planet."

>—IAN DOUGLAS, emeritus professor, School of Environment and Development, University of Manchester, UK; president, International Council for Ecopolis Development; and author of *Cities: An Environmental History*

ECOLOGY *and* EXPERIENCE

ECOLOGY *and* EXPERIENCE
Reflections from a Human Ecological Perspective

RICHARD J. BORDEN

Foreword by Darron Collins,
president of College of the Atlantic

North Atlantic Books
Berkeley, California

Copyright © 2014 by Richard J. Borden. All rights reserved. No portion of this book, except for brief review, may be reproduced, stored in a retrieval system, or transmitted in any form or by any means—electronic, mechanical, photocopying, recording, or otherwise—without the written permission of the publisher. For information contact North Atlantic Books.

"Desire" by George Bilgere reprinted by permission of the author.

Published by
North Atlantic Books   Cover photo © Zack C/Shutterstock.com
P.O. Box 12327   Cover and book design by Suzanne Albertson
Berkeley, California 94712

Printed in the United States of America

Ecology and Experience: Reflections from a Human Ecological Perspective is sponsored by the Society for the Study of Native Arts and Sciences, a nonprofit educational corporation whose goals are to develop an educational and cross-cultural perspective linking various scientific, social, and artistic fields; to nurture a holistic view of arts, sciences, humanities, and healing; and to publish and distribute literature on the relationship of mind, body, and nature.

North Atlantic Books' publications are available through most bookstores. For further information, visit our website at www.northatlanticbooks.com or call 800-733-3000.

Library of Congress Cataloging-in-Publication Data

Borden, Richard J.
  Ecology and experience : reflections from a human ecological perspective / Richard J. Borden.
     pages cm
  Includes index.
  ISBN 978-1-58394-772-2—ISBN 978-1-58394-785-2

1. Human ecology—Philosophy. I. Title.
GF21.B637 2014
304.2—dc23
2013023677

1 2 3 4 5 6 7 8 9 UNITED 18 17 16 15 14
Printed on recycled paper

To Amy and George—for life and love ...
Andrew and Patricia—for love in life ...
Joe and Bill—for the love of life ...

Acknowledgments

It is impossible to give a full account of everyone who has contributed to this book. First and foremost are the people named on the dedication page: My mother and father—Amy Estelle (Moore) and George Warren Borden, my wife and son—Patricia and Andrew, and my former colleagues Joe Rychlak and Bill Drury. Insofar as I had an audience in mind while writing, they were front and center in my thoughts. The list from there includes my long-standing friends at College of the Atlantic (COA), who invited me to join them and became my closest intellectual companions: Ed Kaelber, COA's founding president and "dream-weaving" tender of the vision ever since; Bill Carpenter, who took me under his wing as a new faculty member and remains an invaluable source of good ideas, as were Dick Davis and Dan Kane, who have passed away. John Visvader and John Anderson joined the faculty later. Both have been treasured colleagues and companions, as well as helpful advisers on philosophical and ecological portions of this project. Former COA presidents Lou Rabineau (deceased) and Steve Katona, with whom I worked closely for years, were fountains of thoughtful mentoring and shared vision. Much could be added here about all of them. But these individuals and their influence are interlaced throughout the forthcoming pages.

The web now spreads in all directions. Other COA faculty who reviewed portions of the manuscript and made valuable comments include: Steve Ressel (on ecology and conservation), Don Cass (for chemistry), Helen Hess (with evolutionary biology, embryology, and morphology), Nishanta Rajakaruna (about botanical evolution and ecology), Sarah Hall and Duane Braun (with geology and geomorphology), John Cooper (on music), and Dru Colbert (about artistic insight)—along with Peter Fuerst (for microbial ecology), from Jackson Laboratory. I would be remiss to not note the special contributions of COA students Peter Wayne, Sean Fitzgerald, and Natalie Barnett—along with the dozens of participants in my thrice-offered Ecology and Experience class in which these ideas were forged. Without their eager involvement and encouragement I could never have made it come together.

On the further reaches of human ecology, I am indebted to many American and international colleagues, but most of all: Wolfgang Preiser, Guido Francescato, Gerald Young, Zena Daysh, Rusong Wang, Dieter Steiner, Rob Dyball, Torsten Malmberg, Gene Myers, Eva Ekehorn, Luc Hens, and Tom Dietz. The list goes on. I have been blessed with a "world of friends" with whom I have shared the vision of a human ecological future. A huge measure of gratitude also goes to Stu Taylor, Clyde Hendricks, and Bibb Latané, my postgraduate academic advisers, who encouraged and trusted in me long before most of these ideas were conscious in my mind.

I want to also thank the people at North Atlantic Books and above all Richard Grossinger, North Atlantic Books' cofounder and longtime publisher. Our friendship has developed over the past decade during his summer retreats to Mount Desert Island (where, in the 1960s, he did his dissertation research on the cultural ecology of Maine lobstermen—and COA was in the seminal stage of moving from an idea to an actual college). In early fall, before returning to Berkeley, Rich regularly joins me as a team-teacher in my classes. His wide-ranging interests are an unparalleled source of enrichment. When the idea of this book first surfaced in my thinking, Rich suggested the possibility of publishing with North Atlantic Books. His invitation was exactly what I needed to liberate my imagination and encourage "the book that I wanted to write"—without a preordained prospectus, in a freely exploratory fashion. Finally, of course, I am deeply indebted to Adrienne Armstrong for her fastidious copyediting—and especially to Wendy Dherin and Vanessa Ta, my project editors, who guided me through completion of the book with tireless support and grace.

Contents

Foreword by Darron Collins,
president of College of the Atlantic   xi
Preface   xv

PART I. TRANSECTS AND PLOTS
1. The Arc of Life   3
2. Ecology   36
3. Experience   71
4. Human Ecology   112
5. Education   149

PART II. FACETS OF LIFE
6. Time and Space   196
7. Death in Life   213
8. Personal Ecology   233
9. Context   251
10. Metaphor and Meaning   270

PART III. WIDER POINTS OF VIEW
11. Kinds of Minds   293
12. Insight   304
13. Imagination   322
14. Keyholes   336
15. Ecology and Identity   353
16. The Unfinished Course   374

PART IV. CODA

Bibliography   399
Notes   409
Index   429
About the Author   453

Foreword

Rich Borden is a *big* man. He's tall. He's broad and has a big beard. But he's large in the less materialistic sense of the term as well. My first recollection of Rich came as a seventeen-year-old on a quest to find a college that would bring more meaning to my then-small world, something more than a rite of passage and an information dump. Stacks of *Peterson's College Guides* and *Princeton Reviews* mysteriously led me to a small, distinctive school on the coast of Maine.

My father and friends were skeptical or flat-out unimpressed by my interest in this quirky coastal college—but I was sold. Without any doubt the college's small size was a powerful pull. The location, nestled between a remarkable stretch of coastline and the Tolkienesque forests of Acadia National Park, also helped set the hook. But the college's course catalog is what ultimately did it for me.

I read that stunning, paperbacked catalog from cover to cover and pored through it randomly, dog-earing pages and filling margins. The most tattered, most annotated page outlined a class entitled Voluntary Simplicity, and the professor's name was Borden. The language in the course description was provocatively matter-of-fact and sat there on the page as if to say, "Voluntary Simplicity—yes, of course, a college staple like chemistry, French, and Western philosophy." Rich's intellectual size had cast a spell with this class, most especially with the line that read: "Several people that have tried this approach (living simply) visit to discuss their experiences."

Armed with the inspiration from that text, I applied, was accepted, and enrolled at College of the Atlantic. I arrived on campus in September 1988 only to find that Rich had taken on the role of academic dean and didn't teach the course anymore. I came to understand voluntary simplicity on my own. It was a minor hiccup on what would become an otherwise steep, four-year learning curve that launched my career, my ability to think, and my sense of *what* to think. COA was transformative like no other institution could ever be and it was that power that brought me back to take on the role as the college's seventh president.

As a student, I'd arrived at a curious time in the college's history. We were emerging from the ashes of a fire that destroyed the college's iconic home: a building that held the library, our community meeting hall, classrooms, dining hall, and faculty office space. In short, we had lost the institution's center of gravity. Figuratively, we were also emerging from an equally tumultuous trial by fire that was a bout of growing pains brought on by the departure of the college's founding president.

Of course the financial support, the presidential leadership of Dr. Louis Rabineau, a committed board, and a powerful underdog mentality all played important roles in COA's resuscitation. But I believe it was the intellectual bedrock and guiding principle of human ecology that ultimately brought us through those tough times, and it was Rich, in many ways, who inspired that focus. Rich was and is a person of big ideas and big visions and it was that vision of human ecology that helped the college survive those times and thrive into a new era.

Human ecology, as this book details, has intellectual roots far older than COA or Rich. The concept has been and will always be rather pliable. Despite the plasticity, Rich and I have spent an enormous amount of time giving some sense of shape to the idea. Some of that time is spent talking with a student deciding where to spend the next four years or to a parent staring down the barrel of tens of thousands of dollars in tuition. But a lot of time is spent exploring the deeper intellectual roots of the term, and this text explores those roots. Following four years of experience as a COA student, my own career implementing human ecology in the field of conservation, my two years as COA president, *and* the analysis of *Ecology and Experience*, I now (finally) feel quite comfortable explaining human ecology in a way that is meaningful and concise. *Ecology and Experience* asks that we abandon the idea of human ecology as a specific body of knowledge: Human ecology is best understood as a lens or a perspective for addressing thorny, complex issues.

At COA our core business is to provide the space, the experiences, and most importantly the community to help acquire that perspective.

Our pedagogy is rooted in experiential learning. Rich's own thought processes, as described within this text, also begin with experience. Learning by doing creates stronger, deeper neural connections with more lasting consequences for the learner.

Using a showing rather than telling approach, *Ecology and Experience* demonstrates the power of transdisciplinarity. Not surprisingly, at COA we also ask students to apply transdisciplinary problem solving to the real-world questions they're asking: Knowing x could be useful; knowing y might be as well, but synthesizing and applying xy produces a fundamentally different set of tools and data.

In *Ecology and Experience* we follow Rich's own personal journey through life. I consider the book a dialectical memoir toggling to and fro between Rich's own life and the foundations and futures of human ecology. In parallel with his own experiences, we also ask COA students to come to grips with human ecology by giving them the reins of their own curriculum.

Acquiring the human ecological perspective involves developing a students' sense of purpose so they leave COA with the skills and a powerful "fire in the belly" approach to taking on the world's challenges. *Ecology and Experience* outlines Rich's own fire, and that fire is none other than human ecology itself.

That's about as simple as I can get it: Human ecology is a powerful and practical lens for addressing complexity that is acquired by experiential learning, transdisciplinary thinking, a self-designed curriculum, and a well-developed sense of purpose. It's hardly a tagline, but some big ideas refuse to be condensed beyond a certain point.

Ecology and Experience walks through the production of that same lens and winds together an idea, an institution, and an individual unlike any other book I've read.

Rich provides us with a variety of handholds for the adventure. First among those are the autobiographical elements of *Ecology and Experience*. You will come to know Rich in his childhood, adolescence, and adulthood, come to know him as a musician, as a graduate student, as an observer, as a pioneer, as an academic dean, and, ultimately, as a wonderfully complicated individual.

Rich finds clarity through the tools of analogical understanding. From Ernst Haeckel's original metaphor using the Greek word *oikos,* or "house," for our understanding of ecology and ecological relations, to Rich's own "world's largest ball of string," the analogies herein aren't of the shallow, whimsical variety. *Ecology and Experience* is a blend of logical and analogical methods that provide a deeper understanding of the historically difficult and complex topics of humanity.

And then there's the college—the same one I found first by chance and second by life-changing choice. Rich also found COA first by chance and, over the course of forty years, has made the college his alembic for distilling human ecology in principle and in practice. *Ecology and Experience* tells the story—or at least one story—of how the school was birthed, was resurrected, and now stands poised to help make sense out of a system of higher education undergoing tremendous and rapid change.

People and institutions the world over have come to understand human ecology in concept and practice. Other scholars and practitioners have taken the concept and made it their own, but have done so collaboratively and in a way that hasn't watered down the meaning nor the power of human ecology. These communities of human ecologists are housed in university settings—as in the Australian National University's program in human ecology—and in the growing number of human ecologists and human ecological institutions bound together in the Society for Human Ecology (SHE). *Ecology and Experience* follows these pathways and demonstrates the intellectual heft and influence human ecology has had on thought and practice at a global scale.

Rich has been something of an oracle to me as a young president of this young college. In *Ecology and Experience* I have something of a playbook for thinking through the next steps of this special institution. In *Ecology and Experience* you will have a playbook for acquiring that lens and for understanding a big man with very big ideas.

—**Darron Collins**
Bar Harbor, Maine

Preface

It has been said the range of human concerns is framed by two basic questions: "What makes life possible?" and "What makes life worth living?" Between these bounds lie the innumerable ideas and queries that have occupied human thought over the ages. Like all generations, we share in these essential questions. Unlike previous generations, we face the additional problems and challenges of our time.

I have a firm belief in the powers of insight. Some insights arise from within as deeply subjective transformations of inner experience. These events are part of the subject matter of psychology. A different rendering of insight is aroused by external sources. This happens when the outside world presents us with new or contradictory information. The fundamental core of science is built upon systematic investigation and integration of knowledge from this realm.

Subjective introspection is often viewed as complementary to—or a reversal of—objective, scientific methods. The apparent incompatibility of these approaches has produced a long-standing tradition of keeping them relatively independent of one another. Yet we know—irrespective of how firmly we seek to draw a dividing line—they are intimately intertwined.

One way to encourage integration is to place ideas in juxtaposition. Artists and poets commonly employ this device as a means to surmount the powers of rationalization. Psychotherapists also take advantage of analogical resemblances to uncover partial aspects of linked experiences. Metaphorical extension invites unanticipated connections. It is an effective way to resolve our tendencies to compartmentalize feelings, thoughts, and perception.

Scientists, in contrast, prefer a more reasoned ordering of relations and tend to be critically minded. They are wary of falling prey to false analogies or being distracted by them. Their way of analyzing and integrating knowledge seeks more logical explanations—dis-embedded from mere likeness. Yet a careful study of the history of science shows that metaphor and analogy have often been some of the most powerful tools of scientific creativity.

Inspiration is seldom simple. Poetry is lost to cold hearts and closed ears; worn-out phrases and empty slogans are worthless when passions surge. Middle ground may be found where crossroads meet. But when they don't, we must risk a leap to bridge the gaps.

The Shape of Things to Come

There is a tendency, especially in the academic world, to carve life into ever-smaller pieces in order to make sense of it. All too often, the people who do this come to believe that is how the world really is. Human experience has many levels. So does the natural world. Gathering from both realms gives rise to novel constellations. Attempts to bridge the mental and environmental arenas are risky. But rigid conventions and narrow views have their dangers too—especially when they obscure underlying connections or smother imagination.

This book is a blend of themes and approaches based on a lifetime of interdisciplinary inquiry. My primary aim is to explore these intersections. A further goal is to convey a cautionary tale about what may be lost in not trying. At one level, I seek to offer an overview of the intellectual and institutional history of human ecology, along with various lines of thought relating to this perspective. The narrative also contains features of a personal memoir and in so doing includes many people who have significantly touched my life along the way. Bringing the mirror of self-reflection into the mix was not without trepidation. I am hopeful the benefits outweigh the perils. Finally, this is an invitation to exercise our capacities for ecological insight, to deepen the experience of being alive, and most of all to enrich the whole of life.

The forthcoming chapters are organized around a three-part structure. Part I takes a transect-and-plot approach, somewhat akin to the basic method of field ecology or landscape study. The scope and contents of these chapters are large; they are therefore longer than later chapters, which follow a less linear process. The structure for Part II borrows from the idiom of cubist art and unfolds in a multifaceted exploration of unifying perspectives. Part III is the least organized. In a paradigm analogous to jazz or musical improvisation, perhaps, its themes are more varied, speculative, and open-ended.

The organizing motifs for each part were unplanned at the outset. They emerged in the process of writing and gradually coalesced into a workable outline. In keeping with this process, I have included a part opener to introduce the chapters of each part. The outcome is a reflection of a lifetime preoccupation with the ecological relationships of human experience. Taken together, my intention is twofold: to invite an awakening of personal mindfulness about our place in the natural world, and further, to encourage a collective appreciation of the complex problems of which humans are a part—and the pressing need to enlarge our understanding of life.

The Deeper Search

There is an oft-quoted line by G. K. Chesterton, from his opening essay in *Tremendous Trifles,* that goes like this: "The world will never starve for wonders; but only for want of wonder."[1] It is the state of wonder that has given birth to philosophy. I am grateful here for a poignant comment in a recent conversation with Daniel Dennett. Philosophy, he pointed out, is not about answers. It is the discovery of new questions brought about by wonder.[2]

But wonder is bigger than questions of philosophy. Its true proportions reach far beyond thoughts or words or conscious knowing. The depths of wonder transcend even time. They extend to the experience of the eternal, within the drama of the self ever coming into being. This is the domain of myth. I do not mean the impoverished (and mistaken) definition of myth as falsehood. I mean it in the deeply transpersonal way Rollo May presents it in *The Cry for Myth*. "Myths," as he describes, "are our self-interpretation of our inner selves in relation to the outside world … that give significance to our existence … [within] … the inscrutable mystery of creation."[3]

Western society's rationalism and technological preoccupations suppress the mythic quest—and with it a good deal of our "want of wonder." But not entirely. The loss of mythic consciousness, according to May, "was the main reason for the birth and development of psychoanalysis in the first place." The narrative patterns of myth "are the essential language of psychoanalysis."[4] Our hunger to give significance to existence comes through in other ways. Joseph Campbell's 1988 six-part lecture series, *The Power of Myth*, with Bill Moyers, was the most popular TV series in the history of public television.[5] His expanded *Mythos* lecture series narrated by Susan Sarandon, which appeared in 1996, received a similar enthusiastic response.[6] Even now, a quarter century after his death, new episodes of Campbell's lectures on psychology and mythology continue to be added to the growing collection.

I have viewed countless hours of Campbell's talks and conversations from these and other productions. Like many people, I enjoy his storytelling and tenacious commitment to keep the mythic impulse alive. In all of those presentations, however, there is one brief moment that especially stands out for me. It surfaced at the close of one of the *Mythos* lectures, when an audience member asked Campbell about the meaning of life. A flash of annoyance crossed his face. "Life has no meaning," he retorted reflexively, "What is the meaning of a flower? What we are looking for is the *experience* of life!"[7] The spontaneous honesty of his reaction was palpable. The message was clear. Myth is not an explanation or a theory. It is beyond thought—but not without thought.

The principal value of comparative mythology is not the stories per se, lovely as they can be, but is in the experience they disclose. This is where science and psychology could and should meet—but seldom do. From the standpoint of Western mentality our bias is toward finding causes in the world. As Campbell reminds us, "That is not what myths are about. Myths do not have to do with analyzing and scientifically discovering causes. Myth has to do with relating the human being to his [or her] environment."[8]

W. B. Yeats met the issue this way: "Science is the critique of myth."[9] But here we must be cautious. The impulse of many, who yearn for mythic experience, is to deny science. Their response is to dive into non-Western or ancient traditions. "No," says Campbell: "We must find the beauty in our scientific knowing; ... our imagery has to keep up with what is known."[10] Rollo May held the same: "There is surely no conflict between science rightly defined and myth also rightly understood."[11] In Campbell's view, "The only myth worth thinking about is the planet." Ecology, as he added, notices "our cutting ourselves off from the living world"; it is "the revelation" of nature. "We are coming out of the earth," he concludes: "We *are* the earth."[12]

From the other side comes a sympathetic voice from science. "The evolutionary epic," E. O. Wilson submits, "is probably the best myth we will ever have."[13] Wilson makes a good point and he is not alone among scientists. But again we must take care. The power of myth has always been told in the language of poets and artists, whose special gifts go further than what they consciously know. "In this sense," May suggests, "they are the predictors of the future."[14] Our susceptibility to beauty, empathy, and identification lies in aesthetics—along with the capacity to endure and participate in the sorrows of the world.

Neither scientists nor artists can bridge the gap on their own. It may well be imprudent—even together—to try. On this point, the literary scholar Betty Sue Flowers is persuasive. Flowers was consultant to the Campbell–Moyers *Power of Myth* documentary and editor of the popular Doubleday companion volume to the series. In her words: "We need a new myth that takes into account our diversity ... that makes it coherent ... that allows us to stick together ... [and] ... work for a common good.... We need a higher organization for our complexity ... of who we are and who we might be."[15] I fully agree. "But how do we make a new myth?" Flowers asks. I think she is correct on this too: "The first thing to understand about myths is that we can't simply make them. They arise out of what is there."

Sotto Voce

The position voiced by Flowers suggests an intractable dilemma. If ecology does carry a potential to reconceive mythic mindfulness, how then might it arise? The answer, I believe, does not lie in a headlong or purposive undertaking. To do so is too cerebral. What is needed is an approach that unifies knowing *and* intuition—wherein aspects of personal and collective unconsciousness align in a deep "felt significance" of being in the world. It comes in moments when eternity breaks into time. These encounters, as Rollo May suggested, will most likely happen in a manner akin to "the capacity for creative waiting" of psychotherapy. In everyday life they may appear in Maslowian "peak experiences," in the creative impulse of art, or amid the long lines of eager young readers awaiting J. K. Rowling's next novel.

The central thesis of this book is rooted in these convictions. But the evidence, such as it exists, is mainly subjective and experiential. Much as I desire a fuller infusion of ecological consciousness in human affairs, I remain wary of mythic speculation or proselytizing. I am likewise aware of my incapacity to find words to even try. Hence, I take the counsel of Ludwig Wittgenstein: "Whereof one cannot speak, thereof one must be silent."[16] This discourse is best left beneath the surface—in the submerged refrains of an evolutionary past or yet-to-be-imagined future realities.

This point may be expressed in a more straightforward way. Many years ago, I was invited to be a delegate to the First Latin American Congress of Ecology in Montevideo, Uruguay. My role in the program was to review the international development of academic human ecology. I wrote my presentation in English. I then translated the paper into Spanish—thinking that would be a more fitting way to present it—and began to practice my delivery. Shortly before departing for the conference I reviewed it with my former colleague Bill Drury. Bill's vast knowledge of ecology and helpful comments enriched the contents. He also gave me some further guidance, based on his experience at international meetings. "Speak slowly," he advised, "in a language you know." In the end, I abandoned my stumbling Spanish version and followed his suggestion. His advice was good. It was a far more comfortable and effective outcome.

I will try to do the same here. Rather than drop into the shadows of unfamiliar terrain, the goal is to stay near the surface and convey my views in ordinary language. This is how I teach—in an admixture of academic knowledge, suggestive metaphors, and personal anecdotes. It is how I experience the world. But the veneer is thin. I enjoy staying attuned to unforeseen surprises and spontaneous connections. The final form for this book is but one of many possibilities. While the narrative is mainly descriptive, it is also meant to invite active imagination and intuitive participation. My weavings arise from the desire for a fuller sense of life. The overall hope is to enhance ecological awareness. The task before me therefore is to find ways to engage the reader at the borders of our life experiences.

PART I
TRANSECTS AND PLOTS

The figure/ground relationship of water and land defines two fundamental types of geomorphology. Islands—where water surrounds a landform—exemplify one type. The other is the watershed, where water is contained within fixed geologic boundaries, i.e., land surrounding water. These naturally occurring frameworks are the most common grounded-models for the ecological study of living systems. Each perspective can be scaled upward or downward: the first, from tiny islands to drifting continents; the latter, from the microhabitats of vernal pools to massive river basins.

Transect-and-plot techniques are applicable to either setting. On an island survey, transects usually follow a line from shore to shore, or from water's edge to the highest point of terrain. In watersheds, the transect might trace a river from outlet to source, ridge to ridge, or valley to ridge, etc. The features of interest may be geological or biological. They may also be human, as in an exploration of urban-to-rural landscape gradients. Transitions along the transect line are recorded. Systematic plot samples can be selected along the way to add depth to the survey. The observed changes across space (or time) coalesce into a basic ecological vision.

Part I of this book is organized around five transects. The lines do not describe attributes of physical terrain. They are, instead, transects across selected landscapes of lived experience, academic traditions, and the history of ideas. Chapter 1 follows a personal lifeline from my earliest environmental memories to the midlife discovery of human ecology as a professional path. This is the least academic portion of the book. It was an uncommonly private piece of writing for me. I have debated whether or how it fits. But as an exercise in recollection and reflection, it was a necessary stimulus for gathering my ideas. I have chosen to include it, as well, as an encouragement for others to remember the stories that lie along their own prime transect of life experience. Chapter 2 traces some of the background and patterns of ecological thought. The living world is enormously complex. So too is the history of natural history and ecology. My attempt here was to capture a cross section of high points and issues of this domain. Chapter 3 turns inward toward the mindscapes of consciousness and experience. It contains a basic historical and thematic summary of psychology as an academic discipline. These ideas are both a counterpoint to the preceding chapter and a prelude to the one that follows. Chapter 4, on the origins and ideas of human ecology, lies at the crossroads of the preceding transects. This was a challenging section to conceptualize and compose. In many ways it represents both the foundational core of the book, as well as the central theme of my personal life. The academic materials and anecdotes of this section are only a fraction of a far larger story, which could have taken many other forms. But, hopefully, the selected elements along this transect are sufficient to convey the contours of human ecology and to validate the significance of its unifying perspective. Chapter 5 is a retrospective and self-reflective account of education—the main arena of my professional life.

The lessons of life are a never-ending procession. We learn many through formal education; countless more are gained in the informal encounters of everyday life. Who we become as individuals—and how we function societally—is profoundly shaped by the endless opportunities to grow and learn. How we use these lessons are the hallmarks of a livable future.

CHAPTER 1

The Arc of Life

We shall not cease from exploration
And the end of all our exploring
Will be to arrive where we started
And know the place for the first time.

—T. S. Eliot

The story of life is a marvelous drama in which humans have become central figures. When the first band of hunter-gatherers emigrated out of Africa sixty-five thousand years ago they were just a few hundred strong. It took all of human history—from then up to 1800—for the population to reach its first billion. The second billion took only until 1930. Now, less than a century since then, there are more than seven billion human inhabitants on the planet. It is estimated that one-tenth of all the people who have ever lived on earth are alive today. If survival and population growth can be taken as a sign of anything in the living world, these numbers are surely a measure of success. Our adaptability and cleverness have been amply rewarded. In the game of life, humans have captured the earth. But, for this, we hold great responsibilities. We cannot conceal our footprints; nor can we hide from our liabilities. The earth is not an object for possession. At every turn we face these truths. The most elementary lesson of ecology teaches that no species ever enjoys infinite resources or longevity. Daily news reports remind us

3

constantly about growing problems of resource shortages, species losses, and climate change. Even the voice of our intuition whispers a warning of dangers to come.

The attributes that got us where we now are in the world, however, may not be the ones that will lead to a livable future. These concerns were the founding thoughts of the environmental movement. The central question at the outset was: "Can the natural environment absorb the impact of human influence?" More recently, the problem has become a much tougher question: "Can human consciousness comprehend our relation to the living world?"

Our knowledge of ecological processes is growing. But a great deal about the workings of nature remains unknown. The field of scientific ecology is barely a century old. The British Ecological Society, the first professional association for ecologists, was founded in 1913. Its U.S. counterpart, the Ecological Society of America, formed two years later. In comparison with many other scientific societies, neither is a large group. The professional study of human consciousness and behavior is only slightly older. The American Psychological Association, founded in 1892, is also a relative newcomer among academic disciplines. Until quite recently, contact or collaboration between these academic fields has been minimal. Biological ecologists have generally ignored humans and preferred building their science on the study of nonhuman species and natural systems. Psychologists, conversely, have scant knowledge of the natural environment. Their interest in the biological sciences seldom extends beyond human physiology and neurology.

Most of my professional life has been at the confluence of these streams. In the late 1970s I joined the faculty of College of the Atlantic—a small, private institution committed to the interdisciplinary study of human ecology. I served as the college's academic dean for two decades and have continued in the position of the Rachel Carson Chair in Human Ecology. In the early 1980s I also became a member of a small group of scholars and practitioners in the creation of an international Society for Human Ecology. I was president of the organization from 1986 to 1988 and served as executive director for ten years later on. Taken together, these roles have furnished countless occasions to explore and engage with the diverse meanings of human/environment relations. Most of this work has been within the world of higher education—a combination of teaching, research, administration, and writing dedicated to establishing an academic and professional status for human ecology.

My colleagues have frequently urged me to write an introductory text on the topic. There is a growing and substantial academic literature of human ecology. Yet I have resisted the task. The scholarly language of textbooks has a barren quality that feels detached and impersonal. Writing "about" the academic domain in which I have spent my life somehow dissolves much of the story of how human ecological ideas have really grown. My opinion is further biased by the luxury of having taught in a very small college with seminar-size classes, typically with a dozen or so students. In this setting, it has been most fun to draw on primary sources, to utilize anecdotes and stories, and to explore ideas through team-teaching.

There are plenty of facts about the living world. At the same time, though, a great deal of what I know has been acquired interpersonally. These personal truths come from the actual people working on the common project of putting something around the idea of human ecology and their sharing the pleasure of doing it. My own research, if that is the proper term, has been an *in situ* exploration of the history of these ideas. Some is based on books, published papers, and other formal academic sources. At least as much derives from direct experience, of which a considerable amount is very much alive and in the process of becoming. I knew, therefore, a candid account of human and ecological perspectives, as I have come to know them, required a blending of objective descriptions and subjective viewpoints. In mixing the personal together with the impersonal, I have unavoidably become a part of the story. This is not without some uneasiness. Self-disclosure may be enjoyable and effective in the give-and-take of the classroom. In print, however, it is a much trickier balancing act. If I have missed the mark, I apologize at the outset.

Words and Worldviews

In my college days, before the advent of credit cards, it was a common practice for students in need of money to go to the bookstore and sell our used books. Whenever I needed to do this, there was the inevitable dilemma of what to sell and what to keep. The answers to those choices sit on my bookshelves. The books I have kept are some of my best old friends. Looking at them, I realize only a few are textbooks—those bulky compendia of bits of knowledge that survey some field or other. Those were the first to be sold. The books that have moved with me and stayed by my side for the past half century are carriers of more creative ideas. Sometimes I take them from the shelf and page through them. Many are underlined or highlighted or filled with notes in the margins. They often take me back to the time when I first encountered the ideas they contain. I recall the pleasure of learning, and I reminisce over them like old photographs or objects from the attic. There are Anton Chekhov and Bertrand Russell, along with Hermann Hesse, Emily Dickinson, and Carl Jung.

I see another old favorite as I scan the shelves: S. I. Hayakawa's *Language in Thought and Action*. This one comes from my freshman year. I remember reading it late at night and recall the excitement of new thoughts. Hayakawa was a student of Alfred Korzybski, founder of the discipline of general semantics and author of the famous premise "the map is not the territory." One of Hayakawa's distinctions that struck me then—and has stayed with me over the years—is about levels of abstraction. Sometimes words refer to concrete *things,* and language is not abstract. The owner's manual in the glove compartment of my car is a good example. Words may also point toward *relationships* and interactions between things, which is a higher level of abstraction. When language joins relationships with relationships it performs its most abstract function—creation of *ideas*. Hayakawa's ladder of abstraction changed my understanding and perception of language. I began to develop an ear for classifying thoughts in conversation and writing. I suspect that this may have attuned me to psychology and a fascination with the "shape" of thoughts, a process not unlike that of a field botanist following the pattern and contours of a plant.

A paperback copy of *The Ego and the Id* sits nearby. It was my first introduction to Sigmund Freud's enduring contributions to psychology and his articulation of ego defense mechanisms. Many people fail to appreciate that these processes operate more often than not below the level of conscious awareness. When psychological defenses like displacement, rationalization, and projection are at work, we cannot know our hidden motives. Unconscious desires and threats to well-being are detected before they reach consciousness. Our actual thoughts and actions are adjusted unwittingly so that conscious experience can carry on overtop these buried conflicts. These processes of unconscious editing became central features of Freud's early psychoanalytic investigations and opened the door to his depth theory of human mentation.

However much we may be unconscious of hibernating internal complexes, I believe that we are equally capable of hiding external realities from awareness. Many facts of life elude us in countless ways when cherished beliefs are threatened. Instead, we carry on through unconsciously motivated avoidance, distortion, or denial of them.

Between these mental and environmental arenas lies a third domain—of human capacity for language. It is a world of words. Words bring the light of consciousness to each realm, and often bridge them in world-changing ways. The democratic ideals of "life, liberty and the pursuit of happiness" provide a good example. Once these principles entered our thoughts and dialogue, they began to transform the foundations of self-image and society. The story of these evolving conceptions is magnificently described in the Pulitzer-winning historian David Hackett Fischer's book *Liberty and Freedom*. Abraham Lincoln would restate the ideals in his Gettysburg Address four score and seven years thereafter. "All men are created equal" he reminded us, and with those words enjoined a nation at war to ponder new levels of liberty. A century later, Betty Friedan—author of *The Feminine Mystique*—spoke of "the problem that has no name." She was referring, of course, to the underlying issues that energized the women's movement. By penetrating the surface of everyday attitudes and habits, Friedan opened American consciousness to a buried intuition about the future. As with the civil rights movement, a more compassionate view of society began to unfold. We are in a similar state of semiconsciousness again. The issues this time are not about interpersonal relations or equal rights for humans. They are about human relations with the rest of the living world.

Some may say environmental concern is not new. Ideas about conservation and nature protection have been around as long as, even longer perhaps than, the civil rights or women's rights movements. There are others who believe that environmental concern is merely the initial stage of scratching the surface of a far deeper reorientation. Among those who hold this belief, including myself, the term "human ecology" has become a way of giving voice to this nameless problem. The scope of its meaning extends beyond the specific agendas of "environmentalism" and "sustainability"—or the even broader designation of "environmental studies." These terms may be confused or conflated. But to do so misses a crucial insight, which like all insights arises in a condition of fragility. One way to convey this point comes from personal experience.

I have always been motivated by a myriad of interests. My habits of mind resemble, perhaps, those of a beachcomber who fills his pockets with "interesting things" selected for unknown reasons. What I collected (or ignored) through most of my early life was not guided by a conscious purpose. My attention and curiosity were held together by a sense of formless desire and some inexpressible "felt experience" of value. It has always been interdisciplinary, but not random. In my early thirties the best-fitting academic label for combining these pursuits was "environmental psychology." Then one day, quite unexpectedly, I received a letter from a fellow psychologist at another university informing me of a recently founded college of "human ecology." He did not describe what they were doing, nor did he define the term. Nonetheless, I had an immediate and intuitive sense of its meaning. "Yes," I said to myself. "That's it!"

This book is a chronicle of the journey from then to now. Along the way I have met many others with similar experiences. The advent of human ecology for them, like my own, often appeared as a private discovery. These events and the shared intuition behind them have coalesced into a growing community of individuals dedicated to putting something around this phrase. Many aspects of human ecology may be described by other terms. Yet still, there are times when new words really do change our experience of the world. Like "liberty" or "art" or "love," they invite a broader vision that leads us beyond conventional patterns.

The interplay of mind and nature goes back to my early childhood, long before I ever heard of human ecology. The roots of many questions that still intrigue me were taking shape well in advance of terms for them or knowledge of their place in established fields of study. Growing up in the country gave me many opportunities to know the varied nuances of the out-of-doors. Long before nature was an idea, it was a major part of daily life. My first world of the environment was through the senses. I knew it by smell and sight, sound and texture.

There are times in life when we feel fully in the world. They are often moments when we feel most alive, when we are happy and whole—content, secure, and connected to our surroundings. An old friend once likened the experience to a summer's day and her memory of being "a little bit hungry, a little bit tired, and a little bit sunburned." Ralph Waldo Emerson expressed the transcendental and spiritual significance of these events in his essay "Experience": "Life is a train of moods like a string of beads," he declared, "and, as we pass through them, they prove to be many-colored lenses which paint the world."[1] The psychologist Abraham Maslow called them "peak experiences" and made them central features of his theory of self-actualization. Thomas Tanner and Louise Chawla have built on these notions with research on "significant life experiences" as transformative moments of environmental insight. They are also a major aspect of Mihaly Csikszentmihalyi's concept of "flow" within his psychology of optimal experience. As with a string of pearls, we gather these moments and hold them in memory. A lifetime full of these experiences is a good life.

Starting Points

In my own mind I can locate one of the first of these memories. I was about three or four years old. I had just awoken on a warm, sunny morning and was searching the house for my family. Through an open window I heard voices in the backyard. As I went to the screen door, I saw my mother hanging laundry on the large, four-sided laundry tree in the backyard. I could smell the freshness of clean, wet wash. My grandmother was sitting across the lawn in the shade of the grape arbor. I ran to her as she called me. I remember them talking to each other about what a hot day it was going to be, and that I should stay in the shade. My sister, three years older than I, was at school. She would be returning later on the school bus. My father was at work but would be home before dark. There are other details—sounds and smells from a summer's day, feelings of knowing where I was, an awareness of my own body as I ran through the warm grass. But the important thing is the completeness of the experience. The world was full and undivided. It contained a clear awareness of my immediate environment, the season of the year, and the key people in my life. Although the time frame was narrow, I knew what had come before and could anticipate what was forthcoming.

My parents—Amy Moore and George Borden—met at a small party in Brooklyn, New York, in August 1935. He was a civil engineer with the New York Dock Company. She worked at an insurance company and shared an apartment with her mother. Photographs of her childhood show a comfortable life. Her father died when she was thirteen, but his investments were sufficient to support his wife and daughter. College pictures of my mother portray a young woman with stylish clothes at the wheel of her Oldsmobile roadster with a Pekingese puppy in her arms. This happy story would change, however, with the crash of the stock market that forced her to drop out of college and find a job. I know these—and many other things—because my mother kept a diary. She wrote something every day for more than sixty years. Because of her habit, I have an uncommon insight into the daily life of my family.

My father's childhood was spent on a remote family farm in upstate New York. The homestead was pleasant and picturesque, but there was little money and much work. My grandmother foresaw a different life for her son. So she sent him off to boarding school. In college he chose civil engineering and immediately after graduation began a forty-year career on large-scale public works projects in New York City.

Not long after my parents met they began an adventure in rural living. They purchased part of an old farm about sixty miles north of the city in the Hudson River valley. It was surrounded by a patchwork of dairy farms, usually between one and two hundred acres each. In those days a herd of fifty or so milking cows provided most families with a good life. Much of the farmland was unwelcome for tilling and crop farming, having been the dumping ground for countless stones deposited by glaciation. Gathering fieldstones heaved by frost action was an annual activity. Centuries of accumulations became the stonewall borders of pastures and hayfields. Many more stretched through the woodlands, evidence of old fields and abandoned farms. It was a scenic terrain of mountains and valleys, accented by small lakes fed by meandering streams. These were the idyllic features that inspired the Hudson River School of landscape painting, whose aesthetic pastoral vision celebrated a sublime harmony of humans and nature.

My parents' property lay in the middle of a triangle equidistant from three small villages. Each was about five miles away. An Erie-Lackawanna train station in one town offered a way to commute to and from the city. The trip took about an hour and a half. They began by building a small weekend retreat and summer home. It was a log cabin constructed from freshly felled hickory trees, stripped of bark and tightly fitted. My father was a meticulous carpenter. Much of the interior was finished out with recycled lumber, collected from demolition sites associated with his work and trucked to them. He fashioned everything by hand—from digging a cellar and making doors to surrounding the cabin with stone porches and terraces. It was a labor of love. Photographs of my parents show them cheerfully leaning over their tools, each day of progress faithfully recorded in my mother's diary.

Their choice of location was also influenced by the needs of my grandparents. During summer haying season and on weekends my parents often drove farther upstate to help on the family farm. It was not a common practice in that time for unmarried couples to live together. But that is what they did. The constant company of my mother's mother made their situation more acceptable. After three years at this adventure, their small cabin was a livable home. Once the initial log cabin was winterized and fitted with closets and cabinets, my father switched to building with readily available fieldstone. He added a summer kitchen and mudroom, more bedrooms, and began with outbuildings. On August 19, 1939, they married. My mother quit her job in the city. She and her mother moved in. My father continued to work in the city. His urban-rural life continued for thirty years, punctuated by timetables and long commutes.

My parents enjoyed history. Their bedroom was lined in bookcases with finely bound volumes. They also shared an interest in genealogy that led them to public libraries and cemeteries as a form of entertainment. They took some pride in having traced the family name back to the first Bordens (Joan and Richard), who came to Massachusetts in 1639. My sister's and my names derive from this fact. On my mother's family tree the lines led to the *Mayflower* and to John and Priscilla Alden, a point of gentle rivalry between my parents. My sister has continued this custom and since filled in many more genealogical details.

Joan was born in January 1942, one month after Pearl Harbor. I was born in the summer of 1945. Two weeks later, the first atomic bomb was dropped on Hiroshima. The war's casualties and years of rationing had significant impacts on our community. There were numerous indirect effects as well. One was the flight by many people away from large coastal cities. Our parents' prewar venture had taken them beyond the customary comfort zone of daily commuting. But after the war this threshold expanded. The American dream of a house and yard in the quiet suburbs was unfolding.

Suburban expansion accelerated around cities, as its tentacles wound their way ever deeper into the rural countryside. In many places it followed the train lines and highways that linked urban workplaces to suburban home life. Other people, however, were in search of a new version of country living. They wanted a complete escape from the city—to live and work beyond the bedroom communities of suburbia.

Prior to the war, when farmland changed ownership it was typically handed down to the next generation or annexed by neighboring farms. In the urban flight of the 1950s land-use patterns changed. Farmers now had a choice to sell their entire holdings to a single agent, who subdivided the open fields into small lots for tract housing. These "developments" began to redefine the rural landscape into a scattered mix of old family farms and new housing projects.

Another aftereffect of the war followed from how it ended. In an instant, we had entered the atomic age. The echoes of world war had barely hushed, as a new Soviet enemy appeared. The Cold War had begun. Mushroom clouds became a dramatic new symbol of a fearsome future. Within this scenario New York City became, perhaps, the most widely imagined prime target. The terror of mass annihilation by a distant enemy amplified the undesirability of city life and further accelerated a reordering of the lower Hudson River valley. The threat of nuclear war also mushroomed in global consciousness. The seeds of change fell not only in my own backyard and overshadowed the serenity of childhood, they were scattered throughout the world.

I began kindergarten in the fall of 1950. It was a turning point and time of important educational changes in rural New York State. Before the war, primary education was offered locally in one-room schoolhouses. There were two nearby. One was a mile or so away, next to the Congregational church we attended. The other was about the same distance in the opposite direction. The year I started school we were bused to a brand-new "district school" that combined elementary and secondary grades. It was a model facility built of bricks with large windows, an athletic field, and a combination gymnasium/auditorium. Each grade had a separate homeroom and teacher who taught only that class for the year. It was considered a major advancement in education.

During that first year, our school was selected for a motion picture about progressive education in America. The film title was *The Rural*

School. Joan and I were chosen to play parts in the movie. We were cast as siblings, but in a more conventional home life and with different parents. George Montgomery's *Davy Crockett, Indian Scout*, was popular at the time. I had my own coonskin cap, which the filmmakers happily incorporated into the all-American story line. Joan obtained a copy of the film years later. We did not realize, until then, that it was something of a propaganda piece promoting U.S. interests abroad. The target audience was postwar Europe. Seeing the movie with my sister, decades later, was a tangible reminder of the simplicity and idealism in those years. Small-town life was a dominant way of life. Democracy, individual freedom, and patriotism were unimpeachable values. We were growing up in the relief and recovery after World War II, but also beneath the gathering clouds of nuclear threat and fear of communism.

Our grandmother died the winter before I started school. With both children away during the day, my mother became active in the local Congregational church. She regularly hosted meetings of the women's guild at our home. This was basically a community support group that organized church suppers, an annual Christmas Bazaar, and other social events. Church was a central feature of rural life. My involvement consisted of more than a decade of Sunday school attendance. I was a member of the choir and also one of the boy acolytes who tended the candles at the opening and closing of services. I enjoyed the social activities and can still recall many of the hymns and Bible stories. But in all those years, I don't remember ever having a single "religious" experience in the actual church.

In other ways, my childhood was somewhat unconventional and out of sync with my peers and the times. When television became popular in the early 1950s, everyone bought them. We did not. I don't think our parents avoided buying one based on any strongly felt principles. They merely had no interest in TV. They were avid readers. Their bedroom had a fireplace surrounded by a semicircle of comfortable chairs. Mine was the farthest to the left, beside the shelves of *National Geographic* back issues and the *World Book Encyclopedia*, which I browsed time and again. Evenings were spent there reading together in front of a fire. Sometimes we played cards or board games; other times we did the same in the living room.

My father went to work in a dark suit and white shirt with cuff links. Like the streams of other commuters who filled the trains, he also wore a fedora and carried a simple briefcase. On weekends he was a different person. In cold weather he wore a plain canvas coat with a sheepskin collar, old army boots, and a toboggan skullcap knitted by my mother. He commonly worked with no shirt at all in summer. In this persona, he looked no different from any of the other local farmers, or the farm boy he had once been. His weekends were filled with projects. He had a habit of whistling to himself as he moved through his tasks in an easy rhythm. He seemed to enjoy being busy and working with his hands. Sometimes he would bring home huge rolls of engineering drawings. There was a visible sense of satisfaction whenever he unrolled them on the dining room table or the living room floor. Some of his bigger projects included the design of the second deck of the George Washington Bridge and the construction of New York's jetports. I never had the opportunity to see him when he was engaged in his professional work. I wish now that I had. My hunch is he enjoyed both sides of his life—in different ways.

As soon as I was old enough, I began to work along with him. We were constant weekend partners. We cut cords of firewood every year, pulling in tandem on either end of the two-man saw. I came to know all of the local hardwoods by bark, grain, and fresh fragrance of their sawdust. He had an unhurried, steady pace that he could maintain from dawn to dusk. When the original hickory logs began to decay, we replaced them with stone walls—selecting and carrying stones, and hand-mixing countless batches of concrete. His precision and attention to details bordered on perfectionism. He taught me everything about house construction from foundation work and framing to plumbing, electricity, and finish carpentry.

These skills served me well with the competence to design and build two homes myself years later. Beyond this basic knowledge, I absorbed two more general lessons as well. One was the importance of setting the pace and rhythm for "getting into" long-term tasks. The other was to reserve time, at the end of a day, to review and appreciate what has been accomplished. These habits of mind have carried forward and remain significant features of my attitude about effort and enjoyment.

We had elaborate gardens of corn, potatoes, peas, onions, cabbage, squash, and beans. Cucumbers, kohlrabi, raspberries, rhubarb, and grapes were also abundant, along with varieties of fruit including apples, peaches, pears, apricots, cherries, and mulberries. I don't think we ever applied pesticides. Instead, we picked off potato bugs and Japanese beetles by hand and dropped them in a tin can of kerosene. When the can was filled, the contents were strained and the liquid reused. Joan often took part in these activities. Sometimes the three of us would make forays together to learn the local wildflowers, edible plants, and trees. In spring there was maple sugaring and syrup making. In fall we took long walks deep into the woods to gather bushels of nuts from hickory and white walnut (butternut) trees. These were dried in the woodshed in tall cylinders of wire mesh to be cracked and picked out, by the fireside in winter, for cakes and cookies.

The field beside our house, fondly named the "lower forty," was a popular neighborhood gathering-place. Our father set rough-sawn timber ends into the sod as bases for the local softball diamond—where he was the permanent and easy-to-hit pitcher for countless games enjoyed by kids of all ages. Our chicken house supplied plenty of eggs. I expanded the flock considerably and for many years had a successful egg route, making daily deliveries by bicycle. Joan and I also worked on the farm next door milking cows and bringing in the hay. The neighbor's son and I spent a week of summer at the county fair, where we showed Ayrshire heifers and took some prizes. My dream, in this preadolescent stage, was to be a farmer. The Future Farmers of America (FFA) was of more interest than Boy Scouts.

Aside from tending her flower gardens, my mother was not an outdoors person. But she was a terrific homemaker. She knit dozens of sweaters, mittens, and gloves, and sewed most of our coats and clothes. Meals were homemade. We had a cooked breakfast every morning and a traditional family dinner at seven o'clock. We rarely had candy or soda, but fresh baked cookies and pies were always there. We did not have a freezer. Vegetables and fruits were canned. Mason jars lined the shelves of the cold cellar, built into the corner of the basement, along with baskets of root vegetables.

My mother was also a writer. For many years she authored a weekly syndicated column that appeared in a number of Hudson Valley newspapers. The contents were varied. Most themes revolved around community issues, advice on family matters, and commentary on popular books. Our house was filled with magazines, newspapers, and manuscripts in progress. The sound of the typewriter was a constant background in the afternoons. I don't think I realized at the time the scope of her readership in the region, or how widely the details of our day-to-day lives were public knowledge. Some of her work also appeared in women's magazines. When our church wanted a volume to commemorate its bicentennial, she was chosen.

Looking back at those formative years, I recognize other divisions in my life. When the district lines were laid for the new regional schools one of the boundaries ended at our home. We were at the farthest edge of our school district. The bus Joan and I took began its daily route at this outer limit. We were the first to be picked up in the morning and the last let off in the afternoon. I once calculated that all those years of bus trips were roughly equal to half the distance to the moon. Those long rides, year after year, provided thousands of hours of conversations with schoolmates. They also imparted a deep familiarity with the local landscape, changing seasons, and shifting patterns of community development.

Living at the end of the line had another peculiar feature. My sister and I were the only children in the area who went to our school. All of our neighborhood friends went to a different school. Everyone gathered in the morning in our driveway, which was the turning point for buses from the two school districts. But Joan and I went off one way and everyone else disappeared in the opposite direction. A curious result of this situation was that no one in our bus or school ever knew these kids—and vice versa.

My favorite after-school routine was to team up with my dog and go for walks alone. The solitude of the woods and fields was a welcome respite from the social engagement of school and long bus rides. When I was young, my explorations were limited to our own property. It was a diverse mix of woods and overgrown farmland. The land behind our house rose eastward into steep shale cliffs covered in hardwoods, cedars, sumac, and wild blueberries. To the south was an open field that sloped gradually to a marshy valley with a small pond. Overlooking the pond, among a cluster of new-growth maples, ash, and oaks, stood a solitary hemlock. It was the oldest and tallest tree around. A deep carpet of fragrant needles and small cones encircled the base of its huge trunk. Strong branches encircled the tree that invited easy climbing. I am certain I scaled my way to its top more than a hundred times. From this vantage point I could survey the valley in all directions. Midway up, I fashioned a crude tree house from leftover lumber, where I spent countless hours of solitary reflection. If one can call a tree a friend, my relationship with that hemlock was among my deepest connections to the natural world.

In time I was permitted to explore farther afield. My roaming extended ever outward in all directions. I became intimately familiar with the nuances and special features of the patchwork of neighboring farms and forest. Deep in the woods I discovered the cellar holes and remains of many old houses. Their rectangular dry-wall stone foundations formed sunken gardens of brambles and trees. I often unearthed remnants of old tools, bottles, or dinnerware by scratching around in them. There was usually a nearby spring or old dug well that had supplied water for the homestead. These drinking spots were the special secrets on the mental map of my wanderings. I knew every berry patch and isolated apple tree for miles around, as well as the best stream pools and ponds where perch, crappies, bullheads, and pickerel were easily caught.

On top of one nearby mountain was the entrance to an old iron mine, in operation from before the Civil War and abandoned in the 1880s. We were forbidden to go there by our parents. But my friends and I did it anyway. Its dark and silent passages went deep into the mountain. At one point, a long vertical airshaft had been cut that rose up through the ceiling. From below, it created a circular skylight illuminating a small patch of the total darkness. The accumulated rainwater that fell down the deep shaft formed a solid, year-round ice mound that sparkled in the narrow column of light. This was a place of real danger—not at the bottom—but from above. On the mountaintop it was an unmarked hole in the forest floor surrounded by a small funnel of leaves and debris, easily unnoticed until you were upon it. In our foolishness, we sometimes would hold onto a nearby overhanging branch and drop stones down the shaft. I can still recall the feeling of vertigo as we watched our rocks disappear into the darkness, counting the seconds until the echo of impact rang back to the surface. It is a miracle none of us slipped and fell to their certain death. Down in the mine, the old passages spread in whatever direction the ore determined. The lower arms were partially flooded in still and crystal waters. Some boys carried a battered canoe up the mountain and into the mine. We used it to paddle along the flooded arms until we had seen all there was, and our curiosity with the place dissolved.

Whether alone or in the company of friends, these adventures of youth were full with a sense of wonder and imagination. Edith Cobb, in her psychological studies of "the ecology of imagination," describes the powerful imprint of the intimate exposure to nature during childhood. It is the age of enchantment: "a special period, the little-understood, prepubertal, halcyon, middle age of childhood ... when the natural world is experienced in some highly evocative way, producing in the child a sense of some profound continuity with natural processes."[2] It is a time of magic—when every stream and puddle has a place in wonderland. This, I am sure, is the soil and seed of my intuition toward human ecology and fascination with the whole of life.

Turning Points

But childhood ends. Living in a fantasy world of imagination and play no longer fulfills our desires. We begin to seek a different kind of interaction. As adolescence arrives, we become less family-centered and are progressively infused with social comparison. It is a time when "fitting in" with peers pulls us in new and uncharted directions. This shift came for me when I reached junior high school. Times were changing. I was changing. The folksy image my parents projected began to vex me. I no longer looked forward to my outdoor escapades or weekends at home. I wanted to spend time in town with friends playing basketball, listening to the birth of rock and roll music, or just hanging out. In high school these desires and frustrations intensified. Team sports became increasingly important. The inconvenience of living far from town was an annoyance. The late evening of my father's arrival home added to my disappointment. My parents were never available for my events. In time it turned to not wanting them to come.

Their frugality and indifference to modernity touched me at all levels. They seemed entrenched in the past. While my friends' families eagerly purchased stylish new cars, they blissfully soldiered on with their vintage black Plymouth. What was wrong with television, deep freezers, a chain saw, or even a motorized cement mixer? I resolutely refused to wear any more homemade apparel. I wanted clothes like my friends were wearing. When Joan left for college, I was alone. Fortunately I had other resources. The early successes of my egg route had multiplied. The network of customers for eggs had become clients in an enterprising market for flower bulbs, and then, for greeting cards. These activities brought a national award as a young entrepreneur. They also produced a rather substantial bank account. As soon as I got my driver's license, I cashed out. My first car was a 1954 Oldsmobile 88 convertible with wraparound windshield, leather seats, and a 324-cubic-inch engine. It was bigger, newer—and much faster—than my parents' car. They were stunned; so were my high school friends.

This was the early 1960s, long before anyone was troubled about environmental problems. The fabric of my community was knitted around the church and rural history. There was no social or educational forum for the musings of Loren Eiseley or the warnings stirred by Rachel Carson. Many people may have read them, as I had, but they were buried in the background of everyday life. No one ever mentioned Darwin's evolution or Freud's psychology. My friends and teachers did not puzzle over these concerns. Or if they did, it was not fashionable to entertain them in our high school discussions of the day.

Having a car opened an ever-widening circle of exploration. I loved the freedom of the road and was consumed with desires to reach beyond the confines of familiarity. My parents had put aside college funds for my sister and me. Their expectation was for me to attend a northeastern private college, as my father had done and my sister was doing. But in the middle of my senior year their dream was shattered. I did not want to mix college with weekend trips back home. My dream was to go far away—to the sunny south—to Texas. I later realized how heartbreaking it was for them. But for me, at the time, I could only see the freedom of breaking away. I will always admire how they swallowed the disappointment and gave their trust and full support to me.

Before the three-day drive into my freshman year, I had never been more than a few hundred miles from home. I made the trip alone, with the top down all the way, following the old U.S. highway through cities and small towns. Small stretches of the new interstate system were in place, but most of it was yet to be built. I thoroughly enjoyed the adventure of the trip and the excitement of entering a different world. Joining a national fraternity, where I soon found a network of friends, facilitated the social dimensions of my freshman-year experience. Despite occasional twinges of homesickness, I happily adjusted to university life. When Christmas break came, my parents surprised me with a round-trip plane ticket for my first commercial flight on a Boeing 707. Jet travel was still in its early stages. Having the chance to try it—and shortening of the trip home from three days to three hours—was a doubly welcome gift.

I did well academically, ending the year on the dean's list. But I had scarcely any idea of what I wanted to study. I thought, at the outset, engineering should be my major. I enjoyed the engineering drawing classes, but abhorred physics and its four-hour labs. My small-town background was inadequate preparation for the scale and complexity of the University of Texas curriculum. Our sophomore chemistry class was larger than my entire high school. For the first few years of college I seemed to go in a different direction every term. For a while, I considered becoming a math major, switched to premed, and later to anthropology. By then I had also outgrown the party-life patterns of fraternity life. Fortunately, a couple of my psychology professors took me under their wing. They invited me to join them at one of their informal evening seminars for graduate students. It was a life-changing event. I felt as though I had walked through an invisible wall and into a room filled with ideas and intelligent conversation. For the first time, I saw a meaningful path of lifelong learning and an entirely new way of being in the world. I immediately settled on psychology as my area of concentration. I was nearly a senior in terms of completed credits. But without a declared major, it was impossible to graduate.

Psychology was an optimal solution. As an academic field, it is something of a hybrid. What I especially liked—then and now—is that psychology is one of the few academic fields that span the knife-edge of subject/object relations. Everything I had learned from science classes had utility inside psychology's partial identity with the methods and theories of social science. On the other side, psychology was also inescapably concerned with the fluidity of consciousness and the inner, subjective world of art, literature, and the humanities—which I also loved. These intuitive qualities slip through the fingers of science, but they are nonetheless essential aspects of psychological mindedness. The combination of these complementary spheres can be daunting (even to many psychologists—who regrettably diminish their unease by choosing one over the other). But for me it was a liberation and a way to proceed freely without having to throw away any of the pieces. I loved it *in toto* and took an extra year and a half to sample it broadly.

At the graduate level, most psychologists choose either a clinical or a research track. Fortunately I didn't have to make this choice. I went to a new PhD program, just approved by the American Psychological Association, at Kent State University in Ohio. All first-year graduate students shared a common core program. Our professors were enthusiastic about their new curriculum. They gave us a broad and rigorous foundation of freshly crafted classes and up-to-date content that spanned the entire field.

In my second year I began work at a community mental health center. Nothing could have been more of a misnomer. It was a state-run facility—short staffed and bleak. The hard surface of the concrete walls echoed with distant moans of patients throughout the building. A noticeable odor of urine and disinfectant permeated the building. I was assigned to one of the four locked wards that each housed about fifty patients. The chief of our therapeutic team was a foreign-born medical doctor. It was unclear what, if any, psychiatric training he had. In any event he was seldom available except to approve electroconvulsive shock treatments or mind-numbing drugs. It didn't take long for me to realize even my own mental health was at risk here. These were the days before insurance company or third-party payer support. The practice of psychology happened either in state mental hospitals like these, or in private psychotherapy settings in the uptown neighborhoods of big cities. Neither appealed to me at the time.

On breaks between sessions, I often found myself drifting to the large windows of the main room. Through their barred opening I would stare thoughtlessly at the squirrels scampering on the lawn amid the trees of the hospital grounds. The bleak emptiness of the pale green walls drained me. I yearned for sunshine and long walks in the woods. Maybe psychology was a mistake. I was surrounded by troubled souls, whose needs I felt and to whom I perhaps could give some fleeting comfort. But I was losing my self.

The most rewarding parts of those long days were the actual counseling sessions. An especially memorable exchange occurred with a young man who suffered from depression and paranoia. Between episodes he functioned fully. He had a good mind for philosophy and had studied it seriously for years. In our conversation one day I asked him what he thought was the most important event in our lifetime. He answered without hesitation: "Going to the moon." The first manned moon landing had just happened. It was one of the great achievements of science and technology, and something of an American obsession since the Russian *Sputnik* launching in 1957. "Yes," I affirmed, "a great technological achievement—space—the new frontier." "No," he replied with some annoyance, "because it framed the earth." His meaning did not register with me. So I asked him to explain it. His account was couched in the language of Marshall McLuhan, the currently popular social philosopher of media communications. "The point," he elaborated, "is that for the first time we are seeing earth as a fact. The photographs of us looking back at ourselves are a lesson in finitude—of the finiteness of the planet. This will transform our consciousness—like the coming of Christ or Copernicus's reordering of the solar system. The world will never be the same."

This was the first time I heard someone link human consciousness and the environment. I began to notice the earth-as-symbol phenomenon everywhere: the *Whole Earth Catalog, Mother Earth News,* and of course, NASA's striking photos of earth from deep space. He was right; an environmental movement was beginning. Not long after that conversation I left the mental health center. Luckily, my advisers at Kent reached out and offered me a teaching fellowship. It was the invitation for an academic career in psychology. I accepted without hesitation and enthusiastically embarked on a new path into research and higher education.

Later that year the first Earth Day was celebrated. It was a national event and stimulated gatherings on campuses everywhere. For students in Ohio the first Earth Day had special significance. A year before, on June 22, 1969, an oil slick and debris from nearby mills along the Cuyahoga River had burst into flames. In their report of the incident, *Time* magazine described the lower portions of river as having no visible signs of life. A person falling into it "does not drown," they mocked; "He decays."[3] This was not the first time. It had happened at least a half dozen times before. One of the previous conflagrations in 1952 did more than a million dollars of damage to boats and riverfront buildings. The irony of a flaming river became the source of countless jokes. It inspired Randy Newman's popular song "Burn On." A powerful symbol of the seriousness of environmental problems, it also helped to spur creation of the Environmental Protection Agency and the federal Clean Water Act.

The Cuyahoga divides the city of Kent. Not surprisingly, the inaugural Earth Day celebrations of April 22, 1970, drew the participation of many university students. Some of them used the event to fashion a National Science Foundation student-originated grant proposal to explore the river and its environment as an interdisciplinary research project. As a part of these activities, I was asked to help with the design of an environmental attitude survey and related data analysis. This was my initiation into the psychology of ecological concern.

Other connections with the environmental movement also emerged. Many of the young environmentalists were interested in reviving the "lost arts" of traditional knowledge. They wanted to grow their food, learn to build their own homes, and know the natural history of their surroundings. As a child from a home with two fireplaces and a woodstove, I was sometimes troubled by these backward practices of my family. Home canning, cutting firewood, and a life without television felt out of touch with the Wonder Bread and *Leave It to Beaver* modernism of the 1950s. Brand-new things in those days captivated American culture.

The sources of adolescent embarrassment that undoubtedly contributed to going so far from home for college were coming full circle. And with this shift, I discovered a fresh appreciation for my youthful experiences and rural upbringing. Eric Sloane's *A Reverence for Wood*, and *Living the Good Life* by Helen and Scott Nearing, became manifestos of popular culture. The charm of the Nearings's handicraft and simple ways was suddenly no longer atavistic. Years later, I had the good fortune of having Scott and Helen join me in teaching one of the first college courses on "voluntary simplicity." This brought considerable satisfaction to my mother, who unbeknownst to me had long been familiar with their ideas.

The 1960s were a tumultuous time in American society. Young people were experimenting with mind-bending drugs and pulling away from their parents as never before. Strikes and boycotts, led by Cesar Chavez and the United Farm Workers, brought national attention to the plight of Hispanic farm workers. Race relations were increasingly strained. Malcolm X preached black power as urban riots and confrontations with police swept the country. Martin Luther King Jr. became the spokesman of nonviolent change. His 1963 "I Have a Dream" speech on the steps of the Lincoln Memorial symbolized the aspirations of a peaceful resolution. But on April 4, 1968, he was assassinated while standing on a motel balcony in Memphis. Robert Kennedy, another national figure of hope—and a presidential candidate—was murdered two months afterward in Los Angeles. Later that summer, the Democratic National Convention in Chicago erupted in unprecedented street violence with live television coverage seen by millions.

On college and university campuses across the country tensions combined and multiplied. Protests and demonstrations became widespread. Students took out their frustrations, in many cases, by vilifying campus administrators. Mass sit-ins were common. Buildings were occupied and classes were disrupted. At Kent, in 1968 and 1969, student protests were mounting too. Sometimes they were led by a small, but active, group of the Students for a Democratic Society (SDS). On some occasions they were aroused by visits from Jerry Rubin, Tom Hayden, or other leaders of the antiwar movement. The Black United Students (BUS) also organized occasional demonstrations that significant numbers of sympathetic, non-BUS students joined in support. Throughout all of this, of course, were the mounting frustrations and disillusionment of the Vietnam War.

The first Earth Day at Kent stood out as an atypical gathering against this background. The overall tenor had been celebratory and upbeat, despite the underlying concerns with pollution and environmental degradation. But all was changed a week later on Thursday, April 30, when President Nixon publicly announced the U.S. invasion of Cambodia. Until then, people foresaw the war to be winding down. Nixon had promised in his campaign to bring it to a conclusion. The announcement was electrifying. At noon the next day, a large student protest assembled on the commons. Led by inflammatory speeches, it ended with a symbolic burying of the Constitution in protest to an expanding, "undeclared" war. Later that evening, confrontations between angry students and police broke out in downtown Kent. As events escalated, store windows were broken and bonfires were set in the streets. When the mayor declared that all the bars were officially closed, the streets filled and the police resorted to tear gas to break up the crowds. There are many stories of what did or did not actually happen that night. But in their concern about greater disturbances that might follow, city officials called Governor Rhodes, who promptly placed the Ohio National Guard on standby alert.

I was not there that evening. In the aftermath, however, dramatic rumors circulated. From one side came accusations of police brutality; on the other, reports that radical "outside agitators" were involved. The next day was Saturday, May 2. I was on campus most of the day with my girlfriend in the pottery studio. In the late afternoon, we heard the distant sound of shouts. We went outside to see what was happening. A large group of students was already milling around, with many more joining them. A sense of agitation filled the air. I still have a distinct visual recollection of the scene. Almost everyone was wearing jeans. Against the green spring grass, their blue legs were highlighted by the yellow light of the setting sun. The mosaic had a striking organic quality, like agitated millipedes coming together from all directions in a pool of protest. The crowd coalesced and began to head toward town, as if to return to the scene of the past night's events. As they marched down the hill of the front campus, the mob suddenly stopped, reversed direction, and returned to the center of campus. The focal point became the ROTC building—an old frame structure near the commons. Enjoined by loud chanting, its windows were smashed as the building was pummeled by stones and somehow set afire. When fire engines arrived, the crowd interfered and the firemen abandoned their task. The building was soon engulfed—the cheers of the crowd mounting as the flames grew.

By then it was nighttime. In the darkness beyond the circle of light, a distant rumbling could be heard. It was the National Guard. They poured into town and onto the campus in heavy military trucks and half-tracks. There was a thunderous and jarring sense of an invasion. Panic spread as students scrambled in all directions. Cathy and I shared a small cabin in the woods about ten miles away. Our car was parked at a friend's house just beyond the outskirts of town. In a frenzied dash we escaped through the rear of campus. Helicopters with searchlights hovered overhead as we scrambled our way through outlying marshland and woods to the car. The main highways were blocked with police and military vehicles. But we were able to weave our way home on back roads.

We avoided returning the next day. But in town and on the campus, events had become surreal. Nearly a thousand guardsmen occupied the university. All student rallies were banned. The news was filled with disparaging depictions of the students and the institution. On Monday as we approached the town all cars were stopped by a blockade. Our student ID cards were demanded and scrutinized, but we were allowed to pass through. Military personnel and police were everywhere. University status was repeatedly confirmed by spot checks as students moved from building to building for classes. A large circle of uniformed men with weapons surrounded the former ROTC building, their backs to the charred remains.

Around noontime a group of students began to gather in protest. As they yelled and taunted the guardsmen, a jeep began circling the commons, making repeated announcements by bullhorn to disperse. When classes let out for lunch, the crowd grew larger. Tear gas was fired in several directions. Some of the canisters were picked up by demonstrators and thrown back. As the jeering and mayhem spread, one group of guardsmen backed themselves into an awkward position between an athletic field fence and the angry protesters. From there they moved up the hillside on the far side of the commons, where they stopped, turned suddenly, and began to fire their weapons.

In an instant, angry shouts turned to panicked screams. The guardsmen did not fire into a huddled throng bearing down on them. Most of their victims were hundreds of feet away. I know this. Cathy and I were squarely in the middle of where the volley landed. At the first sound of shots, it was instantly clear they were not using blanks. The bullets were audible, kicking up dirt as they struck the soil. Someone next to us was hit and collapsed on the sidewalk. We dove to the ground ourselves.*

When the shooting ceased, we discovered other people nearby who had been hit. Four students were killed; nine more were wounded. It was chaotic. Ambulances were called. The wounded and dead were rushed away. A dazed and grief-stricken collection of students and faculty gathered on one side of the commons. Nervous guardsmen clustered together on the other side, their rifles leveled at the crowd. Several professors pleaded with the students to restrain themselves. Geology professor Glenn Frank, crying openly, begged them to hold back, sit down, and stay peaceful. To my astonishment, Seymour Baron, chairman of the psychology department,

---

* Many of those moments were captured in photographs, from which the two of us were later identified and questioned by FBI agents. A number of the photos were also subsequently published in *The Report of the President's Commission on Campus Unrest*—a.k.a. "The Scranton Commission Report."

stepped forward into the open field. I knew Sy. I was his teaching assistant. He was a popular professor and member of the administration. In an unwavering voice he exhorted the guardsmen to lower their weapons. They did. The steady demeanor of those Kent faculty and staff that day remains one of the most selfless acts of spontaneous courage I have ever seen.

Within hours of the disaster, the university was officially closed. Students were immediately sent home and told that arrangements would be made for completing the term's work *in absentia*. But the future of the university was uncertain. There was talk it might not reopen. A multitude of rumors and conspiracy theories were launched and spread: demonstrators had fired the first shot; the event was incited by outsider revolutionaries; Soviet-made assault weapons had been discovered in student dormitories; the National Guard had conspired to teach the antiwar protesters a lesson.

The summer of 1970 was an uncharted storm of confusion. As university administrators and faculty joined forces to restore the institution, funds were dedicated to survey the entire student body about their knowledge, perceptions, and recollections of the incident. Responsibility for the task was given to Stuart Taylor from the psychology department. Stu was my graduate adviser. He and his graduate students, including myself, devoted the summer of 1970 to the project. A two-hundred-item questionnaire was designed and mailed to all students. More than seven thousand questionnaires were returned and analyzed. The final report, *Violence at Kent State: The Students' Perspective,* is still considered one of the most reliable sources of what actually happened that day.

The student protests of the '60s and early '70s were complex phenomena, fueled by emotional acting-out as much as by historical events. The student-power confrontations of that era shook the foundations of many institutions. They came to a tragic head at Kent. Witnessing the events leading up to the incident, being in the middle of it, and taking part in the aftermath was a formidable experience. The lines between students and university officials, so firmly drawn before the shooting, instantly dissolved. There were no longer any internal enemies. The frustrations over an unpopular war and the injustices of society, and the despair over senseless assassinations, were misplaced aggression. The mask of shadow-projection (as Jung might say) had dropped. The insight was palpable, the lesson profound. The university community was all in the same boat together. Only common interests prevailed—of salvaging the institution and healing the community—all the while under scrutiny of a national spotlight. The shootings at Kent State sent a shock wave throughout the country. Some say it was a symbolic turning point of the Vietnam era. Years of investigation followed. Multiple interpretations of the causes and responsibility for the tragedy still remain.

It is sometimes said that good judgment comes from experience—and a lot of that comes from bad judgment. The worst mistakes are the ones from which we often learn the most. The cultural conditions of that conflicted era, and the lessons learned, changed society and education. By showing how things go wrong, more creative and participatory means to conflict resolution now exist. May 4, and its repercussions, had a substantial personal impact on me as well. One of them was a crystallization of my academic interests. With Stu as adviser, my master's thesis and doctoral dissertation investigated the social and situational basis of human aggression. My research and publications with other Kent professors on attitude change, self-perception, and social cooperation were rooted in similar concerns. (I am sure the appeal of College of the Atlantic—where student participation is practiced on the highest level—is likewise underwritten by my Kent experiences. But this realization would take another decade.)

Gathering Points

The event that determined my path after graduate school happened quite by accident. During my final year, while I was doing my dissertation research on the influence of spectators on human aggression, Bibb Latané from Ohio State University was invited to give an afternoon symposium to the Kent psychology department. Bibb's research on the diffusion of responsibility of bystanders in altruistic situations had just appeared. It was receiving considerable recognition, and Bibb was a popular speaker at graduate programs everywhere. I very much enjoyed his presentation.

I was especially intrigued by his findings about the relationship between the number of bystanders and the (nonobvious) discovery that the more witnesses there were to a helping situation, the less likely it was that anyone actually rendered assistance. His talk had two main themes—one on the inhibition of altruistic behavior and another on group-size phenomena.

Between our master's thesis and doctoral dissertation at Kent, we had two additional degree requirements. One was a two-day written preliminary exam that determined candidacy for the PhD. The other was a lengthy literature review on a selected topic area, prepared in the style of the *Psychological Review*—a leading APA journal. I had just completed mine, which was a summary of the literature on audience influences. In preparing the paper, I had come across a diverse assortment of studies that seemed to show a similar outcome, across a variety of settings. Not surprisingly, the size of an audience is an important factor in social anxiety and stage fright. But most of the influence happens at the low end of the scale, i.e., the relation is nonlinear such that beyond a point ever-larger numbers of spectators have negligible effects.

The shape of the relationship was a mirror image of Bibb's results on bystander inhibition. After his presentation I went up to talk with him. He was intrigued by what I had to say. The conversation quickly turned to an opportunity to work together. Shortly thereafter he sent me application materials for a university postdoctoral fellowship at Ohio State under his direction. I wrote a research proposal that sketched out what I thought were the common features of our interests, which was accepted by the review committee. I was then invited to Columbus to give a two-hour symposium on my current research on aggression to one of the Friday afternoon department symposia. To my delight it was very well received and I was soon awarded the fellowship.

When I arrived at Ohio State I was surprised to discover that Bibb had two quite different lines of research. One, as expected, was about the psychology of social influence. The other was focused on animal social behavior. They were not unrelated. Bibb was interested in a general theory of social behavior tying together group phenomena in human and nonhuman behavioral ecology. I was given two offices—one in the psychology department and another across campus in the animal behavior labs. I split my time between both groups of colleagues. But it was in the latter setting where I became deeply engrossed in the literature of ecology and animal behavior. We found many instances of group-size effects throughout the animal literature that paralleled the human studies. Later that year we submitted a large NSF proposal to pursue these ideas in depth under the title "A Theory of Social Impact." The grant was funded and I was invited to stay on at Ohio State as a visiting faculty member in a combined teaching and research position. I really enjoyed my time there. It was one of the largest psychology departments in the country and a friendly place to work. In addition to the research with Bibb, I also had several successful projects and publications with other colleagues.

In the spring of 1974 I felt it was time to embark on a new path. The job market was good and I had several excellent opportunities. The best offer came from Purdue University, another Big Ten university with a first-rate psychology department. Arrangements were made to take a portion of our NSF funds with me to support graduate research assistants, which was a great boost in getting going on my own. My grant funds supported two new lines of research. I used part of them to set up a clinical psychophysiology lab to investigate the causes and treatment of social anxiety. Before long I had two graduate students busily collecting data. The remaining resources were applied to getting started in the new subarea of environmental psychology. Drawing on knowledge of ethology and animal social behavior from Ohio State, I began a series of field experiments of human behavioral ecology. A number of graduate and undergraduate students joined me and in a fairly short time we had a comprehensive agenda of research under way. I enjoyed working with an enthusiastic team of students, and doing psychological studies in naturalistic settings was fun. As each project was completed, we presented the findings at academic conferences and prepared them for publication. The real-world validity of our results attracted the interest of a number of popular magazines and the media. That was fun too.

But I had a nagging suspicion I was merely dancing around the really important issues of environmental psychology. I voiced my opinion in a few thought pieces that were published as brief journal articles. The reaction surprised me. I apparently had touched a nerve—in a positive way. A flood of replies agreeing with my sentiments appeared in my mailbox. Emboldened by the responses, I made a commitment to map the psychological dimensions of ecological concern emerging in public consciousness. My research team and I embarked on a variety of studies, measuring general and specific components of environmental attitudes and behaviors. We also explored the personality dimensions of ecological concern and began to model the underlying motives behind environmental apathy.

This was about the time I first heard of College of the Atlantic. My request to study the environmental attitudes and personality profiles of the college's students was accepted without reservation. The level of ecological knowledge and environmental concern of COA students was off the chart in comparison with previous research findings. It was an extraordinary opportunity for exploring the intersection of psychology and ecology. The research findings were soon turned into conference papers and published. These findings also gained media attention and were reported broadly.

My varied interests had found a way to coalesce—and the outcome was not unnoticed. In the summer of 1977, I was invited to take part in the Second International Conference on the Environmental Future in Reykjavik, Iceland. I was the only psychologist and the youngest participant among the assembly of distinguished conservationists and environmental scientists, organized by the International Union for Conservation of Nature (IUCN). It was a heady experience to share a week with Linus Pauling, Buckminster Fuller, Gene Odum, Donella and Dennis Meadows, Ernst Schumacher, and other Club of Rome founders so early in my career. "From the mountain," as Ralph Waldo Emerson once said, "you see the mountain."[4] Whither one goes from the peak is a new adventure. This was my first summit. It also marks the end for our prime transect—across the personal terrain to the midpoint of my life. The fabric of human ecology begins its weave here, with the next transect line, through the background and contours of ecology.

Cardinal Points—of Appreciation

The rest of this story never could have happened if not for two important individuals—Joseph Rychlak and William H. Drury Jr. Joe Rychlak is a psychologist and was my colleague at Purdue. His capacity to step outside of psychology and articulate it from a philosophical perspective is remarkable and rare. Joe has always had a way of sparking my curiosity. It began with our first brief encounter during my job interview and has never waned. He is a prolific writer and a steadfast advocate of consciousness, intentionality, and humanistic psychology. He has been somewhat of an outsider amid the reductionism of contemporary psychology—generally misunderstood or merely ignored. But for me, he has been a steady beacon of inspiration and a constant reminder for the place of subjective consciousness in psychology.

Bill Drury, who is no longer alive, was the best field naturalist I have known. He had a strong background in geology, botany, and animal behavior—and was an exquisite natural history illustrator. Before coming to COA, he taught at Harvard and directed the Massachusetts Audubon Society. Bill was an "otherwise-minded" ecologist, whose ideas were based firmly on broad field knowledge and Darwinian evolution. His views did not conform to the culture of holism that reigned over ecological science for decades. He struggled, throughout his career, with the academic hierarchy that promulgated the balance-of-nature/climax-community theory of ecosystems.

Like Joe, Bill was an iconoclast in his field. Their respective views, however, are almost mirror images. Bill was a reductionist in an era of holistic (and tacitly teleological) ecological theory, whereas Joe is the advocate of teleological consciousness in a time when psychology is enamored by reductionism. I owe a great deal to these two people. They have been lifelong sources of inspiration, each in quite different ways. They are also my nemeses. Like little voices on my shoulder, there have been countless times I have asked myself: "How would Joe explain this?" ... or ... "What would Bill say?" I value this lasting gift of a questioning attitude. The antithetical nature of their respective views is another factor that still keeps me searching for ways to bridge them. A less pleasing consequence, however, has been the difficulty of finding a satisfying resolve. Another "yes, but" way to see things is never far off. Great teachers do not tell you what to think; they inspire thinking. That is what they have done for me, in ways that have lasted decades. For this I am deeply thankful. Much of this book is a result of our real and imagined conversations. It is fitting, therefore, that it is also dedicated to them.

CHAPTER 2

Ecology

> The only piece of scientific truth about which I feel totally confident is that we are profoundly ignorant about nature.
>
> —Lewis Thomas

The living world is enormously complex. More than one and a half million species have been identified and scientifically classified. About 80 percent are animals. Invertebrates (insects, mollusks, crustaceans, etc.) make up the larger group, of which nearly a million species are insects. Backboned vertebrates (mammals, birds, reptiles, amphibians, and fish) number around sixty thousand. The plant kingdom contains some three hundred thousand species. The vast majority of these—more than two hundred fifty thousand—are flowering plants (angiosperms). Conifers (gymnosperms), mosses, ferns, and green algae contribute another forty thousand plant species.

However, this is only part of earth's biological diversity. About fifteen thousand new species are found each year by biologists, and many more remain to be discovered. Huge numbers of tiny invertebrates and microorganisms have yet to be classified. The estimates vary widely, but the common consensus is that a substantial majority of the world's species is still unknown. "When dealing with nature," as the Australian scientist Vladimir Dimitrov concludes, "the deeper we go into the processes of life … the larger becomes the field of our inquiry."[1]

Natural History

The roots of modern ecology lie in the traditions of natural philosophy and its outgrowth—natural history. Natural history is a long-established practice of the observation and description of nature. The search for naturalistic (versus supernatural) explanations of the world begins with the pre-Socratic philosopher Thales of Miletus. Thales's cosmological thesis held that everything derives from a single substance: water. The earth emerged from primeval water. It floated upon the seas and was rocked by waves. These movements were the cause of earthquakes and the formation of mountains. His observation that all living things also contained water affirmed the judgment that they likewise were derived from this fundamental substance.

Anaximander, a student of Thales, would critique the idea of primal material causation. He proposed a more fundamental process of *apeiron,* or "the boundless," that preceded substance and was the creative force from which all material itself came into being. His observations that organic forms dissolve and reconstitute back into life is one of the first statements of ecological cycles. He also speculated that life began in the sea, later moved to the land, and that humans were not present at the beginning of the world, but had evolved from fishes. Other early natural philosophers proposed alternative views of nature. For Anaximenes air was the prime substance. Empedocles claimed four elemental substances—earth, air, water, and fire. Like Parmenides, he subscribed to the view that they were fundamental and not created from nothing, *ex nihilo nil.* Mixed together by love and pulled apart by strife, the interaction of these elements—eternal and balanced—accounted for all things. Initially associated with celestial phenomena, this idea of an immaterial "unmoved mover" became a central notion in Greek metaphysics.

Aristotle is generally credited with developing the origins of scientific study. His biological investigations contained some of the first comprehensive studies of animals. His student Theophrastus extended these investigations with parallel contributions on the natural history of plants. Modern botanists still consider him the father of their discipline. Others would follow. The early Roman philosopher Lucretius revealed the scope of Epicurean philosophy and naturalistic explanation in his six-volume, epic poem *De Rerum Natura*. His keen knowledge of plants, animals, and landscapes is framed by a complete explication of the origin and structure of the universe. The Roman naturalist Gaius Plinius Secundus (Pliny the Elder) compiled a substantial *Naturalis Historiae* that was the standard text for centuries. Galen, well known for his contributions to physiology and medicine, gained most of his knowledge from animal dissections and comparative anatomy. These are but a few of the early sources. Many more were no doubt lost in the destruction of the greatest archive of classical knowledge, the Library of Alexandria, an event that still remains shrouded in mystery.

Beyond the various studies of Greco-Roman natural philosophers, medieval Arabic naturalists made substantial contributions. The prophet Muhammad transformed the Arabic world. By the time of his death in 632, the former tribes of the Middle East, North Africa, and parts of Europe began to forge a unified Islamic civilization. Learning of all kinds was encouraged. Schools, libraries, and universities were founded throughout the vast Islamic state. A new era of science and medicine began to flourish, replacing the once vigorous Mediterranean counterparts. In addition to mathematics and astronomy, a rich tradition of natural history was also pursued.

In the eighth century, for example, the great Arabic intellectual from Basra, Al-Asma'i, published *The Book of Wild Animals*. A century later, Al-Jahiz extended these investigations. His *Book of Animals* was the first to introduce the concepts of "food chains" and "struggle for existence," as well as some of the earliest ideas of evolution. His Iranian contemporary Al-Dinawari—considered the founder of Arabic botany—composed a six-volume *Book of Plants*. The Persian scientist and historian Abu Rayhan Al-Biruni added systematic studies of geography, geology, and mineralogy. His eleventh-century encyclopedic writings were based on decades of travel and field study. Among his many contributions to the earth sciences was the first calculation of the diameter of the earth by triangulation. Important advancements in empirical and experimental techniques for botanical study were made by the Seville-born Muslim Abu al-Abbas al-Nabati in the thirteenth century. He and his student Ibn al-Baitar conducted extensive explorations throughout the Middle East and Africa. These resulted in a massive botanical encyclopedia of plants, which stood as the authoritative text for centuries to come.

The knowledge and ideas that stirred the minds of these early naturalists would not be translated into Latin for centuries. During the early Middle Ages most of Europe was asleep in what Petrarch unflatteringly termed "the Dark Ages." The tables started to turn during the eleventh and twelfth centuries in the intellectual vitalization of the early Renaissance. Universities began to form throughout the continent. A hunger grew for Greek, Roman, and Arabic knowledge from the past. With the revival of classical learning, interest in natural investigations was also renewed.

Roger Bacon, inspired by the work of Greek and Islamic scientists, made important advances in scientific methodology. Bacon's version of empiricism rested on repeated observation, experimentation, and hypothesis testing. Combined with William of Ockham's principle of parsimony, the outlines of the hypothetico-deductive model of scientific theory testing were framed. Experimentation became the basis for distinguishing between competing scientific theories, with mathematics the preferred language for representing scientific thought. The physical sciences—astronomy, physics, chemistry, and optics—fell readily into the new paradigm. Copernicus, Galileo, Kepler, and Newton made notable advances using the theory-research model. But it took until the late eighteenth century for uniform methods of biological categorization to develop.

The Swedish naturalist Carl Linnaeus gave the unifying framework with his binomial system of classification. Species were grouped on the basis of shared characteristics and then placed into hierarchical groups—or taxa—of genus, family, order, class, phylum, and kingdom. The idea of humans at the top of the pyramid, and the Creator at work behind the scenes, was in keeping with a pattern dear to the Renaissance thought: the great chain of being. It was at the heart of Linnaeus's quest to classify the whole of creation. He never tired of praising the divine throughout his work. His aim was "of doing justice to the diversity and coherence of Nature," while simultaneously demonstrating "the concept of an infinitely wise and generous Creator."[2] His biological investigations and writings were a testimony of this motivation.*

Beliefs in an exquisitely diverse world of individual species, as the handiwork of a benevolent designer, remained the core of natural history well beyond Linnaeus's death in 1778. The study of nature extended scientific knowledge. But it also revealed the divine intentions of life. In English universities, the theologian and natural philosopher William Paley's *Natural Theology* was mandatory reading for young scientists and scholars. His famous "watchmaker analogy" was commonly taken as proof of a designer. The French naturalist Georges Buffon was another widely read author. His thirty-six-volume *Histoire Naturelle* was the most comprehensive biogeography survey of its time. One of the first naturalists to raise scientific questions about evolution and the possibility of common descent, Buffon would be an influence on later scientists, including Jean-Baptiste Lamarck and Georges Cuvier.

The emergence of biology as a coherent scientific discipline began in a fusion of the traditions of medicine and natural history. The term itself (*biologie*) first appeared in print around 1800, apparently from independent sources. Those most often given credit for its coinage include Karl Friedrich Burdach, Gottfried Reinhold Treviranus, and Jean-Baptiste Lamarck. Refinements of the microscope by Robert Hooke and Anton van Leeuwenhoek, and the discoveries of microorganisms and cellular structure, greatly advanced the scope of biology. So too did detection of electrical properties of the nervous system by Luigi Galvani and Alessandro Volta at the end of the eighteenth century. Hermann von Helmholtz's measurement of the speed of a neuron pulse in 1851 solidified the promise of electrophysiological methods, as a means for stimulation as well as recording data. Experimental physiology, a valuable addition to both

---

* Despite firm religious beliefs, Linnaeus did dabble with questions of how new lifeforms emerged. These questions animated his longing to discover transitional human beings—that included, among other things, a searching for humans with tails and a strikingly peculiar fascination with mermaids.

general physiology and medicine, fell comfortably into the hands of quantitative, laboratory-based biologists.

Alexander von Humboldt's explorations of the geographic distribution of plants relied heavily on quantitative work. His multivolume *Kosmos*, published between 1845 and 1862, laid the foundation of biogeography. A masterpiece of integration, from a lifetime of exploration, it tied together climate, landforms, and biology. Its systematic study of relations between organisms and their environment was a stimulus for a new level of theorizing and applied quantitative methods. The way to understand nature's complexity, according to Humboldt, was to take careful measurements in the field and look for general laws. Among his many contributions was the designation of vegetation zones associated with latitude, altitude, and climate.

The French paleontologist Georges Cuvier also applied comparative scientific methods to field-oriented research in the advancement of organismal biology. Cuvier was professor of anatomy at the Muséum National d'Histoire Naturelle in Paris. He is recognized for being the first biologist to acknowledge extinction as a scientific fact. But he was no evolutionist. Cuvier, like most scientists of the time, was a firm believer in the *scala natura*. Nature in this view was tied together in a linear scale of increasing perfection. At the bottom were minerals and then plants, followed by "lower" and "higher" animals, and finally humans—at the top. In this hierarchy, Cuvier classified organisms within four distinct branches: vertebrates, articulata (arthropods and segmented worms), mollusks, and radiata. These basic forms were completely different from each other. Similarities between organisms were the result of common functions, not common ancestry—i.e., function follows form; form is not shaped by function.

Cuvier's ideas were at odds with those of Buffon and Lamarck, who were suggesting that morphology might be changeable and adaptive to environmental conditions. Based on his knowledge of fossils of extinct species, Cuvier knew that the earth must be older than biblical assertions. To account for this he proposed that periodic "revolutions" had occurred, which had wiped out many species. His position was known as "catastrophism." It was an uncomfortable hypothesis for many who could not believe that a divinely designed and perfect world would permit extinction. A partial resolution was established by tying Cuvier's ideas in with biblical accounts of floods. But this interpretation was short-lived. Ironically, it was Cuvier's student, Louis Agassiz, who replaced the flood theory with his theory of glaciation and recurrent ice ages, which had been repeated worldwide. But that did not make him an evolutionist. Glaciers, according to Agassiz, were "God's great plow."

Natural history in the eighteenth century has been characterized as a "gentleman's science." Its practitioners were often members of the wealthy class. The study of nature for them was associated with the pleasures of botanizing, bird-watching, and collection of natural artifacts. Another group was composed of the parson-naturalists, who believed that scientific investigation was a way to enhance knowledge and appreciation of God's creation. Opportunities for professional natural historians were limited. Only a few professorships existed. The prospects began to expand with the creation of public museums in Europe and America. The British Museum, opened to the public in 1759, contained a small Museum of Natural History based on the collections of Sir Hans Sloane donated in 1753. These were further expanded by the work of Joseph Banks, naturalist on James Cook's first expedition of 1768–71. Paris's Muséum National d'Histoire Naturelle made its debut in 1794, with Jean-Baptiste Lamarck as one of the foundation professors. Its origins date back to 1635 when Louis XIII created the Jardin Royal des Plantes Médicinales—later renamed the Jardin des Plantes and greatly expanded under the directorship of Georges Buffon. The Humboldt Museum für Naturkunde opened in 1810 with the founding of Berlin University.

One of the first American museums (known now as the Harvard Museum of Natural History) was composed of three older research collections: the Mineralogical and Geological Museum (1784); the Harvard Herbaria (1858)—developed by the distinguished botanist Asa Gray; and the Museum of Comparative Zoology (1859)—built around the collections and effort of Louis Agassiz. The oldest public natural history museum in the United States, the Academy of Natural Sciences of Philadelphia, was established in 1812. Other major American museums include: the American Museum of Natural History (1869) in New York City; the National Museum of Natural History, which began when the collections of the Exploring Expeditions of the American West (1832–42) were transferred to the Smithsonian Institution in 1858; and Chicago's Field Museum of Natural History, incorporated in 1893. As more were established, the larger institutions benefited especially from the scientific investigations coupled with global exploration and mercantile expansion. The growing professions of academic geology, paleontology, and biology gave rise to others. The mission of these institutions, whether private or public, usually involved some combination of teaching, research, or public exhibition. The proliferation of museums stimulated extensive interest in natural history. This burgeoning curiosity was accompanied by the formation of many local natural history societies. These frequently resulted in various focal, amateur collections of ornithology, entomology, plants, mammals, and shells. By the latter half of the nineteenth century, "nature study" had become a popular movement throughout education and society.

Life Evolving

The first stage of any developing science involves the definition of its subject matter. Twenty-three centuries of natural history study, from Aristotle to the nineteenth century, had produced a vast descriptive account of the complexity of life. Taxonomy was the unifying framework for organization and classification. The careful categorization by taxonomists of similarities and differences between organisms had produced an increasingly clear picture essential to systematic biology. It not only showed the diversity of life here and now, but also gave unmistakable indications of changes over time. Scientific biology was moving from an exploratory and descriptive stage toward deeper questions of how these changes unfolded.

Ideas of evolution were in the air. The orthodox notion of a constant and recently created world was unraveling. The earth was clearly much older than once believed. Evidence of change was incontrovertible. New life-forms came into existence; others were replaced. And overall, life appeared to be moving forward with direction and purpose. Most biologists, at the time, still viewed the wonders of nature as evidence of divine creation. Evolution might reasonably involve supernatural intentions, guided by the teleological plans of the creator. These ideas fit comfortably with the burgeoning Enlightenment fascination with "progress." Moreover, our own—human—arrival was proof of the intrinsic tendency toward improvement and perfection.

Lamarck challenged the belief in the constancy of species with his 1809 *Philosophie Zoologique*. New organisms, he suggested, could arise and move up the ladder of complexity in two ways: through spontaneous generation (i.e., saltation) or by interaction with the environment. The notion of evolutionary "jumps" was not new. The proposition that adaptations by life-forms to local conditions could carry forward, however, was revolutionary. Adjustments by an organism to its habitat were heritable, according to Lamarck. The use and disuse of these acquired traits accumulated over time and gave rise to new species. It was the first truly coherent explanation for gradual evolutionary change. Cuvier, Lamarck's colleague at the Muséum National d'Histoire Naturelle, roundly criticized the idea. Most naturalists at the time were disturbed by it.

As Cuvier was attacking Lamarck, the British geologist Charles Lyell began an assault on Cuvier's catastrophism. Geologic changes, Lyell maintained, were not fast. They were slow, very slow. But over long periods of time these imperceptibly gradual processes produced vast changes. The uplifting of mountains, advance and retreat of glaciers, sedimentation deposits of rivers, erosion by water, and actions of ice and wind—all are still occurring. The processes that alter the earth, in other words, are uniform through time. Lyell's "uniformitarian" position led to a new conclusion about geological time. The earth is *much* older than had ever been imagined. And so, most likely, is the history of life.

When Charles Darwin set sail on the *Beagle* from Plymouth Sound in December 1831, Lyell's ideas were in his thoughts. A copy of Lyell's *Principles of Geology* was in his bag. He would later write: "I really think my books come half out of Lyell's brain."[3] Lyell's conception of small natural changes over vast stretches of time in many ways prefigured Darwin's later insight. But it was not a blissful revelation for Darwin, who struggled for years with his radical, alternative view. The conflict was not only in anticipation of public reactions. It was deeply personal as well. A completely naturalistic theory of life contradicted his religious upbringing. But the most painful problem was how it flew squarely in the face of his closest family members' beliefs.

Against this backdrop, it is little wonder that he waited so long to divulge his thoughts. Were he not prompted by the correspondence with another naturalist, Alfred Russel Wallace, Darwin would probably have delayed even more. The two men had exchanged ideas for years. But on June 18, 1858, a letter arrived from across the world. In it Wallace shared his speculations about how the environment culls unfit organisms and, over time, species change to create new ones. Darwin immediately recognized the urgency of the moment. As he later wrote: "My plans were overthrown, for in the summer of 1858 Mr. Wallace, who was then in the Malay Archipelago, sent me an essay 'On the Tendency of Varieties to Depart Indefinitely from the Original Type'; and this essay contained exactly the same theory as mine."[4]

Choosing not to betray his friendship with Wallace, he hurriedly prepared for both men's ideas to be read at the forthcoming general meeting of the Linnean Society on July 1 in London. In the midst of other topics and speakers that day, the ideas received little notice or reaction. But for Darwin it was a pivotal moment. The word was out. For the next year he wrestled with his evidence and notebooks to fashion a book-length manuscript. The following November, the book was released. The first printing of *On the Origin of Species by Means of Natural Selection, or the Preservation of Favored Races in the Struggle for Life* numbered 1,250 copies. All were sold on the first day. Another 3,000 were quickly released in the second printing.

Whereas the presentation at the Linnean Society failed to stimulate a response, the appearance of *Origin* was met with a flood of reactions. Some saw it as magnificent research, a brilliant synthesis, and a breakthrough of scientific thinking. Others countered with derision, anger, and disgust. Darwin's friend Thomas H. Huxley rose in defense. It was a more difficult challenge for the distinguished Cambridge professor of geology Adam Sedgwick. Sedgwick had been Darwin's teacher. They had shared correspondence during the voyage of the *Beagle*. Sedgwick believed, like Darwin, in "an old earth" conception. He was not opposed in principle to the idea that evolutionary changes had occurred over time. But he was a strong believer in divine creation. His response in a letter to Darwin after reading *Origin* was unvarnished. "I have read your book with more pain than pleasure."[5] Alexander von Humboldt, whom Darwin considered "the greatest traveling scientist who ever lived," was likewise pained by the secular mechanisms of natural selection. Humboldt saw divine purpose everywhere in nature. Natural history was the analysis of the Creator's universal plan; species were "the thoughts of God." He would be one of the last great naturalists to accept Darwin's theory.

Even Lyell was publicly cautious. There had always been a strong connection between the two men—personally and in thought. Darwinian evolution in many ways analogized Lyell's geological theory, as a sort of biological uniformitarianism. Changes take place slowly and indiscernibly before our eyes, following simple rules, over long periods of time. It was Lyell who arranged for Darwin's and Wallace's papers to be brought before the Linnean Society so quickly in the summer of 1858. He also urged Darwin to hasten his efforts to publish them more fully as soon as possible thereafter. Yet Lyell never openly embraced Darwin's ideas, much to the disappointment of his friend. Long after *Origin* was published, and its ideas became widely familiar to the public, Lyell could offer but a single sentence of acknowledgment in his 1874 geology textbook: "Mr. Darwin, when describing the recent and fossil mammalia of South America, has dwelt much on the wonderful relationship of the extinct to the living types in that part of the world, inferring from such geographical phenomena that the existing species are all related to the extinct ones which preceded them by a bond of common descent."[6]

At the heart of Darwin's thinking was an insight gained from the political economist Thomas Malthus. For Malthus, societal progress was inescapably hampered by a fundamental principle of population: "The power of population is indefinitely greater than the power in the earth to produce subsistence for man."[7] The same principle, Darwin observed, appeared to apply to all living things. Plants and animals have the potential to multiply very quickly and produce huge populations. But this potential is seldom achieved. Exponential growth is held in check and the limiting factor is competition between organisms. The capacity for overproduction, therefore, is ever constrained by a struggle for resources and continued existence. The living world is not, it seemed, a perfect design. Instead, every organism is faced with an individual challenge of survival. If profusion and competition are the driving forces behind life, the challenge was to discover the means by which they operate.

According to the philosopher of biology Ernst Mayr, Darwin's answer was not a single integrated theory—but rather a multifaceted constellation of five logically independent ideas: (1) *the nonconstancy of species,* i.e., the living world is evolving rather than remaining constant; (2) *common descent*—species are branches of a single source of life derived from a common ancestry; (3) *gradualism*—species arise through slow transformations, not by "jumps" or "saltation"; (4) *species multiplication*—speciation occurs from the splitting of existing species, e.g., divergence by geographic isolation; and (5) *natural selection*—which involves the production of variation and its sorting by selection and elimination. Taken together, Darwin's ideas displaced a divinely teleological world with a strictly secular one, which runs according to natural laws. Moreover, in the final pages of *Origin,* he hinted that humans are invariably also part of nature. "We are all netted together" as he put it, and thus likewise descendants of a single, common origin.

The Origins of Ecology

One person who became an interpreter and strong promoter of Darwin's theory was the German biologist and naturalist Ernst Haeckel. Haeckel is given credit for coining the word "ecology" (originally *öikologie*)—a combination of Greek words for "household" (*oikos*) and "study of" (*logos*). It first appeared in his 1866 *Generelle Morphologie der Organismen.* The term was meant to designate the comprehensive science of the relationship of the organism to the environment. "In a word," as Haeckel put it, "ecology is the study of all those complex interrelations referred to by Darwin as the conditions of the struggle for existence." And further: "By ecology we mean the body of knowledge concerning the economy of nature—the investigation of the total relations of the ... inorganic and organic environment."[8]

The natural sciences were now enriched with two broadly complementary approaches. On the one hand, evolutionary studies emphasized differences over time. Like diachronic interpretations of human history, evolutionary questions searched for causal relations. Antecedent events in the past could be linked to subsequent consequences. Exploration of the sequences of prior states into novel patterns was fertile ground for new hypotheses. Aligning geological and paleontological evidence across time gave naturalists a way to test their hypotheses about evolutionary changes.

Ecology, as Haeckel proposed it, was the study of short-term evolution. It brought about a different, synchronic orientation to science. The emphasis here was on identifying structures and interactions within a given place and time. Ecology's synchronic perspective highlighted the functional questions of how these interrelationships fit together. As Aldo Leopold later noted in *A Sand County Almanac*, "Ecology is a science that attempts this feat of thinking in a plane perpendicular to Darwin."[9]

Natural history, for centuries, had been primarily an exploratory and descriptive endeavor. Now suddenly, it was open to entirely new opportunities for experimental methods and inquiry. The combined orientations of evolution and ecology revolutionized the life sciences. These were not merely methodological transformations. They were an invitation for expansive theoretical innovation.

The meticulous research of naturalists had produced countless arrays of organisms. Their systematic collections illustrated textbooks, filled taxonomic cabinets, and lined the displays of museums. But it was, for the most part, a static picture of nature—frozen in time. The nineteenth century brought forth a new vision. Uncharted worldviews lay at its core. The fundamental insight, as Aldo Leopold summed it up, was "perception of the natural processes by which ... living things ... have achieved their characteristic forms (evolution) and by which they maintain their existence (ecology)."[10] As if some magic key had turned, a static pattern of thought was unlocked. The study of life itself was coming to life.

The rise of ecology, however, was a slow dawning. The ecological historian Robert McIntosh likened it to a gradual crystallization. Frank Golley used Claude Lévi-Strauss's notion of "bricolage" to characterize its piecemeal beginnings. Ecological orientations were first adopted in Europe, where they fit with the established traditions of plant physiology and biogeography. These fields did not exist in North America in the mid-nineteenth century. There were few professional botanists in the United States at the time. Most of them were preoccupied with the numerous government-sponsored expeditions of the westward territories. The minor subgroup that held academic positions was engrossed in classifying their copious collections of flora.

Ecological ideas spread slowly in the decade or so following Haeckel's contribution, and mostly as a general orientation and background phenomena. The word itself did not appear in a book title until 1885. The German botanist Hanns Reiter seems to have been the first to use it for his *Die Consolidation der Physiognomik: Als Versuch einer Oekologie der Gewaechse.* The earliest text in English, *Flower Ecology,* by the Iowa State College professor of botany Louis H. Pammel, was published in 1893. Other ecological investigations were furthered by the German biogeographer Oscar Drude. His studies of the relationships between local environments and plant groupings, and especially his *Handbuch der Pflanzengeographie* published in 1890, would become an important source in hastening the development of American ecology. The works of Danish botanist Eugenius Warming were also an important source of new ideas. Plants living in close relationship with one another, Warming proposed, were not a loose aggregation but a vitally interconnected unit. Environmental selection at this level was essential to understanding how new species could arise. His 1895 *Plantesamfund* (i.e., Plant Communities) was based on the careful study of infinitesimally small steps associated with local conditions. His notion of "biomes," based on extensive field explorations, became a foundational concept for ecology. Drude's and Warming's contributions were crucial to the launching of American ecology. Once their ideas did find their way across the Atlantic, a rich two-way flow of ideas between America and Europe soon developed. It stimulated a 1909 English version of Warming's earlier book, fittingly retitled *Oecology of Plants*.

Huge changes were taking place in America in the decades immediately preceding the turn of the twentieth century. The westward migrations that began early in the nineteenth century now filled the Midwest and reached the Pacific coast. As these states took shape, there was a corresponding spread of agriculture, industry, and cities. In anticipation of the needs of the growing country, Congress passed the Morrill Act of 1862. The act provided resources for the founding of a land-grant college in each state. In the same year, Congress also established the U.S. Department of Agriculture. These combined events completely reshaped American higher education. An affordable college-level education was now within the grasp of a much larger portion of the population. Moreover, these new institutions would also serve as centers of applied research for the sciences, technology, and agriculture. The opportunities for professional scientists, formerly scarce and restrictive, rapidly enlarged. New positions were opening everywhere—not only in established fields, but also in a multitude of newly defined disciplines.

The shape of science itself was under modification. There was increasing emphasis in academic institutions to make biology more scientific. The attraction of physiology, and thereby chemistry and physics, was seen as a way of blending the biological and physical sciences. These pressures were threatening to many botanical appointments. The traditional approaches of natural history—demeaned by some critics as a form of "stamp-collecting"—were not viewed as valid within the new sciences. For the upcoming generation of botanists, plant physiology was the proper "maturation" of botany as a science. Physiologically oriented botanists were few in number, but there was already a sense that they were of two groups. One group was attracted by the achievements of general physiology. They urged for laboratory-based research, controlled experimental methods, and the precise study of process and function. Herein, they argued, lay the ingredients of a true science of botany. The other group, having become familiar with the work of European ecologists, argued for a field-based extension of physiology. The former group desired a divorce from natural history; the latter saw the opportunities of joining and amplifying it. In either case, they saw some form of merger with physiology as a necessary step in the future of botany.

Historians of science point to the summer of 1893 as a watershed moment for American ecology. At the American Association for the Advancement of Science (AAAS) conference that year, held in Madison, Wisconsin, a newly created division for botanists (Section G) held its first formal meeting. Following adjournment of the AAAS convention, another forum of botanists was convened. The purpose of the second gathering was to specifically address issues of botanical nomenclature. Appealing to his field-oriented colleagues, A. S. Hitchcock from Kansas State Agricultural College introduced the problem: "The subject matter is familiar enough, but it is rather difficult to give a definition showing its limitations. It concerns itself with the adaptive processes of the plant, and with what the Darwinian school has brought forward and made popular. What we want is a term for this latter part of the science."[11]

A discussion of the competing views ensued and the need for clarification was acknowledged. In the end, an answer to Hitchcock's appeal was offered by the University of Minnesota botanist Conway MacMillan: "It is recognized that there is a group of phenomena very essentially different from the group which we place under the general head of physiology. These have to deal with the interrelations of organisms and their mutual adaptations. To separate these two groups it is desirable to use the term ecology."[12]

MacMillan was one of the pioneers of the new botany. In addition to his university position, he was also the State Botanist of Minnesota. A year before the Madison meeting, he had published a major survey of the vegetation of Minnesota. It was one of the first books to go beyond a mere listing of species in the region. MacMillan's work included a broad range of abiotic and biotic factors involved in plant competition. Emphasizing the dynamic interrelations between species, he also outlined a theoretical framework for explaining the problems of boundaries and patterns of migration at multiple scales. At the macro level, MacMillan applied these principles to describe the large-scale repopulation of plant systems following glaciation. He used them, as well, to account for localized zonal patterns of development around swamps and ponds. The book received a highly favorable review from the prestigious *The American Naturalist*.

The botanical editor of the journal, at the time, was Charles Bessey from the University of Nebraska. MacMillan had worked with Bessey and received his master's degree at Nebraska a decade before. Before assuming the chair of botany at Nebraska, Bessey had studied with the prominent Harvard botanist Asa Gray. Gray made an acquaintance with the young Charles Darwin on a trip to Britain's Kew Gardens in 1838, only two years after the *Beagle* expedition. The two men shared correspondence prior to publication of *Origin*—which included some of Gray's research—and were longtime friends thereafter. Gray paved the way for publication of the first American edition. He was a leading advocate for Darwin's theory in the United States. Gray was also familiar with the extension of physiology from laboratory studies to the relations of organisms in the environment by European botanists.

As an editor of *The American Naturalist*, Bessey was in a unique position. Virtually all new books and research reports in the field came across his desk. Included among them was the work of the European biogeographers Oscar Drude and Eugenius Warming. Bessey and his students quickly embraced the opportunity. The new ecological reorientation—on the close relationship between local environments and the impact of habitat factors on the growth patterns of plants—accomplished several things. It brought Darwin's ideas of competition between organisms and evolutionary biology into the equation. A connection with European physiological ecology enhanced the status of field-based research. Moreover, it promised to validate the mission of land-grant institutions—for applied science dimensions for forestry, agriculture, and land management.

When Bessey was commissioned to oversee the Botanical Survey of Nebraska, he shared the responsibility with his promising assistants, Roscoe Pound and Frederic Clements. The team drew heavily on Drude's book. *The Phytogeography of Nebraska,* published jointly by Pound and Clements in 1898, reached an important conclusion. Plants living in close proximity were not autonomous individuals. They were organized as vitally interrelated units or "communities." In addition, these holistic communities followed a regular developmental sequence of successive replacement. Their concept of "ecological succession" promptly became a defining model for American ecology. Clements elaborated this position throughout his career. From Nebraska, he moved on to the University of Minnesota, replacing Conway MacMillan—and thereafter to an influential position at the Carnegie Institution in Washington, DC.

John M. Coulter, chair of botany at the University of Chicago, was instrumental in launching similar conceptual models. Coulter had worked as a research colleague with Asa Gray on the USGS botanical surveys of the west, and was also familiar with the ideas of European biogeography. Warming's approach became influential at Chicago, especially to one of Coulter's graduate students, Henry Chandler Cowles. Cowles studied the long-term processes of change in vegetation on Lake Michigan's sand dunes. His fieldwork further examined the underlying relationships to abiotic, geological formations. His conclusion was similar to that of Clements: "There must be, then, an order of succession of plant societies, just as there is an order of succession of topographic forms in the changing landscape. As the years pass by, one plant society must necessarily be supplanted by another, though the one passes into the other by imperceptible gradations."[13] The sequence of succession within a plant community, in Clements's mind, followed a predictable sequence of steps—much like the way a human matures from infancy into adulthood.

The combination of natural communities and successional change were compelling ideas for the new science of ecology. Their appeal spread swiftly. They were soon extended to an expanding circle of habitats, from forests and bogs to ponds and islands. It was not long until zoologists joined the botanists. Stephen A. Forbes, Chief of the Illinois Natural History Survey and biology professor at the University of Illinois, extended ecological modeling to rivers and lakes. The natural boundaries of lakes, for Forbes, created a well-ordered social "microcosm" in which the aquatic community evolved and was maintained by competition and natural selection. Victor Shelford, one of Cowles's students at Chicago, further unified plant and animal ecology. His 1913 book *Animal Communities in Temperate America* was one of the first to treat ecology as a comprehensive science. Two years later, Shelford was selected as the first president of the Ecological Society of America. Shelford adapted Clements's concept of succession into animal ecology. Their collaboration continued and later was combined in a coauthored book, *Bio-ecology.*

The turn of the century was an active time for ecology in England as well. Botanists were joining in a comprehensive survey of vegetation in the British Isles. The Cambridge botanist Arthur George Tansley led the survey. Its results were edited by Tansley and published in 1911 as *Types of British Vegetation.* Shortly thereafter, Tansley helped to create and became the first president of the British Ecological Society (BES), the earliest professional organization of ecologists in the world. He also founded and served for many years as editor of the BES *Journal of Ecology.*

While Tansley was a student at University College London in the 1890s, the Fabian social movement influenced him. Their progressive agenda included a strong belief that science should serve social ends. When the First World War ended, Tansley became especially concerned about the mental problems suffered by returning veterans. Further troubled by the conservatism of academic life, he resigned his position at Cambridge and turned toward psychology. His interests led him to Vienna, where he underwent psychoanalysis with Sigmund Freud. As their relationship grew, Tansley was increasingly impressed by Freud's effort to discover the underpinnings of human consciousness. His familiarity with German allowed him to become an active member of the Vienna psychoanalytic circle.

Tansley admired Freud's search for laws of how psychic energies interact in the unconscious mind. The dynamic struggle to achieve psychological equilibrium—intrapsychically and socially—began to dominate his interests. He became a keen public supporter of Freud and made many contributions to research on sex and psychology in lectures and writing. These activities culminated in his book *New Psychology and Its*

Relation to Life. The book was an immediate academic success and a popular best seller. It established Tansley as a leading scholar of psychology. Peder Anker—a contemporary historian of science and an expert on the Freud-Tansley relationship—offers this interpretation: "Tansley's theory of psychology is largely a synthesis of Freud's own work with an exploration of how it relates to biology. The human mind, Tansley argued, follows the laws of biology, and these laws are best expressed in Freud's psychology."[14]

It would not be long, however, until Tansley withdrew from the profession of psychology. He returned to botany and an appointment at Oxford—and soon became one of the foremost ecological theorists in the world. The influences of psychology on Tansley's thinking would not be lost. As his attention returned to ecology, ideas from social psychology reshaped his views. Ecological communities were an outcome of complex biotic and abiotic interrelations. Plant and animal interactions operated as dynamic systems. The concept of equilibrium, for Tansley, was a key to understanding community functions. To capture the integration of biological and physical-chemical components, he introduced a new term—the "ecosystem." But Tansley's view of ecosystem was based on physical concepts. It was decidedly different from Clements's version of an ecological community.

The Clementsian paradigm relied on an intuitively appealing blend of organic metaphors. It was supported, in the background, by a kind of typological idealism. The model proposed that changes in vegetation patterns are best understood as a sequence of orderly stages. Following a disturbance—such as fire, flood, or clear-cutting—vegetation grew back toward a "mature climax state." These were progressive stages, resembling the development of an individual organism. The number of distinct climax communities was assumed to be small, which allowed for easy categorization. The overall picture was held together and carried by an implicit assumption that natural communities operated in a holistic fashion akin to that of a "superorganism."

Clements and Tansley shared many ideas and had met several times in Europe and America. Tansley, however, was deeply disturbed by

Clements's organic metaphors. When he was invited to react to them in a special issue of *Ecology* in 1935, he titled his paper "The Use and Abuse of Vegetational Concepts and Terms." The paper began with laudatory remarks for Clements's contributions to ecology: "At the outset let me express my conviction that Dr. Clements has given us a theory of vegetation which has formed an indispensable foundation for the most fruitful modern work. With some parts of that theory and of its expression, however, I have never agreed ... But I am sure nevertheless that Clements is by far the greatest individual creator of the modern science of vegetation and that history will say so." Tansley went on—with a detailed and blunt treatment of the traditional theory of ecological communities. He likened it to "the exposition of a creed—of a closed system of religious or philosophical dogma," in which "Clements appears as the major prophet." The critique struck a mortal blow to the superorganism concept.[15]

Tansley proposed an alternative model. His framework combined living organisms and the physical environment into an integrated and holistic system. "It is the systems so formed which, from the point of view of the ecologist, are the basic units of nature on the face of the earth. These ecosystems, as we may call them, are of the most various kinds and sizes. They form one category of the multitudinous physical systems of the universe, which range from the universe as a whole down to the atom."[16] "The ecosystem" promptly became a key concept in ecology. It continued as the central model for understanding the mechanisms of ecological relations for the next half century.

Ecosystems and Environmentalism

Tansley's ecosystem concept erased the quasi-teleological aspects of Clements's superorganicism that disquieted many ecologists. It offered a more scientific alternative. As the leading historian of ecosystems ecology Frank Golley explains: "Tansley's ecosystem concept is a physical concept, based on the concept of equilibrium and emphasizing the interaction of physical-chemical and biological components."[17] Equilibrium within an ecosystem is a dynamic and developing process. Progress toward stability develops slowly as systems become more highly integrated and adjusted. Relations between the living and abiotic components, as a whole, are knit together by principles of order, balance, and design.

Ecosystems theory and research flourished during the early and middle decades of the twentieth century. They were a means of eliminating barriers between zoologists and botanists, and for the elaboration of new hypotheses and mechanisms. The Oxford animal ecologist Charles Elton modeled food webs, predator-prey relations, and the pyramid of numbers. His work on invasive species and the "niche" concept paved the way for many other community ecologists interested in the structure of ecosystems. The study of population dynamics was greatly facilitated in the 1920s by Alfred Lotka (an American mathematician) and Vito Volterra (an Italian physicist), who independently derived a set of differential equations for examining species competition. The Lotka–Volterra equations became important tools for examining predator-prey relations and environmental carrying capacity.

Raymond Lindeman, in his dissertation research at the University of Minnesota, examined energy flow across trophic levels in the food chains of lakes. His "trophic-dynamic" theory was a seminal model of potential stabilizing factors in ecological succession. Shortly after taking a position at Yale, however, his work was cut short by an untimely death. G. Evelyn Hutchinson, Lindeman's colleague at Yale, continued to explore the dynamics of species interactions and biogeochemistry of lakes. His approach relied heavily on feedback systems, logistic growth models, and cybernetics. He maintained that ecosystems evidenced processes of self-regulation that produced and maintained equilibrium conditions. Hutchinson's student Robert MacArthur also took up the stability-diversity-complexity model of ecosystem succession. Using energy paths through the food web, he fashioned an influential mathematical model of ways that competition could lead to conditions of equilibrium.

Howard T. Odum, another of Hutchinson's students, pioneered the application of thermodynamics and general systems theory to ecosystem ecology. In 1953 his older brother Eugene published the first textbook on systems ecology, *Fundamentals of Ecology*. Gene had obtained his PhD in zoology at the University of Illinois under Charles Kendeigh. Kendeigh was a former student of Victor Shelford, and with Shelford, a founding member of the Nature Conservancy. *Fundamentals of Ecology* was an immediate success. The book went through multiple enlargements and editions over the next quarter of a century. It was the primary introduction to ecology for an entire generation of ecologists.

The Odums portrayed ecology as a holistic science. Following Tansley's notion of a hierarchy of systems, from the atom to the universe, the ecosystem concept was their central organizing principle. They placed it squarely in the middle of all biological systems—ranging from the level of individual organisms and populations, to communities and biomes, and ultimately the biosphere as a whole. The focus was on the integrated systems within each level and the emerging properties not found in the parts. Understanding the mechanisms of organization and causation required examination of the higher levels of living systems. The emphasis was on ecosystem properties of material and energy flow and the factors controlling them. The perspective focused on interdependent causal relationships and cybernetic feedback. Particular attention was given to inputs and outputs across a system's boundaries, measured against levels of organization within it.

By laying emphasis on the physical-mechanical aspects of "ecosystem behavior," the biological-evolutionary aspects of individual organisms were deemphasized. Instead, organisms tended to be categorized on the basis of their functional role as primary producers, consumers, or decomposers. These more generalized roles then invited the supra-population study of predation, parasitism, and mutualism as evolved mechanisms among animal and plant species in a particular place. The relations of living and abiotic components were further knit together by coevolved dynamics that imposed distinctive properties of order within an ecosystem. The interaction among organisms—and the feedback networks of energy, information, and materials within the ecosystem—was conceived as an implicit design, evolved over time: in short, a kind of organization that creates order.

Progress toward equilibrium and the balance of nature were key concepts in the Odums's model. In the earliest stage of development, ecosystems are hugely unstable. There is little diversity as highly opportunistic and individualistic species appear in a disorderly manner. As the ecosystem develops, these features get ironed out. Each stage of the developing community prepares the environment for the next stage in succession. Faster-growing "pioneer" (r-selected) species give way to steadier (K-selected) organisms that protect the ecosystem against external vicissitudes. Succession leads to diversity. Diversity leads to increasing stability.

The ecosystem model of succession, popularized by Gene and Howard Odum, became the standard paradigm of ecological science. Following World War II, their approach defined American ecology and its large-scale research agendas, supported by the Atomic Energy Commission and the National Science Foundation. Ecosystems theory also guided the activities of the International Council of Scientific Unions and their massive studies of global biomes by the International Biological Programme (IBP). Frank Golley's *A History of the Ecosystem Concept in Ecology* and E. Barton Worthington's *The Ecological Century* give an excellent history of this era of "big" ecology.

Applications of ecological knowledge became common in many areas of agriculture, forestry, game management, and conservation. But there were some practitioners who considered ecology to be more than just an applied science. For Aldo Leopold, the natural world had an inherent integrity. Understanding and appreciating wildness, for its own sake, contained the seeds of an "ecological conscience." Leopold articulated the ethical and psychological dimensions of ecology in the compelling "land ethic" essay of his *A Sand County Almanac*, published in 1949. "A thing is right," he proffered, "when it tends to preserve the integrity, stability, and beauty of the biotic community. It is wrong when it tends otherwise."[18]

The science of ecology was little known to the lay public before 1960. Rachel Carson is widely credited with opening the door. *Silent Spring*, which appeared in 1962, and her earlier *The Sea Around Us* were both Book-of-the-Month Club selections and longtime members on the *New York Times* Best Sellers list. Carson introduced the basics of ecological interactions to millions. Her books turned terms like biomagnification, food chains, and trophic levels into household words. At the peak of *Silent*

Spring's popularity, Paul Sears, chair of Yale's conservation program, wrote an influential paper on the "insight" potential of ecology. The article was titled "Ecology—A Subversive Subject" and was published in the leading scientific journal *BioScience*. His point, simply, was that the lessons of ecology would call into question Western civilization's core cultural and economic premises. Ecology would broaden our worldview and overturn how humans see their place in nature. Paul Shepard, whose doctoral work at Yale was supervised by Sears, later expanded the notion in *The Subversive Science*. The volume contained thirty-six essays on the ecology of humans written by authors from diverse backgrounds. Shepard, like Sears, maintained that ecology would do more than change the way we do science. Its influence would reach far beyond the sciences.

With the advent of the environmental movement, the young environmentalists looked to ecology for scientific validation and guidance. Many ecologists happily joined in. Barry Commoner announced "the four laws of ecology": (1) everything is connected to everything else; (2) everything must go somewhere; (3) nature knows best; and (4) (the ever-popular) there is no such thing as a free lunch. Paul Ehrlich's *Population Bomb* heralded a dilemma of crushing ecological proportions, which Garrett Hardin framed as a "tragedy of the commons." There was no technological fix for population problems, Hardin maintained. Our cherished beliefs of individual freedom were leading us inevitably into a social and ecological trap. Environmental problems were not only in the environment; they were problems of human consciousness and actions.

Academic ecologists refashioned their textbooks to meet the swelling concerns of students. Eugene Odum's *Fundamentals of Ecology*—the most widely used text at the time—was revised around a global set of interlaced ecosystems and environmental management issues. Ecosystem concepts of tightly knit and fragile living systems fit the aims of environmentalism. So did Commoner's notion that "you can never do just one thing." These ideas were readily extended to environmental policy and the agendas of conservation groups. Preservation of pristine ecosystems, and protection of the fragile balance of nature from human "trammeling," contributed to the Wilderness Act of 1964. The Endangered Species Act was likewise fueled by a mandate to protect any and all components of an ecosystem. James Lovelock and Lynn Margulis expanded the ecosystem concept to the planetary level. Their Gaia hypothesis, of earth as a self-regulating biospheric system, became a compelling vision. But not all ecologists identified with environmental issues. Some were reluctant to enter what appeared to be a social movement and saw themselves as primarily natural scientists. Nonetheless, as scientist or environmental activist, they shared a common view. Nature was composed of ecosystems, held together by coordinated processes of community, orderly succession, balance, and stability.

Denouement: The Imperfect World of Nonequilibrium Ecology

These were the basic principles of ecology as I learned them. Nature's course was not an aimless wandering, but a steady flow toward stability. When I arrived at College of the Atlantic in 1979, I thought the central aim of human ecology was to bring this holistic vision of ecology into human consciousness. As Aldous Huxley had clearly stated: "Ecology is the science of the mutual relations of organisms with their environment and with one another. Only when we get it into our collective head that the basic problem confronting twentieth-century man is an ecological problem will our politics improve and become realistic."[19] My job, as I saw it, was to find ways to incorporate these ideas into my teaching and research on the psychology of ecological concern.

I was happy to have several ecologists among my new colleagues. But one of them, Bill Drury, was truly remarkable. Bill grew up in Rhode Island. Both of his parents were artists who encouraged him to draw. His father taught at St. George's preparatory school. In high school Bill arranged to be excused from organized sports, which were replaced with daily walks of nature exploration. These years of field study set the foundation for a deep understanding of the nuances of landscape processes, along with exceptional skills at natural history illustration. As an undergraduate at Harvard, Bill developed his field-based interests in ecology with courses in geology, botany, and animal behavior.

Following three years of service in the Navy during World War II, he returned to Harvard, where he earned his PhD in 1951. His primary mentors were Hugh Raup, Director of the Harvard Forest, and the eminent ornithologist and philosopher of biology Ernst Mayr. Raup was an outspoken critic of ecosystem theory and its presuppositions of equilibrium and the balance of nature. His ideas of natural processes were an elaboration of an alternative model of ecology, first introduced by Henry Gleason in 1917. The so-called plant communities identified by Clements, according to Gleason, were not "communities" at all. In place of Clements's holistic representation, Gleason emphasized the "individualistic concept" as the proper focus for scientific ecology. The observed spatial patterns of vegetation, in his view, were merely the sum of individual species jostling and seeking their own advantage. Whereas Clements, Tansley, and Odum theorized about communal stability and order, Gleason saw competing individuals and species as the fundamental units of nature.

Hugh Raup's synthesizing of geological and evolutionary processes substantially extended this position. His fieldwork extended across New England, as well as the sub-Arctic regions and boreal forests of Greenland, Canada, and Alaska. Bill Drury shared many of these experiences. They came to appreciate how natural selection and human historical impacts unveil a more complex version of ecology. Humans are one source of ecological disturbance. But chance factors and natural processes—of ice ages, storms, fire, insect outbreaks, floods, drought, and microorganisms—also play major roles. The patterns of change are dynamic, and stability is the exception more often than the rule. Their nonequilibrium paradigm was a very different way of viewing ecology. Its relevance was not only at the level of theory or research, but also in terms of how these unconventional principles translate into conservation practices.

Bill stayed on at Harvard for four more years after completion of his dissertation, and he taught a series of integrated courses in geology, botany, evolutionary theory, and animal behavior. In 1956, he moved to the Massachusetts Audubon Society to become director of conservation education. It was the first instance of a North American conservation organization employing a PhD scientist to manage its programs. The position combined administrative functions with an active scientific research program and part-time teaching at Harvard. Bill also served, during this period, on the President's Science Advisory Committee under presidents Kennedy and Nixon. He was a coauthor of the influential *Use of Pesticides* report and also a solid supporter of Rachel Carson, during the onslaught of attacks on her scientific credibility, following publication of *Silent Spring*. His principal research focus was on the population dynamics and migratory behavior of seabirds of the North Atlantic and Alaska. He also maintained an active agenda of botanical and biogeographical studies, many of which were linked to conservation issues. All of these activities carried the marks of his alternative view and disdain for the dominant ecological paradigm.

In 1973 Bill teamed up with Ian Nisbet to author a pivotal review of ecosystems theory and research simply titled "Succession." They completely disagreed with Odum's assumptions of ordered and predictable change toward equilibrium. Ecological succession, they asserted, does not lead anywhere. There is no progressive development of species that reaches a point of climax. Diversity does not produce an emergent collectivity of greater cohesion and stability. In short, the prevalent belief in "the balance of nature" was unfounded.

Drury and Nisbet had the evidence to back up their claims, from years of extensive fieldwork and research by other ecologists. Ecosystems were not tightly integrated communities in which everything connects to everything, like a delicately balanced house of cards. Nature is in continual phases of change. Disturbances of all sorts, human and nonhuman, are common features of the living landscape. They may be limited and localized—or widespread. Things are not unconnected. But the relationships among organisms are highly variable; some are strong, while others may be weak or nonexistent. Some species may appear (or disappear) with little overall impact, precisely because of their limited associations. In sum, nonequilibrium ecology showed habitats to be far more heterogeneous and resilient than the tight linkages presumed by equilibrium theory. It goes without saying these findings flew in the face of conventional ecological theory. Moreover, the implications of their conclusions were entirely at odds with established ecosystem-based models of conservation.

Bill and his family lived in Lincoln, Massachusetts, where they became friends with their neighbors Ed and Pat Kaelber. Ed was an associate dean at Harvard. When he was invited to become COA's founding president in 1970, the Kaelbers moved to Bar Harbor to begin plans for the new college. The demands of administration at Audubon and increasing restrictions on his fieldwork led Bill to Maine in 1976, where he helped design the college's field-based curriculum. He also established a vigorous program of research and conservation ecology on the islands of coastal Maine and in Alaska. Many COA students took part in these activities. They were among some of the first in the country to receive a firsthand introduction to a new wave of ecological thought.

Bill Drury was a masterful classroom teacher and even more extraordinary in the field. We first met on one of my research visits from Purdue before I joined COA's faculty. I did not initially realize how different his thinking was from the common conception of ecology. It took considerable time for me to grasp that almost everything I had learned about ecology was at odds with his view. I had never been introduced to Gleason's critique of community ecology or the followers of his approach. These ideas did not appear in most textbooks. But Bill had a vast collection of articles, which served as core reading materials for his courses. There were many times when one or two of them appeared in my mailbox. After reading them, I would test out my understanding in a conversation with him. Invariably, I found myself stalled midstream in our exchange—after which the next round followed. I gradually learned the outlines of the ecosystem critique; grasping the alternative came more slowly.

I remember one night in particular. A small group of COA faculty had formed a reading group to discuss E. O. Wilson's *On Human Nature,* shortly after it was published. The dinner party included a mix of faculty in biology and human studies. Our discussion did not go well. The meeting ended in a discordant split along evolutionary versus humanist lines. Bill, who had been looking forward to a more creative exchange, was sitting across the room by himself with a pained look on his face. I went over to him and sat down. We were both exasperated; but somehow I mustered the nerve to ask him: "How *do* you see natural selection working?" He paused briefly and looked squarely in my eyes. "Have you ever seen a goshawk flying through the woods?" he asked. "Yes," I replied. "And as the goshawk glides silently through the trees," he added, "it reaches out and grabs a sparrow from a branch." "Uh-huh?" I responded questioningly. "That's how it is—like *strings*." Bill's image may not seem profound. But in the frustration of that evening and the puzzlement of my own search for understanding, it was a significant insight. Bill had little appreciation for ungrounded abstractions, especially in relation to understanding nature. The realities of life are actual occasions, where "this" and "that" truly meet and interact. By "strings," he meant seeing the world as it really is—and not through abstract hypothetical constructs or emergent conceptions of holistic systems.

It is tempting, as a psychologist, to invoke ideas about family of origin and early experience to account for these different orientations. Bill's parents were artists who encouraged his talents of careful observation and visual perception. His countless hours of youthful field studies and natural history drawing set the foundation for a decidedly Darwinian view of adaptations among individual organisms and local conditions. Howard and Gene Odum came from a very different background. Their father, Howard W. Odum, was a professor of sociology at the University of North Carolina. He was a prolific author on topics of class, race, and community organization who became president of the American Sociological Association—as well as founder of a leading scholarly journal, *Social Forces,* which he edited for more than three decades. His sons frequently cited his influence on their search for emergent properties and their development of a holistic theory of ecology. Their "sociological" orientation to ecology—in combination with abstract thermodynamic principles—discounted the particulars of individual organisms and species. One might say, to borrow a time-honored comparison, that the Odums saw the forest but not the trees, whereas Bill saw trees but not forests.

Bill became my mentor through the 1980s. His bit-by-bit contributions of research studies corroborating nonequilibrium ecology were invaluable lessons. The truth is it took a decade to unravel my preconceptions and develop a grasp of his alternative view. I often found myself drawn back to childhood and outdoor memories. Those early experiences and solitary encounters with landscape textures and seasonal variations were a rich source of insights. I sometimes lamented the lack of natural history instruction in those formative years—and especially its absence from my elementary and high school science curriculum.

I remember sharing these thoughts with Bill. My concerns resonated with his own ideas on natural history education. He believed an appreciation of nature begins in early childhood—during a developmental stage when a child's mind is especially open and curious about the living world. The most proficient field ecologists, in his experience, had the good fortune of having had natural history instruction during this sensitive period. When the college began to explore adding educational studies to the curriculum, there was a lot of discussion of how to develop a model of ecological education for future teachers. Many faculty thought that a certification program for high school science was the way to go. For Bill, that was too late. He argued instead for an elementary-level certification program. In the end, we did both—but he remained a steadfast advocate of students who chose the elementary level.

Ample evidence exists from developmental and cognitive psychology to support his position. The struggle to deconstruct the "deep program" of systems ecology and to revise my own beliefs is confirmation at another level. The implications of these ideas surfaced one day when Bill and I were chatting in my office. "If we were at a research university," I said, "and ten years younger, I would enjoy doing another doctorate with you so I could really understand your view of ecology." He paused for a moment and with a faint smile replied: "You already do." Whether it was an accurate statement—or an act of kindness—I will never know.

Bill understood the limits of my formal training in field biology. But he was also aware of my rural childhood and years of outdoors explorations. Those years were not spent on the featureless midwestern plains, whose uniformity gave birth to Clements's holistic communities. They were in the scrappy environs of the Hudson Highlands—only a few miles from the Harvard Black Rock Forest, where, as I later learned, Raup and Bill had done years of research. Upland climax forests are not a common feature of that region. Nor were they when Henry Hudson anchored his *Half Moon* there on September 30, 1609. Raup uncovered this fact in the logbook of Robert Juet, a mate on Hudson's vessel, who noted of the nearby mountains: "some of them barren with few or no trees on them."[20] Bill knew those landscape details were molded into me—and not unlike his own. I believe he also appreciated my persistent attempt to comprehend his view. He was clearly on the threshold of a radical reconceptualization; but it was still not fully pieced together. He had been working for years to integrate his vision of ecology and was on the verge of completing a book-length manuscript.

Meanwhile, my pursuit of human ecology was gaining momentum. I had been networking with other human ecologists around the world and was invited to organize a symposium at the Fifth International Congress of Ecology in Yokohama, Japan, in the summer of 1990. The symposium included the leaders of academic human ecology from eleven countries. Each participant summarized the human ecology activities in his respective region. My part of the symposium covered the history and developments within the United States. Bill was chosen by the group to give the closing talk. His role was to offer an overall commentary on the session, along with a presentation of his ideas of ecology and their human ecological implications. Following the conference, Shosuke Suzuki (from Japan), Luc Hens (from Belgium), and I coedited the collection of lectures as a book, *Human Ecology—Coming of Age: An International Overview,* published by the Free University of Brussels (VUB) Press. In the final chapter, Bill reproduced his synthesis of the preceding chapters along with a thought-provoking *précis* of his work in progress and forthcoming book.

Sadly, Bill never reached this goal. In the midst of working on the manuscript, he was struck by an aggressive form of prostate cancer. He died on March 26, 1992. Some of the chapters had been completed. Others were in various stages of progress. But the overall shape of his ideas was there. It was decided, therefore, to make arrangements to finish the book. Many former students and colleagues contributed. John

Anderson, an ecologist who worked closely with Bill for years at College of the Atlantic, stepped in to fulfill the task. With generous support from private donors, and release time from the college, John began to pull Bill's drafts and notes together. As he moved forward, chapter-by-chapter, a small group was formed to review each draft version. Bill's wife, Mary, hosted the evening meetings that were attended by Ed Kaelber, several former students, and myself. In many lengthy conversations, we were a sounding board for John's steadfast attempt to reach closure. It was there too—on paper and in heartfelt conversations—that we shared Bill's ideas and became the students of his final class. Bill's friend and former Harvard colleague Ernst Mayr reviewed the final manuscript and wrote a glowing foreword.

Chance and Change: Ecology for Conservationists appeared in 1998, nearly six years after Bill's death. For those of us who knew Bill, it was the occasion for a major celebration and appreciation of John Anderson's monumental efforts. Our enthusiasm was further enriched by strong and positive book reviews. As expected, however, not everyone loved it. Edward Goldsmith, editor of the popular British magazine *The Ecologist*, bashed it in a lengthy editorial review. Goldsmith was a deeply committed spokesman of the balance-of-nature concept and ecosystem-based conservation. "The principle of balance," as he proclaimed, "is so evident and so critical to an ecological world-view, that it is almost impossible to believe that any serious student of the world of living things could possibly reject it." Drury's attack on natural balance was tantamount in ecological thinking, for Goldsmith, to Nietzsche proclaiming "God is dead." "To deny that the whole is more than the sum of its parts," he asserted, "… is to deny the most basic feature of the living world." Stripping away the ontological protection of nature's equilibrium and self-correcting processes, Goldsmith feared, flung open the door to all manner of human interference. If this was what ecological science teaches, how could environmentalists ever protect natural ecosystems and pristine wilderness in their war with multinationals? And from here, Goldsmith gave his final frantic lashes: "he [Drury] reveals the close connection between his ecological 'science' and his socio-economic ideology."[21]

This kind of reaction would not have been news for Bill. He had encountered similar scorn from environmentalists and ecologists many times. What would have been news, however, was the extent of change in ecological thinking in the few short years between his death and publication of his book. The evidence had been slowly mounting for years. In 1977, Joseph Connell and Ralph Slatyer published important evidence disconfirming the old claim that pioneer species prepare the ground for a new generation of successor species. Steward Pickett and colleagues found similar results in their long-term study of changes in species composition, as agricultural "old fields" returned to "natural" ecosystems. Instead of ordered homogeneous patterns, they found a continually changing landscape of quiltlike patches of differing composition and stages. "Virtually all naturally occurring and man-disturbed ecosystems," they concluded, "are mosaics."[22] Their theory of "patch dynamics," based on unceasing perturbations and variable recovery, offered a very different model from balance-of-nature succession.

The tide of ecological theory was turning. The changeover was hastened with books from other leading ecologists, including Paul Colinvaux, Daniel Botkin, and Sharon Kingsland. It is unfortunate that Bill was unable to personally participate. But his contributions were not without notice. The year following Bill's death, Donald Worster gave this tribute in his book *The Wealth of Nature:* "Thanks to Drury and Nisbet," he wrote, "[the] 'individualistic' view was reborn in the mid-1970s and, by the present decade, it had become the core idea of what some scientists hailed as a new, revolutionary paradigm in ecology."[23]

Ecology looks very different than it did a few short decades ago. System thinking is still part of the mix, but it has assumed a much more "open" conceptualization. Contemporary textbooks are seldom organized around closed-system models, with organisms lumped into broad functional categories. Homeostasis, cybernetic feedback, and emergent properties of material and energy flux are no longer core principles. These abstractions have been increasingly replaced with a greater attention to the inherent complexity of the living world. In doing so, ecological science has become not only more biological; it has also become more human.

This trend is clearly evident in the Ecological Society of America's recent choice of annual meeting themes, e.g., global warming, sustainability, planetary stewardship, etc. Recognition of the status of humans as a worldwide keystone species has blurred the traditional distinction of natural versus human systems. Some say we have entered a new geologic epoch of our own making. The Nobel Prize–winning atmospheric chemist Paul Crutzen and the marine ecologist Eugene Stoermer have proposed a name: "the anthropocene." The coinage is clearly human ecological. But before going there, we need to take one more transect through the inner world of human consciousness and experience.

CHAPTER 3

Experience

> Life is not a problem to be solved but a reality to be experienced.
>
> —Søren Kierkegaard

To talk of experience is to enter a house of mirrors. Knowledge of reality requires awareness, yet we cannot know consciousness independently of reality. Experience is constructed and held together by subjective consciousness. But in an instant, it can become the target of its own reckoning as objective self-awareness. The objects of thought cannot be untangled from the processes of thinking itself. As the philosopher Quentin Lauer put it, "We meet consciousness only as consciousness of something; and we meet reality only as a reality of which we are conscious."[1]

The enigmatic conjunction of consciousness and reality is as old as philosophy—perhaps as old as thought itself. It is a beautiful mystery that has stimulated endless contemplation. The paths from ancient philosophy to contemporary psychology are lined with models and maps. In the academic world, emphasis is given to abstract and formal representations. Some seek to define its broadest outlines. Others favor careful renderings of its subtle features or fleeting moments.

Our everyday consciousness is commonly tied to the details and rhythms of daily life. Only in dreamless sleep is awareness of our self or environment interrupted. The rest of the time we exist as separate streams of consciousness. Sometimes we can hold fast to enduring moments. But mostly we flow in the crosscurrents of memories and imagination—an ever-changing mosaic of reminiscence and desire. Each of us is on a private journey, in which most of our personal history and felt experience is unknown by others.

Some years ago I attended a human relations workshop. The person running the session gave everyone in the room two instructions. First, she requested us to "Choose a number from one to ten that indicates how well you understand other people." Following this, her second instruction was to "Indicate how well you think other people understand you." Everyone was then invited to compare the two numbers. In nearly every case the first number was larger than the second. An interesting conversation about the meaning of the demonstration followed. Some people took it as evidence of their unique psychological talents. Others countered with the curious notion that such thinking might be a sign of self-deception. A different, though poignant, view focused on the lower number. "Maybe," one person suggested, "all of us just go through life feeling we are not understood by those around us." Further discussion ensued. Perhaps we keep our selves intentionally walled off, or possibly we are all unable to fully express our thoughts and feelings. Could it be, on the other hand, that everyone is too self-absorbed or otherwise preoccupied to care about one another? In any event, the general conclusion among the group that day was that our inner worlds were not sufficiently shared with others—and this, by itself, was inarguably meaningful.

So what is experience? The common dictionary definition is "apprehension of an object, thought, or emotion through the senses or mind." Its etymological roots come from the Latin *experientias*—*ex* (out of) + *periens* (trying or testing). A computer search using the visual thesaurus shows experience in the neighborhood of "to see, know, have, feel, live, or go through." It is also in the vicinity of other common terms like expert, experiment, and empirical—or its opposite "inexperience." Experience is used both as a noun and as a verb. In the present tense, it refers to the subjective nature of one's current existence. In the past tense, it can also stand for the accumulated product or residue of past experiences. These dual meanings raise a critical issue when combined, i.e., "To what extent do past experiences influence current and future experience?" This is not a simple question. Even momentary reflection raises a host of quandaries: What *is* experience and how *does* it combine? Why are some experiences remembered and others forgotten? What is knowledge, or memory, or learning? Are your experiences the same as mine? Is there wisdom? Do other living things also have experience—and what is that like?

Responses to these questions are found in every field of knowledge. But these issues also have a home field of their own. As the leading scholar of consciousness studies, Bernard J. Baars, reminds us: "We already have a systematic study of human conscious experience, and it is called 'psychology.' True, many academic psychologists deny this rather obvious fact, but if we look at what they do rather than what they say, we find that ... psychologists are always asking people about their conscious experiences."[2] Baars is right. The study of conscious experience has long been at the center of psychology. He is also right that it is an uncomfortable issue even for many psychologists.

The diversity of approaches within psychology can be bewildering. The noted theorist of social evolution Robert Trivers remembers his own confusion. "When I was a senior at Harvard, I briefly considered psychology as a possible area of study, but I quickly discovered that psychology was not, in fact, a real discipline, but rather a competing set of hypotheses about what was important in human behavior. Each school of thought typically specialized in the arguments for why the other schools of thought were erroneous."[3] Turned off by his discovery, Trivers went on to graduate with a degree in U.S. history.

Following graduation he took a job writing children's books. When given responsibility for a series on animal behavior—about which he knew nothing—he was at a loss. The conventional approach of anthropomorphizing animal characters with human traits seemed silly. So the publisher hired a professional biologist to oversee the project and tutor him. His mentor was Bill Drury. For the next two years Bob immersed himself in natural history, evolutionary logic, and social biology. As it turned out, the publisher's initial enthusiasm for an evolutionary story line cooled and the books were never published. But Bob's passion continued. He received a PhD in biology from Harvard and then a faculty appointment there. Over his career—at Harvard and later at UC Santa Cruz and Rutgers—he has made major contributions to the theories of parent/offspring conflict, reciprocal altruism, and self-deception. There is, perhaps, some irony in Trivers's life story. His initial attraction to psychology was frustrated by the absence of a common theoretical framework. True enough—there is nothing in psychology comparable to "the light of evolution" that illuminates biological theory. Yet the bulk of his work clearly flows back into social and developmental psychology, and evolutionary psychology has become one of the field's richest areas of new research.

The odd mixture of ideas and schools of thought that makes up psychology is not recent. It was apparent even in the discipline's earliest years. Hermann Ebbinghaus, the German pioneer of experimental studies in memory and forgetting, articulated it in 1908: "Psychology has a long past but only a short history."[4] A century later, psychology now has a good deal more history. But the long past should not be overlooked. The fabric of psychology spreads across an extraordinary range. In some form or another it touches upon all of the human studies from anthropology, linguistics, and sociology to history, economics, and politics. Many aspects of medicine and biology line its background—along with religion, philosophy, and the creative arts.

If I might digress for a moment, maybe we can grasp the problem by way of analogy. Biological evolution is sometimes pictured as a giant tree. Leaves and branches are an outline for adaptive radiation, budding species, and the overall diversity of life. A single trunk, rising from the earth, conveys an ancient starting point and line of common descent. The accumulated detritus from fallen deadwood and twigs completes the picture. These ordered layers are a record of the time where, here and there, some hardened paleontological clues from the past lie buried. Fanciful as this might seem here, this was actually Darwin's favored metaphor. As Darwin pondered his field notes and specimens, it was an image of a tree that gave him the clue to reverse-engineer the history of life. An early sketch of branching species appears in his notebook very shortly after his *Beagle* voyage. "The tree of life," in fact, was the only illustration to appear in *Origin of Species*.

So Bob Trivers was correct: biology does have a coherent conceptual framework; psychology does not. By way of contrast, what kind of pictures helps to capture a sense of psychology? To skeptics like Trivers, psychology might be likened to ancient Babel—a disorderly amalgam of academic subcultures speaking in a confusion of tongues. A more benign image may be an oasis where flocks of many kinds are drawn together and jostle for position. Another analogy might be akin to a multicultural assembly or an international trade meeting. Each group has its own agenda, but some notion of common purpose exists and meaningful attempts of translation are made. I do not offer these comparisons to be critical or demeaning. Nor was Lee Cronbach, in his 1957 presidential address to the American Psychological Association, when he likened the annual meeting to an eighteen-ring circus. Cronbach's message bespoke respect for a diverse and growing profession of psychology. It also affirmed the eclectic shape of its recent history. My aim is to draw on Ebbinghaus's useful distinction between the "long past" and "short history" of psychology. Although psychology may lack the solid core of biology's life-tree, the pathways of its story line are as richly varied.

The Long Past

Human history is filled with countless belief systems in which the psychological and spiritual ingredients are inseparably wound together. Animism, perhaps the original religion, is still widespread throughout the world—particularly in Africa, South America, and parts of Asia. These mystical encounters receive little acknowledgment in the rationalism of modern society. Nonetheless, they are still at the center of childhood experience and remain significant features of daily life for many adults as well. Their weavings go far back in time and are part of the long past of psychology. Some of the threads can be found in the ancient Egyptian *Book of the Dead* and Pyramid Texts, dating back to 3000 BCE. The oldest inscriptions were made on the inner walls of the pyramids. Later versions appeared as carvings on the deceased person's sarcophagus or written on papyrus scrolls and placed inside. Their contents include descriptions of polytheistic mythology, funerary practices, and advice on preparation for the afterlife.

The early Sanskrit scriptures of India are nearly as old. The Hindu *Vedas* and *Upanishads* introduce the Trimurti of Brahma (the creator), Shiva (the destroyer), and Vishnu (the preserver)—along with a pantheon of other deities. The texts contain an elaborate cosmology and guidance on religion, philosophy, and self-realization. In the Middle East we find the origins of monotheism. Judaism traces its roots to Abraham, who lived in the second millennium BCE, and the prophet Moses, who recorded the ancient Torah scrolls. Less well documented than Hebrew tradition, there is also evidence of Zoroastrian monotheism in ancient Persia. Elsewhere, in China, Taoism was founded by Lao-tze in the sixth century BCE. He is believed to have authored its main text, the *Tao Te Ching*, which describes "the way" to wisdom and compassionate living in the balance of universal yin/yang principles. Confucius also influenced Chinese philosophy. His *Analects* appeared at about the same time as Lao-tze's contributions and further shaped Chinese thought and social relations. Buddhism, which began in the sixth century BCE, quickly spread across India and Asia.

These traditions have long and elaborate histories. Many more traditions have developed—from them, alongside them, and in reaction to them. The Abrahamic tradition, for example, was substantially transformed and elaborated by the teachings of Christ and Muhammad. The Protestant Reformation split the Catholic Church into innumerable denominations. Judaism and Islam have likewise divided into multiple sects and movements.

The list goes on, but here is the point. The psychological dimensions of human experience are always embedded in a cultural worldview—or a *weltanschauung*, to use Immanuel Kant's term. These stories are elaborate compositions that bring meaning to experience. They unify conscious and unconscious presuppositions within a shared vision that makes sense of the world and gives purpose to existence. These frameworks and stories are sometimes referred to as "myths." The language of myth goes beyond concrete or objective descriptions. Its distinctive features rely much more on metaphor and symbolic narrative. The basic theme of all myths is that there is a larger field of relationships behind the visible plane. It is, as Joseph Campbell held, "about things that thought can't reach," where our minds and senses are opened to an awareness of the "ground of being." For Campbell, mythic experience performs four functions. The *cosmological* functions of myth provide an account of the origins of life, the structure of the world, and the "unknowns" of the universe. On the *metaphysical/ mystical* level, myths awaken us to the source of all phenomena and the sense of wonder. The *sociological* functions deliver the outlines of a culture, give definition to its social norms, and support ethical codes. And finally, the *pedagogical* functions of myth delineate the rites of passage—along the progression of life stages from childhood to maturity and the final portal of death.

The religions and myths of antiquity were concerned not only with the beginnings of the world and its component parts. They are complex maps of human consciousness that give psychological insights into the long past Ebbinghaus was pointing to. As Rollo May said, "We owe the emergence of our self-consciousness to our capacity to think in terms of myth."[5] Their rich narrations reveal humanity's endless search for meaning and the social beliefs that undergird moral values. It is in the study of religion and myth that we encounter the depths of the human psyche—of what Paul Tillich called "ultimate concerns"—in the perennial questions about life and death, hope and despair, existence and transcendence.

Ebbinghaus's comment about psychology's "short history" highlighted a specific lineage of ideas on its road to becoming an academic discipline. We should keep in mind, however, that psychology has more than one history. One of the main divisions is between the traditions of Eastern and Western psychology. Eastern perspectives tend to follow introspective, experiential, and intuitive approaches to consciousness. Spiritual aspects are not excluded but, rather, are integral to the development of higher levels of awareness. Meditation, yoga, and other long-established practices are essential aspects of psychological development and health. Mindfulness is a participatory pursuit, where inner and outer worlds meet, and the body is an instrument of consciousness. Western traditions take a more objective, analytical, and extraspective stance. Mind and experience, in contrast, are customarily treated as concepts or hypothetical constructs. They are viewed from an outside perspective—in need of description (or to be explained away)—and not to be explored from within. The difference is sometimes characterized this way: Eastern perspectives are like maps. They guide one's journey through the pathways and stages of consciousness. From a Western perspective, consciousness is represented as models; it is more conceptual, more "thinglike" and "over there."

This mental-map versus mental-model comparison is a bit of an oversimplification. But it is nonetheless helpful for highlighting how differently we can look at human consciousness. Of course, there have always been psychologists in the Western tradition who used introspective and subjective approaches. William James and Edward B. Titchener were among the early American psychologists to do so. Others, like Wilhelm Wundt, Max Wertheimer, Abraham Maslow, and Carl Jung, also drew many of their ideas from non-Western sources. Their respective contributions led to the development of psychophysics, Gestalt, humanistic, and transpersonal psychology. A myriad of additional East/West links have appeared in recent years. But the arrows in the history of academic psychology point mainly in one direction.

From a Grecian Urn

Like ecology, contemporary psychology also traces its history back to ancient Greece. Unlike ecology, the source word for psychology was much more firmly embedded in Greek thought. *Psyche*—the root term—derives from the Greek word for "breath." It sometimes referred to human "thought," but more generally to the "spirit" or "soul" of living creatures. The latter meaning is shared by psychology (study of the soul) and psychiatry (treatment of the soul). Latin equivalents are *anima*, from which we derive animal and animate, as well as *spiritus*, "to breathe," which connects to spirit, inspiration, respiration, and so on.

"Psyche" was more than just a word in antiquity. It was also part of a dramatic legend of how the soul (Psyche) and love (Eros) came together. We don't really know how old the story is, but Apuleius gives a very good version of it. Most of us know the outline of the fable. Variations appear in plays by Molière and Shakespeare. It is the fairy-tale motif for "Beauty and the Beast," "Snow White," "Sleeping Beauty," and "Cinderella," as well as the subject of innumerable sculptures, paintings, and musical compositions.

Psyche was not a goddess. She was the youngest of three mortal princesses. Her beauty was so stunning that people came from far and wide to admire her. Some declared her lovelier even than Aphrodite, the goddess of beauty. That was a problem. Aphrodite didn't like people admiring anyone but her, especially a mere mortal. She soon came to detest the young Psyche. To remedy the situation Aphrodite sent her son Eros, the god of love, to fix the situation. (In the Roman version the mother and son are Venus and Cupid.)

The task for Eros was to cast a spell on the young princess, forcing her to fall in love with the most horrible and ugly of suitors. However, when Eros beheld Psyche it was he who fell in love with her. That was another problem. So the god of love had to disguise himself. He succeeded, for a while, by meeting and making love to the beautiful princess only in darkness. But Psyche became curious, in part by the urging of her jealous sisters. One night, while Eros was sleeping, she lighted a lamp. In the nervousness of wanting to see his face she accidentally spilled some hot oil on him. Eros promptly awoke and fled, though not before Psyche recognized that her bedmate was the god of love himself.

This was a terrible situation. Now she was hopelessly in love too. A long time passed. Eros did not return. So Psyche set out to meet with Aphrodite, beg forgiveness, and urge her blessing. Aphrodite would have none of this. Instead, she toyed with Psyche, leading her to believe that if she could pass a series of tests the lovers would be reunited. The tasks were seemingly impossible. The first required Psyche to sort a roomful of grain in a single night. With assistance from a family of ants, however, she miraculously accomplished the feat. Her second ordeal was to retrieve a skein of Golden Fleece from a flock of vicious rams. By following the advice of the god of the river—to gather the wool hanging from a thicket of briars, while the sheep were sleeping—Psyche managed this goal as well. For the next challenge, she was sent forth to collect a flask of water from a deadly waterfall in the river Styx. This time it was an eagle that gave support, by flying above the black waters to fill her vessel.

Well, Aphrodite was really furious now. So she made sure the fourth and final test would end in failure. This time Psyche was commanded to go to the depths of the underworld. There she was to retrieve a bit of the beauty ointment from Persephone, queen of that realm—and daughter of Demeter (the harvest goddess) and Zeus (king of the Olympians). Again the voices of other spirits helped Psyche. They instructed her how to make the dangerous passage down, what to avoid while there, and the hazards she must evade on her return.

Psyche did all these things perfectly. But on the way back, just as her perils were about to be behind her, she gave in once again to curiosity. She peeked into the sealed box containing Persephone's beauty secret and was instantly overpowered by a deep sleep. The bereft Eros, no longer able to endure the separation from his beloved, flies to her side. He replaces the bits of ointment back into the box, wipes the sleep from Psyche's eyes, and promptly dashes off to Olympus. There he begs for assistance from Zeus. The gods have a meeting; Aphrodite and Psyche forgive each other; the lovers are allowed to marry. At the wedding, ambrosia is served. Psyche drinks it and is thereby granted immortality.

Before going on, I must apologize. The legendary version by Apuleius is far more elegant and compelling than my makeshift rendering. Everyone should read the original story, or one of the many later adaptations. It will be readily apparent why psychology has chosen this story as the mythic nucleus for its line of descent. Psyche's quest is a chronicle of archetypal proportions. The power of her love is the beacon of personal truth. Her epic challenges, and valiant return from the underworld, hold a universal drama of the soul's progress on its path to fulfillment. The familiar depiction of Psyche with diaphanous butterfly wings is a symbol of transformation and transcendence.

Not everyone in ancient times was satisfied by stories of the gods. First among them were the early Mediterranean philosophers who were hard at work with different explanations of the world. This is a history shared by psychology, medicine, and science. Empedocles, as we know, had proposed that underlying all things were four eternal and unchangeable elements: earth, air, water, and fire. The philosophy of Empedocles was a reaction to the Eleatic philosophers' claim of a single eternal reality. The "all is one" reductionism by Zeno and Parmenides lacked vitality. Empedocles, like Pythagoras, sought a more dynamic model based on a small number of fundamental properties. The interaction of these elements accounted for the world, as we know it.

Hippocrates built on the foundations laid by Empedocles. Hippocrates was a member of the Asclepiadic guild. Asclepius was the god of healing. His staff within a spiraled snake is still the symbol of modern medicine. Hippocrates wanted to rid medicine of sorcery and magical healing, and replace them with natural explanations and treatments of illness. In parallel with Empedocles's earthly elements, he created the doctrine of four bodily humors: blood, yellow and black bile, and phlegm. Hippocrates opened the door for the physical diagnosis of illness and the practice of healing—thus the term *physician;* for that he is honored as the father of medicine. Hippocrates's bodily humors were further elaborated into a psychological model. Each humor was linked to a corresponding temperament: sanguine, choleric, melancholic, and phlegmatic.

The intersection of these ideas had profound consequences. First, it offered a multilayered view in which universal features of the world were united with the body and with mental states. In addition—with mystical demons, exorcism, and incantation set aside—physicians were free to explore material causes of disease. Finally, by adding a fifth principle (the "quintessence" of balance among the four material essences), the treatment of disease became a holistic process. Medicine was now a hands-on profession. The medicinal use of plants—for healing decoctions, salves, and poultices—gave a practical aspect for natural history. The aim of medicine was health, and achieving it involved restoration of homeostasis by natural means. A strict taboo on human dissection constrained medical knowledge. But many things were discovered from animal physiology and anatomy. The later research of Galen, and the Arabic physicians Avicenna and Averroes, expanded the Hippocratic model. From there the road leads to the European Renaissance—with Vesalius, Harvey, and Da Vinci. Psychology's past along these routes is wound together into the history of medicine, science, and biology. Hippocrates may have removed the Olympian gods from human medicine. But he did not erase the predilection in human thought for an immortal soul.

Allusions to psyche appear throughout ancient Greek writings. Homer employs it with various meanings—as a reference to breath, as the life force, and also to signify the part of a person that survives death. Heraclitus and various other pre-Socratic philosophers used it too. But Plato was the first philosopher to systematically explore the soul. He believed the physical world around us was flawed, constantly changing, and filled with illusion. Behind this imperfect realm was another immaterial and perfect realm. This was a stable world of truth and ideal forms. The goal of philosophy was to clear away false apprehensions and find the way to truth, beauty, and justice.

A person's soul, for Plato, was immaterial and eternal. People are different because each individual is inhabited by a unique soul. It enters the body at birth and departs at death. Thus Plato made a strong case for immortality, as well as possible reincarnation. In his *Phaedrus* he wrote: "The soul which has seen most of the truth shall come to the birth as a philosopher or artist, or musician or lover; that which has seen truth in the second degree shall be a righteous king or warrior or lord; the soul which is of the third class shall be a politician or economist or trader" … and so on down the line.[6]

Aristotle held a more relaxed position on "formal causes." His philosophy took a fourfold approach to causation. In addition to form (pattern) as a cause of things (i.e., Plato's notion of what makes a chair a chair, or a dog a dog), he also entertained three other ways of representation. Because everything that exists is composed of some kind of substance, he proposed "material cause" as another necessary condition. Next, to account for how material things move, he introduced the mode of "efficient cause" (from *efficere*—"to produce" or "bring about"). The emphasis here is on the energy or impetus that produces temporal motion and changes. This is what we usually mean when we speak of "cause"—as in cause and effect, or "something happened *because* of such and such." Lastly, Aristotle called his fourth type of causation "final cause." This describes the "that for the sake of which" things exist or are done. It refers to the purpose or end (*telos*) that something serves. Final causes are attributions of intention, purpose, or instrumental action. They are typically used to convey acts of mind, psychological processes, or other "teleological" modes of explanation.

For Aristotle, soul and mind were much more in the world. So was everything else. It is easy to see why he liked science, and why scientists have liked him. Theologians have tended to prefer Plato, especially the Neoplatonic shapers of early Christian theology Plotinus and St. Augustine. We will return to these themes later. But before we leave the shores of antiquity, I wish to share a final fragment of Mediterranean mythology. It is surely apocryphal and perhaps not terribly important. But I like it—and will want to bring it into play down the line.

One day, according to Greek legend, a young man named Gordius was driving his oxcart toward a small city in Phrygia. Unbeknownst to him an oracle had prophesied that whoever arrived there by wagon would be the next king. When Gordius reached the town there was a grand welcoming. The people promptly made him king and renamed the place in his honor. In gratitude for all these good things, Gordius surrendered his wagon and tied it by the yoke to a large pole beside the temple of Zeus. His elaborate knot was made of cornel bark, so tightly woven that no ends appeared to enable its unraveling. A second prophecy foretold that the person able to untie the knot would rule all of Asia. Over time it became a celebrated feature of the town. The knot attracted many hopeful efforts, but resisted all attempts. And that is how things stayed until the arrival, one day, of the young Alexander (son of Philip of Macedon and a student of Aristotle). Alexander made no attempt to undo the knot. Instead, without hesitation he drew his sword and by a single stroke slashed it. It may have been cheating. But Zeus honored the prophecy nonetheless, rewarding the boldness of the initiative. The rest, as they say, is history. The story's veracity is surely overshadowed by its mythological appeal. But another, equally dramatic hew would happen again two millennia later in seventeenth-century France. The blade this time was in the hands of René Descartes. Its slice was not through a hardened ball of cord, but the fabric of philosophy.

In the Gordian Shadow

Philosophers have always struggled with the tangled fastenings of spirit and matter. With the rise of science during the Renaissance, things were especially knotty. Galileo got a special taste of its bitter noose in a monumental confrontation between theologians and the rising scientists. Copernicus had come along and voiced out loud that maybe the earth was not the center of the universe. Then Galileo, with his telescope, revealed the phases of the moon. He also discovered Jupiter's moons and other evidence for Copernicus's notion. All these things led to trouble. The Church accused him of heresy. His observations and ideas were banned. His recantation before the Inquisition barely saved him from execution.*

Galileo was not the only scientist to get into trouble with the Church. But his story was plenty good enough to understand the dangers. While he was suffering his dilemmas before the Roman Inquisition, the French mathematician and philosopher René Descartes was struggling with related problems of his own. Descartes was a brilliant mathematician. By combining Arabic algebra and Euclidean geometry, he came up with analytical geometry. Descartes's contributions to mathematics were crucial to the development of calculus, physics, and engineering. The fruits of these labors are the abstract system of mathematical representation we all know as the Cartesian coordinate system (in honor of him). Descartes was aware of the Church's condemnation of Galileo and the heat surrounding these

---

*According to John Visvader, the problem was not primarily about Galileo's use of Copernicus's mathematics. The real issue was that he got himself mixed up in the Church's fight with the "magical tradition that thought the Sun was the central living being."

issues. Like Galileo, he was committed to science. He was also a devout Christian. Descartes was no fool. Because of Galileo's plight, he held back the publication of his own treatise on Copernican ideas, *Le Monde,* until after his death.

Descartes was also a spectacular philosopher. After an episode of deep doubt and reflection, he emerged with the famous resolution *cogito ergo sum* ("I think, therefore I am"). The independent existence of a thinking being is irrefutable. Descartes's insight introduced a clear bifurcation between mind and matter. Thought and material reality are separate realms. Each is composed of distinct attributes and properties. Mind is unitary and indivisible. It is characterized by thought, feeling, consciousness, and intention. The body, on the other hand, is spatial, extended, and nonthinking. Like the rest of the physical world, it is characterized by spatiotemporal and physical properties of mass and force.

Descartes accomplished several things by establishing the independence of mental and material realms. God and human souls were freed from all material views. This would become an easy proof of immortality. Religion was liberated from mechanistic explanations. Moreover, as only humans possessed souls, animals could be seen as insentient automatons. The door on that side was open to an exclusive reliance on physical causality and physiology. Theologians and metaphysicians no longer needed to quarrel with empirical scientists—and vice versa. Descartes's feat was an elegant piece of surgery. But as Solomon Diamond notes: "One might say that in the battle between rationalism and empiricism, he carried ammunition for both armies."[7]

Cartesian mind/body dualism really stirred up philosophers. Benedict Spinoza espoused a single underlying substance of reality with infinite attributes, two of which are mind and body. Gottfried Leibniz attacked Descartes's dichotomy on metaphysical grounds and attempted a resolution with his theory of monads. In Spinoza's and Leibniz's views, spirit and matter were causally independent attributes that ran in parallel, but did not interact. For Descartes, however, they somehow did interact. This happened at a tiny point, which he located deep in the brain. But most thinkers after Descartes have rejected his notion as an untestable hypothesis.

British philosophers took a different stance. Francis Bacon opposed the medieval uses of Aristotelian logic and the position that the more causes that were brought to a description the better it was. Like William of Ockham, Bacon held that the least was best. The goals of science must be to explain things solely through discovery of nature's underlying physical causes. Thomas Hobbes was a friend of Bacon—and Galileo too. In 1650 he laid out his psychological ideas in his classic *Treatise on Human Nature*. All mental phenomena, according to Hobbes, can be reduced to mechanical explanations. "All is body," he said. Consciousness, memory, and thought are derived from sense impressions. Free will is an illusion. Human behavior is not by choice, but is a natural avoidance of pain or the pursuit of pleasure. With his doctrines of hedonism and scientific materialism, Hobbes became the father of British empiricism. George Berkeley's theory of visual space perception, based on the compounding of sensory qualities, became the prototype for associationism. John Locke added to the position with his *tabula rasa* conception of the mind as a blank slate. "Let us then suppose the mind to be, as we say, white paper void of all characters, without any ideas. How comes it to be furnished?" he asked. "To this I answer, in one word, from *experience*."[8] In Locke's view, lower things add up to higher-level things. Everything can be accounted for. As with Newtonian physics, these laws can be discovered and expressed in mathematical theories. David Hume took an even more skeptical position. "What we call mind," he said, "is nothing but a heap or collection of different perceptions, united together by certain relations." Hume's doubts went even deeper, suggesting that there is no connection between cause and effect. And therefore, perhaps, even science couldn't be used to figure things out.[9]

Back on the Continent, in Germany, Hume's pessimism stunned Immanuel Kant. There were a lot of things he disliked about British empiricism, but if even natural science was in danger—well, that was just too much. So Kant set out to put philosophy back together again. He accepted the notion that the objects of our knowledge are derived from sensory experience. But he distinguished between two realms: *phenomena*, i.e., appearances—which can be known, and *noumena*, the actual—but unknowable—things themselves. But sense data are meaningless without the activity of a synthesizing mind. As he said, "thoughts without content are empty, perceptions without conceptions are blind."[10]

Kant brought "mind" back into experience and added that there are certain inborn, natural ways in which it worked. Human consciousness, in his model, organizes sensations and puts meaning onto reality. Experience is actively "construed" by mental functions. The self, for Kant, has its own conceptualizing structures to "make" sense, to "understand" things, and to "imagine" alternatives. It also contains the inherent capacities to transcend itself within consciousness. Thereby, Kant allowed for a reflective self—capable of exercising doubt and oppositional meaning—that could reason dialectically and synthesize entirely new positions.

The Light of Consciousness

The term "phenomena" generally refers to the objects of perception or the ever-changing outward appearances of things. Its singular form, phenomenon, has multiple meanings. In physics it refers to "an observable event." The meaning is enlarged in ordinary language to describe an unusual occurrence, an outstanding achievement, or broader still, a remarkable person. The word is also rich in ancient meaning. The roots come from the Greek noun *phainomena*, for "appearances," or verb *phaino*, "to make visible" or "to come to light." Fantastic and fantasy (sometimes spelled with "ph") share these etymological roots as well. These word origins are likewise associated with the Orphic god Phanes (or Protogonos), who hatched from the cosmic egg and was the source of the universe in Greek mythology. When the golden-winged primordial being burst forth, one-half of the broken shell became the skies and the other the earth.

A similar cosmogony is found in the Hindu creation story of Hiranyagarbha (a.k.a. Brahma), who, in cyclic time, creates and re-creates the world. A world-egg origin occurs in the Chinese Pangu legend and in many other creation stories from Africa, Polynesia, and the Americas. A fifteenth-century representation is given in Hieronymus Bosch's *Garden of Earthly Delights*. Most people are familiar with the triptych's vivid depiction of Paradise, Earth, and Hell. When the panels are closed, however, a less well-known motif is revealed on the exterior. Through a crystal shell we see a world-in-creation, not yet with humans, suspended in a dark cosmos awaiting its birth.

The spontaneous manifestation of the world is a primal wonder. In other creation stories the universe begins with a feathered serpent, a disk of light in the eternal darkness, or a lotus springing from Vishnu's navel. But the questions are the same. How did everything begin? These are the really huge questions about appearances. They are deeply rooted in our psychic search for meaning. Later on in our chronicle of psychology we will encounter them again. Freud wrestled with his versions. Carl Jung plumbed the depths of dreams and archetypal symbolism on his quest. Joseph Campbell ran a parallel course in studies of comparative mythology. Other groundbreaking contributions came from Viktor Frankl, Rollo May, Claire Douglas, and Ann Ulanov. We will meet these people and their ideas later. For now, though, we should return to Europe and pick up where we left off.

Europe in the eighteenth century was an exciting time. Philosophy, as we've seen, had taken Descartes's mind/body dualism to quite different alternatives. Locke and the British empiricists were realists. Experience comes from reality *into* the mind, where everything is added up and is accounted for in a constitutive model. In Kant's Germanic idealism, mind is an active agent, with the capacity to organize and put meaning *onto* experience. Theorizing about mental processes from this point of view allowed a more subjective and introspective position.

Psychology, insofar as it existed at that time, was still a branch of philosophy. But the intellectual context of the Enlightenment and the rise of science were changing things. By the close of the eighteenth century, Luigi Galvani had discovered the electrochemical properties of the nervous system. This was soon followed by Carl Ludwig's invention of the kymograph for recording muscular motion, blood pressure, and other physiological events. Meanwhile, Dmitri Mendeleev's working out of the periodic table was transforming chemistry into an empirical science. In medicine, Louis Pasteur and Robert Koch discovered the germ theory of physical diseases, while Jean-Martin Charcot used hypnotism to explore the etiology of psychosomatic disorders.

The scientific revolution was breaking new ground in all directions—from physics and chemistry to biology and medicine. Even in the traditional human studies, a new generation of social sciences was unfolding. Adam Smith launched the science of economics. Niccolò Machiavelli, Alexis de Tocqueville, and Karl Marx were devising empirical approaches to political science. The founder of modern sociology, Auguste Comte, promised to discover the scientific laws of social progress. For Comte the progress of history and knowledge unfolds in three successive stages. The first is the theological phase, which is then followed by a metaphysical or speculative period. Finally, as he proffered, knowledge reaches maturity—in a quantitative, scientific, or "positive" stage. It is from these far-flung sources that we find a fresh start for contemporary psychology. So, one might ask: if economics, politics, and sociology can do it, why not psychology?

An Untidy Confluence: The Short History of Psychology

Philosophy had supplied a profusion of theories about the mind and consciousness. Science offered something else: methods for testing ideas. Laboratory experimentation was the heart of nineteenth-century natural science. The development of new scientific instruments was responsible for many of its successes. Experimental physiology was coming up with interesting and useful discoveries. It offered an opening to move beyond philosophy; and here is where psychology took its first steps toward independence. Maybe the mind couldn't directly know the objects of the world. Yet clearly the brain, mind, and world are somehow inextricably linked. The nervous system is intermediary between inner experience and the outer world. Physiology could be studied scientifically. States of the nervous system could then be related to the mental processes of sensation and conscious experience.

The science of conscious experience formally began when Wilhelm Wundt at the University of Leipzig opened the first psychology laboratory in 1879. For this, Wundt has earned the distinction as "father of experimental psychology." He and his colleague Gustav Fechner would have an enormous influence on scientific psychology. Their phenomenological physiology combined the methods of experimental physiology and psychological introspection. Through careful experimentation they explored the fundamental components of consciousness, perception, and sensation. Both men made individual contributions to the new psychology. But they are perhaps best known for their joint work in psychophysics and discovery of the Weber–Fechner law: that there exists a logarithmic relation between the physical strength of a stimulus and the intensity of its sensation.

The laboratory in Leipzig was a magnet for aspiring pioneers of psychological research. Emil Kraepelin's early work on conscious experience in Wundt's lab led to the scientific study of psychosis. Among his many contributions were the clinical classification of manic depression, dementia praecox (later called schizophrenia), and the foundations of modern psychiatry and psychopharmacology. The origins of American psychology began there too. G. Stanley Hall did his postdoctoral studies at Leipzig. He later returned to Johns Hopkins University to establish the first experimental psychology laboratory in the United States in 1883. Three years later, the first U.S. doctorate in psychology was given to Joseph Jastrow under Hall's direction.* James McKeen Cattell, another of Wundt's students, went to the University of Pennsylvania to become the first "professor of psychology" at an American university in 1888. E. B. Titchener soon followed and established an experimental program at Cornell. The American Psychological Association (APA) was founded in 1892 with Hall as its first president, who also launched a series of APA research journals.

---

* There are conflicting accounts of who actually received the first American doctorate in psychology. Hall, who completed his PhD under William James in 1878 at Harvard, also studied in Wundt's lab, after which he went to Johns Hopkins. By some accounts, Hall is considered the first American doctorate; for others, the credit is given to his student, Joseph Jastrow. The distinction, it seems, rests on whether the philosophical psychology (of James) or the first doctorate from a formally established department of psychology is the preferred measure.

The early years of psychology were not free of discord. The Wundtian approach, championed in America by Titchener and others, was built on two important principles. One was concerned with the theoretical goals of psychological science; the other was about the proper methods to study consciousness. On the first issue, Titchener believed that understanding the basic elements of experience and the structures of the mind was fundamental to psychology.*

The second—methodological—issue concerned the procedural techniques for collecting psychological data. Introspectionism in the Leipzig tradition was anchored in first-person accounts and interpretations of immediate awareness. Experimental research usually relied on highly trained observers, who were familiar with the purpose of the experiments in which they participated.

Both of these principles soon fell under attack by a new school of psychology. The "functionalists," as they were known, were influenced by Darwinian ideas and evolutionary biology. If consciousness is the product of evolved adaptations, they reasoned, the question then should be "what is consciousness for?" (i.e., what were the evolutionary problems that consciousness solved?; what environmental pressures led to certain mental functions?; how do individual differences and heritability enter into the picture?). The leaders of this alternative view were John Dewey and James Angell from the University of Chicago, and E. L. Thorndike at Columbia University. Psychology's aim, for them, should be directed toward mental *processes* and not, as it had been, on mental *states*. The functionalist/structuralist controversy also carried elements of an American versus European dispute. The symbolic peak emerged in 1895–96 in an exchange between Titchener and the Princeton developmental psychologist James Mark Baldwin. The Titchener/Baldwin debate is taken as one of the major turning points and paradigm shifts in American psychology. In its aftermath, the theoretical direction of the young field was forever changed.

---

* Some people liken Titchener's approach to assuming, as in biology, anatomy ought to be learned before physiology—or in the physical sciences, perhaps, working out the elements and structures of chemistry should precede the study of physics. We may be reminded here of Aristotle's distinction between material versus efficient causes.

So too were its empirical methods. Introspection relied on trained observers who "split" their consciousness between having an experience and reporting on the experience. Most studies relied on experiments with only a few participants, and individual differences were treated as a nuisance of imprecise measurement. For the functionalists, individual variations were of interest and a legitimate focus of study. With the aid of statistics they could be analyzed as experimental or correlated variables. Psychological research rapidly reoriented toward the study of large groups of individuals and the use of "naive" subjects.

There is a curious twisting of language here. In introspection the person reporting on his subjective experiences was termed "an observer." Under the new functionalist model, individuals were treated methodologically as objects, but paradoxically called "subjects." In effect, American psychology took a giant step back, away from the actual contents of consciousness, and became more like the physical sciences. This change in methodology would have profound theoretical consequences as well.

Depth Psychology

Meanwhile, back in Europe a young Sigmund Freud was completing his medical studies at the University of Vienna. After several years of post-doctoral work as a neurological research associate, he obtained a scholarship to study with Jean-Martin Charcot at the Salpêtrière Hospital in Paris. Charcot, a renowned neurologist, had discovered that certain neurotic patients were highly susceptible to hypnosis. In many instances their symptoms disappeared, though only for the duration of the hypnotic session. This evidence of a psychosomatic connection, buried in the patient's unconscious mind, had a powerful influence on Freud. After returning to Vienna, he explored the idea of unconscious conflicts further, using methods of free association and "talking" therapy. In time, he relinquished the medical model and began to replace it with a theory of unconscious psychological causation. In place of a neurological framework, he developed a "depth model" of mind with both conscious and unconscious levels. Neurosis is not a medical syndrome but, rather, a mental ailment—arising from the intrapsychic conflicts of early experience, buried beneath the surface of awareness. Therefore, its treatment should likewise be psychological. The next leap was to extend his theory of unconscious motivation to all human affairs: from the hidden meaning of dreams and inadvertent slips of the tongue, to personality development and the cultural patterns of society and religion.

Freud's basic mental topology is the cornerstone of all subsequent versions of depth psychology. Mental activities are rooted in the mind's unconscious region, from which conscious awareness gradually arises. Freud outlined the way early experience shapes the psyche in his book *Das Ich und das Es*. These psychological structures are well known by the corresponding Latin terms: ego and id. In English, of course, they would be the "I" and the "it."

Experience begins as unconscious id relations, in which the infant's needs and desires are directly "cathected" to external objects—the breast, the mother, a smiling face. These relationships gradually develop into mental representations and the foundations of cognition and conscious experience. With further consolidation, the psychic structure of the ego begins to form. Inner experience expands and becomes more consciously mediated. The ego allows the child to delay gratification, fulfill wishes, execute intentions, or—as any parent knows—stubbornly reject action. But it is never fully free from unconscious influences. In Freud's view the conscious and unconscious mind are inseparable. Our human and animal natures are inexorably fused. He sometimes likened ego/id interactions to a horse and rider. We may consciously direct much of our action. But always there is a powerful and often unruly beast below.

The third element in Freud's structural theory of personality is the superego. In juxtaposition with the ego, it gives a mental representation of the "self as object." The superego holds the internal self-evaluation capability of judging the ego's thoughts and actions, and functions as a moral compass. Its foundations are laid down and shaped by introjection of parental values—and the corresponding internal experiences of "good me" or "bad me." When ego ideals are met, the superego renders a sense of fulfillment or pride; when they are not, we experience guilt.

Another way to understand the general shape of the theory is through a linguistic comparison. Freud's structural elements of mind closely emulate the basic pattern of common, singular (indexical) pronouns. His notions of ego, superego, and id—I, you, and it—are a direct parallel of the first-person, second-person, third-person structure of language. Mental life begins in an unmediated third-person perspective—a sort of voiceless, unconscious "it wanting." As the ego forms, we develop our "I-voice," e.g., "*I* want *it*." Layered onto the voice of our self-interests is a third perspective. This enters our experience, from others around us, as the referred object "you"—and is often conditioned by approbation or displeasure. These voices are internalized within the developing psyche. They remain in constant interaction. For Freud, the ego's conflict is an enduring one. We are always challenged to seek a balance among the quarrelsome forces of selfishness, practicality, and judgment.

Freud's Vienna was the intellectual center and birthplace for multiple elaborations of psychological theory. Many of his followers began their understanding of psychoanalysis as his patients. In time, however, they developed ideas of their own. These elaborations often arose from conflicts over Freud's dogmatic reliance on the Oedipus complex at the core of his psychosexual theory. One of the bitterest splits was with Alfred Adler. Adler began as a devoted supporter of classical psychoanalysis, but gradually began to see other factors that contributed to personality formation. For Adler, early experiences of interpersonal power were at least as important as intrapsychic erotic conflicts. His idea of the "inferiority complex" became a compelling alternative for interpreting unconscious motives. Deep-seated feelings of inferiority, from early in life, appeared to give a better account of neurotic tendencies behind the overcompensation and superiority strivings he encountered among many of his patients. This led the way to other repressed power-based complexes and an increasing emphasis on family dynamics, birth order, and social identity.

As Adler pulled psychoanalysis in the direction of the external social environment, Carl Jung stretched it down an opposing inner path toward the collective unconscious. Within this realm, Jung proposed yet another elaborate constellation of complexes, arising from the depths of universal human experience—far beyond the bounds of Freud's personal unconscious. Other members of the Vienna psychoanalytic circle invoked additional theoretical formulations and therapeutic techniques. Helene Deutsch revised the male-oriented notions of castration anxiety and penis envy from classical psychoanalysis. Her ideas on female sexuality, mothering, and attachment unlocked a door to a bona fide psychology of women. Wilhelm Reich's controversial theory about the function of the organism and character armor located neurosis in the body, and thereby laid the early foundations of sex therapy. Freud's daughter Anna peeled back the retrospective techniques of psychoanalysis with direct methods for child analysis and therapy. Melanie Klein also advanced child psychology and the role of early relational experience with her introduction of object relations theory. Erik Erikson rounded out the picture with a life-span model of psychological development. The centerpiece of his theory is the identity crisis, a pivotal stage in personality formation beyond childhood and adolescence. It lies midway along a series of critical periods that unfold, from an initial stage of trust-versus-mistrust during infancy to the end-of-life encounter with feelings of integrity-versus-despair.

This is only a brief snapshot of the richness of thought inspired by depth psychology. Many more variations were conceived around this founding core and continue to be developed. The quest to comprehend the role of unconscious processes still remains a major feature of contemporary theory and practice within psychology.

Behaviorism

Explanations based on hidden motives and untestable assumptions were not for everyone. Skepticism about mental entities runs deep in the history of psychology, and has been a significant dividing line for a long time. Around the beginning of the twentieth century, the Russian physiologist Ivan Pavlov had demonstrated early examples of associative learning. By repeated pairings of a neutral stimulus (a bell) with an innate reflex stimulus (food), he showed that the bell alone could predictably elicit a behavioral response of salivation. In other words, the natural relationship of a stimulus and response could be "conditioned" (i.e., associated) to a novel stimulus. He used this basic model to further explore the basis of stimulus discrimination, generalization, and higher-order conditioning. Pavlov also revealed that conflicts in difficult discrimination tasks could produce stress in his animals, often leading to dramatic nervous agitation. His laboratory discovery of "experimental neurosis" in animals was elaborated to human conflict conditions associated with situational neurosis, emotional breakdown, and traumatic stress disorders.

While Pavlov was working out his model of classical conditioning, Edward Thorndike was studying problem-solving behavior in cats at Columbia University. It took a long time for a cat placed in a "puzzle box" (requiring a complex set of behaviors) to initially escape. But on subsequent trials less and less time was needed. Thorndike charted the decreasing escape times and found a pattern of gradual learning. He therefore concluded that complex learning occurred by trial and error, in a gradual strengthening of stimulus/response connections. The speed of connections, moreover, was governed by associated reward or punishment consequences, or what he called "the law of effect."

Behavioral science's great leap forward in American psychology came with John Broadus Watson. Watson took his graduate studies at the University of Chicago, where he was strongly influenced by John Dewey, James Angell, and the animal behaviorist Jacques Loeb. In 1909, at the invitation of James Baldwin (of the Titchener/Baldwin debate), Watson joined the faculty at Johns Hopkins. For the next four years he consolidated his thinking into a "behaviorist manifesto" that appeared in *Psychological Review* in 1913. The first three lines tell the story. "Psychology as the behaviorist views it is a purely objective experimental branch of natural science. Its theoretical goal is the prediction and control of behavior. Introspection forms no essential part of its methods, nor is the scientific value of its data dependent upon the readiness with which they lend themselves to interpretation in terms of consciousness."[11] In short, introspection was discarded; consciousness was rejected as an explanatory device; and the laws of behavior were equally discoverable from, and applicable to, animals and humans.

Behaviorism is rooted in the philosophy of British empiricism. But where classical associationism relied on mental experiences, behaviorism replaced these internal entities with physical events in the environment. Externally observable stimuli were then tied to observable behaviors, with no appeal whatsoever to mental events. Locke's blank slate of experience was now a black box. There was nothing of significance inside. Physical processes and only physical processes were the causes of psychological phenomena. The black box awaited filling in, but only in terms of theoretical concepts and behavioral laws of prediction, understanding, and control.

For the next several decades a new generation of behaviorists happily set about the task. University psychology departments prospered, and laboratories for the experimental study of animal-based learning thrived. Research results were fashioned into elegant learning theories by Clark Hull, Kenneth Spence, and many others. These theories began to fill in some of the blanks with internal mechanisms of habits, motivation, and emotion—but customarily in the language of hypothetical constructs or abstract intervening variables. John Dollard and Neal Miller at Yale used Hull–Spence learning theory to reinterpret psychoanalytic theory. Their goal was to derive testable hypotheses from both theories and to subsume personality, developmental, and social psychology within the folds of stimulus/response and reinforcement explanations.

The rigid definition of performance measures gradually relaxed, which made human self-reports acceptable data and substantially broadened the scope of research. Even B. F. Skinner argued for the inclusion of private events of language, thought, and feelings. But he never retreated from the strict position of environmental determinism. In his utopian novel *Walden Two,* he boldly reasserted a behaviorist theory for society—in a comparison, some believe, to Freud's *Civilization and Its Discontents.*

Behavioral principles eventually reached all across psychology. They found applications in management, organizational behavior, industrial psychology, and educational psychology. An assortment of behavioral therapies were developed using counterconditioning, systematic desensitization, and behavior modification techniques. These methods fit nicely into APA's graduate training model for clinical psychology, in which research and behavior therapy were combined. In time they also merged with the growth of cognitive psychology and expanded into cognitive behavioral therapies. At many institutions, behavioral agendas ruled the roost, where more often than not they displaced psychodynamic, humanistic, and other counseling approaches.

In recent years, the tide appears to have turned. Animal research holds a less prominent place in psychology. This is due, in part, to reduced funding as well as the growth of animal rights concerns on many campuses. Behaviorism's assumptions regarding scientific knowledge have also been an object of postmodern critiques, which have successfully countered with their own research and therapeutic alternatives. These are topics for psychology's future—and must await our transect through its history.

Gestalt Psychology

Psychology at the University of Berlin in the late 1800s and early 1900s was very different than at Leipzig. The founder of the Berlin department, Carl Stumpf, was strongly influenced by his teacher Franz Brentano, who opposed Wundt's structuralism. Brentano believed that mental processes are directed toward performing a function—intending, expecting, remembering, and so on. Thus "the science of mental phenomena," as Brentano called it, should be directed toward the investigation of the functions of consciousness. Stumpf shared Brentano's belief in the unifying aspects of consciousness. He adopted the term "gestalt" to describe this principle, adding the famous phrase "the whole is greater than the sum of its parts."

Gestalt psychology began the study of perception with Stumpf's student Max Wertheimer. When two lights were flashed in close succession, they produced a perception of apparent motion. The experience was different from the actual events. Many other forms of perception also showed the influence of mental organization. Figure/ground illusions jumped back and forth unstably between alternative interpretations. Incomplete or ambiguous images were filled in and seen as meaningful patterns.

These propensities—for the experienced percept to contain more information than the sensory stimuli on which it was based—were formalized in the "Gestalt laws of perception." Comparable holistic tendencies would be demonstrated in thought, memory, and problem solving.

Wolfgang Köhler, a cofounder of Gestalt psychology in Berlin, traveled to the Canary Islands to study cognition in apes—where he remained throughout World War I. Contrary to the conclusions of Thorndike's cat studies, Köhler found clear evidence of insight learning in animals. Problem solving was not gradual. Instead it leaped forward as the apes perceived the solution all at once. During his stay at Tenerife he wrote an important book, *Mentality of Apes*. After returning to Berlin, he published another book, *Gestalt Psychology*. His work was a major impetus to understanding the psychology of original thinking.

Bluma Zeigarnik conducted a striking demonstration of Gestalt principles on cognition and memory in her doctoral dissertation at Berlin. Her professor, Kurt Lewin, had noticed a waiter who was very good at remembering the particulars of orders. Once the bill was paid, however, the details were forgotten. Zeigarnik explored this in a series of experiments. Subjects were asked to perform a battery of simple tasks. They were allowed to complete some of the tasks. On others they were interrupted before finishing. Afterward, when she tested their recall of the activities, uncompleted tasks were more readily remembered than completed ones—even weeks later. The "Zeigarnik Effect" is believed to stem from the inability to reach "cognitive closure" on unfinished acts. This kind of "unforgettability" appears to be widespread in the dynamics of memory, especially for ego-involving events.

Gestalt psychology offered a very different model of mental processes. Kurt Koffka, another member of the Berlin group, introduced the ideas to American psychologists in a 1922 issue of *Psychological Bulletin*. Five years later he moved to the United States, and in 1935 he published his influential *Principles of Gestalt Psychology*. Wertheimer escaped the troubles in Germany in 1933; Köhler and Lewin were also forced to leave for the United States. Their influence on American psychology was enormous. The Gestalt principles they brought with them infused a new generation of psychologists, who applied them profusely to attitude theory, group dynamics, and social psychology.

Frederick (Fritz) Perls extended Gestalt ideas to psychotherapy. Perls began his career as a medical doctor in Berlin. The Bauhaus movement intrigued him. But the expressionist philosopher Salomo Friedlaender was an even greater influence. Perls became deeply fascinated with Friedlaender's concept of creative indifference: "the zero point as center nothingness stretching into opposite somethings."[12] Following World War I, Perls spent several years in analysis and study with Karen Horney and Wilhelm Reich. He later combined these ideas in *Ego, Hunger and Aggression*, and in his own version of "awareness therapy." Perls came to the United States after World War II. In 1951 he teamed up with Ralph Hefferline and Paul Goodman to write *Gestalt Therapy*. Gestalt psychotherapy sessions rely on challenge and response, rather than cause and effect, as a way to confront anxiety directly in the present moment. He later moved to the Esalen Institute, where he offered workshops and supervision to the new generation of humanistic psychologists.

The tenets of Gestalt psychology spread into philosophy as well. The founder of phenomenology, Edmund Husserl, had studied with Brentano and Stumpf. He elaborated on their idea that the acts (contents) of consciousness exist as "intentions" in the mind. Philosophy should therefore study human experience from the inside, from a first-person perspective. For Husserl, there were various types of experience—perception, imagination, thought, volition, and so on—but conscious awareness was the fundamental building block. The essence of the mind is intentionality, that is always directed toward things. These objects-as-intended can be investigated through direct experience. Husserl outlined a complex system of phenomenological philosophy that he applied to logic, language, ontology, and knowledge. His ideas influenced and were further elaborated by his student Martin Heidegger.

Heidegger moved beyond representational forms of intentionality. Philosophy, for Husserl, was about subjective experience. For Heidegger, it was about "being"—something even more fundamental than consciousness. We are not separate subjects interpreting the world. We are already in the world, in amongst things—that may or may not come into consciousness. Consciousness is a manifestation. It derives from being (*sein*) and is always experienced as being in the world. Our subjectivity is where things are—there (*da*)—in the world. All being is "being there" (or Dasein). Heidegger was a major influence on philosophy who brought new ideas about experience and the role of language in history.

Existential/Humanistic Psychology

Heidegger's phenomenology was also a new bridge back to psychology. The Swiss psychiatrist and lifelong friend of Freud, Ludwig Binswanger, combined Heideggerian concepts and psychoanalysis into a new form of psychotherapy. Medard Boss, another Swiss psychiatrist, enlarged the frame further with ideas of nondualism from Eastern psychology. Existential psychology—Daseinsanalysis as originally formulated by Binswanger and Boss—became an appealing alternative within European psychotherapy. In 1958, Rollo May introduced American psychologists to these new therapeutic methods, and the ideas behind them, in a pivotal book, *Existence: A New Dimension in Psychiatry and Psychology*. Existentialism, as May described, was not a comprehensive philosophy. It was an endeavor to grasp reality that cut below the cleavage between subject and object. It was more like an attitude, arising from diverse sources, concerned with accepting that humans are always in the process of becoming. From Kierkegaard came the relentless question of "how to become an individual" and his emphasis on "commitment." Nietzsche stressed the duty to live out one's potentials.

Existentialism, a term first used by Sartre, comes from the Latin *ex* + *sistere*, literally "to stand out." Through consciousness, humans emerge or stand out from the world—as individuals who must create values and meaning in life. At the heart of existentialism was the principle of freedom. Freedom allows people the ability to see choices and to decide how to act, to fulfill meaningful lives, and to grow. On the other side of the coin, existence is always in a dialectical relation with nonbeing—death, a fact of life that is not relative, but absolute. Herein lay new definitions for traditional psychological categories: anxiety—the dizziness of freedom or the experience of threat of imminent nonbeing; guilt—the forfeiting of one's potentialities; and neurosis—a lacking of the capacity to fulfill one's own being.

Existential psychologists were suspicious of theory and abstract concepts, which all too often suggest that something that cannot be seen is producing that which is visible. They likewise rejected scientific notions of causality, mind/body dualism, and the separation of the person from the environment. Existential psychotherapy focuses on understanding people, their capacities, and the barriers that prevent them from fully experiencing their capacities. How people choose to view the world creates the kind of person they are. Viktor Frankl, who also studied with Freud and Jung, revealed his firsthand struggles with survival in Nazi concentration camps in *Man's Search for Meaning*. His logotherapy is considered an important addition to existential therapies. Irvin Yalom's *Existential Psychotherapy* remains the scholarly standard of the field; his many works of fiction and nonfiction have brought existential themes to widespread public attention.

Another new orientation—humanistic psychology—began in America in the 1950s. The name was meant to highlight the dehumanizing aspects of psychoanalysis and behaviorism. Instead of people acting as pawns of unconscious motives or environmental forces, the humanists viewed people as inherently good, creative, and capable of self-directed, meaningful lives. Its pioneers were Abraham Maslow and Carl Rogers. Maslow did his graduate work on primate behavior at the University of Wisconsin. His supervisor was Harry Harlow—well known for his controversial experiments of social isolation and maternal deprivation in monkeys. But Maslow's career took a very different path. Disturbed by the reductionism of behaviorists and psychoanalysts' preoccupation with pathology, he turned toward a holistic study of psychological health. His far-reaching investigation sought to identify the characteristics of healthy, "actualized" personalities. Some of his evidence came from biographical and autobiographical records of historical figures like Thoreau, Lincoln, and Beethoven. Others, such as Eleanor Roosevelt and Einstein, were living at the time. Maslow discovered several distinctive features of these people. Overall they tended to be humorous, realistically oriented, self-accepting, spontaneous, and democratic in their views. Interpersonal relationships were usually few in number but deeply emotional and long lasting. They were, on the whole, quite independent personalities who resisted conformity and often had a strong need for privacy.

Maslow was intrigued by a tendency for psychologically healthy people to have profound unifying, mystical, or spiritual experiences (though not necessarily of a religious character). These "peak experiences," as he termed them, became a central feature of his theory of personality and motivation. Most of the time humans are motivated by physiological, safety, social, and self-esteem needs. In Maslow's view, these "deficiency" needs have a hierarchical order, whereby lower needs can overrule higher ones. Sometimes, as in moments of peak experience, all sense of deficiency is transcended. Here is when human "self-actualizing" or "being" needs find expression. Maslow's ideas initiated not only a new era in psychology, but they also reshaped education, business, and organizational management.

Carl Rogers's contributions to humanistic psychology arose from his experience as a practicing therapist. The best vantage point for understanding a person, in Rogers's view, was from the continuously changing world of the individual's own conscious experience. Unlike classical psychoanalysis, the relationship between the therapist and patient (which he renamed "the client") is "nondirective." This reorientation was part of an effort to separate psychology from the "treatment model" of medicine, and to highlight the natural, self-healing tendencies of the person. The self, in Rogerian theory, is a fluid gestalt of perceptions and feelings that is continually in the process of becoming. When personal growth is threatened, or actualizing tendencies are incongruent with lived experience, the defense mechanisms of anxiety, denial, or distorted perceptions come into play. Insight and resolution can arise from within the person, however, by establishing a relationship of self-reflection with an understanding, accepting therapist. This atmosphere of "unconditional positive regard" restores the client's natural healing, growth, and self-actualizing process. Rogers's novel approach to counseling and personality theory quickly spread. His commitment to "pure phenomenological psychology" was clearly articulated in a celebrated debate with B. F. Skinner before the American Psychological Association, and later reprinted in *Science* magazine. Rogers's methods have been broadly extended to active listening and collaborative decision-making techniques, and are ideas behind the encounter group and student-centered education movements.

Cognitive Psychology

Many people mark the beginning of cognitive psychology (some say revolution) with the 1967 publication of Ulric Neisser's *Cognitive Psychology*. Neisser did coin the term. He also led the movement that brought ideas of information processing and cognitive science into psychology. But the place of cognition (thought) had long been a part of psychology. Back in the 1880s, when Hermann Ebbinghaus made his comment on psychology's "short history," it was he who pioneered experimentation on higher mental processes. To remove the confounding influence of meaning on learning and memory, he invented the nonsense syllable. Using himself as the subject of his research, he spent countless hours learning, rehearsing, and attempting to recall multiple lists of meaningless trigrams, e.g., DAX, KOJ, etc. His discoveries included the superiority of spaced practice versus massed practice, the serial-position influences of recency and primacy in memory, as well as the invention of learning (and forgetting) curves. William James called Ebbinghaus's painstaking research a "heroic" addition to psychology and praised it as "the entering wedge of a new method of incalculable reach."[13] Mary Whiton Calkins, who worked with James, expanded on Ebbinghaus's "serial learning" methods. She developed a "paired-associates" procedure that became the standard research method of verbal learning. Calkins made many other contributions to psychology and philosophy. She was the first female president of both the American Psychological Association and the American Philosophical Association.

The British psychologist Sir Frederic Bartlett also explored the relationship of memory, meaning, and cognitive structures. In a study on the recollection of folktales, he noticed that while a story's details might be forgotten or be remembered inaccurately, the underlying shape of the story remained. Bartlett proposed an unconscious mental structuring process, which he called "schemata," to account for this phenomenon. Schematizing tests (based on noticing or ignoring gradually changing modifications) have revealed individual differences in "cognitive style" that correlate with many other personality traits. The perceptual, thinking, and learning styles of people who emphasize differences (sharpeners) are quite different from the styles of those who don't (levelers).

Mental schemas are the foundation of Jean Piaget's theory of cognitive development in children. Piaget was not trained as a psychologist. His doctorate was in malacology (a subfield of biology), and he explored the processes of growth and adaptation of snails in the lakes of Switzerland. Piaget's interests later turned to psychology. He moved to Paris to work with the pioneer of intelligence testing, Alfred Binet. But he soon lost interest in testing children's abilities to get the right answers to age-related questions. Instead, he wanted to understand how children organize knowledge—to arrive at *any* answer—at different stages of development. Piaget's careful observation of these unfolding changes is the core of his main lifework: *genetic epistemology*. Genetic refers to genesis (i.e., origin and growth) of cognitive structures—not to genes or DNA; and by epistemology, he means the child's systems of knowing at different stages of mental development. The mind and environment, for Piaget, are in a continuous process of adaptation—composed of two recursive processes: assimilation and accommodation. Assimilation is the "taking in" of information and experience utilizing existing structures. Accommodation is the growth and transformation (i.e., restructuring of the mind) that makes for better assimilation. These back-and-forth adjustments produce a characteristic elaboration in human ontogenetic development, as the mind literally grows itself (analogous to the periodic and visible growth rings of snails he observed as they biologically adapt to their environment). Piaget expanded this basic underlying relationship between function and structure into a sophisticated stage model of cognitive development. His ideas have been applied in many areas: e.g., in moral development by Lawrence Kohlberg, education theory by Eleanor Duckworth, and sociology by Jürgen Habermas.

Other groundbreaking approaches to cognition appeared in the 1960s. One of them began with a critique, by Noam Chomsky, of Skinner's behavioral explanation of verbal behavior. Chomsky maintained that humans possess an innate linguistic structure that is impossible to acquire through rote learning as Skinner proposed. The speed and ease with which children learn language rely on universal syntactical structures. His ideas about the "deep" structures of transformational-generative grammar—and the modularity of mental architecture—revolutionized psycholinguistics, education, and computer science. They remain broadly influential—from Steven Pinker's ideas of how the mind works to Elizabeth Loftus's revelations about "false memories."

Ulric Neisser introduced a different paradigm to cognitive psychology, drawing heavily on the language of computational systems. Neisser applied these principles to human perception, attention, memory, and thought. Psychoanalysis had primarily relied on a symbol-driven approach to thought. Behaviorism either avoided internal referents, or explained them in terms of abstract stimulus/response laws. For cognitive psychologists, the mind is like a computer. Thinking runs like software on the brain's hardware, or "wetware," as some called it. Principles of signal detection, information processing, and input-output algorithms became the new metaphors. Cognitive psychology grew rapidly, hand in hand with the upsurge in computer capacity. Some psychology departments were renamed as "cognitive and brain science," expanding their scope into informatics, artificial intelligence, and neuroscience.

Psychology Today

Lee Cronbach's comparison a half century ago of a psychology convention to an eighteen-ring circus was an imaginative metaphor. When I attended my first APA meeting a decade later, I was enthralled by the varied topics and rich contents. I relished the mix of ideas and people. The organization's past presidents represented the full range of backgrounds. There were clinicians, behaviorists, statisticians, physiologists, and humanists. The names we all learned in our classes had been selected by their peers: John Watson, Mary Calkins, John Dewey, Margaret Washburn, Wolfgang Köhler, Donald Hebb, Carl Rogers, Jerome Bruner, and Abraham Maslow. I admired how the field of psychology celebrated its diversity.

Behind the scenes, however, hidden frictions were mounting. Cognitive psychologists had begun to separate from their colleagues into a new Psychonomic Society. The leaders of humanistic psychology were also splitting off to form the Association for Humanistic Psychology (AHP). In 1988 a substantial portion of APA's scientific psychologists withdrew and created a separate Association for Psychological Science (APS). The APA remained the largest professional society. But the organization's internal structure, of more than fifty subdivisions, was enormously complex. When evolutionary psychology burgeoned in the 1990s, its practitioners formed their own society, rather than joining any existing group. Human Behavior and Evolution Society members share a common background of evolutionary theory, but have little contact with psychologists from other backgrounds. The intellectual movement of postmodernism has had a major impact on psychology as well. Its pluralistic model of the psyche and its emphasis on multicultural awareness have called many assumptions of both science and psychotherapy into question. The postmodern themes of the "social mind" and the "narrative self" have produced entirely new versions of social identity and psychotherapy.

These intellectual and organizational divisions have substantially altered the field of psychology. When I was a graduate student, psychological training followed the scientist–practitioner model. University-affiliated PhD programs combined research and clinical training. In the 1980s, as the APA/APS split was occurring, pressures grew for PsyD (Doctor of Psychology) degree programs that emphasize clinical training over research. To meet the need, dozens of freestanding schools of professional psychology were founded to offer APA-approved PsyD degree programs.

The APA began in 1892 with 31 members. By 1950, membership had grown to 15,000. It is now approaching 150,000 members. Recent surveys by the National Center for Education Statistics indicate nearly 100,000 bachelor's degrees, and more than 20,000 master's and 5,000 doctoral degrees, are conferred annually. In addition to its overall growth, the field of psychology has also changed substantially in composition. In 1970, 20 percent of PhD recipients in psychology were females. A recent APA report indicates that nearly three-quarters of all new PsyD and PhD degrees were earned by women. The increase is not only in clinical and counseling areas, but also across all subfields including experimental, cognitive, and organizational psychology.[14]

At the beginning of the twentieth century, Hermann Ebbinghaus began his *Outline of Psychology* with the familiar statement about the long past and short history of psychology. I wonder what he might think of the century of psychology that followed. I expect he would be surprised by the many twists and turns, and by the field's tremendous growth. Overall, could he still find connections between its contours back then and its outlines now? Would he be delighted or dismayed? As I look back across the intervening century, I see grounds for both. On the one hand, psychology has surely prospered and opened in a wealth of directions. Countless new concepts and approaches have spawned. Psychological research has enriched our understanding of humans and established itself as a legitimate social science. Psychology's status as an effective healing profession also has grown tremendously. The quality of life for an immeasurable number of people has been improved through its practice.

On the other hand, the field as a whole stands on troubled ground. The fissures beneath its fabric grow wider and deeper. As psychologists divide into separate and ever-smaller subgroups, they lose contact with other points of view. The separations are frequently fed by disdain toward alternative approaches. Worse still, they often produce ignorance of them. I have encountered these issues in several ways. As academic dean at a small college, it is increasingly difficult to find young faculty knowledgeable of the field as a whole. Moreover, to remain current about contemporary psychology, as a professor myself, now requires membership in multiple organizations. I enjoy the clarity of purpose in their respective conferences. A week with Jungian therapists or a meeting of evolutionary psychologists is fascinating. So are the contents of the leading APA, APS, and AHP journals. But connections and cross-references between them are scarce. The inroads, it seems, have become clearer than the outlines of psychology.

Closing Thoughts

At the end of Chapter 1, I briefly introduced Joseph Rychlak. He has influenced me more than any other psychologist I know. We were colleagues at Purdue. Joe is a warm and friendly person. We shared various departmental duties together, where I learned a great deal from his supportive mentoring. Back then, he had already written several books on personality and psychotherapy—and has written many more since. In addition to writing, teaching, research, and supervision of graduate students, he also maintained a private practice in psychotherapy.

I can still recall Joe's thoughtful and patient response to visiting colleagues at departmental colloquia. Most failed to grasp his question; fewer still had an answer. The same was true for me. Whenever we talked about psychological theory, I was soon disoriented by the scope of his knowledge. Joe was never disputatious or critical. He was just—well—beyond me. I was enormously curious about his ideas, but I could never seem to sustain my end of the conversation. So these conversations tended to be brief, and frequently left me feeling somewhat breathless and dizzy.

One of my graduate students was also a teaching assistant for Joe's personality and psychotherapy class. She had a copy of his lecture notes, which she shared with me. The first time I read them I barely understood any it. His thinking about psychology was unlike anything I had seen. Joe taught in the old-school style. His lectures were carefully written in tight, single-spaced paragraphs—four hundred pages in all. I have reread those notes and his books many times since. Each time, I find yet another untwisting of some conceptual knot in my views of psychology.

In the thirty-plus years since I left Purdue, I have thought of Joe many times. I wanted to thank him for shaking up my worldview. I also wished to see if I could sustain a conversation—if I had gotten his ideas. So finally,

I mustered the pluck to call him on the phone. He is retired now. He was as talkative and friendly as ever. It was a wonderful exchange, and overall I think I did pretty well. As we hung up our phones, I was both satisfied and inspired. Here was someone who taught me a lot—and from whom there was yet still more to learn about the psychology of experience. The threads of his ideas are woven through these pages. But here are some of the major features.

First, Joe has always been a forthright advocate of human subjectivity. The position is summed up in the titles of his books: *In Defense of Human Consciousness* and *Discovering Free Will and Personal Responsibility*. In his words, "I think the role of intention in all human affairs is fundamental."[15] Yet, he does not reject science as a way to understand consciousness, e.g., *A Philosophy of Science for Personality Theory* and *The Psychology of Rigorous Humanism*. He has likewise found a way to embrace postmodern perspectives—*The Human Image in Postmodern America*, and to dissect the nuances of humans versus machines—*Artificial Intelligence and Human Reason*.

Second—like Piaget—Rychlak's focus is on human mentation, but from a very different perspective. Whereas Piaget was concerned with *answers* to questions (e.g., how mental solutions are achieved and explained, how to understand understanding, and so on), Rychlak asks the opposite: how do questions *arise* and intentions *unfold*? His stance on these matters is unequivocal: mind is dynamic and purposive. Feeling and thought are not reactions; they are actions. In Joe's view, psychology has unwittingly (perhaps unconsciously) fallen prey to a biased perspective. Scientific objectivism has obscured the reality of human subjectivity. Mind is not material. Purpose is not mechanism. Consciousness, imagination, and insight are not mere chemistry. They are real—as real as rocks, or trees, or embodied humans.

The essence of Rychlak's position comes from retracing the labyrinth of psychology's long past. He brings back Aristotle's formal and final causes, not as divine intention, but as individual *human* purposiveness. This duet of formal/final causation is further married to the Kantian concept of an active (pro forma) mind. In short, consciousness is telic.

Cognition and affective assessment (thought and feeling) are inextricably joined. Experience unfolds dialectically in gestaltlike mental images as the mind frames—or "predicates" (i.e., grabs onto)—the objects of our intention. Sometimes the object and intention are tautological, i.e., they have a well-defined "identity" relationship. Most often, however, mental predications take the form of "partial tautologies," i.e., as approximate or metaphorical extensions of intentionality. Behaving symbolically for the sake of our intentions—to affirm, negate, or choose alternatives—is the core of mental action. But it has multiple levels. In conscious thought we have the capacity to transcend and reflexively evaluate whatever is being predicated and "taken on." Unconscious predications, though still intentional, are not available to conscious (transcendent) awareness. When they do arise into consciousness, the experience is "insight." However, as Rychlak cautions, "It is impossible to be entirely conscious of one's most fundamental assumptions."[16]

Rychlak's contribution to psychology bears a resemblance to Ernst Mayr's clarification of the uniqueness of biology. Whereas Mayr made a case for the irreducibility of biology to physical science concepts, Joe gives a parallel argument about the special features of consciousness. Taken together, their views support a vision of complementarity, rather than incompatibility, across these levels of understanding. Rychlak has actually developed this position in detail elsewhere. But for now, we have an ample base for our next transect into the landscapes of mind and nature, or more specifically: human ecology.

CHAPTER 4

Human Ecology

Sooner or later Human Ecology under some name or other, will win its way to academic recognition and to its proper place in general education.

—H. G. Wells

The fundamental challenge in human ecology and meeting it will require knowing the earth well—knowing its history and knowing its limits.

—Donald Worster

Lawrence "Yogi" Berra was one of the most successful and colorful baseball players of all time. He began his major league career as catcher with the New York Yankees in 1946. He was a fifteen-time All-Star and three-time American League MVP, who played in fourteen World Series. When his player career ended, he went on to be manager for the Yankees and the Mets, and finally, coach for the Houston Astros. Yogi was also an artist with words and one of the most quoted personalities in American society. Everyone knows some of his memorable utterances, "It ain't over 'til it's over" or "It's déjà vu all over again." These and many others of his beloved phrases are treated jokingly as disjointed malapropisms. One of my favorite "Yogi-isms" is this: "When you come to a fork in the road, take it." But when Yogi was given a chance to explain his verbal contortions, he often had a story that gave them a unique and fitting logic. The "fork in the road" expression, for example, was based on advice to guests coming to his New Jersey home. The house was located midway around a long circular driveway, equally accessible by either route from the fork. Once explained, his otherwise perplexing construction made perfect sense and conveyed a wisdom of expression all its own.

The academic world is full of divisions. Countless small fault lines exist within every field of knowledge. The really big splits occur between disciplines and in many ways constitute the forks in the road that define the separation of one field from another. When we enter the realm of interdisciplinary inquiry, the signposts at these intersections point both ways: biochemistry, behavioral genetics, political economics, and so on. They tell us, like Yogi's advice to drivers, that whichever path we take ends in the same place. This is true even when we take the broadest of stances and look at life as a whole. From this vantage point, one of the most familiar crossroads lies at the juncture between the human and nonhuman worlds. Nonetheless, whichever route we take, sooner or later, it will bring us to the other. For our purposes, here in this chapter, the crossroad signs have simple names. One points toward ecology, the other to humans. Together they lead inevitably to their intersection: "human ecology."

Human ecology may be an unfamiliar phrase to some individuals. For others it might seem abstract or confusing. But for a growing number of people, it is becoming the unambiguous and unifying expression for the intersection between the two most important realms in the living world. In its broadest sense human ecology aims at comprehensive approaches to human/environment interactions. Its mandate is unequivocally interdisciplinary and integrative. Its subject matter cannot be subdivided according to academic traditions. The scope of its domain, across time and space, is nearly boundless—from the emergence of humans on earth, to the immediate experience of each of us here and now, and from there into the furthest reaches of imagination about the future. As such, it demands a multiplicity of perspectives in search of connections among otherwise segregated ways of knowing. Yet despite all complexities, a salient and identifiable challenge persists at the center. In the words of Paul Shepard:

"Perhaps the central problem of human ecology may be characterized as the relationship of the mind to nature."[1]

As Gerald Young, a leading scholar of the history of human ecology, explains: "The actual origins of human ecology are lost in the mists of time, with the Neanderthal and in the Neolithic, or even further back...."[2] Interactions among early hominids in those ancient surroundings were the formative influence for a new species. Their daily life practices and their successes and failures shaped the creatures we have become. Human consciousness, perhaps our most distinctive feature, was forged and refined in those environments of evolutionary adaptation. As human capacities for awareness, imagination, and thoughtful action emerged, altogether new contextual relations developed between the "first world" of biological ecology and the "second world" of human ecology. The philosopher John Visvader expands on this basic notion: "If human ecology is to be understood generally as the study of the relationship between human beings and their environment, or more particularly, the relationship between human beings and nature, then its subject matter must be as old as human culture itself."[3]

When the ancestral human populations emigrated out of Africa, they spread in all directions—onto the Eurasian continent, across Southeast Asia, and then on to New Guinea and Australia, arriving there at least forty thousand years ago. The migration from Asia to North America and thereafter to South America would come later, somewhere between thirteen thousand and eleven thousand years ago. Humans were a truly global species by then, living in a multitude of diverse habitats. Separated by vast distances and living in dissimilar environs, the sources of cultural diversity were widely dispersed. These human groups discovered various means of adapting to different environments. They also invented their own specializations of language. These linguistic systems invariably reflected differing cultural structures and practices, as well as their various environments and perceptions of them. The ecological anthropologist Roy Rappaport reminds us of the rich and unique features of the world's language systems. He also points out some commonalities among them: "With language, discourse can escape from the here and now to enter not only the actual past and distant, and the realm of future action. It can also enter into the might have been, the should have been, the never will be, the could be, the should be—into, this is to say, the realms of the desirable, the moral, the proper, the possible, the impossible, and the imaginary."[4]

The global migration of human groups is a captivating narrative. But it is only the opening chapter in an understanding of human ecology. According to the Australian human ecologist Stephen Boyden, the history of human/environmental relations has unfolded through four relatively distinct phases. The first and longest was the primeval, hunter-gatherer period. About eleven to twelve thousand years ago, a second phase began to emerge with the introduction of farming. As agricultural practices became increasingly successful and human populations grew, a third, "urbanizing" phase began about eight to nine thousand years ago. The fourth and final stage of this biohistorical perspective has culminated in what Boyden calls "the high energy phase," with its beginnings in Europe during the past couple of centuries. From the emergence of the second, agricultural phase to the present, Boyden calculates that the human population has increased about a thousandfold. Of greater significance, he estimates the ecological impact of humans on the biosphere has multiplied ten-thousand-fold—and most of that within the past century.

If we allow ourselves to imagine the full significance of Boyden's biohistorical perspective, we begin to get a glimpse of the contemporary meaning of human ecology. The picture begins with the dawn of human civilization and stretches around the globe and across time to the present moment. Within its frame every human who ever lived or is now alive is a part of the story. Along with these individual and collective human components, it also includes the complex relationships of humans within the living world—from the uses of natural resources and our impacts on them, to the structures and practices of human society. Taken together, it is a position that seems to defy comprehension. At the same time, however, the veracity of the stance conjures a buried intuition about human existence. It is this intuition that has sparked a growing interest in human ecology.

Stephen Boyden's professional and personal life story is an illustration of this realization. Born in London in 1925, Boyden grew up in the

English countryside. His interest in animals led him to train as a veterinarian. He continued his education at Cambridge and received a PhD in immunology in 1951. His early career also included research at the Pasteur Institute in Paris and at the Rockefeller Institute in New York City, where he began a lifelong friendship with the eminent microbiologist René Dubos. After returning to Europe, Boyden took charge of the WHO Tuberculosis Immunization Research Center in Copenhagen. In 1960 he moved to the Australian National University (ANU) in Canberra. At ANU his interests became increasingly interdisciplinary. Like his friend Dubos, he began to see the myriad connections between evolutionary biology, disease, and human society. When the opportunity arose for Boyden to take on a human ecology project of his own, he did so without hesitation.

The Hong Kong Human Ecology Programme was a groundbreaking study of the ecological history of a major human settlement and its surrounding environment. The study traced the ecological and social characteristics of Hong Kong from its formal founding as a British Crown Colony in 1842 to the 1970s. "It [Hong Kong] was an extraordinary opportunity," Boyden noted. "It had fantastic records of all the inputs and outputs"—of materials, energy, foodstuffs, wastes, of human uses of materials, fuels, and so on.[5] The results of the project appeared in more than fifty scientific papers and a major book, *The Ecology of a City and Its People,* which was rapidly adopted by UNESCO's Man and the Biosphere (MAB) Program as the first comprehensive study of the ecology of an urban system. The enthusiasm generated by the Hong Kong project provided Boyden with an opportunity to refashion ANU's curriculum and in 1973 a new degree program for conferring the Bachelor of Science in Human Ecology. Since then, the program has been extended to all levels of study, from undergraduate majors to the PhD in human ecology.

Ian McHarg introduced ecological principles to regional planning with an influential book, *Design with Nature,* in 1969. The challenges and opportunities of his vision of landscape design were explicit:

> Human ecological planning is a cumbersome and graceless title. Remedy, however, while possible, is distant. When it becomes accepted that no ecosystem can be studied without reference to

man then we may abandon the "human" descriptor and revert to "ecological planning." Better still, when planning always considers interacting biophysical and cultural processes, then we can dispense with the distinction of "ecological" and simply employ the word "planning." However, that state is far in the future, as most planning today excludes physical and biological sciences, ecology, ethnography, anthropology, epidemiology, and concentrates upon economics and sociology.[6]

McHarg's graduate program in human ecological planning at the University of Pennsylvania inspired a new generation of landscape architects and environmental planners. Other leading scientists and scholars would launch visions of human ecology as well. One of the foremost pioneers was Boyden's friend and former colleague René Dubos. His *So Human an Animal* and *Only One Earth*, with Barbara Ward, received widespread public acclaim. But as his biographer Carol Moberg notes, "René Dubos's transition to human ecologist began in the 1950s."[7] Nascent signs appeared throughout his early work on evolutionary and environmental factors contributing to human health. In his later books these ideas unfolded as a rich philosophical orientation. Dubos was a charismatic speaker with a gift for sketching complex ideas via simple messages. At the 1972 U.N. Conference on the Human Environment in Stockholm, he highlighted his conviction that ecological consciousness begins at home with the unforgettable motto "Think Globally, Act Locally."

The prominent developmental biologist Conrad Waddington was also an early proponent of human ecology. Waddington (like Dubos) was a member of the Club of Rome that commissioned "The Limits to Growth" report presented to the 1972 Stockholm Conference. That same year, he founded the University of Edinburgh Centre for Human Ecology. The American physician and environmental physiologist Frederick Sargent was another advocate. Sargent was a collaborative leader of human ecology interests in the United States, and in 1965 edited a special issue of *BioScience* devoted to human ecology. His 1974 book, *Human Ecology*, was one of the first comprehensive texts on the developing interdisciplinary topic. He later became the founding president of the Society for Human Ecology.

Paul Sears, chair of the graduate program in conservation at Yale University, concluded that ecology might well be a "subversive subject." The science of ecology was everywhere revealing the complexity of human/environment interrelations. Sears was a leading ecologist and had served as president of the Ecological Society of America (ESA). In an address to his ESA colleagues at the 1954 annual convention, he put forward the challenge of human ecology: "We are in an explosion. For the first time in earth history, a single species has become dominant, and we are it. The power and intensity of our pressure upon the environment is without precedent." This reality must be acknowledged and made explicit. "The advantage of *human ecology* as a label" … [is] … "the encouragement it offers to workers in seemingly unrelated fields to become better aware of one another and of common interests and responsibilities." However, "Human ecology is not so much a specialty as a scientific activity which must draw upon a wide range of specialties." The central problem of human ecology, Sears declared, is "a problem of synthesis."[8]

Other ecologists followed. Eugene Odum rewrote his *Fundamentals of Ecology* with a new concluding section on applied human ecology. Paul and Anne Ehrlich, authors of the popular textbook *Population, Resources, Environment*, revised their second edition with the subtitle *Issues in Human Ecology*. The opening line of their preface heralded a new approach to environmental studies: "With many of the crucial variables that affect human ecology changing almost daily, any text dealing with the subject can rapidly become out of date."[9] A new generation of economists and political scientists added their versions of the transformative potential of ecological views. William Ophuls's *Ecology and the Politics of Scarcity* laid out a new vision of political ecology in a critique of the values and institutions of modern capitalist society. Others also noted the complexity and inherent interdisciplinary nature of human ecological problems. The Nobel Prize–winning economist Gunnar Myrdal observed: "The isolation of one part of social reality by demarcating it as 'economic' is not feasible. In reality, there are not 'economic,' 'sociological,' or 'psychological' problems, but just problems, and they are complex."[10]

The medieval scholar Lynn White Jr. explored the historical and religious roots of modern technological society. His ideas stimulated a new field of study, environmental history, and provoked an extended debate that was soon joined by philosophers, theologians, and political economists. These are but a few of the early voices that articulated a vision of human ecology.

Another significant turning point may be marked by the creation, in 1969, of the Commonwealth Human Ecology Council (CHEC). Based in London, the organization's founding goal was to provide an interdisciplinary forum for a diverse group of people concerned with history, medicine, economics, planning, education, economics, and ecology from throughout the forty-nine nations of the British Commonwealth. Founding board members included Sir Hugh Springer, secretary general of the Association of Commonwealth Universities and governor-general of Barbados, as chairman, and the eminent British ecologist E. Barton Worthington, scientific director of the International Biological Programme (IBP). CHEC's mission is epitomized in its definition of human ecology: "It is the key concept of our age; through an understanding of it we can influence change constructively, linking the social, cultural, spiritual, and economic with the physical and biological, without jeopardizing the rich variety of life which has evolved during the world's history."[11]

Under the vigorous leadership of New Zealand–born Zena Daysh, a broad agenda of educational, development, and intercultural activities was planned. These began with the First Commonwealth Conference on Development and Human Ecology on the island of Malta in 1970. The event was launched with an auspicious endorsement from Prince Philip, Duke of Edinburgh: "No subject is causing such worldwide concern as human ecology.... It is an immensely difficult subject as it involves value judgments, conscience, and a whole mass of conflicting interests. I suspect that the sheer complexity of the problems has tended to discourage people from tackling them. I am therefore delighted that the Commonwealth Human Ecology Council is taking this important initiative and I hope very much the first conference in Malta will trigger off a chain reaction of enquiries and discussions."[12] A survey of human ecology education presented at CHEC's next meeting, two years later, revealed more than one hundred courses of study in ninety-two institutions in sixteen Commonwealth countries. Beyond CHEC's network, other new educational initiatives were appearing elsewhere in Europe, Asia, and South America. Many of them had also developed regional organizations for coordination and cooperation.

In Search of Human Ecology: Finding My Way

Somehow, the ideas of those prominent scholars and emerging groups never entered my awareness. My introduction to human ecology was a more indirect result of personal happenstance and chance encounter. When I arrived at Purdue from Ohio State in 1974, I was looking for a new research direction. I had a growing sense of opportunity in linking psychology and the environment. At first, I began to explore issues of interpersonal touching, personal space, and social territoriality. These kinds of experimental and observational field studies fit nicely into the new subfield of environmental psychology at the time. I had a good team of graduate and undergraduate research assistants. As our studies began to appear in journal articles, several of them attracted the attention of the popular press. Purdue's Office of Public Information was great at creating opportunities for popular coverage, and it was fun to see our work appear in the newspapers and other media. But I also wanted to delve into a more deeply psychological approach to the environment. My background in personality theory and attitude change seemed to offer a way. I was further stimulated by Joe Rychlak's encouragement toward a straightforward consideration of individual consciousness, intentionality, and insight.

In those days (long before the internet), researchers pored over *Psychological Abstracts* to keep up with their field. The university library had just acquired a new computer technology for doing comprehensive searches of all academic journals. I tried it. A cross-referencing of multiple terms—like "ecology," "environment," "attitudes," "behavior," and so forth—yielded a massive printout. Most was irrelevant to my interests, ranging from the "behavior" of airplane wings in varied weather conditions to comparisons of the "environmental response" of paint products. A small portion was concerned with environment and behavior issues like those I was exploring on human responses to crowding, ambient noise, and the built environment. Only a tiny fraction looked at attitudes about the environment. These were in a scattering of unrelated publications—about natural resource management issues, studies of the motivations of campers, hunters, and fishermen, and personal preferences for house pets. Scarcely anything could be found in the mainstream psychology journals.

But surely, it seemed to me, psychology must have something to offer in understanding and influencing environmental concern. So in a moment of frustration I wrote a couple of short articles lamenting the absence of psychologists from the environmental arena—and urged anyone with such interests to contact me. To my surprise, I received more than a hundred replies. I was not alone after all; and in a few short weeks I had uncovered a burgeoning network of like-minded colleagues.

Among them was a team of UCLA researchers, who had recently published an *American Psychologist* article entitled "Ecology: Let's Hear from the People."[13] Along with their plea, the authors also provided a well-designed scale for measuring ecological attitudes and knowledge. The test was composed of four parts based on established methods of psychological assessment. One subscale measured individual differences in environmental concerns, feelings, and emotional reactions. A second part of the test scored each respondent's level of ecological knowledge. The remaining two scales focused on environmentally responsible behavior, including a measure of actual commitments that were a part of one's current actions, and a further verbal commitment to behavioral changes the person would consider making in the future. It was exactly what I needed. My students and I quickly adopted the instrument as the centerpiece of a new research agenda. Our initial work examined the intrapsychic relations involved in ecological consciousness and cognitive mapping of attitude/behavior change. Further studies compared personality, developmental, and lifestyle characteristics of environmentally concerned and unconcerned individuals. As our pool of computerized data grew, the psychological differences between these extremes became increasingly evident.

The short papers I had written that stimulated my new research venture also brought a second surprise. I had briefly mentioned that understanding the inherently interdisciplinary nature of environmental problems might be hindered by the traditions of academic specialization. Steve Nelson, a psychologist at the University of Michigan, sent me a letter in reply. "There's a little college started by a group of Harvard-types up in Bar Harbor, Maine," he said, "and they're doing something called human ecology." This was the first time I had heard the phrase. I had an immediate, intuitive sense of intrigue. I promptly wrote to the college, in a somewhat formal way, describing my research background and that I hoped to visit and study the psychological profiles of the students. A few days later I received a reply (handwritten on the back of my letter) from Steve Katona, one of the founding faculty members. "Sure," he said, "come on up, help yourself ... and you are welcome to stay with me."

College of the Atlantic was a terrific research opportunity. I did a series of studies on a sample of students that included multidimensional personality assessments, attitude surveys, lifestyle inventories—the whole gamut. I'm sure some of them thought it was slightly weird, but they all went along with it. The students, faculty—the whole college—was unlike anything I had ever seen. All of the students had a first-rate exposure to evolutionary theory and field-based ecology. Ecological ideas permeated the entire curriculum, from which each student freely constructed an individualized course of study. I felt, at times, like an anthropologist in an exotic, far-off island culture—which in some ways it really was.

My research team and I started to find interesting differences right from the beginning. Based on their responses to the California Personality Inventory, COA students were significantly more philosophically minded and introspective than the traditional college students or community groups we had been studying. Their personality profiles showed much stronger idea, ethical, and value orientations than their counterparts elsewhere. They also differed substantially in attitudes toward nature, pollution, and technology, as well as in their commitments to environmentally responsible behavior—in terms of energy use, what they owned, how they spent leisure time, and so on. They were also more androgynous. Unlike the cultural-stereotyped attitudes surrounding feminine versus masculine orientations, COA students showed a greater flexibility in gender-based attitudes and behaviors. Working through identity questions like these, it seemed, paralleled or were perhaps a part of an exploration of larger questions of relationships to the environment, the deeper implications of ecology, and so on.

The shift to studying ecological beliefs and behavior came at an opportune time. The research was met with an enthusiastic response, not only from other psychologists but from environmentally oriented researchers in sociology, education, and policy studies as well. My students and I presented the results at conferences and began to publish them in academic journals. Thanks in large part to Purdue's public relations outreach, some of the findings began to capture media attention right from the outset. One of our studies was used in a two-part Sunday supplement, "Environmental Lifestyle Test," that ran nationwide in 1,700 newspapers.

In the midst of these activities, I received an announcement for the forthcoming Second International Conference on the Environmental Future to be organized by the International Union for Conservation of Nature (IUCN). On the chance my research might be of interest, I wrote a brief inquiry. A few weeks later my phone rang. The scratchy voice at the other end was Linus Pauling, two-time recipient of the Nobel Prize—for chemistry and for peace. He and Nicholas Polunin—president of the Foundation for Environmental Conservation and editor of its premier journal, *Environmental Conservation*—as cochairs of the meeting would be happy to hear an environmental psychologist's contributions.

The event was held in Reykjavik, Iceland, during the second week of June 1977. In New York's JFK terminal, I immediately recognized the angular profile of Pauling, waiting with his wife for the flight. As I introduced myself, I had the faint sense he was expecting a more senior scholar. I was scarcely thirty years old at the time. The conference included an extraordinary cadre of international scientists and environmental leaders, e.g., Letitia Obeng and Mostafa Tolba from UNEP;

Maurice Strong, chair of IUCN; the "Small Is Beautiful" economist, E. F. Schumacher; Gene Odum; Buckminster Fuller; and the *Limits to Growth* authors, Donella and Dennis Meadows, to name just a few. Most of them knew each other or were familiar with one another's work. Many were decades older than I was. But I never felt out of place. My contributions to the program were thoughtfully accepted and I was treated with the utmost respect. When the conference was over, I was completely transformed. I had gone, in a few short days, from being a solitary environmental psychologist to having first-name relations and membership with the environmental elite.

At the end of the meeting, I needed to decompress from the heady intellectual encounters of the preceding week. So I decided to stay a while longer in Iceland and explore its intriguing landscape and culture. The other ruling passion at that stage of my life was folk music. After my father, who was also an old-time fiddler, died, I had developed a fascination with collecting traditional fiddle tunes wherever I went. Iceland seemed a likely source of new discoveries. It did not take long to find a group of folk singers, who welcomed me into their home. Fiddling, as it turned out, was not common in Icelandic traditional music. But singing in complex harmonies was. After performing a selection of songs, one of the group's members asked why I was in Reykjavik. I explained I had come to attend an environmental conference and, with little thought, casually added I was a psychologist doing research on "human ecology."

I had never before described myself that way. But somehow at the moment it seemed like a sensible response. "Oh yes," one of the singers affirmed, whereupon he invited me into the adjoining room. There, on the desk, he pointed to a slim book titled *Almenn Visfraeði*—the Icelandic/Old Norse term for human ecology.[*] I picked it up and thumbed through the pages. I could not understand the Old Norse text. But the pictorial illustrations and data charts clearly revealed its subject matter. I had, in that quiet moment, a profound revelation. The study of human ecology was not an exclusive purview of a small college on the coast of Maine. It was

---

[*] A more accurate translation, I later discovered, might be "general" ecology. By then, however, my collection of international human ecology texts contained dozens of volumes in other languages from around the world.

also a legitimate academic subject elsewhere in the world. The teaching of ecology, I soon discovered, was a part of general education throughout Scandinavia at all levels. What had begun as a musical event turned into a lively environmental discussion.

Icelandic summer nights are without darkness and it was surely well into the hours of morning before our conversation ended. I thanked them for a wonderful time and started for the door. But to my surprise they asked if I would prefer to cancel my hotel reservations and be their guest for the remainder of my trip. One of my new friends was a historian. For the next few days we shared an awe-inspiring road tour together. Our journey traced the coastline and interior valleys, highlighted by overnight stops on remote farms. It was further enriched, all the while, by a flowing account of social and environmental history, folklore, and epic legends.

Iceland is a land of fire and ice where glaciers and volcanoes meet in unsteady tension. It is a wonderland of dramatic cliffs and mountains, icy rivers, and bubbling hot springs. The country is virtually devoid of trees, which adds a further element of magic to the landscape. But it hasn't always been that way. There was a time when substantial forested regions did exist. When the Viking settlers first arrived in the ninth century, much of the island was tree covered. The old sagas recount their laboring to clear woodlands and using the trees for buildings, fuel, and making charcoal. These practices contributed to deforestation, further worsened by the unsustainable reliance on grazing animals. But climate evidence from the Middle Ages points to additional, nonhuman causes resulting from fluctuations in the Gulf Stream. Wood was too scarce for burning. What little they had was saved for flooring and roof beams. Walls were constructed of sod blocks. The lower level was for animals. Human inhabitants lived above in the cramped, steep-roofed upper level. During the long, dark winters, the main source of domestic warmth came from the beasts below.*

---

*Sod construction was the vernacular style of house design for centuries throughout Iceland. Its widespread use for domestic structures, as I learned, is why fiddle tunes are uncommon in Iceland. A fiddle would rapidly fall apart in the dank environment. Instead, the tradition became song and harmony rather than instrumental folk music.

By the time we got back to Reykjavik I was already hoping to return. Signs of environmental concern were everywhere. It would be easy to extend my research to this new and exciting place. I finished off my trip developing contacts at the University of Iceland, as well as with several environmental organizations, and making plans to revisit later in the year. Everyone was supportive. I wanted to expand my work to include all age groups and perhaps even set up a longitudinal study for tracking the development of environmental attitudes from childhood. For this, I would need to translate my research materials from English into Icelandic. It was not hard to find a willing assistant. We exchanged materials by mail over the next few months, after which I returned fully loaded with ready-made Icelandic survey instruments and questionnaires. While I was there, an opportunity appeared to take part in a newly formed environmental movement with a focused agenda. Icelandic environmentalists had arranged for 1980, two years hence, to be celebrated as "The Year of the Tree" (Ár Trésins). In support of the organized efforts at public education, the government released a commemorative postage stamp to officially honor the cause. The chance to monitor an ongoing environmental campaign and study its persuasive impact on attitudes and behavior was an extraordinary opportunity. For the next few years, these activities became a significant research commitment.

A Leap of Faith

My relationship with College of the Atlantic was the other—where I also kept coming back. I really liked the college: the interdisciplinary mission, the people there, and how the place ran. It was absolutely charming. At one point there was talk of perhaps adding a faculty position in psychology. I was unsure what the leap from a Big Ten university to a tiny experimental college would be like, but I was curious. In the spring of 1979, I got the chance to find out as a visiting professor for a semester. While I was there, they held a national search. I applied and was selected. I resigned my position at Purdue and made the move to Maine that fall.

The shift from research on people studying human ecology, to actually doing it, was a major transition. There was no such thing as a major in psychology at College of the Atlantic. Students there didn't want the "inside story" of psychology required for undergraduate majors or graduate students elsewhere. Everyone was on his or her own path to a single degree—the BA in Human Ecology. Departmental majors completely defined institutions like Texas, Kent, Ohio State, and Purdue—academically, architecturally, and culturally. COA students didn't take my courses to prepare for the next level of required classes. They wanted to learn psychology. But rather than me defining the subject matter for them, they wanted what I knew to be related to their individual interests. One student was there to learn about the evolution of consciousness; another was working on group dynamics and collaborative decision making; the next searching for the meaning of dreams. They challenged me, each in their own way, to use my psychology background in a much more open-ended manner. It was a firsthand discovery of how self-directed, interdisciplinary learning turns conventional education inside out. The need to reframe my teaching within the college's educational mission of human ecology was a further challenge. The experience of finding my path into human ecology education in many ways resembled the introspective methods of the early Leipzig psychologists. I was both the subject and the observer of my own experiments. Fortunately, I was not alone. All of my faculty colleagues at COA were going through similar experiences. The college's nondepartmentalized structure encouraged sharing our respective backgrounds and ideas. We were, as a group, undertaking a unique experiment in higher education. The purpose wasn't to emulate any other institution or to recapture our own college experiences. The goal was to invent an entirely new philosophy, not only to guide interdisciplinary education, but as an integrative perspective for embracing all of life. As the architect Roc Caivano's "ultimate circle" symbolized—during a lively talk-and-chalk discussion one afternoon—the aim was all-inclusive. The whole of humanity and nature lay within the orbit of ecology. Our vision of human ecology began with the first spark of life billions of years ago, across the ancient human past, and into the jumbled environments of the modern world. Its threads also disclosed the segregation of academic knowledge and the fractured landscape of education. The gaze from there leveled unflinchingly to the future and the urgent problems of the world that lay ahead.

These were exciting times. Human ecology was fast becoming more than a vicarious research topic for me. I was swimming in it. By my second year at COA, I began to redesign my course offerings along increasingly interdisciplinary lines. It was during this period that I also was asked to chair the college's curriculum committee. The administrative responsibility for coordinating a nondepartmentalized faculty around a rigorous and relevant undergraduate curriculum in human ecology really altered my day-to-day concerns. For the next two years I worked closely with COA's president Ed Kaelber and his administrative team. As a part of this new role, I began to look outside the institution for other human ecology ideas and colleagues elsewhere.

In the spring of 1982 *The Chronicle of Higher Education* printed a tiny announcement of the First National Conference on Education and Human Ecology. The four-day meeting was to be held at the University of the District of Columbia in Washington, DC (UDC). I leaped at the opportunity and submitted an application to give a presentation. The proposal, which I titled "Human Ecology as a Psychological Identity," was a blended summary of my research and an overview of COA's history and curriculum. The preconference materials that accompanied the notice of acceptance scheduled my talk in the "Human Ecology: Definitions and Roles in Education" session on day three. The meeting promised to be exactly what I had been hoping to find and I eagerly looked forward to attending.

I knew nothing of the University of the District of Columbia. What I discovered was a very unique institution. Its origins lie in Congress's 1972 granting of home rule for the District of Columbia. The university opened in 1978 as the nation's first exclusively urban land-grant university. The institution was chartered by direction of President Carter under the Morrill Act, which a century before had been the creative force behind our nationwide system of public state universities. The UDC campus is in the heart of the capital city. The founding mission was to serve District of Columbia residents with opportunities for professional development and practical programs responsive to a rapidly changing society, structured around five programmatic colleges—one of which was the college of education and human ecology.

None of my new human ecology colleagues at the conference were aware of College of the Atlantic. My presentation of the college's model of education went well and was followed by a lively conversation. I also learned, from other presentations and discussions, of very different meanings of and educational applications for human ecology. For many, human ecology was used as a contextual lens for framing the challenges of urban life. Topics ranged from gerontology, family nutrition, and community health to issues of multiculturalism, government relations, and adult education. Nearly all of the conference presenters were affiliated with UDC or were faculty from other historically black institutions that also had programs in human ecology. I was very curious how these programs came into existence. The first bit of history came from Cecile Edwards, dean of Howard University's School of Human Ecology. Cecile received a PhD in nutrition from Iowa State University in 1950 and began a distinguished career of NIH-funded research on the metabolism of amino acids. She moved to Washington, DC, in 1971 as chair of Howard's department of home economics. Three years later she launched the university's School of Human Ecology. Other institutions, including UDC, followed her lead, and this was the occasion for their first national conference.

On my way to the airport after the conference, I happened to pass the American Home Economics Association (AHEA) near the Dupont Circle subway entrance. I was excited by my recent discovery. So I decided to stop for a visit and learn more about the transition of home economics to human ecology. Perhaps, I thought, they might be interested in COA as well. They were not, nor did they seem to care about the meeting I had attended. The reception was rather chilly and unwelcoming. It took a while to learn why. The story is a long one, in which the irony runs deep. But here is a brief synopsis. AHEA's first president, Ellen Swallow Richards, was an extraordinary woman. She graduated from Vassar in 1870 with an AB in chemistry. She continued to study chemistry at MIT, where she was the first female student. After completing all of the work to receive a doctorate, the university balked at granting the distinction to a woman. They were, however, willing to hire her as their first female instructor. Richards was fluent in German. She had read the works of Ernst Haeckel and even visited his laboratory in Jena, where she purchased equipment for her courses at MIT. She may well have been the first American to employ the word "ecology." In 1892, on the morning after one of her many public lectures, the *Boston Globe* headline read: "New Science. Mrs. Richards Names It Oekology."[14] Among numerous other activities, Richards also coordinated the yearly Lake Placid Conferences on women's education from 1889 to 1908. It was there that the term "home economics" was chosen as a new educational venture (rather than human ecology, which Richards considered to have broader meaning and preferred). The American Home Economics Association was established in 1909 and selected her as its first president.

At the beginning of the century AHEA was a pioneer in unlocking barriers to university education for women. By the 1960s, however, home economics was increasingly seen as a symbol of the gender stereotypes women were struggling to overcome. Its implications of housewifery were dissonant with the women's movement and feminist ideals. Cornell University was the first major institution to respond to the problem. Under the leadership of dean David Knapp, the university reorganized its College of Home Economics and renamed it the New York State College of Human Ecology in 1969 (the same year COA was founded). Michigan State University made similar changes the next year. Many other public and private institutions followed. The UDC meeting was a subset of that larger movement, which had just happened among the historically black colleges.* Knapp went on to become president of the University of Massachusetts. I visited him in his office there shortly after my return from Washington. We had a stimulating conversation about human ecology. He recounted the history of this line of educational reformation that ended with his sharing copies of the Cornell planning documents with me.

---

*AHEA was renamed the American Association of Family and Consumer Sciences in 1994.

Ed Kaelber retired in June 1982. Judith Swazey was selected to be COA's second president. Judith had a PhD in the history of medicine from Harvard and was a respected researcher and author. My interests in human ecology were somewhat parallel to her research on the history of ideas. She saw their relevance to my administrative role and encouraged me to continue. On a bright October afternoon that fall, Peter Wayne—a student familiar with my pursuit of human ecology—appeared in my office with the 1974 volume of *Advances in Ecological Research* under his arm. The lead article was a 105-page survey of a half century of academic human ecology: "Human Ecology as an Interdisciplinary Concept: A Critical Inquiry," compiled by Gerald Young from Washington State University. Young began with an overview of biological ecology. He then traced how ecological concepts had been adopted, in myriad ways, among the social sciences, across the humanities, as well as throughout many applied professions. In the paper's final section, he offered his appraisal of ecological thought within these various fields, along with an assessment of the prospects for future integration and synthesis of human ecology.

It was a magnificent piece of scholarly work. Young's painstaking research had recovered a vast, uncoordinated, and nearly lost history of human ecological thought. It was a powerful validation of the multitude of ways ecology had been a source of cross-disciplinary inspiration. How his review could have gone unnoticed for nearly a decade was a mystery. Yet there it sat all the while on a library shelf unbeknownst to everyone at the college. Odder still was the fact that I had spent the summer of 1979 on the Washington State University campus in Pullman, where I routinely used the university library for research. That fall was when I began my permanent position at COA. I have often wondered how things might have been different had I found the paper then, or met the author—whose daily path to the stacks unknowingly crossed my own.

Nonetheless, I was delighted in Peter's discovery of Young's reconstruction of the far-reaching roots and peculiar history of human ecology. Most fields of study have a fairly clear historical starting point—in the form of either a founding personality or a seminal problem that stimulated its elaboration. The history of human ecology appeared to be quite the opposite. Instead of beginning in one place and spreading, it seemed to have hatched in a hundred places. Most of these inceptions, moreover, appeared to have taken shape without an awareness of interests developing elsewhere.

One of the earliest strands was Harlan Barrows's 1922 presidential address to the Association of American Geographers. Barrows's presentation, titled "Geography as Human Ecology," was both a historical review of geography and a call for greater interdisciplinary reorientation, which ended with these closing words: "The road which to me seems most promising is that denoted by human ecology."[15] Sociologists, in the meantime, were making their own versions of human ecology. R. D. McKenzie's "The Scope of Human Ecology" appeared in the *American Journal of Sociology* in 1926 with the extension of ecological concepts of competition, displacement, and succession to the study of human habitation. McKenzie was a student of Robert E. Park at the University of Chicago. Park and his colleague Ernest W. Burgess had introduced the term "human ecology" in their 1921 *Introduction to the Science of Sociology*. Their application of quantitative methods and naturalistic observation to urban ecology initiated the pioneering "Chicago School" of human ecology—where Amos Hawley, James Quinn, George Theodorson, and a long line of other sociological human ecologists developed their ideas.

The shape of anthropology was likewise transformed by an infusion of ecological concepts. J. W. Bews's 1935 *Human Ecology* text was a major source; the "cultural ecology" of Julian Steward was another. Steward, who studied with the renowned Alfred Kroeber, was also the inspiration behind the ecological anthropology of Roy Rappaport, Andrew Vayda, and many others. A half century of this line of research can be found in the pages of *Human Ecology: An Interdisciplinary Journal*. The merger of ecology and psychology took various forms. Kurt Lewin developed a version of "psychological ecology," which he applied to mental representations of the environment and to the intrapsychic processes of attitude change. Roger Barker and Herbert Wright took a more outward-directed approach. Their "behavioral ecology," based on extensive observational field studies of social interactions, is still an active subfield within psychology, also known as "social ecology."

These are a small sample of the sources and topics from Young's paper, which contained more than five hundred references pertaining to human ecology—not only in the social sciences but across planning, conservation, engineering, health, architecture, and numerous other academic domains. Young's conclusion was forthright: "The present situation in human ecology is, then, best described simply: it is a fragmented field, far from interdisciplinary.... Though many of the concepts are shared ... most human ecologists are strongly discipline-oriented."[16] Young, however, did uncover a few notable exceptions to these piecemeal trends. The bright spots, in his opinion, appeared in the writings of A. N. Whitehead, Lewis Mumford, René Dubos, and H. G. Wells. I had some familiarity with the work of Whitehead, Mumford, and Dubos (who was a member of COA's board of trustees). But I did not know that Wells had written extensively about human ecology. In his 1934 *Experiment in Autobiography*, he lamented the choice of *The Science of Life* as the title for his sequel to *The Outline of History*. "The exactest name for such a synthesis would be the *Outline of Human Ecology*. But I did not call it that because the word Ecology was not yet widely understood." Looking ahead, he had this to say: "One of the things I would like to see done in the world is the foundation of a number of chairs for the teaching of an old subject in a new spirit. If I belonged to the now rapidly vanishing class of benevolent multi-millionaires I would create professorships ... my professors would be human ecologists." And, as he further added: "Sooner or later Human Ecology under some name or other, will win its way to academic recognition and to its proper place in general education."[17] Wells's presaging of human ecology education was an inspiration.

The next big impetus was the appearance of Young's *Origins of Human Ecology* in the spring of 1983. The volume contained two dozen of the key founding papers of academic human ecology, along with editorial commentaries by Young. The book's introductory comments included a brief acknowledgment of COA and a reference to an emerging effort to establish an interdisciplinary Society for Human Ecology. Without hesitation, I telephoned him in his office. He was, he said, just about to call me to find out about the college's approach to human ecology. We had a long conversation about COA, human ecology activities taking place elsewhere, and the newly formed professional society. He encouraged me to join, and he shared his phone list of the founding members, with whom I soon made contact.*

A Gathering of Perspectives

In the spring of 1979 a handful of people met in Washington, DC. The topic of their conversation was the need to fashion a distinctive and interdisciplinary group for professionals. The underlying aim was to extend the integrating framework of ecology to create a fuller understanding of the place of humans in nature—and to do this under the name of human ecology. Forging such a society would be counter to conventional pressures, both conceptually and organizationally. It would require expertise from a broad range of disciplines and people who were inclined to work together to embrace the problems and possibilities of a livable future.

Later that year, at the University of Maryland, they met again to adopt a set of bylaws and elect the first slate of officers, with Guido Francescato of the University of Maryland as executive director, Frederick Sargent from the University of Texas as president, and Wolfgang Preiser of the University of New Mexico as vice president. Others present included Bill Loring from the Centers for Disease Control, Ann Eward from Michigan State University, Gerald Young from Washington State University, Dan Rose from the University of Pennsylvania, Joseph Valadez from the University of Maryland, John Krummel from the Tennessee Valley Authority, and Anthony Neville from the Smithsonian Institution. Though small, the group was composed of representatives from a broad range of backgrounds.

---

*Gerry and I shortly became close friends. Since then, we have coordinated meetings, coedited books, and traveled together—giving talks, networking, and enjoying the company of other human ecologists around the world.

Documents of incorporation to establish the Society for Human Ecology (SHE) as a not-for-profit educational and research organization were prepared, and plans were made for the First Pan American Conference on Human Ecology, to be held at the Pan American Center for Human Ecology and Health in Toluca, Mexico. Official incorporation was received in the state of Maryland in 1981. Due to the unexpected death of Frederick Sargent, however, plans for the first conference had to be canceled. Wolfgang Preiser, the society's second president, offered this reflection on SHE's founding:

> It was soon realized that founding a Society for Human Ecology would be a difficult undertaking considering the fact that in the United States similar attempts in the past had failed. On the other hand, European efforts in this direction were beginning to take shape, mainly those of the Commonwealth Human Ecology Council (CHEC) based in London, England, and the International Organization for Human Ecology (IOHE) based in Vienna, Austria.
>
> The legacy of the late 1960s movements, and the increasing trend towards highly specialized disciplines without adequate understanding of their relationships or effects upon each other, prompted the foundation members of SHE to pursue Society objectives that were first focused on the United States, but were later to be expanded to include concerns relating to other countries, including nations in the Third World. The underlying motivation was a sense that a broader perspective and holistic view of the world was needed, linking humans both to the natural and built environments. This viewpoint incorporated the traditional ecological disciplines, with those that were merging in the late 1970s, focusing on the effect of humans on the built environment, and vice versa.
>
> Consequently, a working definition of human ecology for the purposes of the Society was based on the hope of the Society's founders that the term "Human Ecology" could be understood to be more comprehensive than other possible terms.[18]

I became a member of SHE in the spring of 1983. Later that summer, on July 25, a major fire destroyed College of the Atlantic's central complex—including the library, dining hall, and most of our classrooms and faculty offices. My office was in another building, but the disaster had a life-changing impact. Statistical data, in those days, was coded on IBM punch cards—fed into and compiled by computers. All of my research from Purdue, Iceland, and COA filled several dozen boxes. The college had recently purchased its first computer. All of my boxes of data were neatly stacked in the corner of the new computer center waiting to be transferred to magnetic discs. That's where they were when the building burned. The loss of a decade of research on personality assessment, cognitive mapping, and environmental beliefs was a setback. The uncertainty of COA's survival, however, was a far greater dilemma. But the spirit of the college was strong and we were soon on our way to rebuilding.

In October, Wolfgang Preiser came to Bar Harbor to visit me on a beautiful weekend. As we stood looking out at the ocean—beside the enormous hole in the ground that had been the heart of the college—we pledged to do our best to carry on the making of this association. We later drove to the top of Cadillac Mountain to continue our discussion and to view the sunset. Just before leaving the parking lot, Wolf jumped out of the car and ran around behind to open the trunk. In a moment he returned with two stemmed wine glasses and a bottle of red wine, which he opened. He then proposed a toast to the future of our partnership—and invited me to fill the SHE vice president position left open by his move into the presidency. That was my start on this journey. A great deal has happened between then and now. What I would like to do here is give a sketch of SHE's history, briefly review its activities and accomplishments, and recognize some of the individuals who have played significant roles in these developments.

A review of SHE's activities begins with the commitment by the Board in 1983 to build a professional network of people interested in human ecology. These interests, as we knew, were not restricted to locations within the United States. Consequently, a two-pronged approach was adopted. On the one hand, we began by contacting established human ecology programs around the United States and other interested colleagues. These leads were used to develop a referral list of individuals and institutions to build a membership pool. At the same time, we searched for people and programs in other countries working under the name of human ecology. Our first substantive product was publication of a *Directory of Human Ecologists* in February 1984. It contained the names and brief biographies of some 250 scholars, researchers, and applied professionals from across the United States and abroad. The directory was a joint effort of COA and the Society for Human Ecology, supported by small grants from the Exxon Foundation and the Continental Group. The grant funds also subsidized my travel to Europe later that summer, where I visited a dozen human ecology centers in the United Kingdom, Norway, Sweden, Denmark, and France.

Judith Swazey resigned her presidency shortly before I left for Europe. The trustees began the search for a replacement, and by the time I returned, they had appointed Lou Rabineau. Before becoming COA's third president, Lou had been Connecticut's chancellor of higher education and senior vice president at the Academy for Educational Development. He asked me to join him, as the college's chief academic officer, in the role of provost and academic dean. I worked day-in and day-out with Lou for nine years. In many ways, I stopped being a psychologist. The responsibility of articulating the college's human ecology mission and raising financial support to expand the curriculum was all-consuming. Lou was fully supportive of my interest in building relations with other institutions—and especially helpful in finding external support for these activities.

Networking Human Ecology Worldwide

Based on our growing U.S. network and the encouragement of European colleagues, the Society reinstituted plans for its initial conference, this time hosted by Guido Francescato and held at the University of Maryland. The First International Conference of the Society for Human Ecology in April 1985 was a success. Participants came from as far away as Europe and Australia and debated a wide range of programmatic and conceptual issues. Invited keynote presentations were given by Stephen Boyden (Australian National University), Britta Jungen (Gothenburg University, Sweden), Garrett Hardin (University of California–Santa Barbara), Amos Rapoport (University of Wisconsin), Philip Stewart (Oxford University, England), and Christopher Nuttman and Anthony Vann (Huddersfield Polytechnic, England). Their addresses and other papers from the meeting were published in a special volume by the Society. At the end-of-conference business meeting, I was elected SHE's third president.

Energized by the success of our discussions and the enthusiasm of participants, a second conference was planned for October 1986 at College of the Atlantic. By then our networking yielded participation from more than twenty countries and five continents. Keynote presentations were made by Zena Daysh (Commonwealth Human Ecology Council's executive vice-chair), Paulo Machado (professor of human ecology at the State University of Campinas, Brazil, and former Minister of Health), Andrew Vayda (Rutgers University's distinguished professor of human ecology), Torsten Malmberg (chair of the Nordic Society for Human Ecology and director of the human ecology program at Lund University, Sweden), and William Carpenter (COA professor and faculty dean). All college classes were suspended during the event, to allow for the full participation of faculty and students. As before, SHE and COA prepared a jointly published volume of the conference proceedings. Those early encounters among human ecologists were not unlike the proverbial group in a dark room with an elephant. They were invaluable gatherings for sharing perspectives. Many of the conversations revolved around a basic question: "And what do you mean by human ecology?"—from which everyone learned about the common and distinctive aspects of their respective views.

At the close of the Bar Harbor meeting it was decided to hold SHE's third conference on the West Coast. The Golden Gate National Recreation Area, just outside of San Francisco, was selected as the venue. A flood of submissions was received in response to the call for participation. All together, however, there would be a disjointed schedule of conventional paper presentation in multiple conflicting sessions. So, instead, the conference committee arranged a collaborative experiment of full-fledged interaction, guided by a team of professional facilitators. Flip-chart collaboration techniques and group decision-making methods were becoming established in a variety of community and business settings. But facilitated meetings were still unfamiliar in the academic world.

On October 7, 1988, Donald B. Straus, past president of the American Arbitration Association, opened the proceedings with a keynote address emphasizing the "threshold" condition of human ecology as a perspective and as a profession. He then challenged us to address, as a single body, three questions: "What is the current status of human ecology?" "What are our visions for its future?" and "What steps can take us from where we now are to where we want to be?" This became the agenda for the next three days. In an accordionlike process, conference participants moved back and forth between small group discussions and interactive plenary sessions—all done in highly participatory, facilitation-collaboration style.

Thanks to the extraordinary skill of the facilitators, we gradually worked through the initial skepticism; and by the end of the meeting, the group arrived at a powerful consensus on several concrete and useful outcomes. Not only had participants engaged with colleagues they might otherwise not have shared ideas with, the Society itself created a working structure for next steps in the form of ongoing working groups. The themes that emerged—many still at the core of subsequent meetings—included: sustainability, economics, education, health, environmental consciousness, applied human ecology, theory and paradigms, the future of human ecology, etc.

Later that year, we released an expanded *International Directory of Human Ecologists*. The new edition contained 750 entries from fifty-one countries. Each person's entry included several thematic keywords and a narrative description of his work. The alphabetical listing of surnames was enhanced with a cross-referenced index of each person's country and topical interests. The map of indexed keywords—like the outcome of our facilitated conference—transcended conventional disciplinary lines. The emerging attributes were not only interdisciplinary in an academic sense, but they revealed a synthesis of diverse personal and professional interests of truly international scope as well.*

Many of these people had been working on explicitly interdisciplinary human ecology problems for a long time. The University of Tokyo's department of human ecology opened in 1965. Other universities followed and formed the Japanese Society of Health and Human Ecology. In 1972, the University of Geneva established an International Center for Human Ecology, to offer a specialization in human ecology. The following year the University of Paris V and the University of Toulouse joined them. By 1978 the model expanded to nine more universities—in France, Italy, Portugal, and Belgium—under the auspices of the European Association for Human Ecology (EAHE). The Commonwealth Human Ecology Council, active since the late 1960s, had stimulated programs at universities in Africa, the Caribbean, and elsewhere around the world. In India, Rajasthan University's Indira Gandhi Centre for Human Ecology, Environmental and Population Studies, opened through CHEC's initiative in 1985. Not long thereafter the Indian Society for Human Ecology, based at the University of Delhi, incorporated and began publication of a scholarly journal. Links with a host of other academic programs, research initiatives, and smaller regional associations developed across the United States and Canada, in eastern Europe, South America, as well as Korea, Indonesia, the Philippines, Bali, and elsewhere in Asia.

Just a few years before, SHE had scarcely two dozen members. The network strands, which now extended in all directions, had touched upon an astonishing diversity of interests. The next challenge was to figure out how these pieces fit together. During this period SHE began to cosponsor symposia within the professional meetings of other organizations, e.g., the American Association for the Advancement of Science (AAAS), the International Association for Impact Assessment (IAIA),

---

*Substantial credit for this achievement—as for all of SHE's early publications—belongs to Jamien Jacobs, who took her student internship with the Society in 1985–86, and continued to work on SHE projects for the next three years. Also, Lou Rabineau, COA's third president, was ever-helpful in finding support from the Academy for Educational Development, the Frost Foundation, and the U.S. Department of Education.

and the Environmental Design Research Association (EDRA). SHE representatives served as keynote speakers and session chairs at various human ecology forums within the Human Ecology Commission of the International Union of Anthropological and Ethnological Sciences (IUAES), the European Seminars on Education sponsored by UNESCO and the EAHE, the Commonwealth Human Ecology Council (CHEC), the Institute of Ecosystem Studies (IES), the Nordic Society for Human Ecology, the International Organization for Human Ecology (IOHE), and the First Latin American Conference on Ecology.

In July 1989, Lou Rabineau and I were invited to the Ninth Commonwealth Conference on Development and Human Ecology, hosted by the University of Edinburgh, to give a joint presentation on the history of COA's founding, growth, and influence. At the close of the meeting, just as we were leaving, two Chinese delegates introduced themselves and expressed their interest in SHE's agenda. A few weeks later a package containing several articles and a book, *Human Ecology in China*, appeared in my mailbox. The author, Rusong Wang, was at the Chinese Academy of Sciences in Beijing. It was a double delight. This was the first link to human ecologists in China. But I was especially excited by the author's introduction of human ecology within a three-thousand-year historical framework of Chinese philosophy and human/nature relations. In the letter of thanks to Dr. Wang I mentioned that if his travels ever brought him to the United States, COA would have funds to bring him to Maine. It was not long until it occurred.

Rusong's presentation to students and faculty began with this handwritten, overhead transparency. (It is perhaps noteworthy that the fourth character contains both physical and mental attributes—which conveys an appealing alternative to Cartesian duality.)

He then moved through a remarkable interweaving of Chinese principles of dynamic harmony, yin/yang balance, and Wu Xing (Five Element) theory—on which traditional holistic medicine is based. From there, he outlined a model of contemporary human ecology and its applications to urban planning, rural development, agroecology, and environmental management. It was a human ecological vision for China's future, not in

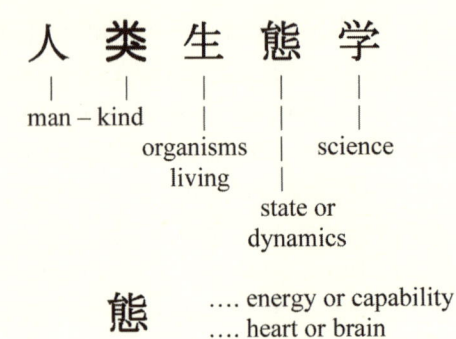

人　类　生　态　学
| | | | | |
man – kind | | |
　　　organisms | science
　　　living |
　　　　　　state or
　　　　　　dynamics

態　　.... energy or capability
　　　.... heart or brain

The science of living state/dynamics of human being driven by objective and subjective factors

-- understanding
-- planning
-- management

disciplinary or interdisciplinary terms, but from a truly cross-cultural synthesis. COA's philosopher, John Visvader, has a deep knowledge of Chinese philosophy and the philosophy of science. He and Rusong developed an instant intellectual bond. So for the next few days we explored Maine's coast and northern forests together.

The 1990s were filled with bridge-building activities. One of the first was a daylong symposium at the V International Congress of Ecology (INTECOL) in August 1990 in Yokohama. It brought together a dozen leading human ecologists from around the world who described the activities in their region. Bill Drury, as the closing speaker, provided a summary of the changing landscape of ecological theory and its relevance to the future of human ecology—along with integrative remarks on the event as a whole. Vrije Universiteit Brussel (VUB) published the papers with the title *Human Ecology—Coming of Age: An International Overview* with joint sponsorship by SHE, the Japanese Society of Health and Human Ecology, and the European Association for Human Ecology.

The following July, in Sweden, Gothenburg University hosted a six-day conference, "Human Responsibility and Global Change." The meeting's participants came from more than forty countries. The leadership from the various professional human ecology associations held a special international forum to discuss membership issues and future coordination. Many of these people knew one another by this time. Merging into a single umbrella organization, given their respective histories, was seen to be unnecessary. Instead, a published directory—describing the mission, structure, and membership of each organization—was proposed. Eva Ekehorn, the forum's moderator and president-elect of SHE, was appointed to edit the directory, which was published jointly by SHE and the Nordic Society for Human Ecology.

The scope of SHE's activities expanded beyond conferences with the launch of *Human Ecology Review* in 1993. The journal has become a respected forum for research, theory, and project reports. Its contents—like meeting agendas and member profiles—offers an ongoing operational definition of the shape and growth of human ecological ideas. Among academic and professional societies, SHE is a tiny organization. Even within human ecology, it is but one of many. Nonetheless, it has become an important forum for exploration of truly broad-based and interdisciplinary views. Over the past thirty years the Society has been the intellectual home for an extraordinary and dedicated group of individuals. We have organized meetings across the United States, in Mexico, Canada, Europe, South America, and Australia. In addition to SHE's second conference in 1986, COA has been host to two more—in 1997 and 2006.

This is an education that has taken me around the world and brought a global family of like-minded colleagues to College of the Atlantic. Rusong Wang invited John Visvader and me to teach a human ecology seminar in the Chinese Academy of Sciences in 1994, where he had become a program director of the Research Center for Eco-Environmental Sciences. The exchange of Western and Eastern viewpoints was a delight. Later on, as president of the Ecological Society of China, Rusong organized the 2007 EcoSummit in Beijing. The meeting brought 1,400 leading environmental scientists and planners from more than seventy countries. John Anderson was president of SHE at the time, and I was the Society's executive director. During our conversations with the leaders of the Ecological Society of America at the Beijing meeting, we were invited to create an ESA human ecology division. The new section was chartered the following year, with strong backing from ESA's current and past presidents Alan Covich, Stuart Chapin, and Elinor Ostrom and executive director Katherine McCarter. A series of successful symposia have been held at annual ESA meetings since then. The section's membership, though still small, is steadily accelerating. It has been extremely gratifying—at long last—to bring human ecology back to its nominal birthplace and home.

Human Ecology: From Discipline to Perspective

No simple statement can sum up the many meanings of human ecology. For nearly a century, the term has been applied to a diverse family of speculative and scientific lines of thought. In a general sense, it points to certain problem areas manifesting the influence of ecological thinking and to various intellectual movements at the intersections of traditional academic disciplines. Perhaps it is not surprising that a multitude of human ecology initiatives have sprouted. To some extent this paradox is a result of the specialized structure of institutions of higher education and research. As universities expanded during the nineteenth and twentieth centuries, assurance of a disciplined course of study was linked with a narrowing of interests. In time, each field of knowledge acquired sufficient autonomy to define its own problems and methods, formulate specialized curricular and research agendas, and frequently acquire its own building. Taken together, these forces produced an architecture of knowledge, which has compartmentalized universities from within and has established discipline-based intellectual cultures among professional scholars and scientists. Once established, the arrangement of incentives and the strategies for personal and professional advancement became associated with disciplinary projects or accomplishments. In other words, the university system has evolved over time into a family of large institutions, each of which offers a universe of intellectual perspectives without a forum or reward structure for integration of them.

Ecology was one of the few integrating perspectives that overcame, at least partially, the hard structures of academic institutions. Shortly after the beginning of the twentieth century, its orientation gained a toehold across the natural sciences. Interdisciplinary from the outset, ecology invited a pluralistic coalescing of physical and biological science—from geology, chemistry, and meteorology to botany, physiology, genetics, zoology, and behavioral studies. As ecological theory and research developed, its ideas began to stimulate isolated domains in the social sciences and applied fields. Some were the singular efforts of individuals. Other times a small program was created by a small group of collaborators. These pockets of interest and schools of thought were generally of restrictive scope due to the slant of their founders. They were of separate origin, seldom aware of each another, and often of limited duration.

By the 1960s ecological perspectives began to intersect with mounting concerns about the profound influence of humanity at all levels of the environment and the global system. Entirely new issues were being raised and explored. Pioneering models for the study of human/environmental relations appeared throughout the educational community. Policy, health, and design professionals began to transform their methods and applications. Ecological concepts permeated the human studies. As they were adopted (and adapted) across the regions of human affairs, scientific ecology was likewise infused with issues from far beyond its traditional boundaries. It is easy to envision, against this background, how human ecology arose as a common term for a multiplicity of views from widespread starting points.

Some of the pioneers took a firm position that human ecology was a science that should follow clear methods of investigation. Napoleon Wolanski, director of the department of human ecology at the Polish Academy of Sciences, was a strong advocate of this stance. During the 1960s, Wolanski fashioned the Commission on Human Ecology within the IUAES and was editor-in-chief of the international journal *Studies in Human Ecology*. The Vienna-based International Organization for Human Ecology (IOHE) was conceived around a similar model. During the 1970s, IOHE's International Congresses on Human Ecology were active forums for the development of human ecological research agendas under the leadership of Helmut Knötig. Wolfgang Preiser and Guido Francescato were early members of IOHE. But, as architects, they were uncomfortable with Knötig's strict scientific orientation. This is what led to the founding of SHE, for which they envisioned a much broader interdisciplinary agenda. The Nordic Society for Human Ecology and the German Society for Human Ecology were also spin-offs of IOHE, for similar reasons. SHE's founders knew what they were striving to do would be difficult and counter to mainstream traditions. At the outset, many of the sociological and anthropological human ecologists—who came from established research traditions—often voiced their discomfort with "programmatic" and "applied" agendas. The prickliest differences, perhaps, were between biological ecologists and those with home economics backgrounds. Yet these were the very obstacles to be confronted, and bringing people together from diverse backgrounds was imperative. The debates were sometimes lively. But whatever differences existed among those who came to SHE meetings, everyone always returned. The absence of traditional academic walls seemed to invite an unusual openness of thought, which still attracts broad-based participation. Members from every background have stepped forward since SHE's founding, three decades ago, to organize and host one of its conferences. As the twentieth international conference approaches, the prospect of human ecology continues to attract enthusiastic participants in search of a wider vision.

Human ecology makes no claim that pursuit of specialized knowledge is misdirected. The intention is not to denounce academic disciplines nor dismiss the value of focused and rigorous investigation. A human ecology perspective reminds us that we really are part of a complex living world. It seeks new relations—not instead of disciplinary ones, but in addition to them. Its interdisciplinary mandate invites crossing boundaries. This requires a different kind of imagination, in pursuit of fresh combinations of ideas. Its value lies in recognition that some people's sense of an authentic understanding of the world requires a larger foundation. Whenever someone leaves the comfort of a familiar worldview, it is a first step toward human ecology. There may not be many who do so—but always enough, I hope, to carry its future.

Finally, I wish to add a few brief, closing points. They begin with some observations on human ecology's institutional and intellectual past by the Swedish historian Emin Tengström. At the time (in the mid-1980s), he was a founding professor of human ecology and senior administrator at Gothenburg University. The history of human ecology, in Tengström's view, was the progressive unfolding of three more-or-less distinct stages. The first phase (from the 1920s to the 1960s) was mainly *monodisciplinary*. The distinctive feature of this stage was the creation of discipline-based "schools" of human ecology, "borrowing their theoretical pattern from ecology." A second *multidisciplinary* stage began in the '60s. It was characterized by multiauthored anthologies and calls for the action-oriented cooperation of specialists—but with little actual exchange of ideas among them. Tengström also envisioned a new and developing third, *interdisciplinary* stage. This version of human ecology explicitly called upon an integrative strategy "with the principle aim to restructure knowledge already gained" and the production of "fundamentally new and specific human ecology knowledge."[19] The best place to achieve such a high degree of integration, in Tengström's opinion, was within a permanent institutionalized framework.

Since then, a further, *transdisciplinary* distinction seems to have appeared. Some people have taken this to be equivalent to interdisciplinary knowledge (or perhaps consider it a meaningless bit of wordplay). But for others, it represents an important reorientation. Transdisciplinary perspectives go beyond the foundations of academic disciplines. Their aim is to include the know-how of nonspecialists, the creative contributions of open collaboration, as well as the role of imagination. The epistemological and methodological challenges of this complex perspective have been outlined by the Chilean ecological economist Manfred Max-Neef, who starkly lamented: "It goes without saying that no transdisciplinary universities exist."[20] That may well be true, but it does not mean no one is trying. The human ecology program at the Australian National University is a leading example, where the faculty has collaborated to publish an important book: *Tackling Wicked Problems: Through the Transdisciplinary Imagination.** Like my ANU colleagues, I also have the good fortune of being a part of an institution that values this kind of experimentation. We are not the only ones. Nonetheless, universities could surely go much further in support of this approach to research and education—and in doing so greatly enhance students' preparation for the future. In this sense, I concur with the spirit of Max-Neef's judgment.

I believe Tengström was only partially correct that permanent institutions are a necessary condition. The occasional forums of human ecology conferences are not permanent—and most participants come from conventionally structured institutions. Yet a distinctive community has formed and a significant body of valuable knowledge now exists through these collaborations. On the other hand, gatherings of individuals from diverse backgrounds—permanent or temporary—do not, by themselves, produce interdisciplinary or transdisciplinary cooperation. A motivation to share knowledge and explore novel syntheses must also reside *within* the individuals. Institutions can support and enlarge these objectives. But they are also an attitude of mind and a way of looking at the world. Human ecological relations surround us. Anyone can open himself or herself to a broader vision of life. Oftentimes they do so entirely on their own. The delight of my life comes from knowing many—and in sharing their views.

---

*This book was selected by the Society for Human Ecology to receive the 2011 Gerald L. Young Book Award "for exemplifying the highest standard of scholarly work in the field of human ecology."

CHAPTER 5

Education

A student is not a vessel to be filled, but a lamp to be lighted.
—**Plutarch**

There should be no greater honor given by society than permission to teach, just as there can be no greater disaster than to fail at the task.
—**Loren Eiseley**

The word "education" comes from the Latin *e-ducare*, "to lead or to draw out." It is a two-part process, often symbolized by a torch handed between teacher and student. One part comes from the teacher, who stimulates the imagination. The other involves stirring a latent interest or talent within the learner. As G. K. Chesterton noted, education in its broadest sense "is simply the soul of society as it passes from one generation to another."[1] But education is not indoctrination. The futurist Bill Ellis makes a useful distinction with his differentiation between "being taught" and the self-growth of "learning."[2] How the mind grows was the centerpiece of Jean Piaget's work on cognitive development. The principal goal of education, for Piaget, "should be creating men and women who are capable of doing new things, not simply repeating what other generations have done."[3]

Development of new ideas often involves holding contradictory thoughts. The ability to entertain a thought, without accepting it, was Aristotle's mark of an educated mind. In the parlance of contemporary academic freedom, "it is the right to say what one thinks without thinking what one says." As Socrates discovered, however, these high ideals may lead to trouble. What happened to him in the Greek forum has befallen many others throughout history. Nonetheless, the core principles of education have never been fully extinguished.

Threats to education come not only from outside or from those fearful of new ideas. They may as easily arise from within. Alfred North Whitehead described the problem clearly: "Above all we must beware of what I call 'inert ideas'—that is to say, ideas that are merely received.... Education with inert ideas is not only useless: it is, above all things, harmful.... The problem of keeping knowledge alive, of preventing it from becoming inert ... is the central problem of all education." In addition to naming the problems, Whitehead also expressed the aims of education: "Education is the acquisition of the art of the utilisation of knowledge." Reversing his wording captures the full meaning of this thought. Bits of knowledge, by themselves, are inert. Usefully combining knowledge is an art. Acquisition of that art—of the utilization of knowledge—should be the aim of education. In short, education is an art—to which Whitehead quickly added, "an art very difficult to impart."[4]

Edward Kaelber introduced me to this idea of education as an art. Ed was the founding president of College of the Atlantic. He built the college around Whitehead's philosophy of education. His leadership style was unlike any I had seen. Presidents, deans, and department chairs make their presentations in a characteristically formal and stiff style. They deliver prepared speeches, usually from a podium, to segregated groups of students, staff, and faculty. This kind of formality did not exist at COA. I remember the first weekly All College Meeting (a.k.a. ACM) I attended at the beginning of the semester I arrived. The auditorium filled in a haphazard fashion. Everyone showed up. But it wasn't clear who were students, staff, or faculty. Some sat in chairs arranged in a broad horseshoe, more or less oriented toward the front of the hall. Others relaxed on the floor, leaned against windowsills, or stood at the back. Many balanced lunch plates and food bowls in their laps.

The meeting began with a series of spontaneous announcements, interspersed with various committee reports and brief show-and-tell stories about recent vacation activities. At some undetermined point, with no introduction, Ed stood up and began to talk in a free-form, conversational manner. He had no notes. One topic flowed into the next, occasionally looping back to gather some previous point. When Ed began talking, the person beside me, whom I didn't know, began to fidget and look at his watch. After he repeated this several times, I nudged him and asked if something was wrong. "No," he whispered back, "I'm just waiting to see when he gets to the 'bricks and mortar' part." In time I came to understand what he meant. Ed had a handful of anecdotes, which he repeated in no particular order, that held his talks together. The bricks and mortar piece was his way of saying that COA wasn't about buildings. People were important—always more important than architecture or fancy facilities. Most important of all were students and faculty. That was what made a college. Administration was secondary—or as he sometimes put it, "a necessary evil." This wasn't empty rhetoric. He really believed it. The role of administration was to serve the interaction and exchange of ideas among students and faculty. It was a wonderful way of making the college's nondepartmental, interdisciplinary mission meaningful.

I came to see the beauty of Ed's nondirective leadership. His talks resembled a bridge player sorting their hand in preparation for an opening bid. The order of ideas was ever-changing. The familiar face cards were his way of reminding people of the values of the institution. One of his favorites was Whitehead's quote about the aims of education. Ed circled around it and sooner or later, like bricks and mortar, the memorable "acquisition of the art" came into play—often as the closing trick.

Before Ed was invited to be COA's founding president, he served as an associate dean under Francis Keppel at Harvard. Keppel was dean of the Graduate School of Education from 1948 to 1962, where he made enormous strides in improving the quality of professional education. As U.S. Commissioner of Education during the mid-1960s, he also oversaw many national innovations in education. He later became a COA trustee. Many of Ed's ideas about education and leadership were gained under Frank's mentorship.

Kaelber wasn't the only person at COA steeped in Whiteheadian philosophy. Richard Davis, the college's first philosopher, was a specialist in process philosophy. So was Daniel Kane, whose expertise extended into both physics and law. He taught a range of classes on environmental policy, philosophy, and sources of invention. Dick and Dan had been college roommates at Yale. Their classroom and lunchtime discussions at COA were a continuation of late-night debates that had matured over the years. These exchanges were further elaborated by Donald Meiklejohn, the college's senior scholar at the time. When Don retired from administration and teaching at Syracuse University's Maxwell School of Public Affairs in 1975, Ed Kaelber convinced him to join the COA faculty, where he continued to teach politics and philosophy for a dozen more years. Before Syracuse, Don had been on the faculty of the University of Chicago from 1946 to 1963. He was an artful teacher in the Socratic style. His classes began with a carefully crafted, provocative statement that led to amazing discussions, restimulated only briefly with subtly nuanced follow-up questions. Don's doctoral dissertation at Harvard was directed by Whitehead.

This was a formidable intellectual environment. When I arrived in Bar Harbor, I entered an entirely new world. None of these ideas were familiar. It was as exciting as it was extraordinary—but rather terrifying as well. Whitehead was *de rigueur* in the early years at COA. I knew I had a steep learning curve ahead of me. It soon became steeper when I was invited to join the teaching team with my new colleagues the next year. Whitehead's *Science and the Modern World* was one of the core texts. It remains one of the most difficult books I have ever read. Trying to teach from it—indeed, to get even a preliminary grasp of the ideas—was uncanny. Preparing for each class was daunting. I got a lot of help and support from two of my closest humanities colleagues, Bill and JoAnne Carpenter. Bill's background was in English literature, JoAnne's in art history. We met for an hour or so before every class to go over the day's readings and sort out how we would present them together. But when we got into the classroom, neither Bill nor JoAnne ever followed our script. They would launch out in some unforeseen direction, happily pursuing whatever line of thought led to an enthusiastic discussion among the students. I had never seen anything like it. I was a fairly successful teacher at Ohio State and Purdue. In those settings, I spent a lot of time preparing for each class, and followed a prepared outline of organized notes. I was pretty good at extemporizing around the points, but I always knew where I was going. With Bill and JoAnne, I felt like a first-timer on a squash court.

Bill Carpenter was the first COA faculty member hired by Ed Kaelber. He had been on the faculty at the University of Chicago. At first, I assumed Bill was following a Chicago give-and-take seminar style to which I was unaccustomed. I later learned that he and JoAnne were doing something else. Every class was a blank canvas awaiting a novel creation. By the end of the semester I was beginning to grasp their method. I was exhausted, but I was also transformed. Were it not for their open-minded and uncritical support, I could not have survived the challenge. In the years since, I have realized that neither of them ever does the same thing twice in teaching.

Thankfully, not everyone at COA was that spontaneous. The scientists, as a rule, did tend to follow a more structured approach. But teaching with them was difficult in another way. Their facility with ecology and natural history often left me breathless. I remember one event in particular. It was the beginning of the term. The admissions director was introducing the incoming class, over lunch, to the faculty. Each student said her name and a few things about why she had come and where she was from. Incoming classes were not big in those days—maybe forty or so new students. At the end of the introductions, Steve Katona—another of Ed's first faculty members (and later, COA's fourth president)—stood up. "Let me see if I've got it," he said, whereupon he went around the room and recited their names and hometowns. He didn't get everyone, but he only missed a few. "Thank God," I thought to myself, "I didn't have to take biology class alongside of him." Steve had done his undergraduate and graduate work at Harvard. It wasn't hard to see how he got there. Indeed, most of the college's faculty had come from Ivy League or private institutions. Sue Mehrtens—the historian—from Yale; Bill Carpenter from Dartmouth;

Roc Caivano—the architect—from Dartmouth and Yale; Dick and Dan also from Yale; Steve Katona and Bill Drury—both from Harvard; Judith Blank—an anthropologist—from Chicago; Carl Ketchum—math and oceanography, and Harris Hyman—engineering—both from MIT. Many of them also had prep-school backgrounds.

In my sophomore year at college, I lived in an honors residence hall. Several of my suite-mates had gone to Exeter. They were proficient in Greek and Latin and well versed in the classical academic canon. It was there that I first realized the limits of my small-town background vis-à-vis elite boarding schools. I envied their facility with ideas and was frequently bewildered by their erudite discussions of philosophy and politics. Many times I slipped away to check some unfamiliar word or name in the dictionary. They seemed to me, at the time, to already have a college education. Yet I was dismayed by what appeared to be a cultivated attitude of cynicism toward life. Their cloistered experience at all-male preparatory schools hampered them socially as well. There was much talk about women. But for the most part they were uncomfortable with meeting female students or developing relationships. Instead, on weekends and many evenings, they huddled together in all-night poker sessions or drinking binges at local bars. I was thankful not to share those problems, and appreciated the social value of my public coeducational background.

None of that sense of detachment or elitism existed at College of the Atlantic. Ed Kaelber had carefully sculpted his new college out of a rare combination of bright and collegial academics. Each professor brought the background and disciplinary expertise of his respective field. Unlike their counterparts at most institutions—who all too often were in a state of constant competition with colleagues—everyone at COA seemed to share a commitment to work together in support of individual students, and to provide a rich curriculum for self-directed student learning. It was an exceptional, nondepartmentalized faculty. As a group, they blended together as a vibrant interdisciplinary learning community, and a bona fide model for integrative education. I had witnessed some unseemly departmental and personal disputes in the past. Many academics take pride in a refined form of nastiness. The atmosphere at COA was otherwise. Scientists regularly taught side by side with artists; evolutionists engaged humanists. As Dan Kane once declared at a faculty retreat session one evening: "This college is an idea." Exchanges could be vigorous and frequently irreconcilable, but not unfriendly. People seemed to genuinely enjoy one another. They were building a college—together.

I sometimes wondered, given my unlikely path through public education, how I was selected. Yet I never felt out of place or unwelcome. So it was a considerable surprise, in my second year at COA, when Ed Kaelber and Dick Davis pulled me aside one evening after dinner to ask if I would chair the academic affairs committee. Sam Eliot, the academic vice president (and grandson of the distinguished Harvard president Charles Eliot), was preparing to return to Harvard and complete his doctoral studies. I was flattered by the invitation. But I protested on grounds of ignorance about college administration. Ed made an unforgettable reply. The job required only one thing, he said, "to arrange affairs so that people will work together." It was the core of Ed's organizational philosophy of education. His guidance was a steady keel and a treasured inheritance of wisdom. This simple job description was the same as he had received from Francis Keppel at Harvard. We are each other's teachers. Our learning comes by sharing, and the cardinal points of our compass, many times, are the insights and counsel of others.

The Gifts of Great Teachers

In a lifetime of formal education a continuous parade of teachers passes before us. Most people remember the name of their kindergarten teacher. Many of us can recall other elementary and high school teachers—and a lot of our college professors. Few can summon up the names of all, even though we spent months or even years together in the same room. But there are always some who inspire our lives in powerful and unforgettable ways. They stand out from the rest. Their ideas and actions are the spark for our inner sources of illumination. If we are fortunate, we encounter many.

Sometimes the connection requires something more of the teacher. The Emmy Award-winning author, performer, and social activist Ossie

Davis recalls one of his most memorable experiences this way: "If you are lucky," he said, "someone recognizes you."[5] The gift of "being seen" can be transformative. I remember such an experience from college. It was during the summer session of my junior year at Texas. I was taking my first statistics class. Statistics is a gateway course for graduate study in psychology and has a reputation as a stubborn subject. I decided to take it in the summer to avoid having to balance it against other courses in the preceding semester. The professor was Robert K. Young, a leading psychometrician with a reputation for being demanding. We had just taken the first exam. At the beginning of our next class, he called out my name and asked me to come to the front of the room. As I walked toward him with considerable uneasiness, he reached into his pocket and pulled out several quarters. He handed them to me. "Go get yourself a coke," he said. "You don't need to hear this—and buy me one too." When I returned, the room was hushed and the students disconsolate. He had apparently given a firm assessment of his disappointment with their performance. My graded exam was on my desk—with a perfect score. I was delighted with the grade. Far more importantly, I had a profound experience of "being seen" by someone I sincerely admired. My relationship with Bob continued to grow. Whenever we passed in the corridors of Mezes Hall thereafter, he always cheerfully greeted me and often stopped to chat. That event opened a door, not only to meet other members of the psychology department with whom I later worked, but *within* me. Bob's personal recognition and professional encouragement were an inestimable teacher's gift. Like all gift exchanges, it was a two-way experience.

The British psychoanalyst Anthony Stevens illustrates this power of mutual connection at the most basic level. Early in his career, Stevens held a research position at the Metera Babies' Center in Athens, Greece. The hospital was designed as an alternative model of care for unwanted babies. In place of the impersonal dormitory-style of traditional orphanages, Metera was organized into autonomous pavilions. Every pavilion contained twelve infants. Four graduate nurses, who resided in the center, and eight student nurses were assigned to each pavilion. Within the pavilion, the four graduate nurses were permanently assigned as "mother nurses" to smaller groups of three babies each. Each pavilion's nurses, as a team, provided around-the-clock care for feeding, bathing, changing, and whatever else the infants needed. As Stevens describes: "These infants were receiving multiple mothering on a scale which was possibly unprecedented in the existence of our species. Never in the whole history of mothering had so few received so much from so many."[6] Stevens observed that in the course of only a few hours each child received some kind of attention from virtually every nurse in her pavilion. He also discovered something else. Most children became specifically attached to one nurse. Once the infant's preference formed, he usually refused care from anyone else. Often it was a nurse from whom he had received only minimal caretaking. It was seldom the assigned mother nurse. The infants typically established their preferences by eight or nine months of age. This is the same age, as Stevens points out, that unequivocal conscious signs of recognition of the mother appear in family-reared babies.

The infants of Metera introduced an unforeseen psychological dimension to the center's system of continuous caregiving. Their singular preference for a "mother figure" is consistent with Carl Jung's theory of unconscious archetypes. In Jung's view, each child carries within himself or herself a deep psychic image of a mother. When the bond forms, a chord is struck that stimulates the child's attachment complex. The British psychiatrist John Bowlby and the American psychologist Mary Ainsworth have expanded the attachment theory of child development. Their research shows the powerful influence of infant/parent bonding on healthy human development. Moreover, they have also discovered that attachment failures—on either side of the relationship—can have devastating psychological consequences.

The significance of parent/offspring bonds is not unique to human development. Harry Harlow's studies of maternal deprivation in monkeys showed similar needs. Given a choice between a surrogate "wire mother" (with a milk bottle) and a "terrycloth mother" (without food), infant monkeys spent most of their time clinging to the latter. The Austrian ethologist (and Nobel Prize–winner) Konrad Lorenz revealed a "critical period" for social bonding in geese. The following response of his fresh hatchlings quickly "imprinted" onto the first large, moving object in their environment. This included Lorenz himself, when it was he who hovered over the fledgling birds. Their subsequent mating preferences were also determined by this early exposure. (Many of Lorenz's ethological insights were a blend of evolutionary biology and Gestalt principles of holistic perception and insight.) The ideas of attachment theory have become one of psychology's most unifying perspectives. Its foundations draw broadly from across developmental psychology, psychoanalysis, Gestalt psychology, animal behavior, and evolutionary biology.

Jean Piaget studied the intricate processes involved in long-term, human cognitive development. The child's mind grows, as he discovered, in progressive stages of problem-solving skills. Observational learning often facilitates the gradual expansion of knowledge capacities (which he called accommodation). In short, imitation is the best form of accommodation. Achievement of complex cognitive schemata, such as learning geometry or a new language, is a lengthy process. But a good teacher can accelerate it by "showing the way." Imitative learning can also be instantaneous—as when we observe the solution to an unfamiliar task like opening a subway door in a foreign country, or following an instructor through a ski lesson. Our primate mind appears to have deep roots in imitative learning.

New findings from neuroscience on mirror neurons have added to this mix. Laboratory studies of functional magnetic resonance imaging (fMRI) reveal that cortical brain activity, while observing a behavior, "mirrors" the brain activity associated with performing the behavior. Many people consider these findings to be an important breakthrough for understanding the rapidity of language acquisition and other forms of learning. They may, as well, be the neurological underpinning of emotional intelligence and empathic responding. It remains to be seen where these discoveries will lead. But the traditional notion of the mind as a passive "blank slate" has been severely challenged.

Ethological and attachment research has revealed distinctive capacities of mental preparedness in many social organisms. I believe attachmentlike connections are widespread in human relations, and may be the psychological basis of why learning frequently occurs best in one-to-one encounters. If so, a person's life may be the ongoing search for one's next teacher—along an unending path of readiness to learn.

In the Tibetan tradition of discovering a guru, according to Chögyam Trungpa, it is not because the teacher is famous or renowned. The guideline is whether or not you are able to actually engage with the person, directly and thoroughly. The process is a "matter of mutual communication … [and] … meeting of two minds," which also "depends upon the student giving something in return."[7] The tradition of the Zen master represents the highest order of this quest. Meditations compel discipline and deep reflection, and the next level is reached only when the master judges whether the proper answer is given. Without a teacher, enlightenment is impossible. But without an active learner, a teacher is not a teacher.

In Western societies these conventions have given way to more practical standards. Nonetheless, a few havens still exist where the triumph of cleverness over wisdom is not complete. One of them is within the Jungian tradition. The idea of self-realization, as a manifestation of wisdom, is still central to analytical psychology. The archetypal images of the wise man or wise woman remain potent symbols. Jungian psychotherapy continues to explore these soul-searching lessons of the deep unconscious, well beneath the surface of day-to-day life.

Wisdom and self-realization remain as fundamental concepts of Eriksonian psychology as well. These were potent goals in Erik Erikson's theory of the life cycle—the final stage of which is weighed by whether a person arrives at life's end with an integrated self (or not). Those who do, he observed, carry a personal and inherent sense of wisdom within themselves. Their lives have progressed and rounded out with a sense of balance and completion. Some people, however, do not meet life's challenges in ways that mature to a meaningful finish. As the end of life approaches, they arrive in a fragmented state of lingering desires and unhealthy regrets. The psychological state of affairs for these individuals, as Erikson discovered, is characterized by a sense of emptiness and despair. Unlike their counterparts who find a way to self-integration, death looms as a more fearsome outcome of life. I have known people from both ends of this spectrum. My encounters with them have been invaluable lessons. Some of the most important of all teachings are gained from the end-of-life experience of others.

Life Lessons

As a child, I spent a lot of time in the company of old men. My father's father, Jay Ross Borden, was born in 1877. When he died in 1962 at eighty-five, I was a junior in high school. Because our home was a hundred miles from the family farm in the Schoharie Valley, I didn't spend as much time with him as I might have. But I always enjoyed our visits. He was tall and wiry, and even in his eighties was a strikingly handsome man. I remember tagging along with him as he tended the cows, mended fences, and followed the rhythms of daily farming. He taught me to milk by hand, to throw hay down the hay hole from the mow to the barn floor, and to feed and grain the cows during morning and afternoon milking. They had two vacuum-operated milking machines, but he still preferred hand milking into large stainless-steel buckets. The raw milk from the machines and buckets was collected in ten-gallon steel milk cans. The cans were then dropped into a large, insulated tank of water, cooled by blocks of ice. The blocks came from the icehouse behind the barn. The supply was replenished every winter with fresh blocks cut from the pond and packed in thick layers of sawdust. I enjoyed the cool smell of the icehouse and still recall the sweet taste of old, granulated ice-bits buried deep in the auburn sawdust from years before. The first chore of the day was to lug the heavy cans to the roadside, where they were gathered by a truck every morning. The milk went to the local creamery, where it was turned into wheels of sharp cheddar cheese.

My grandparents' farm was on the edge of time, halfway between the nineteenth and twentieth centuries. Their way of farming was established long before the advent of tractors and rural electrification. When these amenities arrived, they were adopted slowly as add-ons. But the patterns of daily life remained much as they had been. Although they did acquire a tractor and mowing machine, they continued to fill the barn with loose hay pulled from the fields with a team of Belgian horses.

When my grandfather was a boy, hops farming was widespread in upstate New York. Most farms had one of the towering, pyramid-shaped drying sheds with its crowning cupola. But a mold blight of the late 1800s brought a rapid end to the boon of hops growing. Dairy farming took its place and with it came the familiar cow barn with milking stanchions and generous post-and-beam framings for storing hay and animals through the long winters. The distinctive architecture of hops houses could still be seen throughout the countryside when I was young. Ours had been converted into a wagon shed for horse-drawn buggies, haying equipment—and later—motorized machinery, cars, and trucks. The mosaic of separate buildings for cows, horses, chickens, pigs, equipment, and firewood was standing testimony of lived history. Those characteristic smells and dim-lit arching interiors are engraved in my senses. Even now, the aroma of old farm buildings, plowed soil, and drying hay stir an instant sense of déjà vu.

At the end of the day, my grandfather retired to his rocking chair—in summer on the porch and in winter beside the woodstove—where he puffed his pipe and chatted with my grandmother. They were cheerful people with a good sense of humor. I remember their fondness of my mother, who enjoyed pressing them for bits of family history. Their stories were a treasury of local knowledge. The accounts of departed family members—one of whose Union Army, .44-caliber cap-and-ball pistol and holster rested on the mantelpiece—heightened the sense of history.

My grandfather was seventy-nine when I was ten years old. He was born twelve years after the close of the Civil War and knew many people who had lived through that era. My great-grandfather Hiram Borden was born in 1835. When my father was ten years old, Hiram was still alive to relate his experiences. So my father, as I learned early on, had direct connections to someone who actually knew people from before the Revolutionary War. These bonds were amplified by proximity to the locations of past events. The regions around Saratoga and Ticonderoga and down the Hudson Valley were steeped in history. Washingtonville, where

I went to elementary and high school, had been the site of Washington's headquarters for a time. There were other family threads running across New England and the Mid-Atlantic states. These experiences imbued a deep sense of place within me from an early age. I felt an intuitive connection across time.

Managing the farm became increasingly difficult for my grandparents in their later years. We did not live close enough to help with daily chores. My father struggled with the conflict and did a lot to provide financial support. In the end, his sister's family took over the operation, moved in, and cared for our grandparents. I know, deep down, my father wished to go back. His request before he died was to have Grantland Rice's powerful and nostalgic elegy "The Last Port" read at his funeral. The poem begins and ends with the same line: "I'm going home someday." It was a great insight to his romantic side—as well as the inner turmoil and homesickness he must have carried as he set off for preparatory school and college. I still cannot read it aloud without flooding with feelings of sympathy and love. I also harbored hopes, for a time, of making the family farm my home too. But like my father, there was no way of combining what I had become with the heartfelt yearnings of family tradition.

There has always been a part of me that identifies with the place and with the image of grace and simplicity of my grandfather. One of my treasured gifts from him was a book from his childhood by Charles Carleton Coffin: *Winning His Way*. Coffin was a war correspondent for the *Boston Daily Journal* during the Civil War. At the war's end, he published several novels that revealed the daily anguish of war. *Winning* is the tale of a young Connecticut boy, Paul Parker, growing up in poverty without a father. Although a loving mother and grandfather do all they can to nurture him, his youth is an ongoing struggle with malicious schoolmates. The beautiful and compassionate Azalia notices Paul's noble character. Just as their romance sparks, however, clouds of war overshadow it. Paul goes off with the local regiment. He soon sees the horrors of battle. Wounded, and then captured, he ends up in Georgia's Andersonville prison. Back home the word is received that he has been killed. Azalia is crushed by the news. Her sorrow resolves in a commitment to serve as a nurse in the far-off Annapolis hospital for wounded soldiers. When General Lee surrenders at Appomattox, the war prisoners begin to be shipped north. Paul, emaciated and nearly dead, lies on the deck of a hospital ship in Annapolis harbor. By chance Azalia passes by. She senses a barely recognizable face with wasted cheeks, sunken eyes, and an uncut beard. Through colorless lips, Paul can whisper but one word—her name. Azalia cries out for a doctor. He is miraculously pulled from the jaws of death. She nurses him day by day; his strength is slowly restored. They return home to a joyful reunion and a happy life.

Coffin's *Winning His Way* was the first full-length book I ever read. I was in second grade at the time. I will never forget the thrill of my initial adventure in reading. Moreover, my grandfather had owned and read the same book when he was a boy. So had my father. In the shuffle of life transitions, his original copy was sadly lost somewhere along the way. I was pleasantly surprised, a few years ago, when my wife Patricia presented me with an identical replacement. Rereading it took me back to my eight-year-old self. I was reminded, for a while at least, of the magic of childhood. The look of the cover and smell of the pages were just as I remembered—further adding to the experience and familiar feelings. I wish I could have spent more time with my grandfather, known him better, and learned more from him. He was the first "wise old man" of my life, an iconic figure and thus one of my great teachers. Never knowing my mother's father and the death of her mother when I was very young were losses.

But there were other significant elders who surrounded my childhood, and filled what I may have missed from that corner of life. One of our neighbors, just over the hill to the east, worked for the Belmont Turf and Field Club of the New York Racing Association. The wife's father, Oscar Eden, took care of their house during the summer while they were busy with the horseracing season. We became close friends. "Grandpa Eden," as he wished to be called, was born in 1868 in the Gaspé region of Canada. He was a fisherman and lumberman most of his life. The Great Depression forced his children to leave—and him to follow them. When we began our friendship he was well into his eighties. Like my grandfather he also smoked a pipe, and the smell of his Half and Half tobacco still conjures a profound reverie of visual recollections for me. My summer routine for many years, after breakfast, was to follow the path through our gardens into the woods and over the hill. He had a charming Quebec accent and a penchant for gin rummy. He was good. But gradually over time I came to match him. We played hundreds of nickel-a-hand games together. He told countless stories of distant places as he shuffled and sorted his cards—of fishing, fur-trapping, and hunting caribou (for which I had no reference whatsoever at the time). I was aware he enjoyed our companionship. But I did not realize, at the time, that I was the only person who visited him. He gave me the gift of attention and taught me the value of mere presence.

I also spent a lot of time with our neighbors Benjamin and Bertha Bush—an elderly Jewish couple who somehow escaped the tragic turn-of-the-century Russian pogroms and emigrated to the United States in 1904. The Bushes lived in the main house of the farm from which my parents brought their property. "Bennie" hired me as his work partner for seventy-five cents an hour when I was still in grade school. He was barely five feet tall and spoke with a thick accent. They were proud of their only son, who had attended the U.S. Naval Academy and became a prominent businessman. But sadly, he never visited them—apparently wanting to put his ethnic background behind him. And so, in some way, I was informally adopted and given their supplanted affection. We worked together until I left for college. By then Bennie was in his nineties, but still very active. I learned a great deal from our partnership—about carpentry, gardening, masonry, grafting fruit trees—and even winemaking. I was often confused by his instructions, which were a seamless blend of English, Yiddish, and Russian. He was the reason that I took Russian as my college language. The last time we saw each other was during my senior year of college. As I began our conversation in his native tongue, a broad smile stretched across his face. Before I left, he asked me to wait a little longer while he went upstairs. He returned holding a beautiful old Hebrew–Russian dictionary—one of the few things he brought with him to America—and gave it to me. I never saw him again. His dictionary is on the bookshelf not far from where I sit writing this, and I still think of him often.

I am saddened by the way modern society displaces our senior citizens. Grandparents do not often share in the home life of children as they once did. Elderly family members now live in distant retirement communities. They see their children and grandchildren only occasionally. Oftentimes, their lives have no connections at all to young people. This gap in the circle of life is a societal—and educational—problem that calls for attention. There is, I am sure, a natural and human affinity between children and elders. I have seen it in my father-in-law's eyes, on the eve of his dying day, as his grandchildren and great-grandchildren gathered at his bedside. I have felt it many times myself in the long hours of companionship with caring older people. It was a happy surprise, therefore, when the Environmental Protection Agency (EPA) announced their Rachel Carson "Sense of Wonder" Contest—based on her beautifully written children's book of the same name. Carson wrote it the year before her death as a gift to her nephew Roger. The award is the brainchild of Kathy Sykes—an EPA senior adviser—and is sponsored by the agency's Aging Initiative to encourage teams (of a young person and an older person) to share the exploration of nature through poetry, essays, photos, and dance. It is a wonderful initiative, from which many other modes of cross-generational learning can grow. This kind of education also carries greater life-lessons—about aging and the whole of human existence. I am grateful for the good teachers of my childhood who shared the end of their lives with the beginning of my own.

Great teachers need not always be present. Many are long dead—yet their lessons live on. Who has not been captivated by the elegant weavings of a good book that leaves us unaware of our surroundings, or even that we are reading. The words and pages disappear. There is no struggle to understand or effort to attend. We dissolve into the author's thoughts, whose ideas enjoin an awareness of our mind growing—as it grows. This can happen with nonfiction or fiction; subject and style do not matter. What matters is that we are captured and guided through a labyrinth of new encounters. The psychologist Mihaly Csikszentmihalyi refers to this experience as "flow"—when passion leads the mind—and engagement and enjoyment are self-rewards. It is one of the purest kinds of learning. Many people hold on to their core of favorite, life-changing books. These books and ideas become parts of us. We are drawn out and enlarged by them. Formal education has traditionally been based on a systematic exposure to the ideas and writings of eminent scholars. An account of these approaches and institutions is a long and varied history—to which it is time to now turn.

Higher Education

In the summer of 1992 I spent a month at Harvard's Institute for Educational Management with ninety other senior administrators from around the world. It was fun to be a student again. Our daylong classes covered a range of topics in lively and provocative ways that were followed by spirited discussions well into the evening. As the end of the program approached, we selected one of our class members, Henry Ramsey, to give a "student speech" at the graduation ceremony. Henry began with an expression of gratitude to our teachers for a month of magnificent classes. He then moved into a commentary on the importance of education. In the middle of his talk, he highlighted his remarks with the following anecdote:

> I want to share with you a short story about a man who was born during the Great Depression into poverty at just below the lowest rung of America's economic ladder. As a young boy at age fourteen and in the ninth grade, he became a high school dropout. This young boy did enjoy reading but was denied access to the only public library in his North Carolina hometown because of his race. He consequently became somewhat of a town novelty, standing in the commercial bookstore on Main Street reading books a few pages at a time.
>
> This young man never returned to high school but, probably because of his fondness for reading, was able to pass a test required

of applicants for the United States Air Force. Eventually, he would be stationed in Southern California near the city of Riverside, where he became interested in acquiring more formal education. He was able to enroll in evening classes in remedial arithmetic, grammar, and composition at the local community college.

Classes taken at Riverside City College helped him to pass the entrance examinations for Howard University. After a very shaky start, he did well and two years later, he transferred to the University of California at Riverside. Thanks to federal financial aid in the form of the Korean GI Bill, earnings from working in the cafeteria, and later earnings as a research assistant, the young man was able to pay for room and board. He was later admitted to and enrolled at the University of California's School of Law in Berkeley, graduating three years later near the top of his class.

He continued. After graduation, the young man was appointed an assistant district attorney, and as prosecutor "marched every foot of every mile of the historic march for voting rights from Selma to Montgomery, Alabama." He entered private practice, became a member of the faculty at his law school alma mater, and eventually a superior court judge. Henry then disclosed the rest—it was *his story*. (Which he had never before publicly shared.) "I proudly stand before you today as Dean of the Howard University School of Law and as living evidence of the value and power of your work." Everyone was awestruck by the stirring account of challenges and creative growth. But Henry's narrative was more than a personal portrait. It was also, as he made clear in closing, a tribute to everyone: "Your work—higher education—is the bedrock in which must be anchored the future of our countries and the world."[8]

Higher education has a long history. Its origins go back a millennium, to the twelfth century, when European monasteries were the center of intellectual life. The first universities were established in Italy and France as an expansion of the monastic tradition. However, as Charles Homer Haskins notes, "our inheritance from the oldest universities ... is not buildings or a type of architecture, for the early universities had no buildings of their own."[9] The university of the Middle Ages was a "community of scholars," a professional guild that held the authority to confer degrees. They were initially structured along two different lines, depending on how teachers were paid. In Bologna, teachers were hired and paid by the students. In Paris their salary came from the university—clustered around the cathedral of Notre Dame on the Île de la Cité.

The curriculum was standardized around the liberal arts, i.e., the Trivium (grammar, rhetoric, and logic) and the Quadrivium (arithmetic, geometry, astronomy, and music). Satisfactory completion of study of these subjects entitled the student, if he qualified, to continue on in one of the higher branches of learning—law, medicine, or theology. In addition to the administrative structure imparted by the university, "colleges" provided another basic unit of academic life. Originally they were simply the group residences of students. But in time they became the normal centers of teaching and life, and the first buildings and physical expressions of higher education.

Theology was the supreme subject of medieval learning, and the cathedral school of Notre Dame was the preeminent institution. The streets of the Île de la Cité bustled with intellectual life. Latin was the language of scholars. Books, lectures, and the daily life of students were all in Latin. The philosopher Peter Abelard (and famed lover of Héloïse) taught at the cathedral school. His attack on the realist theory of universals began a legendary debate between faith and reason: "For by doubting we come to inquiry; by inquiry, we come to the truth." Pitting philosophical reason against theological doctrine was heretical, and it aroused the ire of the Church. Students crowded to his lectures and debates. Ultimately they followed him across the Seine to the Left Bank, where he set up his own school. Thenceforth the district became the Latin Quarter and the birthplace of the venerable Sorbonne and University of Paris.

Oxford is the oldest university in the English-speaking world. The actual date of its founding is unclear. Its founding appears to have been accelerated by Henry II, who banned English students from attending the University of Paris in the middle of the twelfth century. At the outset Oxford operated in the monastic tradition. But it soon adopted its characteristic style of separate colleges, only loosely attached to the university structure. The first colleges—University, Merton, and Balliol—were largely secular. They were designed to encourage more adventurous teaching than their monastic predecessors. College life was highly regulated. Students lived together in the self-contained colleges, often with resident teachers. The arrangement was partly to encourage learning and scholarly camaraderie. But it was also a means of protecting students from townspeople. The early history of Oxford was frequently punctuated with riotous town/gown conflicts.

English education was based on principles of intellectual and moral excellence. The capacity for good judgment and leadership was formed in pursuing these ideals—and was strengthened by collegial living and studious conversations. In a liberal arts education, as John Henry Newman maintained, knowledge was its own end. The benefits were character formation and good members of society. The model of freestanding colleges grew rapidly. By the fifteenth century, seven more Oxford colleges would be founded. Cambridge, the second-oldest university in Britain, was chartered shortly after Oxford. It began when a group of scholars took refuge in Cambridge, in the aftermath of early hostilities between students and residents in Oxford. The first of the Cambridge colleges—St. Peter's or "Peterhouse"—was founded in 1284. In the following century, eight more colleges were established. A similar growth of higher education was happening throughout Europe. Nearly a hundred universities existed in various parts of Europe by the end of the Middle Ages.

Harvard College was the first colonial college of North America. It was founded in 1636 and opened in 1642. For sixty years Harvard was the only college in all of British America. The College of William and Mary, the second, offered its first degree in 1700. Yale College was chartered the following year. The College of Pennsylvania was established in 1740. (In 1779 it was rechartered as the University of Pennsylvania—claiming credit as the first American university.) The College of New Jersey (later Princeton), King's College (later Columbia), College of Rhode Island (Brown), Queen's College (Rutgers), and Dartmouth College all began in the next two decades. These were the nine colonial colleges at the time of the revolution. Seventeen more were founded by 1800 and twelve more by 1820. The early American colleges were small. Harvard had about twenty students when it opened and only sixty in 1670. A hundred years later, at the time of the revolution, it was graduating only forty or so students per year. It is estimated that the total student population—of all American colleges at the time of the revolution—was substantially fewer than a thousand.

For the most part, medieval universities were children of the church. This was also the case for the nine original American colleges. Though not legally bound to any denomination, all had religious affiliations. Three were with the Church of England (Anglican), three were Puritan (Congregational), and the remaining either Presbyterian, Baptist, or Dutch Reform. American colleges were built on the collegium plan of Oxford and Cambridge. The foundational curriculum was also medieval. It was composed of two parts: the traditional liberal arts, and the professional studies of law, medicine, and divinity. They were, like their British counterparts, organized bodies of students in communal life. As the educational historian H. G. Good notes, "of modern science, history, or literature there was hardly a trace ..."[10]

Most of the seventeen colleges founded between the end of the Revolutionary War and the close of the century were in northern New England. The others were located in the frontier regions of the Mid-Atlantic and Appalachia. Four were state colleges, though only one was actually in operation in 1800. The University of North Carolina was the first to open, in 1798. The University of Georgia was chartered in 1785; however, it did not officially enroll students until 1801. By 1825 nine of the present state universities were begun in Vermont, followed by two in Ohio and six in the South. The last of the group was the University of Virginia.

Thomas Jefferson was a champion of education at all levels. He firmly believed that only educated people could preserve democracy. In 1779 he prepared a bill in Virginia to create publicly controlled, primary schools with instruction for the teaching of reading, writing, arithmetic, and history. The bill additionally provided for twenty secondary schools throughout the state. Jefferson was also instrumental in founding the University of Virginia. It was the first public university to begin with high standards, and it was the first institution to allow specializations in such diverse fields as botany, astronomy, architecture, and political science. Jefferson designed the whole institution. He drew the architectural plans for the buildings and landscape, and oversaw construction. His original handiwork remains as the center of the university and has inspired generations of architects and campus designers.

The Federal Census of 1830 registered a population of about thirteen million. Fifty-six colleges were operating at that time. A year before the beginning of the Civil War, the 1860 census showed a population of thirty-two million. The number of new colleges had grown exponentially—more than tenfold since 1830. Many were frontier institutions following the rapid westward expansion. Nine out of ten had religious connections. Most failed. Of more than six hundred colleges founded prior to the Civil War, only 180 survive today. The Jeffersonian ideals of education for a growing democracy appeared to be very much alive. Realization of them in the form of lasting educational institutions, however, was frequently unsuccessful.[11]

The Rise of Universities

The next major innovation in higher education was not American. It was German. When Europe's universities were forming in the Middle Ages, the first in a German-speaking country was in Vienna, founded in 1366. The next was Heidelberg in 1386. Others soon followed in Leipzig, Rostock, Freiburg, and Munich. Like their counterparts elsewhere, they followed the rigid requirements of the medieval model. Things began to change in the eighteenth century. Infused by ideas of the European Enlightenment, several new "reform" universities were established in Göttingen, Halle, and Jena. But the real change came with the founding of the University of Berlin. It began as a letter to the king of Prussia, Frederick William III, sent on July 24, 1809, by Wilhelm von Humboldt (older brother of the prominent scientist and naturalist Alexander von Humboldt). The letter contained a proposal to create a new kind of university. Humboldt was a liberal-minded intellectual and a leading educational reformer. As minister of education, he had overseen major reforms of Prussian elementary and secondary schools, along with his introduction of kindergarten to the educational system.

The proposal was accepted. Humboldt promptly set about building the faculty and organizing the curriculum. The University of Berlin opened the following year. The "Humboldtian" university was unlike anything in the past. It revolutionized the centuries-old medieval curriculum. Humboldt did this by integrating the "lower" liberal arts faculty with the "higher" professional faculty. Creation of a faculty of arts and sciences opened the door to pure research. Teaching and research were combined in all fields. The institution was transformed, as a whole, into the research university. It was no longer merely a place for the transmission of knowledge. The new German university was a place of scholarly creativity, where everyone was committed to the frontiers of learning. Its main characteristics were the discovery and advancement of knowledge, in an atmosphere of specialist education and intellectual freedom.

Academic freedom was crucial for Humboldt. There were two kinds. One was student freedom—*lernfreiheit*—to learn and to pursue any curriculum. The other was faculty freedom—*lehrfreiheit*—the freedom of scholarly inquiry. Professors could study what they wished and could lecture and say (i.e., "profess") what they liked. Humboldt's ideals of academic freedom not only reshaped the structure of his university, they also became cherished standards of scholarly life. They have been symbolically reenacted, ever since, in the ritual practice of the faculty procession walking out of step during commencements.

It took time for these ideas to find their way into America. No tradition existed in the United States, as in Germany, of federal support for higher education (with the exception of the United States Military Academy at West Point, founded in 1802). Most American colleges were independent, tiny, and poverty-stricken. The new state institutions were just as poor. Several of the established "old-time" colleges actively denounced specialization. *The Yale Report of 1828* was a staunch defense of the classical curriculum: "Our object is not to teach that which is peculiar to any one of the professions; but to lay the foundation which is common to them all."[12] Edward Everett became the first American to obtain a PhD from a German university in 1815. Later, as president of Harvard from 1846 to 1849, he sought to introduce changes, but with little success. Even Henry David Thoreau held to a traditional stance. When Thoreau graduated from Harvard in 1837, there were only a few hundred students. In 1854, when he published *Walden,* his position was as critical as it was clear: "The mode of founding a college, commonly, is to get up a subscription of dollars and cents, and then following blindly the principles of a division of labor to its extreme, a principle which should never be followed...."[13]

The path of American higher education, however, would be otherwise. The appeal of more specialized learning, if only in piecemeal ways, was finding its way into the mix. Many of the new institutions eagerly set about "liberalizing" the liberal arts curriculum. Jefferson's University of Virginia was among the first. The University of Michigan was another. Henry Philip Tappan, Michigan's first president, had also studied in Europe. He was greatly influenced by the experience. In the 1853–54 university catalog, he wrote: "The system of public instruction adopted by the State of Michigan is copied from the Prussian, acknowledged to be the most perfect in the world ..."[14]

The decades leading up to the Civil War were rich with experimentation. Many different kinds of new institutions were started. Mount Holyoke, the oldest women's college of the prestigious "seven sisters," was chartered in 1836. Mills College opened in 1852 as the first women's college west of the Rocky Mountains. Several more women's colleges also started during this period. A number of the original historically black colleges began in this era as well, including Cheyney (1837), Lincoln (1854), and Wilberforce (1856). Oberlin College began instruction in 1833, initially for men, but shortly became the first college to allow coeducational education. Antioch College opened in 1853 under the direction of Horace Mann. A close friend of Edward Everett, Mann was also an admirer of the German system. He was an outspoken humanitarian and educational reformer. The sciences and classics were equal partners in his new college.

Antioch became an unparalleled leader in educational reform. It was the first truly coeducational college in the country; the first to appoint a woman to the faculty and to its trustee board; and among the first to enroll African American students. Antioch students were also given authentic participation in the institution's governance and decision making.

It took until midcentury for Yale to change its position, after which it eagerly sought faculty who had attended a German university. In 1861, Yale's graduate school of arts and sciences offered the first American PhD. Changes at Harvard were slower. Charles Eliot made many during his long tenure as Harvard's twenty-first president from 1869 to 1909. His comprehensive curricular reforms included the free-elective system for undergraduates and the creation of the graduate school of arts and sciences in 1872. Many of his innovations can be traced to the German model and his own, firsthand study of European education. To Harvard's credit, though, it was the first college in the country to award a Bachelor of Science degree in 1851. In 1860, Michigan followed as the second institution to offer the BS degree.

Major changes were soon forthcoming in the public sector as well. Justin Morrill, a senator from Vermont, introduced a bill to Congress to provide public lands for the new state universities. Congress passed the bill in February 1859. President Buchanan vetoed it, however, on grounds that it was too costly and, further, that it would injure existing colleges. Congress was unable to override his veto. Three years later, in the midst of the Civil War, Morrill tried again. Congress once more passed the bill and Lincoln signed it on July 2, 1862. Every state still in the Union at the time was granted thirty thousand acres of public lands for each member of its congressional delegation. Lincoln and the Congress of 1862 passed two other important measures. One created the Department of Agriculture, with which the new public universities were quickly aligned. The second was the Homestead Act. Any citizen, or person intending to become a citizen, could receive 160 acres of undeveloped land. After living on the land for five years, they could then purchase it for a nominal fee. These opportunities—spurred by completion of the First Transcontinental Railroad in 1869—unleashed a flood of western migration and economic growth.

A nationwide era of new state university systems accompanied the brisk population expansion. Unlike the old eastern institutions, their scope of instruction was broadened. Science instruction was increased, especially in the applied directions of agriculture, forestry, and engineering. Laboratories were established. The traditional subjects of the liberal arts curriculum were divided into separate departments, and new specializations were added. Vocational training became an integral part of college work. According to the noted historian of the American West, Frederick Jackson Turner, the rapid growth of state universities was fueled by a distinctive fusion of two American values: "the conquest of nature" and "the ideal of service to democracy." Turner's attributions bespeak the heady optimism of his "frontier thesis," delivered on the occasion of the 1893 Chicago World's Fair. The mission of the state university was to forge a modern society and to educate its leaders. In his words: "Scientific farming must increase the yield of the field, scientific forestry must economize the woodlands, scientific experiment and construction by chemist, physicist, biologist, and engineer must be allied to all of nature's forces in our complex modern society. The test tube and the microscope are needed rather than ax and rifle in this new ideal of conquest."[15]

The German university would play a significant role in this—institutionally and ideologically. Daniel Fallon, chair of the education division of the Carnegie Corporation, has traced the history of these influences. He reports that before 1850 only two hundred or so American students had gone to Germany for advanced studies. By 1900 more than nine thousand Americans had studied there. The PhD from a German university had become the degree of distinction for American scholars. There was hardly anywhere else to go. Many of the pioneers of American higher education received graduate training in German universities. Upon their return, they brought back not only advanced degrees, but also the ideals of the research university itself. The Johns Hopkins University was founded in 1876 as the first American university in the Humboldt tradition. By 1884 its teaching staff had grown to fifty-three members. Virtually all of them had studied at a German university. Clark University opened in 1889 as the first American all-graduate-student university. The University of

Chicago opened three years later. Both were shaped by educational principles from the German research university.

The total number of postgraduate students in the United States in 1871 was fewer than two hundred. By 1890 the number of students enrolled in postbaccalaureate studies was nearly three thousand. "Throughout this period of birth and development of the American university, the overriding ideal," Fallon asserts, "was the model of Humboldt's enlightenment university."[16] The German configuration was never directly copied in the United States. Yet its inspirational influence was profound. Three of Humboldt's principles were integral to the rise of American universities: the unity of research and teaching, the protections of academic freedom, and the opportunity for specialization across the arts and sciences. The third—specialization within the curriculum—would completely transform the shape of American higher education. Departmentalization along disciplinary lines became the defining feature of the modern research university. The rapidly growing state universities adopted and expanded the model. The ideals took root and blossomed in other newly endowed private universities, e.g., Vanderbilt, Tulane, Stanford, Duke, etc. Ultimately, even the traditional liberal arts colleges would be challenged into offering a variety of undergraduate majors.

Barely two hundred thousand students were enrolled in America's higher-education institutions in 1900. By the end of the First World War the number had doubled. It surpassed a million in 1930 and continued to rise even throughout the Depression years. A major surge followed World War II as returning veterans received GI Bill support for their education. Between 1946 and 1950, student enrollments averaged around 2.3 million. A generation later this was echoed as the baby boomers pushed the number to nine million. Today it is twice that—and is rapidly approaching twenty million.

The growth of higher education is difficult to envision. At the beginning of the nineteenth century, barely two dozen colleges existed in all of the country. A century later there were almost eight hundred. "Yet in 1900," as Roger Geiger reminds us in *The American College in the Nineteenth Century*, "the modal college enrolled only 83 students.

Few colleges reached a faculty size of 25 before 1920."[17] Some, however, grew well beyond the average, often at a staggering pace. The Ohio State University opened for classes in 1878 with twenty-four students. In 1905, enrollment was at two thousand students. By 1930 it had surpassed fifteen thousand. In the 1970s, when I was at Ohio State, enrollment was well beyond sixty thousand students. That is more than the population of Portland, Maine—the largest city in the state where I now live. There are currently at least fifty universities with student enrollments beyond twenty-five thousand, and another fifty with more than ten thousand students. Many of them function like independent city-states—with their own health, police, and bus systems, radio and TV stations, and sometimes even commercially served airports.

The Architecture of Knowledge

Colleges and universities are beautiful places. The architecture is magnificent, with entire buildings dedicated to this or that field of study. Their carved lintels and arched porticoes celebrate the richness of the knowledge. The landscape designs are equally splendid. Tree-lined walkways are interspersed with statues, fountains, and formal gardens. The serenity of their grounds nourishes scholarly contemplation.

But architecture is not without its secondary consequences. Winston Churchill, after the London bombing of World War II, opposed a proposal for a modern reconstruction of Britain's Parliament building. As he famously argued, "We shape our buildings; thereafter, they shape us." A different architecture would alter the traditions of politics. The halls of British government should be restored as before—and they were. At the same time, architects were being sought for a new kind of deliberative body: the United Nations. Design of the U.N. General Assembly Hall was a collaborative effort by a team of eleven architects. The gracefully curving walls and seating arrangement for its 191 member nations orient toward a common focal point. Above the central podium hangs the U.N. emblem— a map of the world viewed from above the North Pole, surrounded by olive wreaths. The nearby Security Council Hall and Trustee Council Hall suggest their respective functions with a similar embedded sense of global purpose and cooperation. These are inspiring examples of thoughtful and aesthetic design. In contrast, we may be reminded of the Paris Peace Accords of the Vietnam era. Meaningful negotiations were delayed for months by awkward disputes over the shape and seating arrangements of the peace table. Architecture and environmental design are important to human affairs. They matter at all levels—from household dwelling to urban landscape.

The architecture of our educational institutions also shapes our views of the world. The walled perimeters and enclosed spaces of the early Oxford and Cambridge colleges were designed in ways that urged people toward communal engagement. The early colonial colleges of America may have shared a similar curriculum, but their buildings were disconnected and planted across a campus (a Latin word meaning "a field"). Jefferson designed the quintessential campus of the first university to have academic majors. The curriculum and campus were isomorphic. At the time of construction, the campus was elegant, harmonious, and fully coherent with its educational mission.

Higher education, by then, was already in a state of rapid expansion. America's colleges and universities have grown, building-by-building, ever outward. Every campus map tells the story. Sometimes an "Old Main" hall and the vestige of a central concourse may be identified. Or perhaps an original quadrilateral campus can be found somewhere within. But these features are usually overshadowed by an expanding array of newer edifices—of increasing size and ever more distinctive design. Sometimes the campus map suggests no clue whatsoever of the institution's historical center.

At the end of the nineteenth century, Harvard did seek to enclose its famous "yard." But the institution had already spread far beyond those walls. The pattern of Harvard's disjointed expansion has been expressed, somewhat wittily, as "a loose confederation of departments held together by allegiance to a central heating plant." The truth is that most institutions stretch far beyond the piping of their heating systems. This is not a critique of the nation's oldest and most revered educational institution, nor of any other college or university. I truly delight in the diversity and breadth of American higher education. My point is simply to illustrate their astounding growth—along with the accompanying consequences it has had on the fractionation of knowledge.

Jefferson's design for the University of Virginia was meant to reflect a new kind of liberal arts institution, and the campus map looked that way. Other institutions, with different missions, often resemble their educational aims as well. The U.S. Military Academy at West Point was designed along sturdy neo-Gothic lines. Most of the buildings are constructed of predominantly gray-black granite. The two main features are "The Plain"—used for ceremonial reviews, and the Cadet Cathedral—which sets the architectural mood of the academy and contains the largest chapel pipe organ in the world. The monuments and statues of the military leaders who graduated from the academy punctuate the campus. West Point looks like a military academy. So do the cadets. For nearly two centuries "the dress gray," with black trim and brass buttons, has been the standard uniform. The "long gray line" is a symbolic thread that ties together the campus, the traditions, and the daily lives of USMA cadets and graduates. The academy was the first American institution to teach engineering, and the curricular model was followed by many other colleges and universities thereafter. West Point now offers forty-five academic majors. Its tradition of educational excellence remains. In 2009, *Forbes* magazine named the academy "the best college in America."*

When Congress approved building a counterpart United States Air Force Academy in the 1960s, the idea was to look toward the future. The modernist architect team of Skidmore, Owings and Merrill was chosen to design a new kind of institution. The campus site is at an elevation of 7,500 feet in the clear blue skies of the Rocky Mountains. The academy's iconic chapel—as at West Point—dominates the campus. But its seventeen-spired metal construction clearly points to the sky, with strong

---

*I have a peculiar connection to West Point uniforms. My mother, in her ceaseless homemaking style, somehow acquired dozens of old dress uniforms. She cut them into strips, sewed them end-to-end, and wove the braided woolen rug for our dining room. I can still recall crawling around on the black-rimmed, gray carpet as a toddler.

elements of aviation design. So does the rest of the campus—from the gridded "Terrazano" parade grounds to the interlocking elements of its highly functional, modular buildings. Monuments of airplanes are interspersed throughout the campus. A parachute airdrop and landing field at the academy entrance leave no doubt about the institution's mission. The cadets' blue and silver uniform colors, as reflections of the sky and clouds, complete the Air Force image.

Education for a Human Ecological Perspective

When College of the Atlantic opened, the founding trustees had a strong sense of its educational purpose. The mission was to address two problems. One was the increasing specialization and compartmentalization of ideas within higher education. The other was to use real-world, human/environmental problems as a bona fide focus for interdisciplinary inquiry.

The college began in an old seaside mansion. A leftover from the nineteenth-century "cottage" era, the estate had formerly been an Oblate seminary spared from the fire of 1947 that devastated Bar Harbor and much of the island. COA, at the outset, did not have anything resembling a campus plan. But the question became a real one once the college showed that it could attract students—and began to grow. A large tract of land known as Strawberry Hill, on the southern edge of the town of Bar Harbor, was donated for the purpose through the generosity of a local resident. It was a beautiful property with spectacular views overlooking Frenchman Bay and the Porcupine Islands.

The well-known architect Edward Larrabee Barnes was hired to guide the planning. Barnes made multiple trips to the college. He met with trustees, staff, and faculty. He also attended several ACMs (All College Meetings) to hear students' ideas. When he returned, his renderings featured a unified academic complex of buildings, with prominent solar and wind power features integrated into the design. After lengthy discussions and feedback from the community, he went back to his office in New York City. He later returned with a new design incorporating the suggested revisions. Barnes's drawings contained all of the features of how an environmental college should look. The design received the 1974 *Progressive Architecture* Merit Award and was featured in a two-page spread in the January issue of the magazine. In the end, however, the notion of a Strawberry Hill campus for the college was rejected, largely based on the students' opinions.[18] They did not want to be part of an institution that appeared to "look down" on the town. Town/gown relations could never be good in such an arrangement. So it was decided to stay where they were—in town—beside the water, reusing and making the best of old buildings. The position was summed up in the 1975 institutional self-study for accreditation this way: "The college will move in two directions: (1) restore the past, (2) build the future."

During the next decade the college acquired several neighboring, oceanfront properties. They were estates of very different architectural styles, in stages of serious decline. When COA's main complex burned in the summer of 1983, they were pressed into service. My office at the time was in one of them—"The Turrets"—an 1895 granite mansion that had been abandoned since the Depression. The upper floors had recently been restored. But the main hall and first-floor rooms were still badly deteriorated from decades of damage and neglect. Between then and now the college has acquired other adjacent properties, which have gradually been shaped into a coherent campus landscape. New buildings are designed through lengthy community dialogues, in ways that harmonize with other buildings' features. We have avoided the classic model of linear walkways, disciplinary clusters, and a central administrative core. Instead, science labs and art studios are in close proximity—sometimes directly adjacent to each other. Most buildings combine faculty and administrative offices, with classrooms interspersed across all floors. The outcome is a truly lovely campus composed of exciting architecture where interactions happen everywhere. We think it looks like an interdisciplinary college, without being overly self-conscious about it.

The Bar Harbor campus has grown to thirty-five acres, with two dozen buildings of varying styles, size, and age. The college also owns and operates two farms, maintains a pair of biological research centers on two offshore, decommissioned lighthouse islands, and runs a variety

Human   Earth   Water

of international programs based in Europe and Central America. The college has its symbolic emblems too. The COA seal dates back to its founding days, when Mary Kay Eliot designed a representation of the college's iconic principles using pre-Christian symbols:

Combined within a circle, they exemplify the relationship of human beings and our surrounding environment—the essence of human ecology. COA also has its colors—blue and green—symbolizing ocean and forest. Every student is familiar with the logo. But most are unaware of the school's colors, as we have no intercollegiate sports teams and commencement exercises do not use robes and hoods.

I concur with Emin Tengström's view (noted in Chapter 4) about the value of an institutional home to develop the academic potential of human ecology. I also know that it takes a lot more than mission statements and buildings—irrespective of their configurations. The main ingredient of interdisciplinary education, as Ed Kaelber always expressed, is the people. It is not easy to find faculty with a solid academic background in a specialized domain that also have the capability to work creatively with colleagues from other domains. They are members of a rare breed. Those who do it well have had to overcome the pressures of academic convention. But when they do come together, and really share their backgrounds, the outcomes are indeed inspiring.

As I am writing these thoughts, I have just returned from a trip to Germany with Ken Hill, COA's current academic dean and executive director of SHE. We were invited to the Frankfurt Economic Forum for a two-day consultation with the German Society for Human Ecology (Deutsche Gesellschaft für Humanökologie, DGH). The DGH is actively working to create a European College of Human Ecology modeled after COA. On the first day, we conducted a site visit to Emmendingen, a town of twenty-seven thousand inhabitants, ten minutes by train north from Freiburg. The local officials gave a warm welcome. They were clearly eager to have the new college in their town. We visited four potential sites, all elegantly portrayed in architectural renderings developed in an earlier charrette by the DGH academic team and citizens of the town. We reviewed all of the venues with the architect, the project's leader Wolfgang Serbser, and several other DGH members who have visited COA. The first site was a fully functioning agricultural center—which has served the region for centuries—with several well-appointed historic buildings available for educational uses. The next was a former psychiatric center with an exquisite landscape of ornamental trees, quiet walkways, and benches. The third was a multistory former secondary academy located in the heart of Emmendingen. Its existing classrooms, auditorium, and library space readily fit the vision of a small, self-contained college. Lastly, we went to the industrial complex of Wehrle-Werk AG, a 150-year-old, family-owned manufacturing plant, around which the town has since grown. All of the locations held exciting potentials. Each of them, individually, suggested its distinctive possibilities for an interdisciplinary human ecology curriculum. At the close of our survey, all arrows began to point toward what, at the outset, had seemed the least likely setting: the factory. Wehrle-Werk began as a construction facility for brewery equipment. In the early 1900s it shifted to manufacturing high-pressure boilers for industrial power stations. In recent years the company has become a leader in environmental technology for renewable power generation, flue gas cleaning, biomass energy recovery, and wastewater treatment technologies. The plant is one of the major employers in the region and has excellent relations with the community.

The factory is housed in an enormous, self-contained building larger than three football fields in size. One end of the structure opens onto Emmendingen's historic center and Main Square. Our tour of the facility was guided by Duane Phillips, the project architect, and Volker Steinberg, the sixth-generation president of Wehrle-Werk. Together, they enthusiastically walked us through a visualization of how the entrance could be gardened into the town center and built into the factory complex in successive stages. Their vision reminded me of a recent *New Yorker* article by Jonah Lehrer. Lehrer's essay was an exploration of interdisciplinary creativity and groupthink. One of the highlights was about MIT's legendary Building 20. The 250,000-square-foot "temporary structure" was home to radar and many other inventions developed during World War II. Instead of being torn down, as it was scheduled to be, it became "one of the most creative environments of all time."[19] Building 20 housed a most unlikely assortment of departments and individuals. It is where Amar Bose developed the acoustics for his famous sound systems, Jerrold Zacharias created the atomic clock, Noam Chomsky fashioned his deep-structure theory of linguistics, and countless other innovations were hatched. The open-ended flexibility of the space and the informal encounters among its people became an unusually creative atmosphere. Steve Jobs modeled his Pixar Animation Studios on these principles. Harvard's Isaac Kohane has done detailed studies of creative spaces. "If you want people to work together effectively," as he concludes, "these findings reinforce the need to create architectures that support frequent, physical, spontaneous interactions."[20] The marriage of an environmental technology factory and an interdisciplinary liberal arts college is an exciting possibility.

Steinberg joined us in Frankfurt the next day for the college forum. The discussion among two dozen leading European human ecologists, educators, and potential corporate sponsors was upbeat and promising. The challenges of reaching the full-fledged outcomes as portrayed in the architectural visions are substantial. The concept of an independent college is unfamiliar in the context of German higher education. So are the (uniquely American) fund-raising traditions of private institutional development. Ken and I reminded our German colleagues that COA was not created overnight. In addition, we explained that our initial step was taken with an experimental summer program. Our recommendations were well received. The meeting ended with two positive action items. One was to construct a committed financial resources committee, composed of prominent academic and business leaders. The other was to commence planning for a student summer program, to be launched a year and a half hence in Emmendingen. I am hopeful.

Many leaders of American higher education have called for the expansion of interdisciplinary learning. Vartan Gregorian during his tenure as president of Brown University spoke out without hesitation:

> The real challenge the universities face today is not the choice between pure research and practical application but rather the reconstruction of the unity of knowledge .... The challenge calls for integrating and resynthesizing the compartmentalized knowledge of disparate fields: the ability to make connections among seemingly disparate disciplines, discoveries, events, and trends and to integrate them in ways that benefit the commonwealth of learning. Today within university communities we must create an intellectual climate that encourages our educators to encourage our students to bridge the boundaries between academic disciplines and to make connections that produce deeper insights.[21]

Gregorian continues to support these aims through the activities of the Carnegie Corporation of New York as the foundation's current president. Judith Rodin, president of the University of Pennsylvania from 1994 to 2004 (and first female president of an Ivy League university), championed an interdisciplinary restructuring of Penn. Rodin is now president of the Rockefeller Foundation. In a recent *Stanford Social Innovation Review* article, she noted the steps foundations and development agencies must take in "the development and application of innovative new methods ... that reflect multidisciplinary and systems approaches to problems and complexity."[22] Amy Gutmann, current president of the University of Pennsylvania, has maintained the momentum of her predecessor. In a *Newsweek* poll of "Nation Innovators"—asking what they would do to revitalize America's cities—Gutmann replied: "Redefine the liberal-arts education by integrating curricula across disciplines ..."[23]

Columbia University's Mark Taylor has elaborated on the problems and possibilities in a *New York Times* op-ed contribution: "End of the University as We Know It." In Taylor's opinion, "If American higher education is to thrive in the 21st century ... colleges and universities ... must be ... completely restructured." "The division-of-labor model of separate departments is obsolete," he maintains. They should be abolished and replaced with "creative problem-focused programs.... Responsible teaching and scholarship must become cross-disciplinary and cross-cultural."[24] These are strong statements. Stronger even, perhaps, than my own views. Nonetheless, it has become increasingly clear in recent years that higher education is facing a new era of creative redefinition.

I would like, in closing, to share a personal anecdote along these lines. During my early years as COA's dean, I received some valuable advice from Frank Keppel, former U.S. Commissioner of Education. Keppel, a dean at Harvard, was Ed Kaelber's mentor. As we were rebuilding the college, following the fire of 1983, Frank joined our board of trustees at the urging of Lou Rabineau. Following a summer board meeting, as Frank and I were walking toward our cars, the conversation turned to the topic of external academic relations. The college was developing connections with other environmental studies programs, and my international networking of human ecologists was well under way. Frank listened attentively as I described these activities. He then gave this reply: "Rich," he said, "what you want to be is the cat's whisker." It was his way of saying COA is not—nor will ever be—"the cat." But we should strive to be attached, so in some ways, we might chance to move it. His fitting image was sound guidance and a lasting lesson from a great educator.

PART II
FACETS OF LIFE

The best way to see everything is to consider the whole darn thing.

—Abraham Maslow

MANY YEARS AGO, WHILE I STOOD IN A GROCERY CHECKOUT LINE, a picture on a tabloid newspaper caught my eye. It was a black-and-white photograph of an aging man. He was leaning with outstretched arm against what was purported to be the largest ball of string in the world. It was an enormous lump, twice the height of the man. I strained to make out any clues in his face of what the accomplishment might mean to him. Was he proud, obsessed, or just weary? It was impossible to tell.

The man in the picture was Francis Johnson. He began his project in 1950. As the ball grew ever larger, railroad jacks were used to roll it around and add new coils. His unrelenting obsession continued for thirty years until his death. By then the ball measured forty feet in circumference and weighed more than seventeen thousand pounds. The residents of Johnson's small Minnesota town (population 250) have since enshrined his creation in a glass gazebo. The Twine Ball Museum is now a tourist attraction, which residents credit with saving their town from economic collapse. The achievement earned a place in *The Guinness Book of World Records*. It was the inspiration for Weird Al Yankovic's song "The Biggest Ball of Twine in Minnesota" and the satirical theme for Chevy Chase's cross-country film *Vacation*. Johnson's other collections—including four hundred horseshoes and 1,200 wrenches—are also on display. But the twine ball is what brings the tourists.

My thoughts have returned to this image many times over the years. Most of us are collectors of something—baseball cards, beach glass, jewelry, favorite quotes, fancy shoes—all sorts of things. The collecting impulse is made respectable in the academic world by couching it in terms of "research." The offices of my colleagues are cluttered with small mountains of books, papers, biological specimens, scientific equipment, and art objects. Some people's passions last a lifetime and are fashioned into meticulous collections. The compilations of others may be more episodic or whimsical. The category of collectibles can be highly specific with clear boundaries. On the other hand, collecting itself may predominate, and the overall results look more like a junk pile than a purposeful endeavor.

It is not difficult to identify the episodes of passion behind the compilations in my life. Our home is filled with bookcases, family pictures, cooking utensils, and exotic figurines. The corners of the attic tell the rest of the story. A cabinet of old records (with which I am still unable to part) and several former stereo systems lie among the dusty cobwebs. Beside them sit cartons of books and old magazines, along with bundles of photocopied papers on ever-changing topics. Farther down the eaves are dozens of old stringed instruments, decades of abandoned clothes, and boxes of memorabilia from my family and childhood. I too have my balls of string.

Ari Derfel, a Berkeley caterer, provided a personal snapshot of the river of materials that flows through everyday life. For an entire year he saved all of his trash. Except for what he actually ate, everything else was sorted into bins. At year's end, his living room and kitchen were filled with nearly a hundred cubic feet of stuff. Some was compostable. But the vast majority was leftover food packaging. Derfel's experiment shows what happens when someone intentionally holds onto everything. The point of his exercise was to raise consciousness about the environmental impact of one individual's consumer waste. At another level, it demonstrates that we readily discard most of what passes through daily life as useless trash. By contrast it also contains an intriguing kernel of insight, which highlights what we choose to keep as a special signature of personal meaning.

Francis Johnson's three-decade collection of string and Ari Derfel's yearlong compilation of trash are extreme examples. The singularity of purpose behind their respective accomplishments has a distinctive clarity. But the black-and-white photo of Johnson and his ball of string is more than just the product of a private quest. It is also an invitation to explore his motivations—as well as a window of self-reflection to consider how each of us meets the world and makes it meaningful.

The preceding chapters attempted to put something around the idea of human ecology, resting on more or less familiar academic grounds. But as anyone interested in interdisciplinary questions knows, the terrain of academic knowledge is deeply divided. The boundary lines that separate disciplines are often the outcome of competing views. Shedding conceptual difficulties—rather than resolving them—has been the conventional way to achieve clarity of disciplinary knowledge and methods. As E. O. Wilson notes, "the fragmentation of knowledge and resulting chaos are not reflections of the real world, but artifacts of scholarship."[1] The chasms and deeply etched lines between traditional fields of knowledge are manifestations of divergent views. If these are the ways thought has "come apart" and become segregated, they may well be an unpromising means for recombining them.

Melvil Dewey's decimal system and the Library of Congress Classification system are magnificent means for cataloging the pieces. They are of little use, however, in putting Humpty Dumpty back together. The intellectual and empirical tonnage of our libraries is staggering. How to synthesize and use this knowledge wealth is a fundamental challenge. Herein lies the central issue of human ecology. On a conceptual level, it might be considered the mother of all part/whole problems. But it is much more than just a "thought" problem. It also contains subjective questions about feelings, imagination, and consciousness—where they come from—and how they combine and shape the world.

I do not harbor any notion of an overall "theory of everything" in which all knowledge is unified. Nor do I subscribe to the despairing Jorge Borges–like "library of babel" vision, celebrated by some of my postmodern colleagues. A vast middle ground lies between these extremes, and it is here that much work has to be done. I have wandered this path for a good number of years. It has taken me throughout the library, around the world, across the internet, and down the inner passages of childhood memory. Some connections have developed from the administrative necessity of bringing focus to COA's human ecology mission and publicly articulating its educational and practical relevance. Other dimensions come from teaching and research, as well as through networking with interdisciplinary colleagues worldwide. These ideas, personal relations, and introspective ventures have been an invitation to explore the diverse dimensions of human/environmental relations.

Serendipity

Horace Walpole introduced the word "serendipity" to the English language in the mid-eighteenth century. He borrowed the term from an ancient Persian folktale: *The Three Princes of Serendip* (a.k.a. Sri Lanka). It is the story of a king who sends his three sons on an exploratory journey as the final part of their education. Upon their return, the young princes disclose the lessons they have learned. The value of the expeditions was not what they found at the end of their adventures, but what was accidentally discovered along the way.

I would like to use the serendipitous image of Francis Johnson's ball of string as a foundation metaphor for an alternative approach to explore human ecology. The analogy has many levels. But let us begin with the actual object, as pictured, and Johnson standing beside it. One way to retell his tale is to uncoil the whole ball. We could work our way back the estimated 1,100 miles, taking notes along the way. A linear uncoiling does recount the literal end-to-end journey, but it is a very narrow version of the story. Another approach, like Alexander's solution to the Gordian knot, may be to cut straight through the middle and read its patterns like the annual growth rings of a fallen tree. A less destructive method could frame the ball in Cartesian orthogonal dimensions—of x-, y-, and z-axes—for guiding delicate probes or mapping magnetic resonance images. These various methods are useful for analyzing Johnson's twine ball. They are less effective, however, at giving us insight into his mind, why he spent his life as a collector, or what collecting in general is about.

The tabloid photo that caught my eye in the supermarket line was not only of a ball of string; Johnson was also in the frame. My initial puzzling over his situation stirred similar questions about myself as well. I began to identify some of the underlying threads running through my own habits and fixations. My focus was not (like Johnson's) toward a particular type of object, but rather about a kind of experience. For many years I was unaware of my attention and unable to name its aim. Peter Matthiessen, when asked about the process of creative writing, put it this way: "You start a novel with a feeling that you want to clarify."[2] I too had been following an intuitive feeling. Over the years, the strands have woven together in the fabric of human ecology. I know hundreds of people with a similar fixation of the same name. Every initial meeting with one of them was akin to the first encounter between members of a rare species, or a like-minded Francis Johnson.

Another serendipitous event also shaped the forthcoming. It happened during my sabbatical, when Patricia and I were in Paris. We had rented a small apartment on the Île Saint-Louis, in the middle of the Seine. We spent our mornings reading, writing, and enjoying a leisurely breakfast. Afternoons and evenings were dedicated to long walks. I had begun writing the outline for this book. But I knew a more open structure was needed for what lay ahead. The transect lines I was following crossed knowledge areas of at least moderate familiarity to me. What might follow was unclear. I had no "next" academic domain to map. Further steps in any direction would be random. As I pondered alternative ways to continue, the image of reaching into the depths of organized knowledge and turning it inside out—like a sock—intrigued me. What might the woolly resemblances of familiar academic patterns look like in the soft background of their undersurface connections? The notion seemed rather straightforward in the context of straightening out the Saturday morning laundry. The term for this maneuver is "eversion." Digging into the topic revealed a number of fascinating discoveries. They ranged from the n-dimensional algebraic topology of sphere eversion—to the biology of organisms that can turn inside out as a defense mechanism. This was fun stuff, but much too exotic for use as a comfortable or comprehensible metaphor. I continue to wonder about the image of an "eversible university," even if only as an interdisciplinary thought experiment.

An alternative answer came quite unexpectedly during one of our afternoon museum visits. While we were strolling through the Musée Picasso, I was taken with the unusual power of Picasso's paintings and sculptures. He did not turn things inside out. But he surely had a transcendent strategy for conceptualizing a complementary view of reality. Picasso invented a new method of juxtaposing different views with a striking economy of means. Abandoning traditional representation, he used the interplay of asymmetric facets to recompose attention in a rhythmic sensation of space. The sharp contours and fragmented planes, as both mirrors of and windows for perception, produced a distinctive sense of volume with multiple viewpoints. His abstraction of familiar perceptual features preserved their essential characteristics, which were mentally reconfigured in a novel gestalt. For the remainder of our Paris trip my attention was consumed with learning more about Picasso's life and vision.

Picasso's distinctive "cubist" style—of de-forming reality and creating a new unity of perception—emerged quite suddenly during his midtwenties. The earliest signs appear in his 1907 self-portrait, which hangs in the National Gallery in Prague. It was soon fully developed in his still life, landscape, and portrait paintings during the next few years. The extension of cubist motifs to three-dimensional forms came in his seminal 1909 *Head of a Woman* sculpture of his lover Fernande Olivier. Picasso's wives and mistresses inspired many of his abstract paintings and sculptures. The particular "head of a woman" that engrossed me that day in the Musée was a later work, based on his long midlife relationship with Marie-Therese Walter. By then, Picasso's style had evolved beyond its early angularity. The sculpture still retained his economy of form. Instead of carved planes, however, it used bold, overlapping globular shapes to convey the voluptuous qualities of his lover. The simplified and somewhat crude features were reminiscent of Stone Age figures—like the Venuses of Willendorf or Lespugue. There was something in his well-defined simplifications and abstractions that touched my needs for creative destruction and repatterning. In the end, it was his own words that were most helpful: "When you come to think of it, there are very few themes indeed. They are constantly repeated by everyone."[3] Picasso, it seemed, had discovered a three-dimensional language of archetypal qualities at the edges of our deepest feelings and experience of time.

Part II of this book is inspired by these ideas. The Picassoesque facets were a way to approach human/environment relations using ordinary language, rather than academic terminology. Each chapter theme is fashioned around a transdisciplinary "facet" that bridges conventional categories. In combination, they became a way to explore connections in a fresh sequence of configurations. I begin by looking at "time and space." From there, Part II moves on with chapters examining "death in life," "personal ecology," "context," and finally, "metaphor and meaning." These facets are but a few of many ways to carve the patterns of life. This collection, of course, was chosen to synthesize my compilation of human ecological ingredients and thoughts.

In the course of my exploration, I came upon another representational analogue—yoga. Patricia, a daily practitioner all her life, has gradually drawn me into the tradition. While we were following a Shiva Ray CD during one of our evening sessions at home, I was struck by how the asana postures are based on common images. Many of the basic hatha body positions are named by natural references—e.g., sun, moon, lotus, tree, dog, lion, cobra, pigeon, and countless others. This simplicity of depiction is a powerful means for mind/body connection. The final shavasana position (i.e., "corpse" or "death" pose) joins these identifications and completes the unity of consciousness and being. Of course, my use of mental facets has no physical or bodily aspects as yoga does. What it does share, however, is the important principle of the stretching and opening of experience. In this sense, the goal of these chapters is not to "define" human ecology but, rather, to enhance the flexibility of mind necessary for its realization.

Charles Darwin, in a letter to his friend J. D. Hooker, once observed that there are two kinds of biologists: "splitters" and "lumpers," as he called them. Splitters, it seems, have the kinds of minds that notice differences and create endlessly detailed descriptions of the world. Lumpers do the opposite. They emphasize similarities and resemblances, ending up with fewer categories and more general classification systems. There is in fact some empirical evidence of individual differences in "cognitive style." In contrast to Darwin's bipolar representation, however, it seems to be more of a continuous variable—yet, nonetheless, a stable personality trait that correlates with perception, memory, and many other mental functions. If we examined people's collecting habits, my hunch is the organization of their belongings would resemble their mental style. But what they hold onto is also crucial. The tidbits of knowledge and interdisciplinary strands that I've gathered over the years have become wound into a single lump. Human ecology, for me, is not unlike Francis Johnson's twine ball. His enigmatic picture was a mirror. In his reflected image, I met the urge to carve into this obsession—not only in myself, but also in the minds of my friends who share this perspective—and further, into the view itself.

Those were the questions that got me started on this writing path. The preceding chapters were a way to give some shape to their answers. But Picasso raised the bar. His art parsed another view—of equal richness—along different abstract cleaves. What facets, I wondered, might cut across those familiar lines of figure/ground relations? The metaphor drifted in my thoughts for a long while. I cut and carved and pasted numerous collages, hoping to discover an ideal pattern. But things were far too protean to tie down that way. The mistake revealed itself when I stopped struggling with the need to find "an answer." My passion for human ecology was not a drive for closure—but rather the joy of endless openings and newfound connections. There is no final goal or perfect completion, only the expanding experience of being alive. In this, it is much like yoga. The asana poses are stretching postures, each a widening doorway for mind and nature to meet. The next series of chapters are stretching exercises, designed to relax the stiffness of academic body armor. They do not involve physical movement, of course, but they are nonetheless an exploration of ways to go beyond traditional positions.

Most intellectual training focuses on analytical skills. Whether in literary criticism or scientific investigation, the academic mind is best at taking things apart. The complementary arts of integration are far less well developed. This problem is at the core of human ecology. As with any interdisciplinary pursuit, it is the bridging across disparate ways of knowing that is the constant challenge. Picasso's approach permits us to look for synthesis—where subject/object splits are for a moment relieved, and inner and outer views may be joined. With this in mind, I invite us to take a fresh look at our metaphorical ball of string.

CHAPTER 6

Time and Space

Time is what prevents everything from happening at once.
—John Archibald Wheeler

You can't know who you are until you know where you are.
—Wendell Berry

Our collage of facets begins with ideas from Torsten Malmberg, founder and longtime director of the human ecology program at Lund University in Sweden. At SHE's second international conference in 1986, Torsten synthesized a conceptual foundation for his talk under the title "Time and Space in Human Ecology." The contents of his research and remarks go beyond the present context. But his straightforward use of these fundamental ordering principles "that can be applied to all parts of the physical world" was compelling at both the conceptual and the commonsense levels. Space and time, he noted, are generally conceived as four dimensions of a basic topological system: "Space has three dimensions where movements are possible in all directions. Time is one-dimensional … the transitorial character of which is much more pronounced than in corresponding spatial contexts." Each has respective characteristics, not reducible to the other. And yet, he reminded us, "Nobody has been at a certain place except at a certain time or has experienced a special stroke of a clock except at a special place."[1]

Malmberg did acknowledge the mathematical elegance of the space/time concept from relativity theory. But he promptly concluded that Einstein's abstraction holds little use for understanding ecological events. Ernst Mayr makes the same argument, even more forcefully: "One needs schooling in the physicalist style of thought and mathematical techniques to appreciate Einstein's contributions. Indeed I doubt that any of the great discoveries in the physics of the 1920s had any influence whatsoever on the thinking of the average person."[2] Clearly, the views of both biologists are firmly based on their lifelong study of the natural world.

On the ecological level, Malmberg noted: "It is well known that time and space are joined by movement, and it is interesting to note that time is measured by movement in space, movement through time and space, and space via time and movement." But they cannot be conflated either. "Time and space," as he added, "have many similarities … But there are, of course, many dissimilarities, too."[3] Malmberg's dimensions of space and time introduce an outline for our initial facet. Before our ecological stretching exercises begin, however, some additional—distinctively human—embellishments are needed.

Throughout his imaginative essays, Loren Eiseley often distinguished between nature's "first world" that dwells in the eternal present, and the "second world" of humans, which knows the past and anticipates the future. Human capacities for reflective thought and planned action transform our connections to space and time. "The human mind," as Eiseley put it, "can transcend time, even though trapped, to all appearances, within that medium."[4]

The psychologist Rollo May employed the term "time-binding" to capture the distinctive human ability to reach beyond the present situation. "This capacity to transcend above the immediate boundaries of time, to see one's experience self-consciously in the light of the distant past and the future, to act and react in these dimensions, to learn from the past of a thousand years ago and to mold the long-time future, is the unique characteristic of human existence."[5] Our ability to bring the past into the present—and extend the present into the future—redefines human relations of time and space. We exist, as May makes clear, not only in space and time; its four dimensions exist within us. Here, at the experiential level of human consciousness, is where they are joined.

About Time

A few years ago an intriguing discovery was featured in a report on the evening BBC Radio news. Researchers at Oxford University Press had conducted an analysis of everyday English language. It was a snapshot survey of word frequency from a cross section of newspapers, journals, and blogs. At the top of the list, not surprisingly, were the definite and indefinite articles "the" and "a," along with the prepositions "of" and "to." The pronouns "I," "it," "he," and "she" were likewise high on the list. What astonished the researchers, and made the story newsworthy, was that the favorite English noun did not refer to an ordinary, concrete object. It was one of the most abstract of concepts: "time."

Time, on the face of it, is a simple and straightforward term. When we dig into it, however, a very slippery concept is revealed. St. Augustine had this to say in his fourth-century autobiography *Confessions:* "What then is time? I know well enough what it is, provided nobody asks me, but if I am asked what it is and try to explain, I am baffled."[6] Nonetheless, many have tried. Contemporary examples range from Stephen Hawking's brilliant *A Brief History of Time* to H. James Birx's massive *Encyclopedia of Time.*

Irrespective of what time *is,* attempts to measure it appear throughout ancient civilizations, as far back as forty thousand years ago. Early conceptions were typically circular and were connected to the rhythms of sun, moon, and celestial cycles. Cyclical time fit closely to seasonal calendars and mythological worldviews. In Hindu tradition, for instance, death was not final; it was also the gateway to rebirth. The cyclic pattern of individual reincarnation was akin to the rhythms of nature and to the universe itself, which in some accounts springs from Vishnu's navel as the blossoming lotus. In 2005 archaeologists unearthed what may be the

New World's oldest agricultural calendar, in the foothills of the Andes. It showed, in elaborate, artistic style, the astronomical alignments of the solstices and the seasonal dates for planting and harvesting. But nothing compares to the intricate calculations of Mayan priest-astronomers. Their impressive astronomical studies and mathematics gave precise predictions of planetary alignments, lunar and solar eclipses, and other celestial events far exceeding anything elsewhere at the time. The extraordinary architecture and monuments of the Maya are testimony to the precision of their knowledge. The ancient monument of Stonehenge was another form of calendar construction dating back four to five thousand years. The early Greeks had their versions too. In the eighth century BCE, the historian Hesiod proposed a cyclical version of history depicting five ages. Pythagoras collapsed the view into a single great cycle that would end with the sun, moon, and planets returning to their original positions. The modern concept of time as linear was advanced by St. Augustine. In opposition to the Grecian circular concept, he proposed an irreversible process from creation to final judgment. His idea had a great influence on European thought.

Sundials and slow-burning candles were used to measure smaller divisions of diurnal time. Evidence of them is widespread and has been found throughout antiquity. Water clocks were the most accurate timekeeping devices for millennia. The first mechanical clocks appeared in Europe in the thirteenth century, although the idea may have come from earlier devices encountered in China. The oldest surviving mechanical timekeeping device in Europe is at Salisbury Cathedral. Driven by gravitational force on falling weights, it had no hands but told the time by striking a bell on the hour and quarter hours. Measurement of time independent of the irregularities of celestial events removed the constant need to recalibrate. Clocks and churches were soon united. The chiming of bells was important for calling congregations and marking religious practice and prayer. One of the first clocks with hands can still be seen at Wells Cathedral, where it has been since the late 1300s. Along with its circling hands, it also displays the corresponding movements of the sun across the sky and the phases of the moon.

A secularized version of time began to emerge with the rise of science. Precise measurement was invaluable for scientific experimentation. Galileo figured out that a swinging pendulum provides uniform and accurate measurement of intervals, which he employed for many of his experiments. Shortly after his death, the Dutch mathematician Christiaan Huygens used the principle to invent the first pendulum clock in 1656. It was a huge improvement that substantially reduced the daily gains and losses of earlier clocks.

The next big step came a century later, when the English inventor John Harrison devised a way to replace the pendulum with a spring-operated mechanism. In 1761 Harrison's portable chronometer was tested on a voyage to and from England and Jamaica, losing only five seconds. Pendulum clocks were useless on a rocking ship. With a reliable chronometer, however, accurate measurement of time was possible. Combined with celestial knowledge, mariners for the first time could determine their position in both latitude and longitude. British naval chronometers were set against a clock at the Royal Observatory in Greenwich, the point from which we still measure east and west longitude. Prior to this, local "solar" time—the approximate moment of "high noon," when the sun crossed the overhead meridian—was the common measure.

Precise knowledge of time was vital for navigating on the open ocean. On land it was less important. That is, until the beginning of railroads. Maintaining schedules and avoiding collisions required the accurate measurement of time. Lack of uniform standards caused a state of confusion for railroads, since local time east and west varies approximately one minute for every thirteen miles. The first solution was with time balls. These were large globes, several feet in diameter, positioned on the top of towers visible from long distances. The ball reached the bottom of a vertical pole precisely at noon local time, and thus afforded a daily measure to which clocks and watches were reset. The dropping ball was a common feature of towns and cities. It is still used as the symbolic marker for New Year's celebrations in New York City.

In the United States, the difficulties of adjusting to local time were enormous. Accurate information on the arrival and departure of trains was practically impossible. Timetables, based on multiple destinations of varying distances, were hugely complex and nearly impossible to decipher. The magnitude of confusion was captured in an article in the *New York Herald:* "If each clock measuring local time from Maine to San Francisco sounded noontime there would have been a continuous ringing from the East to the West lasting 3 and a quarter hours."[7] Coordination of time balls along the routes was a partial, temporary solution. The advent of the telegraph improved the situation somewhat by keeping all stations in synchrony, as long as trainmen meticulously checked their watches with depot masters along their routes. But the confusion of "local" and "railroad" time still remained.

Many solutions were offered. The final one came on November 18, 1883, with adoption of "standard time" and four official time zones. There was public outcry at the outset, but the arrangement was soon accepted. The U.S. time zones were further coordinated with the Royal Observatory in Greenwich, and the system eventually spread worldwide. Additional precision came in 1924 with the BBC's tradition of marking the top of the hour by a radio broadcast of time signals.

Standard time is so much a part of life now that we can scarcely imagine how different things once were. The Royal Observatory's celestial telescope, the time ball, and the gate clock are historical monuments. Universal time today is set by atomic clocks. Based on the vibration periods of radiation of cesium atoms, the precision is so fine that atomic clocks will not gain or lose a second in sixty million years. In 1983 the international standard unit of length, the meter, was tied to the distance traveled by light in a vacuum. The smallest interval that can be measured, Planck time (5.4×10^{-44} second), was set as the prime integer of time.

Sometimes, when we are far from clocks and schedules, we can still recapture a lost sense of place-based time. On a relaxing camping trip or a long day outdoors, perhaps, we can slip back into the rhythm of the sun. I had an unexpected encounter of this sort a few years ago, while flying home to Maine from Cincinnati. A golden sun was setting in the west, on a beautiful summer's evening. The plane was nearly empty as I slipped into a comfortable window seat.

Ever since my first flight, I still enjoy watching the landscape as it flows beneath. There is something about a bird's-eye view that reveals a special beauty of the world—the sparkling miniatures of a cityscape, the run of a river, or the splendor of a mountain range. Some of my favorite memories are from trips that follow the coastline of a continent, from Boston to Miami, or the rhythm of lakes and shores from Minneapolis to Maine. On flights back from Europe I have wondered my way across Labrador, Newfoundland, and Nova Scotia, spotting with delight the largest island on the Maine coast—Mount Desert Island—my home. At that moment, I have felt the faint urge to dive down directly, rather than fly on to Boston or New York, only to return. At night I sometimes follow the traffic lines of interstate highways, searching the patterns of lights and naming cities.

On this July evening, as we left the ground in Cincinnati, charcoal shadows crept across the golden fields of Ohio. Streetlights and headlights were just beginning to appear. Somewhere near Columbus, I noticed something from the corner of my eye. It was a brief twinkle of fireworks. I had forgotten, until that moment, it was the Fourth of July. Probably the volunteer firemen at some baseball field were eager to begin their hometown celebration. In the shadows of other valleys, sparkling mushrooms began to bloom. With my forehead pressed to the window, I scanned the landscape and horizon. From waterfronts, fairgrounds, and backyards, the world began to blossom in multicolored Queen Anne's lace. The merrymaking bouquets of light could be seen in all directions—some dramatic and multifaceted, some modest and faint. A few places began their shows early. Others postponed until well after dark. For two hours people celebrated history—all across Ohio and western Pennsylvania, through upstate New York, Vermont, New Hampshire, and most of Maine. They did it, however, not by clocks—but in "local time."

Time Sense

Sunset celebrations, like the one I saw that Independence Day, reflect an age-old connection between human experience and a diurnal marking of time. This basic circadian rhythm (from *circa diem*: around a day) and corresponding seasonal and annual cycles of the sun are the underlying temporal patterns from which life unfolded. The earth's periodicity—of day/night, light/dark, and warm/cold—are deeply etched into biological time. So too are the overlapping lunar cycles and the ebb and flow of ocean tides. According to the most widely accepted theory, a Mars-sized planet collided with the early Earth more than four billion years ago. The debris coalesced due to gravitational forces to form the Moon. The evidence further suggests that the Moon was far closer to Earth, and its gravitational influences were much greater on early life. The solar and lunar oscillations are associated with countless biorhythms—ranging throughout the plant and animal world, as well as in human patterns of sleep, affective states, and reproductive cycles.

Humans have a variety of built-in temporal patterns that mark our capacity to experience time. The cadence of the heartbeat is a primal biological clock at one end of the spectrum. At the other, the life cycle is the standard measure of generational time. Various other units of "momentality" are associated with human attention span and are probably tied to neuronal capacities and the refractory period of cells. Sound impulses separated by more than 3 seconds, for instance, are no longer grouped together in pairs. The shortest division of time fusion lies in a 2–30 millisecond range, depending on modality. Two sounds separated by less than 2–5 milliseconds are perceived as a single acoustic sensation. Touches closer than 10 milliseconds are indistinguishable, and the threshold for lights separated by less than 20 or so milliseconds are seen as a single flash.[8] High-speed and time-lapse photography have become important tools for "capturing time." They allow us to grasp temporal patterns that fall beyond normal thresholds and capacities. Events too fast for our perceptual abilities, like the mechanics of a hummingbird's wings or a contested fumble on the football field, are brought into experience. Speeding up of imperceptibly slow movements likewise reveals another range of patterns. These techniques have been essential to scientific discovery. They also open an aesthetic realm, in which the distinction between scientific and artistic views dissolves. Insights from both domains are apparent in the clever temporal shifts of visual tone-poem films like *Koyaanisqatsi* and *Baraka*.

I especially like the short film *Still Life,* by the British media artist Sam Taylor-Wood. The opening image is a seventeenth-century-style still life of a beautiful bowl of fruit, bathed in a warm glow. Using time-lapse film, the scene decays before your eyes, as nine weeks of rot are compressed into four minutes. First, the pears begin to blacken; next, the oranges and grapes fur over with mold. In an animated display of death and life along the way, mold spores burst vigorously in all directions, encircling the dish. Halfway through—at about a month—a soft mound covers everything and slowly shrinks. By the end, only a mottled cake of indistinguishable detritus remains. Through Taylor-Wood's eye the transformation of living forms, from the familiar to the microbial, displaces our ordinary sense of beauty. Her exploration of the line between life and death and life, as it actually happens, is genuinely insightful. Temporal analogies, like Sam Taylor-Wood's art films, are compelling means for grasping a sense of time—a problem that deserves plenty more attention. As the *New York Times* science writer Verlyn Klinkenborg maintains, "One of the most powerful limits to the human imagination is our inability to grasp, in a truly intuitive way, the depths of terrestrial and cosmological time ... the difficulty of comprehending what time is on an evolutionary scale, I think, is the major impediment to understanding evolution."[9]

In a Gallup Poll, taken on the two hundredth anniversary of Darwin's birthday, less than 40 percent of Americans admitted to believing in evolution. The main impediment (as in Darwin's time) is a faith-based foreshortening of time. Many religious Americans, it seems, still think that the earth and humanity were created within the past ten thousand years. Aside from reasons of faith, however, another psychological impediment remains: evolutionary time *really is* hard to grasp.

One way to get our heads around temporal phenomena is by tying them to everyday experience. The basic biorhythm of our heartbeat is a good place to start. According to the Mayo Clinic's website, a normal resting heart rate is between 60 and 100 beats per minute. For simplicity's sake, let's use 70 bpm. Multiplying a pulse rate of 70 by 60 minutes, we come up with 4,200 heartbeats an hour. The 24-hour total is 100,800. Multiplying again by 365 days, we get 36.8 million heartbeats in a year. That is a big number.

But again: if we take our pulse for ten seconds, we know what we are measuring. We have a real sense of that duration. We also have a good temporal sense for the length of a year. If we mentally transform the duration of a single heartbeat into an annual revolution of the earth around the sun—both understandable temporal rhythms—we can link a familiar bodily sensation to an equally common natural cycle.

By this standard—of one heartbeat equals one year—our lifetime would pass in about eighty or so heartbeats, slightly more than a minute. Similarly, an hour would take us back about four millennia, roughly to the early Bronze Age and the beginning of writing. Humans were by then a global species. Stonehenge, the Great Pyramid of Giza, and the oldest known temples of Peru were standing. Agriculture was widespread across the Middle East, India, China, and the Americas. The world population was somewhere between seven and ten million. One hour ago.

A day of heartbeats into the past (approximately a hundred thousand years) predates *Homo sapiens'* migration out of Africa. The Pan-African population may have been as small as a few thousand. It was a time of harsh climatic changes. Global temperatures were falling. The massive Laurentide glacier was beginning its slow passage over North America, scouring the landscape, as sea level dropped some four hundred feet. Where I am now sitting would eventually be buried under a mile of ice until its retreat ten thousand years ago—a few short hours' worth of heartbeats.

Our heart pulses three million times in a month. We are now close to our *Australopithecus* ancestor Lucy, discovered in Ethiopia in 1974 and whose remarkably well-preserved skeleton dates back 3.2 million years. Our ancestors had lost their hair and achieved bipedalism. The most elementary stone tools, however, still lay half a million years in the future. In sum, a month of heartbeats covers the time of human evolution.

To get a sense of deeper time, I need to invite my sister Joan into the picture. According to her genealogical research, she and I are twelve generations removed from our namesake ancestors—Richard and Joan Borden—who arrived in Massachusetts in 1639. That was 375 years ago (i.e., roughly fourteen billion heartbeats)—curiously close to the age of the universe. In other words, the duration of my father's family on North American soil compares, in normal-pulse-rate terms, with all of the years since the big bang. By this metric, the birth of our five-billion-year-old solar system is about 137 heartbeat-years away, which corresponds with my grandfather Jay's birthday in 1877. The first signs of life, 4.5 billion years ago, showed up around his fourteenth birthday.

Things get easier now—as the first eukaryotic cells appear around the time of my own birth. Multicellular organisms emerge when my son Andrew began kindergarten, and the Cambrian explosion when he left for college. The beginnings of terrestrial life—land plants, insects, and amphibians—follow him through college. Reptiles, mammals, birds, and flowers come along while Patricia and I were building this house. The great Cretaceous-Tertiary extinction put an end to the dinosaurs a couple of years ago. Birds and bats and butterflies fly into the following year. Grasses join the community of life a year ago, along with major mammal groups of whales, cats, dogs, and deer. We are back again to Lucy a month ago, our exit from Africa just yesterday, and the span of my own life in the final minute or so.

Maybe this seems farfetched. But the vastness of time can be brought into a comprehensible and personally meaningful frame of reference. A heartbeat makes a year. A minute, an hour, and a day of them are knowable intervals. So are the lives of my son, my wife, my parents, and my grandparents. I have known them well—and all along, their hearts were beating the yearly equivalents of evolutionary time since the earth began. If a biblical imagination can hold ten thousand years, a simple cardiographic conversion within the breast of a few generations should be as easily conceived.

Space

If time is considered the fourth dimension, what can be said about the three dimensions that precede it? One place to begin is with a standard definition of space: "a boundless, three-dimensional extent in which objects and events occur and have relative position and direction."[10] The basic representation of spatiality begins with an abstract, dimensionless *point*. In one-dimensional space, a *line* defines the distance between two such points. Two-dimensional accounts allow for more complex shapes, including recursive lines that enclose a defined space and give a bounded measure of *area*. Further extensions, within three orthogonal dimensions, reveal the shape of objects and the measurement of *volume*.

The language of representing these features is acquired by schoolchildren everywhere in elementary algebra, trigonometry, and geometry. The numerical and mathematical systems they learn date back to early Babylonia, Egypt, and China—where they were applied in all manner of calculations, from measurement of land areas and assessment of taxes to building construction and astronomy. Mathematics, "the queen of science," has long been considered the unifying basis of all theoretical and applied sciences. Techniques for calculation of space are generally considered to be among the clearest birthmarks of scientific methods. Enlargement of our perceptual grasp of spatial dimensions beyond the naked eye is perhaps the second hallmark. The ancient Greeks understood how to manufacture magnifying lenses. Seneca and Pliny mentioned them in early Roman writings. But more sophisticated means of magnification did not appear until the sixteenth century, when Dutch lens grinders put together the first compound (multiple-lens) microscopes. Their basic optical principles were soon extended to seeing-at-a-distance, in the form of early spyglasses. Galileo refined these simple novelty instruments to fashion the telescopes with which he saw Saturn's rings, the phases of Venus, and the mountains of the moon.

The inventions of microscopy and telescopy shattered the boundaries of ordinary human perception and fueled the scientific revolution. Contemporary means of magnification go far beyond the simple tools Van Leeuwenhoek and Hooke used to first glimpse the world of microbes or Galileo used to observe the wonders of the solar system. Modern electron microscopes enable scientists to study at a half-angstrom of resolution—smaller than a carbon atom or a millionth the thickness of a human hair. At the other end of the spectrum lie the powerful satellite-based Hubble and ground-based Keck telescopes. Researchers using them have recently detected fourteen-billion-year-old events at the very edge of the universe and become aware of as many as a hundred billion galaxies.

The frontiers of the infinitesimally small and the fantastically large continue to enthrall scientists. The emblem of this fascination is the gigantic European Organization for Nuclear Research (CERN). The 8.5-kilometer-wide magnetic particle accelerator, buried one hundred meters belowground near Geneva, Switzerland, is the largest machine ever built. Teams of scientists from around the world, numbering in the thousands, are joined there in a vast project. The scientific experiments they will conduct are the most sophisticated ever conceived. By beaming subatomic particles into head-on collision, they will re-create conditions believed to have been present in the big bang. The hope is to tie our understanding of the miniscule world of atoms together with the massive creative forces of the universe—and thereby reveal the most fundamental laws of nature.

A part of me eagerly awaits their results. What perennial mysteries will be answered? Will they discover, as some predict, support for an n-dimensional model of vibrating strings beneath reality, or will they find evidence of an even more far-out theory of multiple, parallel universes—and what might that mean? There is, as well, a part of me that is troubled by these activities. The feeling is akin to the unsettling qualms that come when military expenditures or corporate greed are juxtaposed with ecological degradation and human suffering. Big science—like big business and big defense agendas—has a way of overshadowing concern for human and environmental problems.

The price of CERN, according to E. O. Wilson, is equivalent to the cost of protecting all of the world's "hot spots" of ecological diversity and saving untold numbers of species from extinction. The Peace Corps's entire budget since its inception is a minor fraction of the cost of the Hubble telescope, NASA's annual budget, or a month of Middle East military expenditures. It is perhaps inevitable that the human spirit will always seek the furthest reaches of knowledge. But the grand events of science and technology can easily leave the fragile fabric of life unnoticed in the ecstasy of quarks and galaxies. In the quest for new frontiers, we must also hold a balanced view. We are here, on this earth, between the vast extremes. How can we bring our senses back to the soft refrains of life?

One way is to keep the earth in mind and our feet on the ground. This is what ecology does, by reminding us that living organisms lie in the center of a molecular and planetary continuum. But the lessons of ecology are not only scientific knowledge; they are also ways to bring the felt experience of the world into consciousness. In this way, through a contemplative approach to ecology, we can stretch our minds toward the natural world.

The same may be possible for any scientific knowledge—from a quantum level to the cosmic whole. These are the kind of yogic stretching exercises I mentioned earlier. Take, for example, one of the most important of scientific discoveries—Copernicus's and Galileo's reordering of an earth-centered to a helio-centered cosmology. Everyone knows this and believes it is true. But in everyday life we still speak of a *rising* sun or moon—and that is how we generally experience it. It is a truly mind-stretching exercise, however, to overcome our egocentric bias. Sometime, when the mood is right, I invite you to await the dawn and really *feel* the earth rotating, *turning toward* the sun, and not the sun's rising in the sky. Better still, take a pose between the setting (?) sun and a rising (?) full moon. Let the awareness of yourself, as a tiny node on a rotating sphere—between two other spheres—fill your senses. A more adventurous outing could be a picnic, perhaps with wine and dessert. And with your wine you might reflect on Galileo's words: "Wine is sunlight, held together by water," or Carl Sagan's challenge: "Remember, if you wish to bake an apple pie from scratch, you must first invent the universe."[11] While you're at it, you might also invite Lynn Margulis (Sagan's wife) into your thoughts. She was the one who proposed the revolutionary hypothesis of microbial symbiosis and coevolutionary cooperation. We share this story with every other living thing. "Life on Earth," as Margulis put it, "is like a verb ... a controlled artistic chaos, a set of chemical reactions so staggeringly complex that more than 4 billion years ago it began a sojourn that now, in human form, composes love letters and uses silicon computers to calculate the temperature of matter at the birth of the universe."[12]

An artful feeling of space was also the creative motif for the extraordinary wife and husband team, Ray and Charles Eames. Their lifelong partnership produced countless architectural designs ranging from medical stretchers and interlocking airport furniture to the still-popular leather and molded-plywood Eames lounge chair. Their fascination with the fluidity of design extended to filmmaking as well. They created more than a hundred experimental films. Their most famous was the classic, nine-minute documentary, *Powers of Ten.*

The film begins with an opening scene of a man and woman reclining on a blanket viewed from above. The image then settles in to represent one square meter (10^0). As the camera slowly zooms out, it pauses for ten seconds in the second frame—now a ten-meter square. This picture shows the man and woman sharing a picnic on a grassy lawn. The view further expands to a hundred-meter square and then a kilometer square (10^3), at which point we can see that the couple is located near Chicago's Soldier Field on the shore of Lake Michigan. The city of Chicago and the southern tip of Lake Michigan are framed at 10^5, and at 10^7 the earth as a whole. The 10^{12} power captures the sun and the inner planets of Mercury, Venus, Earth, and Mars; 10^{13} completes the solar system. At 10^{16} the border represents a light-year across as it approaches the nearest star. It continues ever outward, over the next minute and a half, past the edge of the Milky Way galaxy and ending at the power of 10^{25}, the size of the known universe. The sequence then reverses and slowly returns to the opening one-meter square.

The second half of the film zooms inward, focusing on the man's hand, through negative powers of ten. At 10^{-1} the image is of a ten-centimeter square of skin. Individual cells come into view at 10^{-3}, and at 10^{-5} we pass through the cell wall. The double helix of DNA appears at 10^{-8}. Burrowing deeper, we pass beyond the organic level into the subatomic realm of protons, neutrons, and electrons. The sequence is completed at 10^{-14} in a quark-level view within a single carbon nucleus of the man's hand. The image here has a striking likeness to the farthest reaches of the opposite extreme. Returning to the opening scene, each pause along the way provides a visual gestalt of the patterns of connection at the quantum, chemical, cellular, and organismal levels as were earlier experienced on the social, ecological, global, astronomic, and cosmological planes.

The Eameses's exponential voyage—less than ten minutes in length—fits easily within our attention span. Beginning and ending with an arms-length square, it grounds the overall experience of spatial extension in human scale. The juxtaposition of images and the transitional flow between them conveys the identifiable patterns within each level, as it also reminds us of the connections between them. The fascinating extremes of the miniscule and the massive, folded back onto the middle ground of a single cubic meter of space, invites an interdisciplinary exploration. Where the actual boundaries of life may lie is debatable. But most of the subject matter of natural and human ecology fits somewhere between the outward frame of the earth and life-powering sun, down to the level of DNA. The borders of lived experience are probably even smaller. Most of human awareness (including its representation in memory and imagination) occurs between the 10^0 square meter of our "personal space" and the 10^7 borders of earth.

The few dozen astronauts who have made it to outer space are exceptions. The rest of us, as Malmberg reiterated, live our life-times and life-spaces on a human ecological scale, united by our actual movements within these bounds. His conference presentation concluded with the mental-mapping of human interactions and relations with the natural environment. Elsewhere, in his book on *Human Territoriality*, he compared these with the processes of other social, migratory, and territorial species. In a later monograph, on *House as Territory*, he framed the most basic human ecological territory of all—home.

The landscape historian and urban planner Kevin Lynch also studied how we create mental maps of lived experience. He coined the word "imageability" to describe these mental processes for representation of space and time. The basic perceptual and cognitive language of imageability, according to Lynch, is a composition of five elements: paths, edges, districts, nodes, and landmarks. He derived these features from extensive research on how people actually locate themselves and navigate in the human landscape. Lynch's final book, *What Time Is This Place?*, combined time and space—as the title conveys: "These thoughts about how our environment represents or might represent the past, the present, and the future can be brought into better order if we look at how our bodies and our minds experience time—how time is built into us and yet also how ourselves have created it."[13]

Many aspects of Malmberg's and Lynch's approach to spatiotemporal behavior are shared by behavioral and life history ecologists. Their detailed studies have disclosed the patterns of mobility, food budgets, and reproductive strategies of many nonhuman organisms. This orientation was also at the center of Gregory Bateson's pedagogical device, in *Mind and Nature*—of presenting his students with a crab. The challenge was to discover the "pattern which connects" the crab, across ecological space and evolutionary time, with the past environments and homologous features of other life-forms. Given sufficient time, they usually deciphered their teacher's koan.

To marry Lynch's and Bateson's terminology: as the students' "imageability" expanded, so did their "ecology of mind." The diachronic (temporal) and synchronic (spatial) dimensions of creation are vast. They are also real. Stretching our minds across space and time is crucial to comprehending the living world. To draw on Alfred Korzybski's legendary comparison: the bigger the territory, the larger the map—and hence, the greater must be the imagination. Sometimes it may take us as far as can be imagined. For now, however, it is time to move on to the next facet of life—and its eternal counterpart—death.

CHAPTER 7

Death in Life

Death is life's greatest invention. Death is life's change agent.

—Steve Jobs

The difference between a riddle and a mystery is that a riddle has an answer, but a mystery does not. The primordial dance of life and death has aspects of both. When scientists are asked about the origins of life, they usually point to the simple self-replicating molecules that appeared in the elemental soup as the earth began to cool and the oceans were forming. Laboratory experiments have successfully re-created those organic compounds and amino acids—the basic building blocks of proteins. But nowhere, in the earth sciences or in the laboratory, have we actually discovered or reproduced the true origins of life.[1]

What we do know is that by 4.5 billion years ago living cells of bacteria and cyanobacteria (blue-green algae) had appeared. They were encapsulated structures with internal workings isolated from their surroundings. The full genetic complement of DNA and RNA was present. Those same components have been shared by all of life thereafter, including ourselves. What happened then and there has never been repeated. It is the source of all living organisms. But how it happened is unknown. It may well be unknowable. If so, then one of the most fundamental questions of life really is a mystery.

The earliest organisms were prokaryote ("prenucleated") cells. Prokaryotes have relatively simple internal structures. Their genetic material is dispersed throughout the cytoplasm. But they were a formidable life-form that dominated the planet for the next two billion years. The original prokaryotes were fermentation bacteria that scavenged energy from organic compounds and relied on anaerobic metabolism. They lived in watery environments and replicated themselves by simple cell division (i.e., binary fission).

One by-product of anaerobic metabolism is oxygen, and these early life-forms made a lot of it. Some of the oxygen combined with iron in seawater, producing vast amounts of ferric oxide that fell to the bottom in broad bands of iron ore. As the oceans became saturated, oxygen also escaped into and began to transform the atmosphere. In many ways the dramatic successes of prokaryotes were also their downfall. Oxygen is a poison for anaerobic organisms. The newly flourishing life was ironically in the process of creating its own death.

It would be a long while before life appeared above the water line. But many changes were happening down below. Primitive bacteria relied on freely available chemical compounds. A variety of metabolic adaptations enabled them to occupy new niches. Irrespective of their specialties, they still all functioned basically as tiny bags of chemicals with the added potential of asexual reproduction.

Somewhere amid the diversity, a new form of death was invented. One line of prokaryotes began to engulf its neighbors. But death, in the microbial world, was not absolutely final. A few of the predatory phagocytes, while consuming the energy needed for survival, somehow incorporated the actual structures of their prey. These novel life-forms would become the earliest eukaryote (truly nucleated) cells. The individual tools that prokaryotes used to survive and flourish became parts of a combined toolkit for a completely different kind of organism. One of the new host's adopted structures—mitochondria—became their internal power plants. These tiny organelles are descendants of former prokaryote cells that adapted to the eukaryotes' protected and nutrient-rich environment. Chloroplasts came from another bacterial line capable of forming carbohydrates from carbon dioxide and water through the action of solar energy on a light-sensitive pigment.

Eukaryotic life-forms were much larger and more complex than their predecessors. They flourished in the oxygen-rich environment created by their ancestral anaerobes. The "internal" mutualism introduced to the living world by eukaryotes was an enormous leap. It continued to spread as other bacterial forms devised additional ways to become permanent houseguests. The mutualism that opened the door of the new lineage was not only at the intracellular level. Multicellular symbiosis would soon follow. This evolutionary innovation is the source of most complex life-forms composed of and derived from nucleated cells. Those that expelled oxygen became the prototype for plants; those that took it in would lead to animals.

Sex and Death

The living world is still home to many ancient life-forms, like the primeval cyanobacteria that have remained virtually unchanged for four billion years. Three-billion-year-old remnants of once-dominant algal-bacterial, stromatolite mounds can be found in Australia and in the Bahamas. Bacterial spores buried two thousand feet below the surface in ancient sea-salt deposits near Carlsbad, New Mexico, 250 million years ago have been successfully revived and grown by microbiologists. The longest living individual plant appears to be a king's holly discovered in Tasmania. This clonal shrub, which relies on vegetative root suckering, is estimated to be forty-three thousand years old. The longevity of these organisms is compelling testimony to the reproductive resilience of simple cell division and a long-term mutation resistance.

Most biologists today divide life on earth into six kingdoms: archaebacteria, eubacteria, protists (plantlike algae and animallike protozoa), fungi, plants, and animals. The two bacterial kingdoms are composed exclusively of prokaryote cells that reproduce asexually by binary fission or budding. The cell types of the other four kingdoms are all nucleated eukaryotes. Protists, fungi, and plants have a variety of asexual and sexual reproductive strategies, and some species are capable of both. A few animals—like flatworms, sea stars, and aphids—can also reproduce by asexual means. But most complex, multicellular organisms regenerate by sexual reproduction.

The first organisms to have done so appear to have their origins in early eukaryotic history. How sexual reproduction first happened is still highly problematic for biologists; and the debate about its adaptive advantages is very much alive. According to the eminent evolutionary biologist W. D. Hamilton, "meiosis most certainly evolved from mitosis." But, as he quickly adds, "if there is one event in the whole evolutionary sequence at which my own mind lets my awe still overcome my instinct to analyse … it is this event—the initiation of meiosis."[2]

Somatic cell reproduction (mitosis) occurs by a division process, which maintains the species' standard chromosome number. In organisms that reproduce sexually, separate (egg and sperm) gametes are formed via the process of meiosis—usually by two parent organisms, or less commonly though hermaphroditic self-fertilization. When fertilization occurs, the two gametes produced by meiosis fuse. The resulting zygote, in multicellular plants and animals, then begins to divide and grow by mitosis. But it is meiosis that gives rise to the enormous genetic diversity of sexually reproducing populations. Sexual reproduction in plants is by fruits and seeds. Animal offspring come from their mother, in the form of eggs or live birth, as a result of mating. Unlike the clonal longevity of asexual organisms, sexually reproduced plants and animals usually have briefer, individual life cycles. In short, the enormous diversity afforded by the evolutionary invention of sexual reproduction came with a price—death of the individual.

The biological threshold of death for a single organism is relatively straightforward. At the species level, it is a more fuzzy line. Most biologists concur that 99.99 percent of all species that ever existed are now extinct. The paleontological record is littered with long-gone branches of the tree of life. Some sputtered away in the mists of time from never-to-be-known causes. Others were left behind by transformation into new, more successful descendants. Countless more were wiped out by mass-extinction events like the one that ended the Permian period 250 million years ago when as many as 95 percent of species were eliminated. Similar losses were associated with the Cretaceous-Tertiary mass extinction 65 million years ago. Some say we are in the midst of a destruction of similar proportions in the current Holocene epoch, this time from anthropocentric causes.

Life Histories

The average life span of a species, according to biologists, is on the order of a couple of million years. But there is a lot of variability around this estimate. Birds from the family Zosteropidae—commonly known as "white eyes"—have evolved into at least eighty species in that time period. Faster still is the unusually rapid speciation of European mice on the island of Madeira—where six genetically distinct species have evolved in the five hundred years since their accidental introduction by Portuguese sailors.[3]

At the other end of the spectrum we also find some of the oldest extant species, sometimes known as "living fossils." Sponges show little evidence of modification since their appearance 600 million years ago. Lingulida (lamp-shell) brachiopods likewise appear to be essentially unchanged in more than 500 million years. The spring migration of horseshoe crabs on the full-moon tide has been going on for nearly as long. I have marveled at their midnight mating dance and peered into their hypnotic eyes on the nearby shores of Taunton Bay. Sitting among cinnamon ferns, morphologically similar to their 300-million-year-old family members, I have breathed a prehistoric night air. I have also gasped at the less romantically inspired sight of a scurrying cockroach—one of the oldest flying insects in the world, whose fossils have been found in 350-million-year-old Carboniferous shale.

The time frame shrinks dramatically as we drop from species level to the plane of single organisms. Although a species may endure for eons, the time horizons of its individual members are strictly truncated. The future, if there is one, dangles on the threads of DNA passed from one generation to the next. The entire plan, encoded in a distinctive combination of genes, repeats itself. The forebearers are left behind to expire. In due time, like the fruited bowl of Sam Taylor-Wood's *Still Life* film, they dissolve back into the soup of life.

The life history of every organism is an ecology unto itself. For some, the life cycle may be quite long. The oldest-living, single plant (which reproduces by external flowers and seeds) is a creosote bush in the Mojave Desert. Its estimated age is 11,000 years. There is a bristlecone pine in the White Mountains of California more than 4,700 years old. Nicknamed Methuselah, its location is kept secret to protect it from disturbance. The oldest known animal—whose life ended with its discovery—was a quahog clam found off the coast of Iceland. Based on the growth rings of its shell, it was estimated to have been at least 400 years old. The longest-living mammal appears to be the bowhead whale. A fifty-ton bowhead, no longer living, was caught off the coast of Alaska in 2007. The whale was estimated to be at least 125 years old. A harpoon embedded in its neck, made in New Bedford, Massachusetts, dates back to 1890. More recent research indicates that members of this species may reach an age of 200 years and perhaps even longer.[4]

The longest-living human is a matter of dispute. According to the Guinness record book, the honor may belong to Jeanne Calment from Arles, France, who died in 1997 at the age of 122. But this is by no means the final answer. The average life expectancy of humans is also a moving target. The United Nations currently sets the world average at 65.7 for men and 70.1 for women. Japan tops the list with men at 79.2 and women at 86.9. The Central African Republic, in comparison, is at 44.5 and 47.3, respectively—with a substantially lower life expectancy than their Japanese counterparts half a world away.[5]

Life expectancy may be measured not only by length, but by brevity as well. The aquatic insects known as mayflies—of which there are some 2,500 species—appear to hold the record, with some living as little as thirty minutes. Fruit flies (Drosophila) also have a rapid life cycle with a development time (from egg to maturity) of as little as a week. Mice reach breeding age in five to six weeks. It is easy to see why these two species have become the favored models for geneticists. Ephemeral plants—as the name implies—have brief life cycles that take advantage of infrequent desert rains or the leafless days of early woodland springtime. Many annual plants complete their life cycle from seed to flower to seed in a matter of months. Brine shrimp and worker bees have fleeting lives. So do many chameleons, lizards, and the most short-lived of all mammals, the shrew.

Viewing ecology through the lens of individual life histories or the life cycles of species makes it easy to grasp the Hindu conception of life as a drama. Every creature and plant has a separate path of sustenance and survival on the way to their final dance with Shiva. Migrating salmon enjoy just a single mating dance before the ball is over. Conifers and giant redwoods may have thousands of reproductive cycles. The number of offspring per individual is also highly variable. A female sea urchin releases millions of eggs at a time. A female orangutan gives birth to a single baby and is fortunate to have three or four in a lifetime. With an estimated 80 percent destruction of orangutan habitat in the past quarter century, their modest reproductive capacities will likely lead to extinction. The average worldwide fertility rate for humans (currently 2.5 per woman)[6] is not much different. Yet the life stories of orangutans and humans are deeply connected, and the former depends greatly on the latter. Only conscious recognition of and caring about the demise of the former by the latter will change the equation.

It may be said, in broad-brush terms, that the primary purpose of life is the continuation of life. A deep program for survival and reproduction underwrites the complex cycles of life, in which death is the grand equalizer. There is, however, a peculiar novelty: human awareness of the cycle of life and a capacity to anticipate our own, individual death.

Mortality in Mind

I have always enjoyed the films of Ingmar Bergman. The first one I saw was *The Seventh Seal*. The movie begins with a scene in which a knight, Antonious Block, returns to Scandinavia from the Crusades. As he awakes to the dawn on a broad beach, he bends to wash his face in the seawater. Turning from the shoreline, the knight drops to his knees in silent prayer.

He rises and stares toward the morning sun. Before him stands a pale-faced figure in a black cape. "Who are you?" asks the knight. "I am Death," replies the hooded stranger. "Have you come for me?" Block inquires. "I have been walking by your side for a long time," answers Death. "That I know," the knight concedes. Death opens his cloak and reaches to put his arm around the knight: "Are you ready?" "Wait a moment," the knight replies—and in that moment kindles the interest of Death in a game of chess to forestall finality.

Death cunningly accepts the challenge. The match between Block and his partner, move by move, punctuates each episode of the knight's ensuing travel on a plague-ridden journey back to his home. It is a passage through pestilence, witch-hunting, superstition, and trickery. But nowhere does the knight find his answers about the fundamentals of life, only more perplexing questions. In the end, Death clears the board. He takes them all, silhouetted in a macabre dance across a featureless horizon, in the closing scene.

Bergman's films are gripping portrayals of the human condition. But they are not stories in the common understanding of that term. Cinematography, for Bergman, was not verbal narrative. "Film has nothing to do with literature," he once proclaimed. "The character and substance of the two art forms are usually in conflict" ... "Music works in the same fashion," he noted. "I would say that there is no art form that has so much in common with film as music." So—what does Bergman mean? He meant, I think, they are distinctive *kinds* of story making—that arise in different ways. As a psychologist, I see Bergman saying that writing comes from thoughtful imagination, whereas music and film (at least in his style) have their sources in the wordless realm of feeling. "A film for me begins with something very vague." As he described his art, "It is a mental state, not an actual story.... Most of all it is a brightly colored thread sticking out of the dark sack of the unconscious. If I begin to wind up the thread, and do it carefully, a complete film will emerge."[7]

George Lucas gives a similar account of the making of the *Star Wars* trilogy: "First came the music ... then the visual ... then the words." Lucas worked feverishly with his musical director John Williams to establish their famous leitmotif for anchoring the characters and the plot within the soundtrack. Lucas's vision was not guided by "telling" a story. He was seeking to inspire the depths of a mythic search for wisdom that allowed the story to reveal itself via intuition. The music created the emotive potentials into which the structure and archetypal architecture of good and evil, father and son, teacher and student unfolded. Lucas's creative process was guided by his education in anthropology and further study of the works of Joseph Campbell and Carl Jung.[8]

A comparable fascination with the psychological depths of unconsciousness comes through as Bergman discusses his filmmaking. "Philosophically, there is a book which was a tremendous experience for me: Eino Kaila's *Psychology of the Personality*."[9] Kaila was the founder of Finland's first psychological laboratory and a leading psychologist in Scandinavia before World War II. His early thinking was influenced by the perceptual and cognitive holism of Gestalt psychology. In later years, he expanded on the role of symbolic functions with ideas from Eastern philosophy and quantum physics. Kaila's elaborate theory of "deep mental life" embraced the unconscious need of human beings to experience aesthetic, ethical, and religious values. The impact of Kaila's ideas on the cinematic explorations of Bergman—like Jung's on Lucas—are readily seen. Their films arouse us from the bottommost depths of the psyche. Like the death poems of Robert Penn Warren or Emily Dickinson, they touch ancient sensitivities akin, perhaps, to those that stirred the first burial rites of early humans.

Our deep irrational feelings of death anxiety have been attributed to multiple sources. In part, they may arise from evolved self-protection mechanisms or survival responses of being a victim of predators. They might, conversely, stem from unconscious fear (or guilt) of retribution resulting from our own acts of harming or predation. According to existential psychologists, the most powerful form of death anxiety comes from our general ability to anticipate the future, coupled with conscious anticipation of inevitable personal demise. This expectation, at the individual level, is often met with repression or denial. Limited use of these defense mechanisms may be psychologically beneficial.

Their excessive use, however, can carry other emotional or life-threatening costs.

Easing the anguish of death awareness, at societal levels, has been met through a multitude of institutions and shared belief systems. Larry King may have sounded graceless, but he was not facetious when he summed things up this way: "If there weren't death there would be no religion."[10] King was echoing the German American philosopher Edward C. Hegeler, who wrote the identical phrase in the journal *Monist* more than a century before.[11] Hegeler's son-in-law Paul Carus enlarged the notion considerably over his lifetime as a pioneer of the comparative study of religion. His influential ideas were shared with many turn-of-the-century intellectuals, including C. S. Peirce, Elizabeth Cady Stanton, William James, Leo Tolstoy, D. T. Suzuki, and others.

Death is universal. The rituals associated with it, however, vary substantially—and are greatly influenced by their religious and cultural context. In ancient Egypt, sophisticated funerary texts for "going forth" after death were placed in the tomb of the deceased. One of the finest is the 3,500-year-old, legendary Papyrus of Ani. There were many others and collectively they are known as the *Egyptian Book of the Dead*. These writings contained in-depth instructions for guiding the soul on its journey to the afterlife.

Every culture gives special attention to death and its surrounding activities. The early Grecians were likewise avidly religious people with elaborate beliefs about death and rites of passage. The god of death, Thanatos, guided the dead person's soul on the trip to the underworld domain of Hades. The idea later became linked to Christianity and was converted into the concept of Hell. Birth and death in Hindu tradition are part of a karmic cycle of transcendence leading to liberation of the soul. For Buddhists, death is an opportunity for improvement in the next life. Hebrew, Christian, and Islamic faiths have their respective customs for mourning and for preparing the corpse. Innumerable other religious practices exist—and even the strictest of atheists arrange meaningful ceremonies for grieving and remembrance.

The Greeks also turned death into art. Their intensely emotional tragedies were filled with murderous drama for the entertainment of audiences. A fascination with death was a central feature of the story in Grecian theater. But it was seldom acted out on stage and left instead to the viewer's imagination. The Romans made it into a real spectator sport where gladiators, slaves, and animals fought to the death before applauding crowds. The allure of blood sports and other spectacles of violence—between humans, animals, or both—has provided powerful vicarious experiences for encountering the mysteries of death throughout history. Boxers, matadors, and pit bulls are still crowd-pullers. The actual act of killing itself, as graphically explored in Roger Caras's *Death as a Way of Life*, may well be another surrogate rejoinder to mortality beneath the surface of "sport" hunting.

The average American child, by age eighteen, is estimated to have seen eighteen thousand murders and two hundred thousand acts of violence on television.[12] The "death play" of popular video games is accelerating these numbers to ever-higher levels. Here in rural Maine, the local evening news routinely headlines with a litany of automobile fatalities, murders, and other catastrophes. These reporting trends are partially a reflection of media policies. But without some predilection and appetite for edge-of-life drama, they would fall upon deaf ears. Death by suicide, in contrast, is seldom publicly reported—even though the national suicide rate is double that of homicide. (In Maine it is actually much higher, where it now stands as the second leading cause of death among young people between the ages of fifteen and twenty-four.)[13]

There are many reasons for keeping suicide out of the news—from protecting family privacy to forestalling tendencies for imitation and contagion. But sometimes the act cannot be masked and reveals the unsettling depths of human morbid curiosity. Eric Steel, producer of the controversial documentary film *The Bridge* about the Golden Gate Bridge's suicidal lure and enticement for spectators, describes it simply: "We all want to know what goes on in each other's mind." These performances, like the knight's chess match with Death in Bergman's film or the draw of witnessed aggression, seem to somehow reaffirm our existence—if only for the moment.

Innocence and Evasion

Children do not begin with a comprehension of death like an adult's understanding. Their concepts of death develop through an interaction of personal experience and cognitive maturation. As the pioneering research of the Hungarian psychologist Maria Nagy revealed, a child's sense of death-related phenomena is grounded in the mental capacities available at a particular time in her intellectual development. Nagy proposed three general stages of death awareness in childhood. In the initial state, death is a faded continuation of life, similar to sleep, from which the individual may still awake. In the next stage, death is final. The dead stay dead. For some children, the departure may also include a shadowy figure, which mysteriously accompanies the dying process. Finally—usually by the age of nine or so—a child realizes that death is inevitable, universal, and personal. Everything and every person, including himself, eventually dies. Nagy's general outline has been refined by subsequent studies and elaborated with connections to other theories of cognitive development. But her basic outline of differential phases of understanding remains valid.

Curiosity about disappearance and death is part of a child's normal interest in learning about the world. Peekaboo and other games of concealment, like hide-and-seek, are early precursors to the mystery of vanishing objects. The expression "all gone," often among an infant's first phrases, is another. Aspects of death-related play appear in the game of "tag" (where one is frozen by the touch of "It"—and rescued back to life with a touch from anyone "Not It"), as well as "ring-around-the-rosy," where "all fall down"—a game believed to date back to the Black Death in medieval Europe.

Actual death events, such as seeing a dead animal or losing a pet, add another level. I still recall the death of my first dog, "Pal." He had been struck and killed by a car. My father and I found him late that night. As we lifted him into the car trunk, I was startled by the cold rigidity of his lifeless corpse. We buried him the next day near the base of our backyard grape arbor. I knew he was dead. But the image in my mind, whenever I thought of him thereafter, was of his intact body. If we dug him up he would look the same as when we placed him there, and I could once again give him a hug. My thoughts and feelings, in Piagetian terms, were operating on the level of object permanence and concreteness. The transformation came some years later and took me by surprise. It happened on a sparkling autumn afternoon while walking alone through the woods. I was halted by an unfamiliar and nauseating smell. Before me, on a bed of leaves and pine needles, lay the carcass of a decomposing deer. Bracing myself against the wretched stench, I reeled at the sight of its putrefying and maggot-filled flesh. The shimmer of white teeth and fleshless bones, framed with clumps of hair, protruded from the soupy ooze. My senses flooded at the vile sight—horrible to consider, yet impossible to avoid. In the aftermath, the frozen image of my faithful dog dissolved—as a second mourning followed, and with it, an irreversible comprehension of the destiny for all life's forms.

A child's discovery of death is often accompanied by anxiety and can be deeply distressing. Loss of a family member and the direct encounters by children afflicted with a life-threatening condition are powerful events. The anticipation of losing a parent is perhaps the greatest fear of childhood. My first experience of the death of a family member came when I was four and a half years old. Grandma Moore—our mother's mother—who lived with us, suffered a stroke while eating dinner. She died quietly in the early morning of the next day. I remember what we ate that night and can still picture the blue-and-white china plate with her unfinished meal. My sister and I were taken upstairs, where the minister and then the undertaker visited us. The minister was unmemorable, except for his dogged reading of a dull storybook. I have a strong recollection of the undertaker, who played with us and gave me my first lesson in whistling. But I do not remember the many visitors who came to our house or any of the events before and after my grandmother's funeral (recorded in my mother's diary). Nor can I recall anything our parents said about her death and disappearance from our lives. Indeed, I hold no lasting memory of my grandmother whatsoever, and am unable to visually recognize her from photographs—even though she was a part of every day of my early childhood. The clarity around the events on the night of her death and the complete erasure of all memories of her are perplexing. I'm sure it was a traumatic loss that somehow still lingers within me. It is also evidence, from a deeply personal level, of the inscrutability of death and the unconscious defenses alloyed to our enigmatic apprehensions.

Many children are instructed in the tradition of nightly prayers. In my childhood, these included the "Lord's Prayer," followed by various other heavenly appeals for the protection of family, friends, and pets. The well-known "Now I Lay Me Down to Sleep" was for my protection, i.e., "If I should die before I wake, I pray the Lord my soul to take." I learned these recitations, like most children, by rote long before I was able to comprehend their meaning. They were the first things we were taught in Sunday school. Everyone did them, as far as I knew. Failure to dutifully perform the responsibility endangered one's world and carried with it an added cost of Protestant guilt.

Early religious instruction, in advance of a child's capacity to grasp an awareness of death, has the potential to embed lasting unconscious defenses. Moreover, as Freud suggested, protection of children from death-awareness conveys some degree of vicarious comfort to parents as well. Freud's giant step into the psychology of death came in *Beyond the Pleasure Principle*. In an effort to explain why patients were drawn to repetition of distressing experiences, he introduced the "death-drive" (*todestrieb*) as a dialectical counterconcept to his familiar "life instinct" (*eros*). "If we are to take it as a truth that knows no exception that everything living dies for internal reasons—becomes inorganic once again—then we shall be compelled to say that *the aim of all life is death*" (emphasis in original).[14] The ambivalence of life and death impulses was extended to the motivational processes behind masochism, sadism, suicide, and narcissism—as well as children's death play and the irresistible attraction of the sense of imperilment. Freud later elaborated a threefold representation of the "pleasure principle," the "reality principle," and the "Nirvana principle" (from the Sanskrit "to blow out"): a motivational tendency to return to an inorganic state inherent in all living creatures. These ideas were further embedded into social and political contexts in *Civilization and Its Discontents* and Freud's public exchange with Einstein in *Why War?*

The concept of an innate drive for aggression and self-destruction was controversial at the time—and still remains abhorrent to many people. It nonetheless continues to hold a significant place in psychoanalytic theory. Melanie Klein located the origins of anxiety in the endopsychic perception of the death drive—as did the early existential psychotherapists Medard Boss, Ludwig Binswanger, and Rollo May. Wilfred Bion and Jacques Lacan, in their respective ways, also incorporated the unconscious dimensions of inward-directed aggression. I am not an expert on these various views. But I am quite sure that our psychic relationship with death is complex and, further, that a good deal of it remains subconscious. Ernest Becker, in his Pulitzer Prize–winning *The Denial of Death*, offers compelling arguments about the cognitive dissonance surrounding the inevitability of death and the terror of annihilation. Becker and his former students, via their "terror management theory," have demonstrated some of the ways that "mortality salience" affects individual and group decision making. These questions are what make psychology interesting, important, and—to some extent—scary.[15]

Death: Life's Sculptor

Scientists sometimes have a skeptical attitude toward psychologists. They consider us a somewhat fuzz-brained profession with a lingering predilection for mystical thinking. As a witness to Bill Drury's lifelong frustrations, however, I have come to realize that even the minds of scientists can be quite saturated in buried prejudices. Bill's battle with ecosystem thinking was not a scientific problem; it was a psychological problem. Indeed, many paradigm shifts in science are frequently outcomes of psychological insight as much as empirical discovery.

The lifework of Rita Levi-Montalcini, corecipient of the 1986 Nobel Prize in physiology and medicine, is such an example. It is a long story, retold in her inspiring autobiography *In Praise of Imperfection*. Levi-Montalcini's early career at the University of Turin was abruptly interrupted by Mussolini's decree against non-Aryan academics. Unable to escape the subsequent Nazi occupation of Italy, she fled to an underground hideaway. In the corner of her bedroom, she fashioned a tiny laboratory to study cellular development in chick embryos. It was there that she did one of the most important studies of prenatal neurogenesis. Those initial results, after the war, would lead to the groundbreaking discovery of programmed cell death (PCD). The active participation of cells in their own death is now considered a universal mechanism of multicellular life. These regulated processes of cellular suicide in the interest of the organism (a.k.a. apoptosis) are everywhere. In human fetal development, for instance, the differentiation of fingers and toes is a sculptured result of programmed cell death. Apoptotic processes continue throughout our lives. They remove tens of billions of cells each day, a cell mass roughly equal to our total body weight in a year.

Research in the field of apoptosis has increased substantially in recent years. In addition to widespread contributions throughout general biology, research into the role of defective apoptotic processes in understanding disease and immune system functions has likewise mushroomed. Yet for decades, the important discoveries that would lead to these revolutionary advances remained unnoticed in the shadowed fringes of science. How was something so fundamental and ubiquitous so ignored for so long? Some of the elusive answer comes to light in the award-winning documentary *Death by Design*. The film is a remarkable visual depiction of cellular biology, threaded together by personal accounts from Levi-Montalcini and other pioneers of PCD. In many of their minds, Western psychocultural attitudes about mortality were unquestionably part of the problem. The idea of death, even at the cellular level, was somehow repulsive. That the whole of life might depend on its creative aspects was equally disturbing. Acceptance of a death-view of biochemical and cellular communication required a long time. With the emotional veil raised, the high intensity of both cell division and cell death are now readily accepted as a dynamic process within living organisms.

Elisabeth Kübler-Ross is another person who looked at death and discovered a creative process. Her classic book, *On Death and Dying*, is still considered a master text on the topic. Her stages of the dying process as initially proposed have been challenged and revised. But the courage of her purpose remains unquestioned. I recall being dragged to her guest lecture by a friend in college. The room was overflowing. My thinking at the time, I confess, was simplistic: "We live—and then we die—period." I was baffled that so many had come to hear a lengthy discourse about death. The answer came a few moments later: "Dying," she declared unhurriedly, "is one of the most important experiences of life." The cavalier attitude of my arrival evaporated. The personal relevance and public appeal of her message were clear. It was time to transform the uncertainty, fear, and denial that characterized our attitudes about the end of life.

Kübler-Ross led the way in clearing those psychological clouds. The social prohibitions surrounding the discussion of death and dying began to relax. Ensuing explorations of attitudes have altered the end-of-life experiences for countless families. Awkward avoidance has been replaced by progressively more compassionate approaches. Hospitals—once a place to be sent and die alone—routinely accommodate the families of dying patients. The invaluable time I shared with my mother in her final days of palliative hospital care was a direct result of these changes.

With the rise of hospice and home-based care as alternatives to hospitalized death, the terminally ill have far greater choices. With the help of people like Sherwin Nuland, a surgeon and Yale professor of medicine, we have enlarged our understanding of the dying process as well. His illuminating book *How We Die* is a sensitive and insightful guide through the actual shutting down of the body's processes as death approaches.

The contributions of Kübler-Ross, Nuland, and many others have increased the understanding and acceptance of dying as a natural process. Attitudes about death and the freedom to choose *how* we meet the end of life have opened enormously. The next major psychological and cultural threshold surrounds the freedom to choose *when*. I know many people who favor greater self-determination on this issue. Public opinion and medical ethics are changing. Voluntary end-of-life decisions and medically assisted practices are finding their way into society. As these practices become more common, our attitudes about death will shift in all likelihood from avoidance to celebration.

The challenge of staring straight into death's mirror is a raw reminder of vulnerability, which avows the motivation of self-deception. The forthright examination of death is profoundly unsettling, no matter how gradual the unmasking. Each shedding layer of self-protection reveals a fresh patch of sensitivity. The distortions that protect our psyche from being overwhelmed by personal mortality also distort our views of the external world and obscure the place of death in all of life. Aldo Leopold was a person who looked beneath the surface of the living world. He put it plainly: "One of the penalties of an ecological education is that one must live alone in a world of wounds.... Much of the damage," he added, "is quite invisible ... An ecologist must either harden his shell and make believe that the consequences of science are none of his business, or he must be the doctor who sees the marks of death...."[16]

Leopold saw a death march of innocent organisms throughout the layers of life. The whole of humanity were culprits—collectively blinded by greed and incapable of caring. The death of nature was likewise at the heart of Rachel Carson's *Silent Spring*—as the title made clear. Leopold's and Carson's personal revelations were powerful insights for countless others. By revealing the ecology of death, they generated a more authentic understanding of life. The attribution of environmental problems to human insensitivities was the accepted version of the ecology of their time. Human apathy about nature is still an enormous dilemma. But, as we've seen in the preceding chapters, our understanding of ecology has become far more complex—and so have the psychological issues. A few closing anecdotes may show some of the quandaries.

Not long after I arrived at College of the Atlantic, Bill Drury began a controversial research project. Growing numbers of seagulls on Maine coastal islands were displacing other seabird species. As a field experiment in conservation ecology, Bill and his students set about "removing" (i.e., killing) all gulls that attempted to nest on one of the islands. This was at the height of ecology's balance-of-nature period, and the experiment was met by widespread public and scientific criticism. The idea of interfering with nature's self-correcting forces was deemed not only "unecological," but it was also roundly scorned as environmentally unethical, i.e., for "playing God" with nature. Undaunted, Bill carried on—and as he expected, the island soon became the home to common, roseate, and Arctic terns along with numerous other formerly displaced species of nesting seabirds. The reintroduction of diversity was eventually seen in a more positive light, attitudes began to change, and in the end, Bill's project earned the Outstanding Contribution Award from the U.S. Fish and Wildlife Service. Other COA conservation biology projects, in the meantime, had successfully reintroduced bald eagles, peregrines, and other raptors to local habitats. Everyone was happy—until the shocking day when one student's eagle devoured another student's tern. The irony was as sobering as it was inevitable. The event also contained an element of psychological irreconcilability about wildlife restoration and human emotions.

On another occasion, while driving along the shore of Somes Sound (the central fjord that bifurcates Mount Desert Island), I noticed a bald eagle in flight. I wondered if it might be a hatchling of one of our students. The passenger riding with me soon spotted another, and then another. The uncommon sighting of three eagles was cause to pull off the road and watch. But the enchantment of the moment was quickly interrupted as we discovered what the eagles were doing. In the water, not far from the shore, a mother duck and her baby ducklings were swimming frantically toward the shelter of the rocks. My passenger revealed her sentiments without hesitation as she yelled instructions to the ducks: "swim harder," "turn left," "dive now"—shaking her fists all the while at the eagles in a futile attempt to wave them off their prey. The event was a mosaic of dramatic ambivalence—from the separate beauty of each creature, thrown into a moment of bird-against-bird struggle, juxtaposed with the clarity of my friend's judgment—all conflated in my experience of the episode as a whole. An enduring uncertainty from that day still remains. And I wonder how well we really can integrate death and life—or whether some aspects of reality fall beyond our comprehension and emotional capabilities.

The line between the living and nonliving world seems like a straightforward threshold. But even that can be a muddled place. I am reminded of a conversation, years ago, with a young woman. As we walked across our university campus on the way to a meeting, we briefly shared our backgrounds. She was from New York City and had always lived in an urban environment. I, in turn, mentioned my rural background of fields and forest. "Oh yes," she replied. "I love trees—but not all of them." "What do you mean?" I asked. "Well," she said, pointing in the distance, "I don't like *that* kind of tree. It doesn't have any leaves." I paused for a moment. "Sharon," I said, "that is a *dead* tree."

As strange as that seemed at the time, I am not alone in my incredulity. The year after I arrived at COA, we hired Craig Greene—a young botanist who had just completed his doctorate at Harvard. Craig and I became good friends. We shared a fondness for Bob Dylan's music, homemade beer, and Tuesday evening dart games. Craig had a slightly dualistic personality. In the classroom, he was the classical teacher who seldom strayed from his well-crafted lecture notes. He was an entirely different person in the field—joyfully amusing and full of childlike exuberance. During a faculty meeting one day, we were going around the room and sharing our individual teaching goals. When Craig's time came, he began with his customary allegiance to science, an equally stiff statement about pedagogy, the importance of botany, and so on. But as he neared the end, his voice began to quaver with emotion: "I just want them [the students] to know," he said, "that these things are alive."

Craig's life was cut short a few years later by pancreatic cancer. But what he said that day, and how he said it, left a lasting impression. Craig saw life where others did not—and that is what he taught. In graduate school, he was E. O. Wilson's teaching assistant. I'm sure some of Craig's exuberance came from there. Wilson has explored and written about the living world with delight. He is a fervent advocate for conservation and the inspired proposer of an instinctive (biophilic) bond between human beings and living systems. It was a surprise to me, in a recent interview, when Wilson said: "If I had my life to live over, I would be a microbiologist—an explorer in a new world."[17] How wonderful, I thought, to see the world anew, to look between the lines at the little things below the surface that made life possible and return back—in death—to start again.

CHAPTER 8

Personal Ecology

I always say that our psychology has a long saurian's tail behind it.

—Carl Jung

O earth, what changes hast thou seen!

—Alfred, Lord Tennyson

During the summer of 1909, G. Stanley Hall, founding president of Clark University, arranged a series of distinguished scholarly conferences in celebration of the twentieth anniversary of the university. The conference series culminated in September with a meeting of the foremost psychologists from both sides of the Atlantic. Hall, already a leading international figure in psychology, used the occasion as an opportunity to bring together the pioneers of European psychoanalysis and American psychology. Freud and Jung were featured lecturers of the European contingent, and each gave multiple presentations on the origins of psychoanalysis.

Hall's invitation to America was an especially moving event for Freud. Later, in his autobiography, he recorded its significance: "In Europe I felt as though I were despised; but over there I found myself received by the foremost men as an equal. As I stepped onto the platform at Worcester to deliver my Five Lectures upon Psychoanalysis it seemed like the realization of some incredible day-dream: psychoanalysis was no longer a product of delusion, it had become a valuable part of reality."[1] Freud and Jung were both awarded honorary degrees from Clark; for Freud it would be the only such honor he ever received.

Down the Dark Ladder

Throughout his life, Freud held a special interest in archaeology. He was an avid collector of symbolic antiquities, many of which adorned his counseling office. The metaphor of archaeology was a pervasive and central feature of his theory. The eminent historian and Freud scholar Peter Gay calls it a "master metaphor." As Freud once explained to his famous patient Sergei Pankejeff (a.k.a. the Wolf Man), "The psychoanalyst, like the archaeologist in his excavations, must uncover layer after layer of the patient's psyche before coming to the deepest, most valuable treasures."[2]

Years later, Pankejeff, in his own autobiography, recalled "all kinds of statues and other unusual objects." Freud's consulting room at Berggasse 19 "must have been a surprise to any patient," he noted, which … "in no way reminded one of a doctor's office, but rather of an archaeologist's study." When Freud fled Vienna under pressure from the Nazis, he was able to take his collection. He died the next year, on September 23, 1939, in his London consulting room surrounded by it.[3]

The summer before their trip together to the United States, Freud shared the following thought in a letter to Jung: "One thing and another have turned my thoughts to mythology and I am beginning to suspect that myth and neurosis have a common core."[4] The outcome of this thinking—on the possibility of some type of mental heritage—would later become constellated into his "Oedipus complex." The idea was a combination of Darwin's speculations about the "primal horde" as the basic social unit of primitive societies, and the influence of the Scottish social anthropologist James George Frazer's studies of totemism, exogamy, and incest taboos from *The Golden Bough.*

Prehistoric social groups, according to this line of thought, were arranged around a single dominant male who had total authority and held claim over all the females. Eventually the young males in the tribe formed a bond, overwhelmed the leader, and killed (and ate) him. The guilt arising from the murderous act, combined with its associated sexual freedom, was embedded into the unconscious mind. Residues of the ancient patricidal experience were thereafter inherited by subsequent generations and passed on within the developing psyche. Echoes of the incident were manifested (i.e., symbolically reenacted) briefly in childhood psychosexual development in an incestuous desire for the opposite-sex parent—but quickly repressed. This inherited "primal repression" of sexuality, in Freud's view, is what gave rise to the superego. It was also the underlying template for all subsequent forms of psychological repression. So it was that Freudian psychoanalysis came to be so centered on sexual repression and the search for its clues in neurotic symptoms, dreams, and the psychopathology of everyday life.

The Oedipal event was not simply a personal trauma, however; it also affected all societies at a historical level. Its apparent recurrence—across cultures, throughout literature, and over time—led to Freud's far-reaching elaborations. The broader societal manifestations of the buried memory, as he proposed in *Totem and Taboo*, were universally reenacted thereafter in symbolic rituals of an "unconscious understanding ... of all the customs, ceremonies, and dogmas left behind by the original relation to the father."[5]

In subsequent works, Freud expanded his personality theory to interpretations of history, religion, and cultural anthropology. *The Future of an Illusion, Civilization and Its Discontents,* and *Moses and Monotheism* were a tour de force of psychoanalytic ideas. Beneath those elaborate construals, he never strayed from his grounding in individual psychology and evolutionary biology. The idea that "ontogeny recapitulates phylogeny" (i.e., the development of an embryo is a speeded-up replay of the evolution of species) was one of the most influential ideas of the time. The theory of evolutionary recapitulation, also utilized by Darwin and Huxley, became a central feature of Freud's bridging of biology and psychology.*

---

*An unfortunate historical footnote lies at this juncture. In his 1868 book *The Natural History of Creation*, the German biologist Ernst Haeckel misled his colleagues with a distorted drawing of similarities among various mammalian embryos. He later confessed and apologized. Nonetheless, Haeckel's overzealous act clearly contributed to the widespread popularity of recapitulation theory and no doubt influenced Freud's developing ideas as well.

Nonetheless, Freud was cautious about the human/nonhuman barrier, noting "I regard it as a methodological error to seize on the phylogenetic explanation before the ontogenetic possibilities have been exhausted."[6] He did step over the line briefly in the *Introductory Lectures on Psychoanalysis*, where he suggested that dreams may lead to two kinds of prehistory: "on the one hand, into the individual's prehistory, his childhood, and on the other, insofar as each individual somehow recapitulates in an abbreviated form the entire development of the human race, into phylogenetic prehistory too …"[7] It was this line, between these two realms of the unconscious, that would separate Freud and Jung. The potential of psychoanalysis to explore the depths of the human psyche fascinated both men. For Freud there was a single inherited complex buried in the "personal" unconscious of every individual. Sex was the indispensable link, he believed, between the body and the mind; it was likewise the primary factor in evolution. He may have erred with a Lamarckian interpretation of Oedipal inheritance, but he was on the mark in believing that sexual urges are primordial.

Freud initially encouraged Jung's pursuit of the mythic dimensions of unconsciousness. He failed, however, to foresee the lengths to which his protégé would extend his delight in transpersonal inheritance. In Jung's view, there were *many* complexes constellated within the personal unconsciousness—endowed by the far deeper archetypal potentials of the "collective" unconscious. Jung's complexes, as the British evolutionary psychiatrist Anthony Stevens explains, "are thus the bridge between the personal (ontogenetic) psyche and the collective (phylogenetic) psyche.… In other words, complexes are archetypes actualized in the mind."[8] The archetypes, moreover, are considered to be highly adaptive mental equipment that combine neurophysiological structures as well as their corresponding perceptual, behavioral, and experiential components. In Jung's words, "Just as the human body connects us with the mammals and displays numerous vestiges of earlier evolutionary stages going back even to the reptilian age, so the human psyche is a product of evolution which, when followed back to its origins, shows countless archaic traits."[9] Exploration of these deeper realms of the unconscious mind, where "Ultimately every individual life is at the same time the eternal life of the species,"[10] became his hobbyhorse. These ideas inspired the mythological studies of Joseph Campbell, as well as the literary, artistic, and theological imagination of countless others. They have since been joined with parallel discoveries from ethology, anthropology, psycholinguistics, and genetics—and most recently, by burgeoning evidence from evolutionary psychology and medicine. The indelible stamp of our past, as Darwin put it, may be faint, but understanding how these strands are woven into human beings may be—as Jung maintained—the wisdom of our future.

A View from Below

The summer of 1909 was the occasion for a different kind of groundbreaking. On the last day of August, in the mountains of British Columbia, Charles Walcott was finishing his season of paleontological fieldwork for the Smithsonian Institution. Riding along a ridge trail above Emerald Lake near Mount Wapta, as the story goes, Walcott dismounted his horse to inspect a slab of shale that had fallen across the trail. When he broke off a layer of the rock, he saw the well-defined outlines of fossilized arthropods. Walcott was one of the leading invertebrate paleontologists of the time. He immediately recognized the fossils as an unknown species. Exploring further, he spotted many others—including segmented worms, sponges, and trilobites—some with even their soft-bodied anatomy preserved in astonishing detail.

Walcott returned many times over the next fifteen years and amassed an enormous collection. The Burgess Shale contained more than a hundred species with never-before-seen anatomical details, captured in a frozen frame by a catastrophic mudslide that had engulfed and locked them in an anaerobic tomb. But his administrative duties at the Smithsonian gave little time to work on or publish his findings. After his death in 1927, Walcott's notes and collected specimens remained in storage, hidden away in the dusty drawers of the Smithsonian. They were rediscovered by a new generation of paleontologists nearly a half century after his initial discovery. Stephen Jay Gould vividly told the story of their rediscovery and their importance to our understanding of the evolutionary origins of animals in his book *Wonderful Life*.[11]

The quality of anatomical details and the diversity of species preserved in the Burgess Shale are exceptional. It contains an unprecedented snapshot of the huge radiation of marine life from the Cambrian explosion. Buried in the fine mud of that underwater avalanche are many of the precursors of all life-forms to come—soft and hard parts alike. Included among them are the primal structures of our own chordate phylum, which we share with all vertebrates. Indeed, all major animal phyla that exist today have evolved from the basic body plans established in that relatively short (ten-million-year) mid-Cambrian period.

The Cambrian was a time of extraordinary innovation. All life at the time was in the sea, which was warm and increasingly oxygen-rich. About a third of the earth's surface was above sea level. It comprised several landmasses. The largest were Gondwana (the present-day southern continents and India), Laurentia (western North America; the location of the Burgess deposits), and Baltica (northern Europe). The Burgess deposits at that time were located, along with several smaller fragments, at tropical latitudes in equatorial regions and were devoid of all life.

By the early Cambrian, the first primitive chordates were in place. These descendants of earlier wormlike ancestors had inherited a basic body plan of bilateral symmetry, a digestive system, and a cephalized nervous system. The oldest known fossils of these marine creatures are Cathaymyrus (discovered in southern China) and Pikaia (found in the Burgess Shale). An explosion of marine animals of all shapes and sizes filled the environment they inhabited. The calcified body parts and hardened shells of many remain sealed throughout the fossil record. The arthropods began here as well, eventually to become the most diverse of animal phyla. All insects, arachnids, and crustaceans share the familiar arthropod configuration of segmented body, jointed legs, and hardened exoskeleton. The once-abundant trilobite, arguably the most celebrated of Paleozoic creatures, had its start here too. The first true vertebrates were also emerging about now—the jawless fish similar to lamprey or hagfish.

The earliest indications of terrestrial life appeared in the upper Cambrian. They were most likely some form of euthycarcinoid—an ancestral forerunner of insects and crustaceans. Why they ventured ashore is unclear. It may have been to escape predators or to feed on patches of shoreline microbes. Another hypothesis points toward laying eggs or mating—as horseshoe crabs still do. A major extinction event put an end to the Cambrian. But another period of tremendous biodiversification (the Ordovician) followed, in which many new forms of plants and animals emerged.

Fungi and algae began to colonize the land, followed by an assortment of arthropods adapting to the new terrestrial niches. The ancestors of today's millipedes and centipedes were among the first, soon to be joined by their six- and eight-legged cousins. Approximately 460 million years ago, fish divided into two major groups along the lines of cartilaginous or bony skeletons. As the Ordovician was coming to a close, the bony fish further split into ray-finned and lobe-finned lines. Tiktaalik, the first four-legged animal (tetrapod), showed up around 400 million years ago and would later give rise to amphibians, reptiles, birds, and mammals. By now the land was well covered in vascular plants and ferns. About the time when the first seed-bearing plants and gymnosperms were spreading across the Devonian landscape, the first amphibians branched off from the other tetrapods. Lush plant growth and forestation continued, ultimately producing the great coal deposits of the Carboniferous, for which it is named. A profusion of tetrapods now thrived in the water and along the margins of swamps, rivers, and ponds. The remaining tetrapods eventually separated into synapsids (leading to mammals) and sauropods (ancestors of reptiles, dinosaurs, and birds).

The stage was now set for the reptiles, whose protective skin and amniotic egg opened the door to a vigorous colonization of the land. Many new types of arthropods and spiders also inhabited the vast and oxygen-rich forests. The first flying insects appeared, including the giant meganeura—an aerial predator with a wingspan of several feet. The Pangaea supercontinent had by this time formed, as life continued to evolve and radiate throughout the Permian. Large reptiles, like the carnivorous Dimetrodon (with its distinctive sail-like fin), dominated the landscape—until the greatest mass extinction in earth's history brought an end to the Permian and more than 90 percent of all life-forms.

As the ecosystem recovered, the surviving lines of sauropods rapidly diversified and ushered in the age of dinosaurs. The first true mammals appeared in the Late Triassic, descending through the therapsid/theriodont line. Along the way, a line of small nocturnal animals developed a capacity to maintain their internal temperature (homeothermy), some with an added adaptation of body hair. They were probably like small, egg-laying monotremes. These proto-mammals later split into marsupials and placental mammals, capable of live birth. By now the world's geography was looking very different. Pangaea had been slowly breaking apart. North America and Greenland had split away from Eurasia, as South America independently peeled away from Africa. Australia, still close to Antarctica, was heading north. On the other side of Africa, India rushed toward a collision course with southern Asia, causing the creation of the Himalayas. But before it got there, the Cretaceous-Tertiary (K-T) extinction wiped out a vast swath of plant and animal species, including the giant reptiles.

The meteoric ending of the Cretaceous, sixty-five million years ago, opened the door to mammalian evolution. As flowering plants began to fill the landscape, many coevolutionary relations developed with birds, insects, and other animals. The small mammalian survivors of the K-T extinction rapidly branched out and began to grow in size. Soon, giant herbivores, grazers, and carnivores would occupy the plains. The first primates were descendants of small lemur-like insectivores. Grasping hands with an opposable thumb, stereoscopic eyesight, and the first traces of color vision were crucial adaptations for their forest lifestyle. These changes were also associated with a parallel growth in cerebral capacity. A great diversity of these Prosimians (pre-monkeys) developed during the Eocene (fifty-five to forty million years ago). From them came the Simians (higher primates), later to become the Hominid family (of great apes) with four extant genera, which includes the genus *Homo*. The most recent Hominid split—between humans and the genus Pan (chimpanzees and bonobos)—appears to have taken place somewhere around six million years ago.[12]

The story of our human lineage is continually enlarged, almost daily, by discoveries from physical anthropology, archaeology, and genetics. New insights fill the pages of scientific journals and regularly appear in the public media—about how many species and subspecies of humans have existed, the extent of contact between them, and their social and environmental interactions. With a single droplet of saliva we can now trace the genetic history to our African roots. The power of this kind of self-knowledge was dramatically revealed in the public television series *Faces of America*, written by Harvard professor Henry Louis Gates Jr. The show followed the family histories of twelve prominent people from their childhood to the point where no further genealogical evidence could be found. From there, with the aid of DNA samples, their heritage was mapped across time and around the globe. When the path of migration by Meryl Streep's ancestors was presented to her, she thoughtfully mused: "We are the sum of all the people who have come before us." For Gates, who directs the W. E. B. DuBois Institute of African and African American Research, the findings were somewhat more perplexing. His family tree was actually more European than African, at least for the past millennium or so. His reaction, when he first saw the results, was genuine surprise. "I am my people," he beguilingly conceded. The genetic maps of Yo-Yo Ma and Louise Erdrich were as diverse in other ways, revealing their respective Asian and Native American past. The initial response by everyone who took part in the program conveyed a palpable sense of wonder and geographic validation. Their gene paths were far-flung; they were also somehow a mark of personal truth—from which a common African starting point was the same for all.[13]

But the past does not begin there. The threads of DNA, as we know, wind all the way to life's beginning. We live in the here and now. But the "theres and thens" are also recorded in the codes. Our bodies and minds are the current manifestations of a transhuman heritage. We are the burgeoning borders of life, along with every other living thing. All the creatures through which we have unfolded still linger, however faintly, within the design of our being. The more we know of this, the richer the feeling and experience of personal ecology.

Where Is the Environment?

Most definitions of human ecology emphasize the interactions of humans and their environment. But human/environmental relations are enormously complex. Sensory capacities extend awareness of our surroundings far beyond the envelope of our skin. Many other human life processes occur without any awareness at all. A substantial portion of these takes place in our internal environment. The basic tubular design of our bodies begins shortly after conception. Yet the fundamental processes of cellular cooperation beneath the plan are ancient. The story begins as the earliest wormlike animals passed through the Cambrian doorway. Elaborations of that vital motif run throughout the evolutionary tale.

The initial steps in development involve the cleavage of the fertilized egg into two cells, then four, then eight cells. The arrangement of these cells defines a major line of descent. Protostomes (mollusks, annelids, and arthropods) form from a spiral cleavage in which the initial eight cells are not directly over each other. Deuterostomes, which become echinoderms (sea urchins, sea stars, etc.) and chordates, have a radial or boxlike cleavage. Both lines eventually form a fluid-filled ball (blastula) as cell division continues, and the three principal embryonic layers of the ectoderm, mesoderm, and endoderm develop. In Protostomes (meaning "first mouth"), the gastral tube forms by a splitting process known as schizocoely. Deuterostomes typically follow a different gastrulation plan called enterocoely. As the blastula's ball of cells expands, a portion of them begins to turn inward. These invaginating cells form the anal end of the primitive gut, ingressing through the developing embryo. The gastrulation process is completed as the digestive tube reaches the opposite side of the embryo and forms the mouth as a second (deuter) opening. Actually, it is somewhat more complicated, as some Deuterostomes, including vertebrates like us, use a modified version of schizocoelic splitting.[14]

Gastrulation was a major evolutionary innovation. Earlier multicellular plans were based on filaments, sheets, or clumps (as in sponges). In the mathematics of topology, life had begun to experiment around the fundamentally distinctive properties of a *torus,* i.e., a two-dimensional surface embedded in three-dimensional space (like a donut—or a coffee cup, which is the combination of a hole and a major hollow indentation). In short, the organism lives in the environment, while the environment simultaneously passes through the organism. In our own case, the top and bottom rims of the donut form our lips and anus.

The donut hole of our gastrointestinal tube is a complex ecosystem and is the home to as many as a hundred trillion microorganisms. Some eight hundred phylotypes reside there. Another five hundred inhabit our mouth; two hundred more live in our genitourinary system; and another hundred or so all over our skin. The quantity of microbes living in and on us is ten times the number of cells that make up our body.

Humans are born without any microorganisms. The placenta is a highly efficient filter, keeping the fetus free of microbes during gestation. Colonization of the infant's microbiota begins immediately following birth. Many microbes are helpful—aiding metabolism, stimulating the immune system, detoxifying the body, and in the biomanufacture of vitamins. Disrupting the microbial ecology with antibiotics can lead to serious health problems as a result of losing the beneficial effects of microbes.

Though seldom considered as such, the gut is really part of the body's exterior, through which the environment passes. The actual surface area of our intestinal lining is about 300 square meters (roughly equivalent to three tennis courts). In contrast, an average person has about 2 square meters of skin. In topological language, there is 150 times as much surface area folded together inside of our donut hole as there is on the outside. The spread-out surfaces of the lungs add another 100 square meters.

If some inventive toymaker came up with a "transformer" of a typical children's action figure—reversing the internal and external surfaces—it would resemble something akin to a yard-wide bundt cake. A full-scale version would be as big as a swimming pool, with a body-size column of dry skin standing in the center. Two balloons of lung tissue, each larger than a city bus, hover above on hoses tethered to one of its rims (the mouth).

The small intestine is approximately three meters long and, like the stomach, has a multitude of ridges and furrows. Numerous projections of villi and microvilli function to greatly increase the absorptive surface area. Each villus cell contains blood vessels that facilitate digestion, as peptides are converted into amino acids by the membranes of the microvilli. The cecum lies at the junction of the small intestine and large intestine. In herbivorous mammals, it forms a large pouch filled with bacteria capable of digesting cellulose. In humans, the cecum has been reduced by evolutionary change to form the appendix.

The large intestine (also called the colon) absorbs sodium and other ions, as well as the vitamin K produced by colonic bacteria. It receives about ten liters of water per day, only a fraction of which comes from food. The rest is from secretions into the gut. Ninety-five percent of this water is reabsorbed; if not, diarrhea results, causing dehydration and ion loss. The last twenty centimeters of the large intestine is the rectum. Its fecal contents are composed of approximately 75 percent water and 25 percent solids. One-third of the solids are intestinal bacteria, and the rest is undigested materials. Polyps are small growths that sometimes form in the epithelial lining of the colon. They can be benign or cancerous and can be removed individually.[15]

Our lungs exchange about four liters of air in each breath, or the annual equivalent of six times the volume of the 192-foot-long Goodyear Blimp (this is where the cup comes in). The diaphragm, a dome-shaped sheet of muscle that separates the chest cavity from the abdomen, does most of the work of breathing. The basic processes of respiration are maintained by the autonomic nervous system (ANS) throughout the day, while asleep, and even when unconscious. We can also control our breathing consciously (unlike the muscles of the other internal organs managed by the ANS). This added dual-control of the diaphragm by the central nervous system (CNS) is what makes speech, singing, or holding our breath possible. The interplay of our ANS and CNS during respiration, by the way, is an important indicator of conscious (thought) and unconscious (emotional) conflict used to detect lying in polygraph tests. The autonomic and central nervous systems also join in the sphincter muscles. In infants, the central nervous system is not yet fully developed in the sphincter muscles, which is why toilet training must await their development and conscious control. The CNS/ANS interactions also reveal themselves with loss of control in states of intense emotion (e.g., fear, laughter, etc.), as well as in determining which pets can be housebroken or not.

The skin is composed of two main layers, the outer epidermis and the inner dermis. New epidermal cells are constantly being produced and pushed to the surface, where they die and are filled with keratin. Keratin gives the body a durable overcoat that protects it from damage, infection, and drying out. Our body produces a totally new epidermis every month. When we look in the mirror, nearly everything we see—our skin, hair, and cuticles—is a coating of dead cells. The only actual living cells we see are the corneal surfaces of our sparkling eyes peering back.

The eye is an extraordinary evolutionary innovation. Countless variations of image-forming eyes appear throughout the living world and give compelling testimony of adaptive significance. Twenty-five percent of the human brain is dedicated to the visual system.[16] Our eyes contain about 7 percent of all nerve endings. We have about 150 million retinal receptor cells. About 20 percent are color-detecting cones located at the center of the retina, encircled by a ring of color-blind but highly sensitive rods capable of detecting a single photon of light. The dual system of vision is the outcome of early primates' migration from nocturnal to diurnal environments. Vision increases environmental awareness beyond the body boundary of our skin, farther than any of our other senses. The naked eye can resolve objects as small as 0.1 millimeter—the diameter of a paramecium or the finest of hairs. Distance vision depends on many things, but the farthest object we can see in daylight is ninety-three million miles away (the sun). At night we can see much farther, when as many as nine thousand Milky Way stars are perceptible—and even into the next galaxy of Andromeda, if we direct our vision sideways and allow our rods to do the work. The increased sensitivity of our rod-rimmed retina is also why faint nighttime objects at the periphery of vision disappear when we look directly at them (with our less-responsive cones).

Our sense of hearing is more strictly bounded—by the earth's atmosphere. Nonetheless, the capacity for detection of sounds within this medium is a highly developed sense, which greatly extends our sensory awareness of the environment. The faintest sound detectable by the human ear is a movement of the eardrum equivalent to one-tenth the diameter of a hydrogen atom. The overall range of dynamic sensitivity, from 0 to 140 decibels, is on the order of 100 trillion to one. The human ear can perceive pure tone frequencies from about 20 cycles per second to 20,000 cycles per second. The additional abilities to discriminate, process, and reproduce spectral variations of complex sounds are responsible for perhaps the most distinctive of human adaptations: language. Taste and smell are overlapping senses, and it is commonly said that 90 percent of taste is smell. Yet each does have its separate sensory system. Taste is mediated by receptor cells bundled together in papillae (taste buds) on the surface of the tongue. The most powerful sense appears to be for bitterness, e.g., strychnine concentrations as low as 10^{-6} mole (one micromole) can be detected. As we breathe, each incoming current of air passes over two small sheets of odor-detecting olfactory receptors at the back of the nasal passages. More than ten thousand different odors can be detected. One of the lowest odor thresholds is for mercaptan (which smells like rotten cabbage and is added to odorless natural gas to warn of leaks), detectable at 0.002 parts per million (ppm) or 7×10^{-13} mole.[17]

All Together Now

Children often follow in their parents' footsteps. One place their paths may cross is where they go to college. I have had a growing number of such instances in recent years, as the consequence of teaching at the same institution for more than three decades. A class with several children of former students can take on an uncanny sense of déjà vu. Countless other ways exist to experience the likeness of family members. Some children and parents are strikingly similar in looks and mannerisms, as are many siblings. Other times only limited features are shared. My sister has our father's broad forehead and our mother's hands, whereas I inherited nearly identical versions of his hands and her mouth. My wife shares hardly any of her parents' or sisters' features, yet her height, nose, and eyes are clearly evident in portraits of her grandparents. Photographs from her four-generational family reunions are a complex mosaic of "Where's Waldo?"

But our inheritance goes much deeper than these features of family resemblance. It lies throughout the background of life that Gregory Bateson called "the pattern which connects." Some traces of connection come from Freud's consulting room and his speculations on the origins of human consciousness. Others belong to Jung's indefatigable study of dreams and imaginal explorations in the underground chambers of his Bollingen retreat. Many more may be found in the Cambrian layers of Burgess Shale, on the Pangaean shores, and on the Pleistocene plains. They reside in our bodies and all around us. We are tied to those primal depths by a slender and unbroken thread of DNA—passed on and modified, over and over, from the very beginning. All of life is our family. The overall portrait is a multifaceted composition, which we are only beginning to discern at the juncture of molecular genetics, paleontology, embryology, comparative anatomy, and psychology. Life is not only something to be studied. Ecology is personal. We are swimming in it—and it is swimming in us.

My first step into these depths was a sixth-grade science trip to the American Museum of Natural History. I was immediately captivated, as most children are, by the displays of dinosaur skeletons. A violent-looking tyrannosaurus, with massive jaws and teeth, hovered over its prey in the shadowed hall. Other strange skeletons and plants gave an immediate sense of a different world, most of it long extinct. The ideas of plate tectonics and continental drift were still around the corner of scientific respectability and not yet a part of the display. Yet the exhibits—laid out across Paleozoic, Mesozoic, and Cenozoic eras—nonetheless carried a distinct sense of evolutionary time. The layering of world upon world was inescapable, as was the emergence of recognizable features along the way.

Reading Loren Eiseley's *The Immense Journey* a few years later deepened these feelings. His vivid images and haunting encounters with lost worlds, as in its opening essay "The Slit," left powerful impressions. The emotions were replayed in my explorations of the nearby abandoned Bull Mine. I eagerly anticipated discovering those bands of fossils for myself as

I crept through its subterranean fingers. I had no idea the magnetite ore in the metamorphic Gneiss formations was deposited by some of the first microorganisms capable of photosynthesis—more than a billion years before any form of shelled life. Neither did the pre–Civil War miners who worked the shafts or the ore-roasters and blacksmiths who processed the ore. Most people, I imagine, are still unaware of iron's biogenic sources.

Our high school curriculum scarcely touched on such questions. Nearby outcroppings and roadcuts revealed an educational wonder of prehistory—from brachiopods and trilobites to dinosaur and mastodon remains—as well as some of the earliest evidence of North American human inhabitation following the retreat of the last glacier. Science education in those days, however, was concerned more about outer space than with local knowledge of geology and ecology. Rachel Carson's *The Sea Around Us* helped to raise my awareness to some degree, but that was a solitary experience. My first meaningful educational encounter with paleontology came in college—on a weekend geology field trip to the Arbuckle Mountains in southwestern Oklahoma. The area's exposed strata of Cambrian through Permian rocks are rich in fossils. The original vertical layers, later folded over and worn down, were an easily explored three-hundred-million-year-old, north–south horizontal table. It was in the fossil record there, where I gathered my first understanding of the depths of time.

A tangible sense of geologic time was an integral part of student life at the University of Texas in another way. The Spanish Plateresque architecture of the main campus is a distinctive blend of Gothic and Renaissance elements. Many of the buildings are constructed of Cretaceous limestone, richly textured by Trigonia clamshell indentations. Most also incorporate a variety of other building stones, ranging from the Precambrian through the Pleistocene. In August 2011, while attending the annual meeting of the Ecological Society of America in Austin, I took some time to revisit the paths of my student life. In addition to enlivening personal memories, I also retraced the self-guided campus tour prepared by Samuel P. Ellison, former chairman of the geology department, and his colleague Joseph M. Jones.[18] The combined events were inexpressibly poignant and moving. That morning of reminiscence had the numinous quality of a peak experience, the kind that leaves one feeling deeply fulfilled—and also wanting more.

The border between personal and transpersonal experience is a complex region. It is a territory often filled with spiritual and religious views. Within psychology it was a significant preoccupation of William James, Carl Jung, Abraham Maslow, and many others. But these margins may be seen in other ways as well. There is substantial evidence from psychological studies of personal space that we carry body boundaries of extended space around ourselves. These spatial extensions are not only personal. They may be felt by groups as well—in terms of shared "social" space, communal territories, or even national identities. I can still recall my childhood uneasiness whenever I sensed hunters trespassing on our property, as if the fields were somehow attached to my body. I respond in a bodily way, even now, to a car coming down the driveway or footsteps on the porch.

Holding a pencil in our fingers as a probe to explore a textured surface is another demonstration of sensory extension. We readily have the sensation, when doing so, that we are "feeling" at the distant tip—and not at the point where our fingers actually touch the stylus. This capacity to extend our sensitivities is a common feature of tool use—from manipulating a fork and knife, to finding the "sweet spot" of a tennis racket or the "edge" of downhill skis. The experience also seems to be a part of action at a distance. A well-placed jump shot in basketball "feels" connected to the hoop, as perhaps the squeeze of the trigger does to its target.

The outside/inside line, in other instances, is quite firm. Some people are uncomfortable with subcutaneous injections. The moment of penetration by a needle through the skin can be disconcerting—even nauseating. So is a bleeding wound or the sight of surgery. Anyone who has slaughtered an animal has smelled the curious scent of raw flesh and blood. These things have a sensuality of their own. Freud may not have been mistaken in paying attention, as he did, to the oral, anal, and genital border zones. The passage of things through these nerve-rich orifices can be psychologically charged as well. Despite what was noted above about the body's hollow tubular design, we appear to have strong sensitivities around these thresholds. The anus is an especially emotional zone—not only physically, but also in the peculiarities of how we think or speak of it. Often associated with some form of cursing or offensive humor, it is seldom an area of conversation open to forthright discussion. The traditional way of handling these conflicted feelings has been with mental avoidance—but not without consequence.

Colon cancer is the second leading cause of cancer deaths, even though it has a 90 percent cure rate with early detection by colonoscopy. Many people, however, are embarrassed by the thought and reluctant to take advantage of the simple and painless procedure. In 1998, Katie Couric, cohost of NBC's *Today Show,* lost her husband Jay Monahan at age forty-one to colon cancer. She was left with two daughters and the searing knowledge that his death might have been prevented. Her response to the personal tragedy, in March 2000, was to have a colorectal exam on live national television. The impact was dramatic. The "Katie Couric effect," as it was dubbed by a 2003 study published in the *Archives of Internal Medicine,* was associated with a 20 percent increase in colon cancer screening.[19] Couric's demonstration was an astute unstiffening of a widespread equivocation. In a broader perspective, it was also a significant clue about mental flexibility. How our attitudes are shaped and defended may be more changeable than we realize. A living world surrounds and passes through us. But unless we examine these borders, our predispositions are unlikely to change. Ecological awareness expands the context of life; it also enlarges who we are as a person.

CHAPTER 9

Context

Life is a verb, not a noun.
—Charlotte Perkins Gilman

The interrelated way events occur and are "woven together" is the basis of the word "context." Historians take great pleasure in uncovering the finer points of connection that explain past events. A good historical analysis brings such person-to-person relations to light. Historian David Hackett Fischer calls it finding "big things in small places." The meaning of events relies a great deal on the context in which they occur. Taking a person's actions or words "out of context" (as commonly practiced in negative political ads) is often an intentional maneuver to alter their meaning, which calls forth the need to reestablish their original context. Conversely, careful attention to actual links in the course of events may disclose unforeseen patterns.

In 1967 a young Harvard psychologist named Stanley Milgram conducted a simple experiment. A small packet was given to several hundred randomly selected individuals. Each person was instructed to forward the packet to an unknown "target" person across the country. An additional constraint was added. The package could not be mailed directly to the addressee. He could send it only to someone whom he knew on a first-name basis who he thought was more likely to know the target person than he was. The result was surprising. It took, on average, only six person-to-person contacts to complete the chain. This phenomenon, known as "six degrees of separation," was subsequently popularized in John Guare's 1990 play of the same name—as well as in the movie-buff parlor game "Six Degrees of Kevin Bacon." It has also been widely applied to all manner of human relations—from internet communications to the spread of diseases like AIDS and Asian flu.

What Milgram did, basically, was to highlight the actual chain of connections between individuals that constituted the overall event of his traveling packages. The results of his "small world experiment" were not a discovery. They were a demonstration of contextual analysis in a novel setting. The significance and counterintuitive surprise value of his demonstration was the brevity of network links.

Darwin's idea of natural selection came about by recontextualizing biology. His painstaking focus on small changes of heritability, embedded in an expanded context of time, dramatically altered the meaning of evolution. The central lesson of Rachel Carson's *Silent Spring* was likewise an extension of contextual insights from ecology. Her careful research opened our eyes to a new kind of science and showed that classical notions of simple cause and effect were no longer adequate. Life is more complex than that. It operates through ongoing interactions that organize into webs and chains and pyramids. The links and patterns of living systems function at multiple levels. They take shape as molecules or cells or whole organisms. Individual organisms coalesce as species in coevolved relations that ultimately become the living world as a whole. The earth is replete with compound relations. Outcomes are sometimes dramatic biological eruptions; other times, extinction is the result. The organic decomposes to the inorganic and recycles back again, as biological and human domains combine in distinct ecological story lines.

The story of Clear Lake, California, was one that especially stood out. In 1949 an aerial application of insecticides was made to eradicate an influx of gnats—a nonbiting, but somewhat annoying, relative of the mosquito. The concentration was low, on the order of 1/70 parts per million (ppm). Right after the application, the problem appeared to be eliminated. But a "flareback" in 1954 followed. The concentration this time was increased to 1/50 ppm. A third assault was applied in 1957. During this period, reports began to come in that the western grebe, which wintered on the lake, was disappearing. Careful study of the situation showed that the concentration of pesticide was 5 ppm in the lake's plankton, substantially higher than in the original applications. In the plant-eating fishes it was much higher, and in the fatty tissues of the grebes it had accumulated to an astounding 1,600 ppm. But the grebes were dead. And so too were many other birds, insects, fish, and frogs.

Perhaps an even more poignant example involved the American bald eagle. Farmers were using DDT to control the European corn borer, which was attacking their crops. But the pesticide also found its way into the soil and groundwater, and then into the streams and rivers. As in the Clear Lake story, it was further magnified biologically as it went up the food chain. Increasing concentrations accumulated in algae and plants, in small and then larger fish, and finally in the eagles. At high levels it altered the eagles' physiology, interfering with the uptake of calcium. This resulted in a thinning of the eggshells, which could no longer support incubation and hatching—ending, as we all know, with the eagle on the endangered species list.

These were some of the first lessons of ecology received by the American public. They revealed the multitude of compounding effects—of what were thought to be simple actions—on nontarget species, on human health, and on the environment as a whole. The interactions were often of geometric proportion as biomagnification operated throughout food chains and pyramids. We were discovering the importance of the new science of ecology. The complexity of contextual interactions within the living world was coming into awareness.

Holism

Discovering the threads that constitute actual interactions is an essential means of making sense of the world. But perception of overall patterns of how things are contextually related is equally important. Until that happens, there is no story. In Carson's case, her ecological insights required both collection *and* connection of the dots. There is always some danger, as we know, that holistic interpretations can be misplaced or biased. They may also be subject to the dangers of reification. But nonetheless, without some kind of framing (and often naming) of the contextual patterns of experience, it is nearly impossible to think at all. Understanding the fundamental processes of part/whole relations is the cornerstone of Gestalt psychology. Consciousness, in this tradition, is considered to operate by holistic principles—*gestalt* being the German word for "whole." Mental processes actively organize the elements of perception and thought that shift from confusion into order, define figure against ground, or leap from pattern to pattern. Everyone is familiar with many of the gestalt illusions and creative problem-solving demonstrations. We also know our own sudden "aha" experiences of insight and recognition.

These tendencies to form patterns of mental consistency run throughout the background of the psychology of attitude change, identity formation, stereotyping, and self-deception. The study of subtle contextual influences was a popular theme in the development of social psychology. Many of the field's leaders were students of the Gestalt pioneers forced to leave Nazi Germany and relocate at American universities. They brought a playful spirit to their research, which often explored counterintuitive hypotheses in real-world settings. Bibb Latané was one of them. The impetus for his work on bystander apathy and diffusion of responsibility was based on a celebrated news story. A young woman, Kitty Genovese, had been the victim of a public stabbing and rape in Kew Gardens, New York. The police investigation revealed that numerous people heard her pleas for help or witnessed her plight. Yet it took nearly an hour until help was received. She died in the ambulance on the way to the hospital.

In the aftermath, many explanations were offered—ranging from sociological attributions of urban alienation to notions of pathological overcrowding by animal behaviorists. With a series of carefully designed experiments, Bibb discovered that the likelihood of helping someone in crisis is often influenced by the individual bystander's momentary perception of the social context. Larger numbers of witnesses may actually decrease the likelihood that anyone steps forward to help. This diffusion of responsibility, as he showed, occurs in nonemergency situations as well—such as helping a stranger who drops a handful of pencils in an elevator or a person kneeling in search of a lost contact lens.

During my first year at Ohio State, Bibb and I and several graduate students examined how diffusion of responsibility might also affect restaurant tipping. The actual tipping behavior of diners, gathered in cooperation with several restaurants, showed the same pattern. Single diners gave an average tip of almost 19 percent of their bill. In two-party groups it dropped to about 15 percent and continued down to 13 percent for five- and six-person parties. The study was reported in the *Wall Street Journal, Psychology Today,* and other magazines—and is still cited in support of the now-customary practice of setting a fixed service charge for parties of six or more.

Many forms of momentary or edge-of-awareness contextual influences have been demonstrated in other situations. Sometimes, as Latané's altruism studies showed, the social situation influences individual conduct. Other times the pattern is reversed and the social context is a creation of individual actions. In my second year at Ohio State I was asked to team-teach the fall introductory psychology class. As I entered the auditorium on the first day, and stepped up to the podium, several hundred students were sitting in the floor-level seats. A hundred or more filled the balcony. In addition to the enormity of the audience, I was immediately struck by something else. The hall was a red sea of OSU apparel and other colorful markers that resembled a nineteenth-century neo-impressionist composition. It was the Woody Hayes era of Buckeyes football, and the student body was clearly geared up for a big season. My coteacher, Bob Cialdini, had a similar response. After class, Bob and I decided to explore the situation and telephoned our colleagues teaching introductory psychology at several other large universities. Throughout the fall semester all of us recorded the daily pattern of clothing and color markers in our lecture halls. Lo and behold, students' identification with their university colors rose and fell significantly, based on whether their football team had won or lost the preceding weekend.

We did several other "basking in reflected glory" studies. One of the most intriguing findings came from a telephone survey. A random sample of students was called and asked a series of factually oriented questions about campus life. The final question—"How did the football team do last weekend?"—invoked a significant difference in students' responses. When their team had been victorious, the dominant reply was: "We won." If the team was defeated, it was more commonly: "*They* lost." Moreover, the highest level of *we* responding was by students who believed they had done poorly on the preceding questions. This may seem a somewhat elaborate way to illustrate a contextual relation between attitudes and actions. Nonetheless, it clearly demonstrated the subtle tendency to self-identify with positive features of daily life and distance oneself from negative ones.

This propensity of egocentric bias—in how people skew what happens to them and remember things—has been extensively documented by social psychologist Tony Greenwald. Greenwald offers a new term, "beneffectance," to describe what he sees as a universal (and quite normal) readiness by people to take credit for success, while denying responsibility for failure. He coined the expression to downplay the simplistic and negative connotations of alternative terms, such as "egotistic" or "self-serving"—and to also convey a more complex motivational process. The word, as he explains, "is a compound of beneficence (achieving desirable outcomes) and effectance (motivation to act competently)."[1] Lest we dismiss Greenwald's neologism as a further buildup of psychobabble, I offer a more prosaic version voiced one afternoon by my friend, and former vice president of development at COA, Dallas Darland. "Every successful grant," he noted, "has a hundred parents; every failed proposal is a orphan."

College of the Atlantic is too small for intercollegiate sports and has nothing like the weekend culture of big universities. Yet the dialectics of holistic perception and thinking are easily explored in the classroom. It may begin with the simple query to my students about their home state. For instance, I might ask: "If you had to divide your state in half, where is the dividing line?" There is seldom much indecision. Most students readily come up with either a north/south or east/west division. New York is typically split between upstate and downstate. California is also usually divided into northern and southern sections. For Pennsylvania, Massachusetts, Colorado, and Washington State, an eastern versus western partitioning is more common. Some states go either way. Maine can be coastal versus inland or northern versus southern (as often happens to New Jersey)—but sometimes it is divided between western and "down east." "What are the differences?" Again there is no hesitation, as the students cheerily make attributions about the people, the landscapes, the politics, and even the musical and food preferences of each region. "What about this state compared to that state? the two halves of your hometown? this year's incoming class and the students of the previous year?" Even the island on which the college is located has a clear line between its eastside towns of Bar Harbor and Northeast Harbor and the "backside" villages of Southwest Harbor and Bass Harbor.

The list goes on, but the point is that the basic processes of global categorization are regularly used and readily demonstrated. Of course, some differences really do exist between the various alternatives and give a preliminary basis for the ensuing opinions. But at the same time a lumping together of qualities is also going on, which is almost always woven throughout with evaluative distinctions. This kind of holistic thinking tends to take on dialectical characteristics of this-versus-that, now-and-then, here-or-there, etc. Each "thing" usually can be named and is often judged as more or less preferable to other related things. In psychology, these things-of-mind are formally referred to as attitudes. An attitude, in its broad sense, is a hypothetical construct. The concept is generally regarded as a tripartite combination of cognitive (i.e., knowledge, thoughts, and beliefs), affective (feelings, judgments, and preferences), and behavioral (intentional or action-oriented) components. An attitudinal object may be concrete, like one's attitude toward broccoli, snakes, or Elvis—or abstract, such as cultural diversity, free trade, or justice.

The notion of attitudes, as a way of representing intrapsychic processes, has a long history in psychology. The appeal to psychologists is its components all have some degree of empirical grounding. A person can usually report how much she likes or dislikes an attitude object in a measurable way. Affective judgments and emotional responses can often be gauged by physiological reactions as well. Knowledge and beliefs about an attitude's domain also can be assessed—as can an individual's actual behavior and behavioral intentions. Attitude measurement techniques and theories of attitudinal change are pervasive and widely utilized in organizational management, human relations, advertising, and politics.

In many ways, our attitudes—in the full sense of the term—constitute the internal context of our minds. The attitudes we hold may be reflections and constructions of our external world. But we also have the capacity to reflect upon them, revise them, and thereby change our relationship toward the world. Viktor Frankl once asserted that a person's attitude is "the last of human freedoms." What he intended by that was, no matter how distressing reality may be, we always have the freedom "to choose" our attitude about life—even in the worst of circumstances. He knew this well, from three years of imprisonment in Nazi concentration camps, and later from his therapeutic work with survivors—like himself—whose entire families had been exterminated. Psychological recovery and rediscovery of a meaningful life after such suffering is authentic evidence of psychological healing. It is little wonder that *Man's Search for Meaning*, which relates these lessons, has been translated into forty languages and read by countless millions.

The Things of Life

The word "thing"—like gestalt—also has Germanic language roots. Its original meaning was not at all concrete in the way we commonly use it now. But rather, it was a loosely defined social term that referred to "an assembly." Contemporary Icelandic, ever faithful to Old Norse language traditions, still uses it this way. For Icelanders, a thing (spelled *þing* and pronounced the same way) is a group of people. A big group is an all-thing (*alþing*), which is also the name of Iceland's parliament—the world's longest-standing democratic body. *Þingvellir* is the open-air plains where the parliament met from 930 to 1798, after which it was transferred to Reykjavik.

One might then ask, as Stan Milgram did on another occasion, "At what point does a loose aggregation of individuals become a thing?" This question is very much in the Gestalt tradition of a contextually defined perception. For his experiment, he used the childish trick we all played on one another—of looking up at the ceiling until our unwitting victim did the same, after which we mockingly chanted:

> I made you look, you dirty crook,
> I stole your mother's pocketbook.
> I turned it in, I turned it out, I turned it into sauerkraut.

He didn't do the chanting bit, but he did use the trick part. On a busy Manhattan street corner, one of Milgram's students was instructed to stand still for sixty seconds and stare up at a sixth-floor window. Behind the window a concealed movie camera recorded the responses of passersby. The simple experiment was repeated with increasing numbers of gazers in the initial group. Each time, the number of pedestrians who looked up or who stopped to join the group of experimenters was recorded. When a single person was the stimulus, about a fifth of the passersby glanced up and only 4 percent actually stopped. A five-person group received considerably more attention—with more than 75 percent looking skyward, a fourth of which also joined the "stimulus group" in a prolonged scrutiny. When the target group had fifteen members, 40 percent of passersby stopped to join in and nearly everyone along the street imitated its upward gaze. At this point even automobile traffic in the street was disrupted, putting an end to Milgram's little field experiment.

The point of the study was to show the additional social influence that comes when individuals are identified as a group. In this case the group effect was a combination of the number of gazers and their proximity. If the initial stimulus group members were more broadly scattered along the street, their group-ness was less apparent. On the other hand, as subsequent studies have shown, their impact can be restored if they share some distinctive feature in common—even when they are not close together. For example, the drive from Bar Harbor to the regional airport in Bangor takes about an hour. I am often in a hurry and lost in my thoughts. When I spot a police car along the way, I am momentarily cautious of my speed. If I encounter several, however, my mind usually jumps to a different interpretation, i.e., "The police are out tonight!" This may or may not actually be true, but I nonetheless conscientiously maintain the legal speed all the way. These cues sometimes appear in the behavior of other drivers, who seem to have come to a similar conclusion.

The rapid spreading of attitudes and behaviors is known as "psychological contagion." The phenomenon can take many forms, from the irrational frenzy of mob behavior and "viral" internet communication to copycat murder and suicide. The pervasive nature of precipitous events has been illustrated in popular books like Malcolm Gladwell's *The Tipping Point* and James Surowiecki's *The Wisdom of Crowds*. Not all of the examples they document are psychological ones, though many are. At the core of those that are, we can frequently see the basic Gestalt principle of *prägnanz* at work. The word is a German term meaning "good figure"—or, more generally, the "law of simplicity." The law holds that in searching for a solution to a puzzling perception, the mind tends to reach for the best-fitting, simple solution. In mathematics it is called elegance, in philosophy, parsimony. It is the stuff of which theories are made. In everyday life it is a primary tool of decision making. As soon as we come up with a "good-enough" answer, our momentary curiosity or confusion is eased and we can proceed—usually with some sort of explanation.

The processes of "bringing our mind to rest," in playful ways, are exemplified in popular parlor games like charades and twenty questions. Perhaps the preeminent example of this kind of mental exercise was the 1960s and 1970s TV show *Password*. The game was played between two teams, each composed of one celebrity player and one regular contestant. The correct answer (the password) was given to one player on each team and shown to the studio and TV audience. The other member of each team attempted to guess the word, based on one-word clues from his partner. In 2008 an updated version of the show—*Million Dollar Password*—hosted by Regis Philbin, set an all-time record for prime-time television viewers.

Aside from the game show's popularity as entertainment, it was also a window to the art of guessing. (I confess—I was one of the viewers.) Knowing the correct password made it possible for the viewer to identify with both contestants—but especially with the one giving the clues. How the two team players interacted was instructive. The pathway leading to the answer frequently followed a strategy of associative similarity, though not always. And this, I think, is noteworthy. Attending to the complementarities—of dialectical meaning or what may be notably absent—led to other ways to a solution. In the *Password* game there was a known answer. In many cases in life, however, there is not, and we are just seeking to arrive at *any* answer. Getting to a satisfying closure (to stress my point for a moment further) may require "subtractive" attention—of what must be removed, is missing, or begs to be imagined. This is how artists use negative space, when musicians play with silence, what Steve Jobs meant by death as a creative process, and the way apoptosis (programmed cell death) was discovered. At a more fundamental level, this is also the contextual "possibility space" of coevolution, symbiosis, ecological niches, and creative imagination. The subtle relationships of an object, its context, and our experience are skillfully captured in this poem by Emily Dickinson:

> Occasionally rides–
> You may have met Him–
> did you not
> His notice sudden is–
>
> The Grass divides as with a Comb–
> A spotted shaft is seen–
> And then it closes at your feet
> And opens further on–
>
> He likes a Boggy Acre
> A Floor too cool for Corn–
> Yet when a Boy, and Barefoot–
> I more than once at Noon

Have passed, I thought, a Whip lash
Unbraiding in the Sun
When stooping to secure it
It wrinkled, and was gone—

Several of Nature's People
I know, and they know me—
I feel for them a transport
Of cordiality—

But never met this Fellow
Attended, or alone
Without a tighter breathing
And Zero at the Bone—

The poem's title is "A Narrow Fellow in the Grass."[2] It is clearly about a snake. Yet nowhere in the lines or title does Dickinson directly say so. The context alone infers its object. We can almost see the snake. Perhaps we do—a figure conjured from the background, brought into being by the poet's art.

Sometimes nothing is there. Like Frost's "road not taken," the haunting possibilities of imagination are all that make him pause. Familiar strangers, whose voices we never hear and names we do not know, fill our daily lives. These people are without a context. They are real, but in a vacuum—figures on a blank canvas for our fantasies to invent their stories. Other times, our mind is blind except to what it seeks. The context may be real, but what is seen is otherwise. This was the case on a crisp afternoon in November 1988. Karen Wood had just slipped on her white mittens and stepped off the porch of her Treadwell Acres home in a small subdivision near Bangor, Maine. Moments later, as she crossed her yard, she was shot. The hunter was less than two hundred feet away. He shot again; she was hit a second time. It was buck season, which requires not only the clear identification of a deer, but a deer *with antlers*. The hunter's bolt-action, .30-06 rifle had a scope. The man was Donald Rogerson, an experienced hunter, a local Boy Scout leader, and produce manager of a

Bangor supermarket—where he had recently been named employee of the year.

After his second shot, Rogerson hurried toward his target, discovering, to his horror, Wood's crumpled body. She was still breathing—barely—as he attempted to stop the bleeding, while his hunting partner ran to a neighbor's house for help. Karen died before the ambulance arrived. Rogerson was distraught and overwhelmed. He never denied pulling the trigger, reloading, and firing a second shot. He was arrested and booked on charges of manslaughter. His defense took a curious stand. Rogerson swore there was a deer in his sights and he had twice seen its distinctive white tail. Extensive forensic examination of the site showed no tracks, no droppings, no fur, no evidence whatsoever that a deer had been in the area. It was Rogerson's imagination against Karen's dead body. When the case was presented to a grand jury the following month, they declined to indict Rogerson—in a truly fantastic display of justice. Emily Dickinson stirred the context of our imagination and invoked a mental snake. Donald Rogerson had a deer in his mind and turned a pair of mittens into a killing field.

Going Home

In Chapter 1, I outlined a chronology of turning points in my life. But time is not a rigid rail. Life's moments slip by so smoothly we barely feel them pass. Until, in a sudden surprise, they fold around and prove the past is never far away. "Time," Thoreau once mused, "is but the stream I go a-fishing in."[3] He knew how a tugging on the line fractures tranquility and awakens us to the past. I have felt the pull, as a distant memory surfaces, and on the other end my father meets me once again. One of the most powerful moments of our relationship occurred in the second year of high school, a few months after my sister left for college. We were having breakfast when my father suddenly lost color and slumped forward on the table. My mother rushed to call for an ambulance. As we huddled together, my school bus arrived. My mother consoled me that help was on the way and in a calm voice ushered me to the door. Not long after getting on the bus, an ambulance sped past us toward my home with sirens screaming and lights flashing. My anguish was immeasurable. At every moment that day I sat in anxious anticipation of being called from class by the public-address system or the principal's appearance at the door. Neither happened. Instead, I took the bus home. As I climbed the porch steps, filled with dread and hope, my mother met me at the door. He was alive. It was a heart attack. She had just returned from the hospital. Without delay we got into the car and went to see him.

Like most children, I saw my father as a vital force in life—talented, caring, and invincible. But in a flash, my sense of security was shattered. When we entered the hospital room, I immediately saw that he too was transformed. He greeted me with a reassuring smile followed by an awkward attempt at humor. I had never before seen any signs of fear in my father's face. But I could detect an uncharacteristic trace of vulnerability in his eyes—an unsettling mix of apprehension, mortality, and embarrassment.

The hospital released him a few days later. He was put on a restrictive diet and cautioned about other lifestyle changes. Following a brief recovery period, he resumed a normal schedule of commuting and weekend home projects. Nonetheless, everyone remained alert thereafter to the dangers that prowled at the edges of consciousness. The apprehension of sudden heartache forever altered the context of my personal life. After I left home for college, it took on a peculiar form. The chance ringing of a telephone, especially late at night, often set my heart pounding. Presumably it was the most likely way the news would be received. The trepidation was twofold. It was tied, on the one hand, to the hole in my life from his absence. On the other hand, I was equally frightened of being engulfed and torn asunder myself.

When I finished college, he retired from his long engineering career and settled into a comfortable retirement with my mother. But the sound of the telephone was still an unwelcome intrusion throughout and after graduate school. I somehow carried a Pavlovianesque expectation of conditioned alarm. My fear turned out to be unfounded. He did not die from a sudden, second heart attack. Moreover, the news was received in person and not by a long-dreaded midnight phone call. His death came as the end of a slow decline, the week before Christmas break during my first year at Purdue.

I was not there when he died. We had spent some good time together the previous summer. His health was poor, but his mind was clear. I suspect he knew the end was near, as we retraced the outlines of his early life—just the two of us. Bouncing along the back roads of upstate New York in my VW bus, we stopped here and there for him to reminisce and tell stories from his remembered past. We went to old churchyards and tiny, isolated cemeteries. Amid the overgrown plots, he pointed out barely recognizable headstones from our family history. At one point he asked me to pull off the road near the top of a barren and windswept hill. As we walked through knee-deep grass, with no buildings in sight, he recounted a lost but not forgotten place. It was where his one-room school once stood. He outlined the shape of other structures with his finger. All were gone without a trace. The landscape of his memory was all that remained. My heart swelled into my throat as he shared his recollections. I sensed the complex feelings of reawakened memories and the sadness of time's erasure. In a final gesture he turned toward the old school yard and pointed to where the well and hand-pump had been. We walked to the spot. The stone rim of the old well was still there. It was—for both of us—the only enduring validation of our shared experience.

The sun was low as we climbed into the minivan. I don't recall any further conversation as we turned toward home. But before we departed from the Schoharie Valley, he asked to make one final detour. He directed me down a winding road to the tiny village of Burtonsville. Several members of my extended family had lived there for generations. As we approached the driveway of a large white farmhouse, he asked me to slow down. "Turn in here," he said. We sat for a few moments before he opened the door and slowly slipped down from his seat. Almost at once a sprightly older woman popped from the kitchen door. "Oh Warren*" she shrieked and

---

*Most people knew him by his first name; only our family and a few of his closest friends ever used his middle name.

dashed up to my father. They hugged and did a bit of tiny dance. All of it was a mystery to me. He introduced me. We had a brief exchange. But this was obviously a special moment for them, so I excused myself. They sat together on the porch in spirited conversation while I waited in the van. When he returned, the solemnity from our previous stops had vanished. "Who was that?" I asked. "Someone from long ago," he replied—and softly added, "There's no need to mention this to your mother."*

I treasure those final summer days together. I wish there had been more. What we did share, however, were lasting insights into the context of his life. An even fuller appreciation of contextual meaning followed a few months later. He was already at the funeral home by the time I arrived at home in December. After the family gathering, I asked to be left alone with him. He appeared quite familiar from a distance, as if asleep. But up close, I could barely recognize the vigorous man who was so much a part of my life. I had never before viewed an open casket. The frozen expression of his face was foreign. I touched him—his arm, his shoulder, his face—all were like wood. I tried to speak. In the emptiness of the room, my voice felt hollow as I whispered a few final words. The numbness of his body entered my own as I turned to leave.

The days that followed were full of challenges. My mother needed assistance in making arrangements, with household matters, and in adjusting to life alone. I knew my responsibilities. But all was an existential encounter. Every inch of my childhood home had been fashioned by my father. Everything echoed of his being. It was not easy to overcome a desire to leave things as they were. There was much sadness in pushing through this veil. The tools and papers, which last he touched, overflowed with a sense of reverence.

I gradually shed my emotional paralysis. When it was time to return to Indiana, things were pretty much in order. Before leaving, I asked my

---

*Actually, years later, I did. "I know," she smiled. "He told me." The woman was an old girlfriend. She and my father had played music together when they were young. Had he decided to stay home on the farm, she might well have been his life partner. But instead he chose the big city. She married a local man, had a family, and was now a widow. As far as I know, it was the only time they had seen each other in half a century.

mother if I might have his fiddle. "Of course," she said. I had a strong inclination toward music, which began in grade school with baritone horn lessons (which I hated). It later reemerged with the Beatles. I had played guitar in a small rock and roll band during college and was beginning to experiment with folk and old-time music. My father's musical abilities were far beyond my own. When I was a child, his renditions of "Pop! Goes the Weasel," with its E-string punctuation—and "*William Tell* Overture" (*The Lone Ranger* theme song)—put me into a frenzy. Suddenly, the thought of playing the fiddle, his fiddle, became a stellar goal. I threw myself into the task.

Dad was dead. But he was not buried. His gravesite at our upstate family plot was frozen solid. In the meantime, his body was placed in the nearby crypt. Interment was scheduled to fit my spring break. That summer I went to the Indiana Old Time Fiddler's Gathering in the small town of Battleground (the site of William Henry Harrison's famous 1811 Tippecanoe siege), a half dozen miles north of Purdue along the Wabash River. Those four days of fiddling were hypnotic for me. By year's end, I moved to a small house directly beside the historic park where the annual event was held. My home became a weekend center for local musicians. Four of us formed a string band that later performed on the stage across the street and recorded an album of our favorite tunes.

Meanwhile, back in New York, my mother was increasingly overwhelmed by the burdens of maintaining our family home. Joan and I lived too far away to give the assistance she needed. The time had come for it to be sold. The change happened quickly. My mother moved to an apartment a few miles from my sister's family, where she became an active grandmother and began a new chapter in her life. I was happy to see her spirit rebound. I was also deeply saddened by a sense of emptiness at the loss of my childhood home. Almost at once, I found myself filled with a growing urge to move back to the northeast, to reconnect with rural life and begin my own family. My romance with traditional music had been rooted in these feelings, but now—it was not enough. I moved to Maine the following year.

In January 1980, on a research trip to Reykjavik, I was invited to attend the premier showing of Iceland's first full-length professional film, *Land og Synir* (Land and Sons). The film, based on a novel by Indriði Þorsteinsson, depicts a father and son living together in the late 1930s in a remote northern valley. They are struggling to maintain their farm in the face of debt, a crippling sheep disease, and the father's failing health. The son urges his father to sell the land and move to the city, but he refuses to surrender his heritage and ties with the land. When he dies, the son abandons his father's goals, refuses the aid of neighbors, and deserts the girl he planned to marry. He sells the farm and, like many others at the time, joins the stream of families rushing toward the city. When the movie concluded and the lights came up, I looked around. The entire theater was in tears. So was I. It was everyone's story.

In 1880, Iceland was 95 percent rural. By 1980, it was 90 percent urban—with two-thirds of all Icelanders in Reykjavik. Most Americans also lived on farms in 1880. There were more than four million farms in the United States; more than a quarter million of them were in New York State—only Illinois and Ohio had (slightly) more. The year my father was born, the number of farms topped six million. The decline has been staggering. New York State has barely a tenth of the number of working farms it once had. In the 1880s, New York City was the largest market for milk in the country. Two-thirds of its supply came from Orange County, where I grew up. Dairy farming was still a prevalent lifestyle in the 1950s. The school bus Joan and I took each day passed by three creameries on its daily route and dozens of farms with pastures full of Holstein, Jersey, and Guernsey cows.

Not long ago, the time arrived for Joan's fiftieth high school reunion. She asked me to join her, but I was unable to get away. Her daughter went along instead and they had a wonderful time. Joan and I did meet up the following weekend, however, and made a road-trip review—back through our lives together—to our home, down familiar back roads, and once again around our old school bus route. It was a touching journey. Many things had changed. The look and landscape of our house was so different, it caused no pain to pause and talk about our thoughts. My heart sank, though, when I spied my favorite hemlock through the trees, broken off halfway up and dead. We stopped along the road beside old, familiar places—as if to test our memories and linger in the past. We went to see the railroad station where our father came and went. The tracks were gone, along with many other features of the town. Our trip around the school bus route was a sobering ride. Where friends had lived, we mostly saw overgrown fields and drab remains of once-loved farms. Our school still looked the same, as did the small-town library where Joan had worked for years. But when we went inside, no trace of people from the past was there—and though the smell was quite familiar, we felt like strangers in a dream. We had a quiet afternoon meal in the village tavern and made no mention of our history to the owner.

We drove from there directly back to Joan's home. Arriving late that evening, our adventure concluded by depositing saliva samples in small glass vials, which were sent to the National Geographic Society's Genographic Project the next day. Hers traced our mother's mitochondrial DNA, mine, our father's Y-chromosomal DNA. When the results came back a few weeks later, we called each other. Each line began, of course, in Africa and weaved its way from there. Our father's went toward central Asia, east of the Caspian, then wrapped around through Europe, France, and England. Our mother's trail was straighter, ending much the same. These were tiny samples of our genes. But they fit quite nicely with Joan's years of genealogical study. Up against the magic and melancholy of the dissolving background from our road trip, we shared a novel gift. It was a stitch—a tiny thread of us, our parents, and family tree—to the context of all life.

CHAPTER 10

Metaphor and Meaning

The greatest thing by far is to be master of metaphor.
—Aristotle

Metaphor is right at the bottom of being alive.
—Gregory Bateson

Metaphors are common features of language and thought. At the level of language, metaphor represents a particular type of linguistic expression and communication. It is the act of describing one thing in terms of another word or phrase. The transference of meaning from one source to a dissimilar target is one of the most creative aspects of language.

The complexity of metaphorical expression is what makes attaining fluency in a language so difficult. Anyone who learns a new language soon discovers the limits of a bilingual dictionary. Dictionary definitions rely on literal meanings, or what is commonly known as denotative language. In a standard pocket dictionary, the Spanish word *culebra* translates as "snake." For someone learning English, however, the statement "My neighbor is a snake" may be confusing. That is because many words carry additional connotative meanings. A better dictionary may help to clarify by adding some of the connotations, e.g., "a treacherous person." Or it may create confusion with "a flexible metal wire used for cleaning drains."

When used as a verb, snake conveys additional meanings, as in "to drag or pull lengthwise" or "to coil."

Whenever words are used in ways that go beyond their literal meaning, we are employing figurative language. The most common figures of speech are simile, analogy, and metaphor. These linguistic devices are used to convey resemblances, to make comparisons, or as a way of saying something beyond the literal meaning of the words. Simile takes the characteristic form of relating *a* to *b*, expressed by the use of "like" or "as": "He worked like a dog"; "My sandwich was as hard as a rock." Analogy is usually a four-part comparison in which a relationship between *a* and *b* resembles that of *c* and *d*. The retina of the eye, for example, may be considered analogous to film in a camera.

Metaphors are similar to similes. In a simile, *a* is "like" *b*. In metaphor, *a* "stands for" *b*. In the place of a simile's "like" or "as," a metaphor compares things using the verb "to be." Instead of saying, "His lawyer is *like* a shark," a more forceful and suggestive comparison is made by metaphor with "His lawyer *is* a shark."*

Mastery of colloquial metaphors and idiomatic terminology requires extensive experience within a language community. It is estimated that there are some 160,000 memorized items available for use in American English.[1] Of these, about half are words and half are fixed expressions (idioms). These multiword colloquial phrases are as much a part of the lexicon as single words. The nonlogical nature of "kicking the bucket" or "crying over spilled milk" and their metaphorical extension is a significant aspect of communication.

The traditional account of how people use and understand figurative language holds that it derives from literal language and is more complex. If this is so, literal meanings should be more easily and rapidly understood

---

*It may be interesting here to note a major distinction about communion in Christianity. The Roman Catholic Church considers the bread and wine of the Eucharist as the literal body and blood of Christ (through transubstantiation), whereas Protestants usually take the sacrament as a symbol of Christ's body and blood (i.e., metaphorically). In my Sunday school days, our Congregational church was even more relaxed about it. They replaced the wine with grape juice, thereby making it a metaphor of a metaphor.

than metaphors. But the research by Princeton's Sam Glucksberg reveals something quite different. The nominal term "shark" may be used both as a literal referent for a marine animal and as a metaphor for any vicious and predatory being, as in "His lawyer is a shark." Yet the term's meaning as a general attributive category is as readily comprehended as when it is a literal referent. The vehicle of meaning (shark) appears to be processed at both levels of abstraction. Glucksberg puts forth a new "dual-reference" theory of language comprehension. When metaphoricity is conveyed, it is directly understood via a superordinate category. Predicative (verbal) terms such as "I *flew* home" and idiomatic phrases like "He had an albatross around his neck" also operate with dual-reference capabilities. Glucksberg sums it up this way: "Metaphor comprehension can be as easy as literal … they [metaphors] are generally understood directly as categorical assertions."[2]

At a more general level, metaphor is clearly a widespread form of symbolic representation for linking two conceptual domains. Aristotle's appreciation of metaphorical thinking was clear: "Midway between the unintelligible and the commonplace, it is a metaphor which most produces knowledge."[3] Goethe went further, declaring: "Everything is metaphor." That may be further than I can go. But I can go along with Mary Catherine Bateson, i.e., "You can't think without metaphors."

Ecology and Mind

Glucksberg's research sheds valuable light on the understanding of understanding. The central implication of his dual-reference theory is that we possess two quite different kinds of comprehension. Although deeply interrelated in normal experience, it is possible to emphasize each mode more or less separately. This division of cognitive styles defines the juncture between C. P. Snow's two cultures of science and art.

The traditions of science have emphasized a language of rigorous precision. The hard language of logic and mathematics, the purest of denotative languages, is the preferred expression of scientific goals of prediction, understanding, and the control of variables. The ideal form of this precision is best characterized perhaps by the equal sign. Demonstration of a tautological relation, at the end of a complex deductive formulation, was classically accompanied by the celebratory QED—from the Latin phrase *quod erat demonstrandum:* "what was to have been demonstrated."*

Figurative language is most often associated with poetry and creative literature, which find their strength through connotative devices. These nonliteral features of expression reveal the inherently poetic nature of mind. In contrast to our capacity for the "cold" cognition of pure logic, these "affect-laden" associations rely on the "partial" tautology of connotative relations. This is the psycho-logic realm where reason, feelings, and imagination are fused. It is also the indispensable arena of interdisciplinary thought and practice.

Despite a preference for logical analysis, science also has a long history of theoretical advancement based on analogical attribution. Johannes Kepler likened planetary motion and the "rhythm of the spheres" to familiar patterns derived from musical theory and harmony. Isaac Newton extended the classical mechanics of earthly objects onto celestial bodies to obtain his universal natural laws of gravitation and motion. Antoine Lavoisier's discovery of oxygen and chemical combustion served as the basis of his biology of animal respiration. The biological structures of cells, tissues, and organs supplied the conceptual framework for Auguste Comte's science of sociology—a field he both launched and named. Adam Smith imagined an "invisible hand" guiding market economies. For Darwin, life was "netted together" in the shape of a tree, whereas Einstein saw quantum physics as "rolling dice." These novel mappings of one known domain onto another led to extensive research and hypothesis testing. But the initial leaps resemble a poetic mind much more than acts of careful logic or empirical analysis.

---

*Most scientists no longer attempt to define theoretical concepts in terms of intrinsic essence. Instead, concept definitions are communicated by operationalizing the procedures of empirical measurement. The Nobel Prize–winning physicist Percy W. Bridgeman introduced this system of "operational definition"—based on publicly observable and repeatable methods—in the early 1900s. Its widespread use is evident in the standard practice of including a detailed "methods" section in scientific research publications.

Ernst Haeckel's choice of the Greek word for home (*oikos*)—in his coinage of the word "ecology"—was a similar metaphoric invention. His intention was to open the door to a new kind of science. The richness of the root term became an invitation to a wealth of connotations as well. For a while their various meanings remained within the borders of science. In time, however, the initial scientific demarcation of ecology would encounter human relations within the living world. As an applied science, ecology invoked inevitable questions of human decision making. The circle enlarged further as adjacent academic and applied fields began to use ecological concepts throughout their respective domains. Ecology was no longer able to remain as either a self-contained science or an aspect of separate fields of human studies. Humans were being seen as part of an ecological world, and conversely, ecology's interdisciplinary approaches were becoming a part of human consciousness. The cultural divide of C. P. Snow's lamentation was turning inside out. It was, for some ecologists, a significant loss to interdisciplinary science—and a messy intrusion to the clarity of their field. A few embraced it wholeheartedly as a stimulus heralding a far larger point of view.

Gregory Bateson was among the foremost of these figures. His *Steps to an Ecology of Mind* and *Mind and Nature* were monumental attempts to bridge the chasm between the mental and the environmental. Bateson's ideas are not easy to follow. They are simultaneously brilliant, elusive, and—as his students sometimes decried—maddening. I cannot say that I really understand them. Yet every time I try, I always come away with a richer appreciation of his attempts to elucidate the patterns of life. In broad strokes, it seems to me that he was trying to show some basic resemblances between the inner and outer worlds.

Epistemology, for Bateson, was not a minor branch of philosophy. He used the term in a much broader sense, as a "knowing how" to make connections common within all living things. A plant knows how to be a plant—in its own sort of way. Though not conscious of its epistemology, as we might epistemologically know how to do something, plants nonetheless carry within themselves an embedded knowledge-ability.

Bateson was not concerned with the specific features botanists used to classify a particular plant. Although he knew them, his way of looking at an organism was more similar to what Goethe had done in his 1790 *Metamorphosis of Plants*. Like Goethe, Bateson went beyond normal scientific thinking. He wanted to penetrate the living sphere of creative morphology and expose the internal language of biological epistemology. This biological language, of how an organism's parts are held together and develop, was at the core of how the world fits together for Bateson. He was not satisfied with explanations in terms of anatomical, physiological, or taxonomic definitions of what an organism is. Instead, he was seeking to comprehend how individual life-forms develop, how they change, and ultimately, the pattern through which all living creatures are connected. From his perspective, evolution was an ongoing process (like learning). And to understand it, according to Bateson, we must learn to think in terms of contextual relations.

Bateson's ideas are not explicitly tied together in a formal theory. His intertwined arguments were presented as a collection of intellectual anecdotes and parables. Each vignette was a heuristic step on the long, circular stairway of speculation. His examples touched every level—from embryology and ecology to anthropology, education, and poetry. Yet these often-convoluted meanderings seldom strayed from an emphasis on shapes, forms, and relations.

As a teacher, Bateson had an uncanny talent for moving from straightforward examples to staggering complexities in a few short steps. The rhythmic pattern of forms within a crab's body, for instance, was a comfortable first-order demonstration of repetitive, serial homology. Upper-limb structures were repeated down the line through middle- and fore-limb patterns. One side resembled the other in bilateral symmetries. This quickly led to consideration of second-order homologies, between two species, as in the comparison of a crab and a lobster (or perhaps a horse and a person). And then, Bateson would challenge his students to consider a third-order comparison—of the meta-relationship between crab/lobster *relations* and horse/human *relations*.

The relationship of relationships is the epitome of abstract analogical thinking. Third-order abstractions of this variety, in human minds, are called "ideas." In Bateson's view they were everywhere in the living world. The subtitle of his final book, *Mind and Nature: A Necessary Unity*, was an unequivocal declaration of his post-Cartesian position. "The pattern which connects," as he fondly put it, referred to the deep, contextual meta-pattern of connection of all living creatures in time and space. The language of living things—individually and together—resembles *a story*, another of Bateson's foundational metaphors. The simplest of organisms possess underlying mindlike features and prototypic resemblances of thought. Evolution as a whole is a vast grammatical interplay of life stories and novel biological epistemologies. Science reveals part of the story. But a fuller appreciation needs the combined skills of the musician, poet, artist, and shaman. That, I believe, is what Bateson was trying to achieve.

One way to grasp Bateson's position is to look at the ways that human thinking relies on processes of storylike patterns. But even here, he was skeptical about our rational bias for explaining life, rather than discovering how to experience it. At the heart of this confusion is something we encountered above in our comparison of denotative and connotative modes of meaning. Namely: the problem of different kinds of mind. Bateson illustrated the problem by comparing two types of syllogism. The first form, from classical logic, goes like this:

> Humans die;
> Socrates is human;
> Socrates will die.

The conclusion is reached deductively from the first (major) premise and the second (minor) premise. The basic structure of this logical tool is built upon classification. The predicate ("will die") is attached to Socrates by identifying him as a member of a class whose members share in that predication. Despite its honored role at the core of logical reasoning, Bateson maintained that this logical device is of little use in understanding how mind actually works. He does this by comparing it with a quite different form of syllogism:

> Grass dies;
> Humans die;
> Humans are grass.

METAPHOR AND MEANING

The logical error here is known as affirming the consequent. But the "syllogism in grass," as Bateson called it, is the very basis of metaphoric relationships. Consider Walt Whitman:

> I bequeathe myself to the dirt, to grow from the grass I love.
> If you want me again, look for me under your boot-soles.[4]

[margin note: Is it bad logic? We die, we enter the ground, our materials are reorganized.]

Whitman's thoughts may be bad logic, but they are good poetry. That is precisely what Bateson wanted us to realize. Metaphors are lateral extensions. They are not logical deductions. Nor are they examples of enumerative induction. They constitute an entirely different type of thought, known as abduction (a notion he got from C. S. Peirce), and they are enormously widespread.

According to Bateson, "to fight all syllogisms in grass would be silly.... These syllogisms are the very stuff of which natural history is made. When we look for regularities in the biological world, we meet them all the time." This is Bateson's real jumping-off point. Metaphors are a universal feature of life's connection to life, essential for understanding the unity of ecology and mind from his point of view. "Metaphor, dream, parable, allegory, the whole of art, the whole of science, the whole of religion, the whole of poetry, totemism ... the organization of acts in comparative anatomy—all these are instances of abduction."[5]

Bateson's quest to find connections was enormous. His expansive views probably scared away more people than they attracted. Nonetheless, there is something captivating about the sheer scope of his imagination. In the deserts of academic thinking, his tent has become a welcoming place for all of my favorite big thinkers. There is room for Plato's allegories on form and pattern, equally matched by an openness to Whiteheadian process philosophy. Here is where Darwin, Freud, and Jung could find something in common with Emily Dickinson, Ernst Mayr, Lynn Margulis, or Pablo Picasso.

It was through Bateson that I first glimpsed the possible connection between my mentors Joe Rychlak and Bill Drury. Bateson's metaphorical abduction is a close parallel to Joe's subjective predication of meaning extension as a process of partial tautology. At the same time, I have come to see how the slender life-threads between Bill's individual organisms are woven into living stories amid the unruly forces of chance and change. The beauty of Bateson's method is not in the questions answered. It lies in an invitation to explore new meanings—in a venue where logical and analogical language are equally valid.

Ecological Metaphors

Ecology was born a metaphor—with Haeckel's etymological choice of the Greek rootword. At the time it was a part of botanical physiology. But Haeckel's "house" soon filled with visitors from every branch of science. The complexity of ecological relations invited an unusual combination of analytic and analogic approaches. In the former case, ecologists became specialists in careful measurements of field-based research. In the latter, they were theory-builders who needed simple ways to speak of complex phenomena. It is not surprising that metaphors were soon ubiquitous in the language of bioecology's pioneers. Their descriptions of the patterns of interaction and change in plant and animal communities had a straightforward clarity. Intuitively meaningful terms like competition, adaptation, migration, succession, and climax became common theoretical concepts. Even unique constructs like symbiosis (i.e., an association of dissimilar organisms for mutual extended benefit) were readily comprehensible. Some concepts drawn from ordinary language were enlarged with specific ecological meaning, widely applied by scientists, and finally borrowed back by the academic and nonacademic world.

The notion of niche is a good example. From Latin (*nidus*) for "nest," the word became niche in French. It was later applied to a "recess in the wall" and the location of an ornamental object or statue. Charlotte Brontë used it that way in 1850 in *Jane Eyre* to describe her cousin Mary, who having "taken her seat, remained fixed like a statue in its niche."[6] Joseph Grinnell is credited with its formal ecological development in 1917, shortly after ESA's founding, as the habitat requirements "within which each species is held by its structural and instinctive limitations."[7] A decade later Charles Elton developed the niche concept along somewhat different lines. Elton's niche emphasized the functional aspects of an organism's place in the environment in relation to food, enemies, and position in the larger community and ecosystem. Under the principle of "competitive exclusion," the limited availability of niches began to be referred to as an organism's "occupational" space. This notion dominated ecological theory for decades. G. Evelyn Hutchinson further revised the niche concept in 1957. His highly abstract definition of a niche—as a "multidimensional hypervolume"—introduced new levels of complexity. It also made way for a more sophisticated understanding of the relations between habitat conditions and the requirements of an organism.

It is easy to see why such thinking spilled over to the social sciences—as it did in the creation of early human ecology. Ecology, conversely, was equally infused by adopted ideas from other academic fields. Howard and Eugene Odum brought their family traditions of sociology to community ecology; Hutchinson's niche revision was based on the mathematics of set theory; and Tansley's ecosystem concept, in large part, came from his time with Freud—whose notion of a "closed" psychic system was itself based on mechanistic metaphors of hydraulics and dynamo-genesis. Ecology's transition from a descriptive to an applied science borrowed from other idioms. Some had a military tone, as in the "battle" against "alien" organisms, "invasive" species, or "noxious" weeds. The language of conservation ecologists continues to be highly metaphorical. Where once they spoke of ecosystem restoration and carrying capacity, contemporary "open systems" ecologists have added new figures of speech, e.g., patchiness, mosaics, punctuation, and resilience.

The language is also more focused at the species level. Conservation strategies are tied to the identification of flagship, keystone, umbrella, indicator, trigger, and priority species. *Flagship* species are organisms—such as whales, pandas, or tigers—that can capture public attention. Their significance does not necessarily derive from the impact they have on other organisms. It comes primarily from their capacity to stimulate ecological concern and thereby rally popular support of conservation efforts. *Keystone* species are highlighted because of their identified and significant relationships to other local organisms. The loss or removal of a keystone organism is expected to result in dramatic changes—and thus their protection has both ecological and educational value for conservationists. An *umbrella* species (e.g., the spotted owl) may not be as ecologically critical as a keystone species. But they share similar habitat requirements with a wide variety of other organisms. By focusing conservation efforts on them, they serve as the protective "umbrella" for all. An *indicator* species is usually among the most sensitive organisms in a region. As an early warning sign of environmental degradation (like the proverbial canary in a mine), they are ideal for biomonitoring changes such as air or water pollution, global warming, etc. *Trigger* species are organisms facing imminent extinction, with extreme vulnerability to habitat destruction, which makes conservation action critical. The term *priority* species is a special designation by the World Wildlife Fund (WWF) for the purposes of planning. WWF's conservation strategy is to target certain organisms because of their threatened status and also their crucial economic or spiritual significance for humans in the region. Enlarging the frame to include human consequences changes the conservation equation—in a more explicitly human ecological way.

These are not mutually exclusive designations. A flagship might also be a keystone. An indicator may become an umbrella. Sometimes the best strategy is to select an organism with multiple features. These categories have led to new avenues of scientific research and guiding principles for conservation. Regardless of the particular aims, however, most conservation ecologists are in agreement: "If we want to save something, this is how to think about it to get the job done." The most effective tools for doing so are often familiar words and metaphors that bring their goals to light.

The same is true of ecological discourse beyond the species level. The widespread adoption of the "stewardship" concept is a familiar example. The term is quite old—from when it meant a "keeper of the pigs" (originally *stigweard*—from *stig*, "sty," and *weard*, a "warden" or "guardian"). Historically, it referred to a special watchman appointed to guard the herd from robbers and predators. Later on, in feudal times, the steward was given broader household responsibilities for supervision of the castle dining-hall. Some rose in power to become agents for the lord of the manor—collecting rents, managing leases, and settling disputes. It was in this capacity that the Lord Steward of the Household functioned as a representative of the Royal Household and a minister of the British Cabinet. The idea of stewardship is also applied to other management and service roles, as for instance on ships, trains, and airplanes. In a more general way, it refers to the responsibilities for taking care of something that belongs to someone else. It is easy to see, in a similar sense, how humans can be seen as ecological stewards (rather than "the lords and masters of nature," as Descartes hoped science would make us).

"Earth Stewardship" was the title for the 2011 annual meeting of the Ecological Society of America. The conference subtheme was "preserving and enhancing the earth's life-support systems." As always, the organization sought to balance the creative tension between its natural science and ecological activist members. The carefully crafted mission statement was accordingly twofold: (1) "Ecologists have a special understanding of the complex, multi-scale interactions underlying the earth's life-support systems" and (2) "must be leaders in society's movement to earth stewardship in the 21st century."[8]

The conference opened with a plenary address by ESA president F. Stuart Chapin III. Terry, as his friends know him, is a professor of ecology at the University of Alaska with a PhD in biology from Stanford. When he was elected the preceding year, the anticipated conference theme was "planetary stewardship"—a term Terry had used extensively in his writing and for which he is well known. In the interim, however, a number of members voiced resistance to the planetary part. My hunch is that some may have been uncomfortable with its biospheric connotations, which seemed to undervalue research at different ecological scales and more specific scientific questions. Others were troubled by the allusion of global crisis, the suggestive need for sweeping intervention strategies, and even, perhaps, the vague hint of (hip) environmentalism. In sum, "Stewardship" could bridge the gap—but only in tandem with the more neutral-sounding "Earth."

The strains across micro and macro levels of ecology are not new. Nor are the tensions between basic research, applied science, and the tendency for some ecologists to publicly engage in political activities. ESA's first president, Victor Shelford, faced the judgment of early members who firmly preferred a "scientific" society and those, like himself, who would be advocates for natural preservation. The organization's meetings have always been riffled by these themes. Yet through it all the fabric has held. ESA's success over the years is no accident. It comes from an enduring commitment to the "integration of knowledge from the local to the global scale, from the sciences, humanities, and engineering, and from sources ranging from traditional knowledge of indigenous peoples to the most modern technological advances."[9] The perennial challenge for the board of governors has been to maintain an integrative forum in which all segments of its membership can find their place. From the outset, the aim was to attract participants from across the natural sciences as well as to include issues of scientific applications and conservation. The society's goal from its first meeting in 1915 was clear: "The interests and activities of this society will be of the broadest character, embracing every phase of the relation of organisms to their environmental condition ..."[10]

The advent of 1960s environmentalism brought the inevitable need to reach further still. Contemporary themes have become progressively comprehensive: from linking research and education, or enhancing ecological thought—to global warming, sustainability, and stewardship. Within the overarching scope of these themes, the actual ESA program is composed of some two thousand individual presentations. Taken together, they disclose the indisputable diversity of the living world. In side-by-side rooms I can choose to hear about global environmental concerns or the most recent scientific understanding of evolutionary adaptation, microbial ecology, or paleontology. It is possible to learn something new about life on every level, at any moment, during these weeklong events. This, in my opinion, is why ecology is such a compelling perspective.

Ecology is science and, perhaps as well, the consummate forum for integrating scientific knowledge. Ecologists have refined the contents and adjusted the boundaries of their endeavor for a century. The common interest behind the quest has been resolute: to build a bona fide, interdisciplinary science of life. Ecology is also a word. As such, it is infused with a multitude of meanings and has become a library of powerful root metaphors. The term has swept across academic boundaries and stimulated interdisciplinary cooperation more than any other. As the science of ecology grows, it gives birth to innovative connotations. With new metaphors come novel approaches to science.

The impact of ecological thought is ubiquitous. We saw several examples in the preceding exploration of the origins of human ecology. There are many more. Ecological analogies are increasingly popular in economics—with concepts like natural capital, ecosystem services, techno-metabolism, and industrial symbiosis. The world of business and marketing is likewise in transition, where biomimicry, niche marketing, life-cycle assessment, ecological footprints, and triple bottom-line accounting are widespread. Many of these changes are grounded in solid ecological science; others are more language based; some are merely superficial greenwashing.

The chasm between biological and human ecology can be disorienting. The tendency—when minding the gap—has often been to overlook the unique features of our own species. One of the most remarkable contributions of humans to the world is our capacity for ideas. It is this faculty that makes communication and language possible, liberates us from environmental constraints, and opens the way to endless world-changing inventions. This too is ecology—the kind Gregory Bateson struggled to articulate. It is what Richard Underwood meant when he described ecology "as a science in search of radical metaphors."[11]

Paul Shepard had a glimpse of it when he suggested that "the kind of thinking and synthesis which seem to me to fulfill the great promise of human ecology are not research reports. They are works of art."[12] So did Marshall McLuhan, who foresaw another side of the race to outer space: "For the first time the natural world was completely enclosed in a man-made container. At the moment that the earth went inside this new artifact, Nature ended and Ecology was born. 'Ecological' thinking became inevitable as soon as the planet moved up into the status of a work of art."[13] The interconnections of all things, including the processes of human creativity, are aspects of ecology. In the words of Neil Postman:

> Technological change is neither additive nor subtractive. It is ecological. I mean "ecological" in the same sense as the word is used by environmental scientists.... If you remove the caterpillars from a given habitat, you are not left with the same environment minus caterpillars; you have a new environment.... A new technology does not add or subtract something. It changes everything. In the year 1500, fifty years after the printing press was invented, we did not have old Europe plus the printing press. We had a different Europe.[14]

Postman's views on ecology may be a bit out of date. But his point about technology and the human environment (indeed, the environments of every living thing) is well founded.

Caveats and Afterthoughts

In Act III of *Hamlet*, the Prince of Denmark asks Polonius, "Do you see yonder cloud that's almost in shape of a camel?" Polonius replies: "By the mass, and 'tis like a camel, indeed." Hamlet continues to poke fun at Polonius, leading him to instead see a weasel and then a whale in the amorphous shape of the cloud. Shakespeare reminds us, with this scene, of how readily we can find meaning when looking at chaos. Herein lie the dangers of analogical thinking. The history of science is full of discarded theories and illusory relations—from geocentrism, vitalism, and phrenology—to ether, miasma, and cold fusion. Ecologists have entertained a few of their own as well.

Linnaeus invented the taxonomic language for naming and categorizing organisms. But it was the polymath scientist and artist, Johann Goethe, who coined the term "morphology"—the study of forms. For Goethe, living forms were a fluid process of transition through the full life cycle of an organism. Linnean classification, in contrast, emphasized the developmental peaks of each species. Whereas Goethe felt the flow of Heraclitus's river, Linnaeus saw the perfection of Plato's ideal forms.

One, as it were, was like a cinematographer, the other a still-life photographer. Both were right in their respective ways. Yet Goethe's view is seldom given its due—which brings me back once again to Bill Drury. Bill rather enjoyed his students' confusion when the bird in the tree did not exactly resemble the image in their fieldbook. His answer was always the same: the bird on the branch is real, no matter what you see in the picture. Like Goethe's motto, the lesson was clear: "Look once at the book, but twice at life." The second look unlocks perception. It inspires a fluidity of mind to understanding diversity and change. It is also the land in which pictures create stories, marches turn to dance, and words become metaphor.

It is estimated that we use as many as four metaphors a minute in everyday conversation, and up to three thousand per week.[15] The Berkeley linguist George Lakoff has championed the role of figurative language in everyday life. "In all aspects of life," as he maintains, "we define our reality in terms of metaphors and then proceed to act on the basis of the metaphors."[16] We make a complex world comprehensible by use of metaphor and analogy—but not always in accurate ways. When metaphors are misplaced, the outcomes range from minor failures of communication to catastrophic blunders. The imaginary "domino theory," as Robert McNamara later revealed, was the driving force behind American involvement in the Vietnam War. Countless other political decisions have epitomized Whitehead's "fallacy of misplaced concreteness." In some cases, metaphors become fetishized—and all opposing evidence is rejected, often with disdain. The inability to perceive reality due to an overexertion of projective functions is a form of psychic blindness. Jung called it "totalization." The orientation, in the framework of analytical psychology, is not merely a perceptual distortion. It signifies the ascendancy of certain psychological functions and a susceptibility to "an overbelief" in cherished views. They may be fundamentalist, holistic, reductionist, or deconstructionist. Irrespective of their predisposition, it is unlikely they would find pleasure in the disorderly terrain of human ecology.

While writing these thoughts, I took a short break to make coffee and glance at the *New York Times*. On the front page of Section C was an article about the "linguistic wars" between Noam Chomsky, Steven Pinker, George Lakoff, and Dan Everett. At the center of the controversy was Everett's new book: *Language: A Cultural Tool*, based on thirty years of research among an isolated Amazonian tribe of forest dwellers known as the Pirahã. The language of this remote, three-hundred-member group is one of the strangest in the world. The Pirahã have no written language. Oral communication combines singing, whistling, and humming, and appears to resemble music more than it does normal speech. According to Everett, Pirahã language is largely devoid of abstract terms—even of the most rudimentary sort. There are no distinct words for colors or numbers. The Pirahã appear to be unable to count or perform even the most elementary mathematical operations. Moreover, their conversations contain almost no words for expressing time—and make only the barest of distinctions between past, present, and future events. "All experience is anchored in the presence." The Pirahã, by Everett's description, is a culture that "live in the here and now."[17]

These discoveries have rekindled an intellectual dispute about culture, language, and thought. More than sixty years ago, Benjamin Lee Whorf extended the ideas of his teacher Edward Sapir that language molds perception. The Sapir–Whorf hypothesis proposed that language differences between cultures shape social and environmental relations. The richness of vocabulary—say, for colors or family members or types of snow—prefigures the capacity to think and experience the world in those categories. In short, speakers of different languages have different worldviews.

The linguist Noam Chomsky proposed a very different view. The initial target for Chomsky's alternative theory of language acquisition was the behaviorist B. F. Skinner. Verbal learning, according to Skinner, was expected to follow the basic principles of conditioning and reinforcement—like any other kind of learned behavior. Observation of children's language-acquisition skills and their creative use of syntax, however, far exceeded a purely behavioral-learning account. There was no way, according to Chomsky, that a child's language could be obtained via Skinner's bit-by-bit inductive explanation. He proposed instead that humans possess an innate ability for grammar acquisition. Infants enter the world with a predisposition for language learning. Members of a language community gain verbal fluency in the finite vocabulary of their specific language. But the capacity for metamorphosing infinitely meaningful variations within a language comes from deeper generative rules.

Chomsky's theory of universal grammar rendered a fatal blow to Skinner's behavioral model of verbal learning. It also discredited the Whorfian notion that every language is a world of its own. Chomsky has overhauled his ideas many times since then, and he remains an important and sometimes controversial figure. The Harvard evolutionary psychologist Steven Pinker popularized the historical controversies about the relationships of language and human nature in his 1994 *Language Instinct* and 2007 *The Stuff of Thought*. How the Pirahã live and think has brought many questions to the forefront again. I have no doubt they are important issues for linguistic theorists. They also highlight the customary academic traditions of disputation. The continuing debates will surely stimulate refinements of the respective positions. But I am quite sure, however, the advocates will not seek a discourse of collaboration and integration.

Let me put it another way. The distinguished population demographer Joel Cohen gave a plenary lecture at the 1995 human ecology conference at Lake Tahoe in which he likened academic pursuits to flying—by comparing two kinds of pilots. Stunt pilots, he noted, are dramatic acrobats. They can captivate an audience, after which they return to their home field. The other kind of pilot takes off for distant headings. They take wing with different reasons: to discover new places, to build connections, to bring the world together. Cohen's metaphor bespeaks of how intellectual conventions pull most academics back to familiar ground. It also avows the pull of a distant reckoning and the urge of the few who will test their wings on new horizons.

The preceding chapters on the facets of life explore an attempt to loosen some of the fixity around academic conventions. They are an alternative schema of transects through my ball of human ecology strands—gathered from years of collecting; they are also my version of mental yoga and liberation. The fullness of life is beyond comprehension. Yet the chance to experience life is ever present. As Alfred North Whitehead expressed, "There is no means to stop Nature in order to look at it"—and Maurice Merleau-Ponty added, "Nature is always new in each perception, but it is never without a past."[18] I knew it first in the sense of Edith Cobb's ecology of imagination in childhood. The allure of psychology held an intuitive promise for sustaining the awe. Lee Cronbach's circus image of psychology and Joe Rychlak's talent for honoring science and subjectivity kept it alive. Ecology held a mirror to psychology in which Bill Drury magnified my view of nature.

These people and their ideas are by now familiar. The inspiration for the current chapter was serendipitous, like many ingredients in the recipe for this book. Unbeknownst to Patricia and myself, Kay Deaux, an old friend and a colleague from Purdue, had been vacationing on Mount Desert Island for years. After Kay left Purdue to join the faculty at the Graduate Center of the City University of New York, Kay and Sam Glucksberg were married. When they arrived for their Maine retreat in the summer of 2005, we took them sailing on our boat. The conversation was filled with catching up about old friends and new directions in psychology that continued for hours over dinner. Sam's research and recent book *Understanding Figurative Language* were receiving considerable acclaim. He explained the ideas and later sent me copies of his work. His dual-reference model was a compelling explanation for making sense of the denotative/connotative patterns of language in ecology. Moreover, Howard Kendler had just published another account of theoretical dualism in the previous month's issue of the *American Psychologist*. Kendler's paper was not about linguistic dualities. It was a historical review of psychology as a whole—along with a philosophical clarification of the theoretical and methodological differences of its natural science versus humanistic/phenomenological orientations.

All of these things fell into alignment. Before summer ended, three self-evident aspects of reality surfaced in my thinking. The first was nature, the second was consciousness, and the third was language. Human ecology was the matrix in which they tied together. Yet each also possessed sufficient semiautonomous qualities to allow for meaningful comparisons. It was a starting point. Language struck me as the middle ground. Whatever could be said or symbolized in words needed to be somehow true to both ecology and experience.

Rachel Carson knew both worlds. She said it clearly in her book *The Sense of Wonder*—inspired by the desire to teach her young nephew Roger the joy of discovering nature: "I sincerely believe that for a child, and for the parent seeking to guide him, it is not half so important to *know* as to *feel*."[19] A similar feeling for life likewise moved E. O. Wilson to coin the term "biophilia"—a love of nature—the opposite of necrophilia (the love of dead things). Bill Carpenter used his poet's license to name human ecology as an *aesthetic science*. Through acts of language, he described an elegant possibility of bridging art and science, beauty and truth, and death in life. The Oxford human ecologist Philip Stewart reached eastward to the Hindu concept of *advaita* (the experiential definition of nonduality)—which for him "expresses the relationship better than 'holism'; consciousness and patterns of matter and energy in bodies and nervous systems are not one and the same, but neither are they separable."[20] Further possibilities lie in other Eastern languages, like Chinese ideograms, where the subtleties of human and nature relations have been developed in single contextual representations over thousands of years. These approaches exceed my understanding, though not my appreciation. But my mind and worldview are of Western traditions. So I look toward Homer, one of the greatest storytellers and masters of metaphor. The course turns toward home (*oikos*). Perhaps through the gap of nature and mind (like Scylla and Charybdis) lies a channel to wider points of view.

PART III
WIDER POINTS OF VIEW

Wholeness demands its own rigor.
—Herbert Marcuse

There is only one subject-matter for education, and that is Life in all its manifestations.
—Alfred North Whitehead

THIS FINAL SET OF CHAPTERS ARISES FROM MULTIPLE SOURCES. In part, they spring from the ideas of Alfred North Whitehead. Whitehead's process philosophy was the inspiration for the human ecology mission of College of the Atlantic. Credit also goes to my COA colleague and friend John Cooper. John is a consummate teacher and musician, fully committed to the college's nondepartmentalized curriculum. He is unconcerned with a concrete definition of human ecology and somewhat distrustful of those who seem to need one. His way of framing COA's interdisciplinary approach to education begins with what he knows best. "It's easy," as he says. "Human ecology is like variations on a theme."

Whitehead's ideas and John's words came together in a special way, a couple of years ago, when I accompanied Patricia on a professional workshop for psychotherapists. One of our teachers at the weeklong program was the analytical (Jungian) therapist and author Ann Ulanov. The psychic urge for relatedness, she explained, is not abstract—but immediate. The loving of life and life's sources is a stirring, from the bottom up, not to be denied. The inward journey "to maintain a subjective wholeness and enlarge oneself—like the best of jazz," as she noted, "mirrors reality … and … aims at happiness."[1]

I am not a metaphysician, a jazz musician, or an analyst. But I welcome the ways these people expand the boundaries of their talents and how their open-ended visions combine. Nor am I a member of the guild of smug reductionists who march a narrow trench. My nature is that of the generalist. I love the surprise of a meandering path, which like the uroboric serpent, comes round upon its tail. These final chapters are invitations as much as closings. They abandon the hewn lines and academic motifs of the book's opening. The sentiment is with Frost's familiar line: "Something there is that doesn't love a wall."[2]

CHAPTER 11

Kinds of Minds

We build too many walls and not enough bridges.
—Isaac Newton

Analysis kills and synthesis brings to life.
—Carl Jung

Near the end of his life, Alfred North Whitehead wrote a synthesis of his philosophy for *The Library of Living Philosophers*. The book begins with a "philosopher's summary" of the work. The preface also includes a facsimile of Whitehead's final handwritten letter to the editor: "The progress of philosophy," he noted, "does not primarily involve reactions of agreement or dissent. It essentially consists in the enlargement of thought, whereby contradictions and agreements are transformed into partial aspects of wider points of view."[1] Whitehead's principles of an enlargement of thought and the pursuit of wider views were the core of COA's founding mission. They enlivened the original faculty and infused the institution's collaborative atmosphere. This is what captivated me from the beginning—and still inspires my passion for human ecology.

Whitehead's philosophy holds that process should be taken as the fundamental category of metaphysics. He displaces the classical preeminence of "substance" and instates an alternative category of "relation." All real-life objects—or "actual occasions"—are enduring moments (not enduring substances), best thought of as "events." "Nature is a structure of evolving processes," individuated as temporal gestalts becoming, maintaining, and decaying.² His philosophy of organism rejects mind/body dualism and attributes "feeling" as a constitutive aspect of reality.

Whitehead's ideas have intersected ecology in multiple ways. In the 1930s they permeated the "Ecology Group" at the University of Chicago, where several chapters of his *Modes of Thought* were delivered as lectures under the title "Nature and Life." The poetic naturalism of Loren Eiseley is an evolutionary alchemy of aesthetics and science. Multiple references to Whitehead appear in his autobiographical notes. Gregory Bateson invoked "misplaced concreteness" in *Steps to an Ecology of Mind* and drew on numerous other features of process philosophy in his ecological speculations. Rachel Carson alloyed her proficiency for poetry and research to transcend the reductionism of conventional science writing. As her biographer Mark Lytle notes in *The Gentle Subversive,* "Carson's approach to ecology paralleled the work of Alfred North Whitehead."³ Her claim that feelings are essential to learning about nature echoes the Whiteheadian view of education as a creative integration of experience.

Whitehead expressed the role of feeling in education in a number of his essays. "The Aims of Education" is perhaps the most well known. One of its companion pieces, "The Rhythm of Education," explores the stages of learning in terms of three general processes—which Whitehead called romance, precision, and generalization. In broad terms, they refer to early, middle, and higher education—each of which in Whitehead's view is based on different modes of study. Primary education should inspire; secondary learning develops knowledge skills; and the concern of university education should be principles and ideas. The cycles of romance, precision, and generalization are also essential aspects of learning within each level—as they are of all occasions of mental growth. Thus, learning a musical instrument, acquiring a new language, or discovering how to bake bread will contain all phases. My learning to play fiddle, for instance, began as a kind of love affair that motivated the hours of rigorous practice of bowing and fingering. The ability to play a tune alone generalized into playing with others—to being able to improvise, to call a contra dance while playing, and so on.

Whitehead's philosophy argues against a rigid curriculum and supports self-directed education. But his ideas of rhythm are not an explicit part of COA's pedagogy and never have been. In fact, I know only one faculty member who is familiar with them. Nonetheless, I find something compelling in Whitehead's cycles of feeling, exercise, and abstraction. The recursive features of patterns within patterns, like Hegel's unfolding dialectic relations of thesis-antithesis-synthesis (another dynamic heuristic), make sense at many levels.

Consciousness, as William James famously described, begins in "one great booming, buzzing confusion." But the initial shapeless impression of the world rapidly attains differentiation. This is where Freud began. His formulation of primary and secondary processes of cognition was one of the first models of how mental representations develop. Like Whitehead, he also included desire in the dance of internal images and external reality that become the structures of the ego and superego. Melanie Klein and other psychoanalytic theorists further elaborated the mental representation of object relations associated with internal states of feeling and motivation. Piaget began with the infant's sucking and grasping responses. From these innate sensorimotor tools, he showed how the child's explorations of reality develop into cognitive schemata and fluid mental operations.

Brain research reveals that pre-natal humans have substantially more neurons than adults. During their development a strong increase in synaptic density is accompanied by a dramatic "neural pruning" (apoptosis) of millions of brain cells. The shaping of neuronal networks by the interrelationships of experience and brain physiology continues throughout life. Research on mirror neurons, learning, recovery of function, and even psychotherapy has begun to show how. From these and many other perspectives, a general understanding of the neurophysiology of consciousness is emerging. We also have learned a lot about the unique aspects of human development. Our individuality is a joint outcome. Each person is a peculiar synthesis—of a unique genetic endowment, enveloped by a specific cultural and historical context, further shaped by distinct family dynamics and private experience.

Humans, like bees and beavers, are a species of builders—wall builders. As Freud and Jung showed, we even build walls within the confines of our minds. These psychological barriers alter our perceptions, compartmentalize our feelings, and hide much of our own thinking from awareness. To further ensure our personal privacy, we also construct physical barriers to relieve ourselves from the annoyances of others. A good wall—six or so inches thick—can completely free us from an awareness of the living, loving, fighting, and dying of our neighbors. Thus, physical walls reduce the immediacy and impact of others and become effective psychological walls.

As any student of the history of ideas knows, the strength of feeling that accompanies different conceptions of "the truth" is enormous. Sometimes these differences are discussed and resolved. Other times a wall is erected to make it easier for the disagreeing parties to ignore one another. Matters of state take place in state buildings, matters of religion in religious buildings, and so on. Worldviews become separated for convenience, and often stay that way. What initially separates ideas to reduce dissonance, in the end produces deafness. When dialogue is attempted, it is usually a dialogue of the deaf, who either attack the enemy's bastions or retreat behind thicker barricades.

My transition into high school was accompanied by a special privilege. In elementary and middle school, everyone ate together in the cafeteria. From ninth grade on, however, we could leave the school grounds and walk into town for lunch. It was a welcome respite that also offered the freedom to explore relationships beyond my familiar circle of neighbors and school bus mates. I enjoyed the variety of small group encounters and the companionship of new friends. One day, while in the company of several classmates, I was disturbed by their collective derision about a boy who had just walked by. In his defense, I declared: "Well—I like John." The boy next to me responded without hesitation. "The problem with you, Rich," he noted bitterly, "is that you like everybody." The sting of his disdainful tone, and the implication of my lack of social discernment, stunned me.

That brief encounter was a pivotal event. It opened my eyes to a growing cliquishness of high school culture. The "jocks" and the "bookworms" were becoming well-defined factions. The "gearheads" worked on cars and had a subculture of their own. Students who played in the school band or engaged in theater activities had their social groups as well. The school day began with everyone together in our homerooms. But things spread apart as we moved into the elective curriculum. There was little overlap between students taking shop or home economics classes and those in college-prep courses in science, foreign language, or art. A further distinction existed between "natives," like myself, who had known each other since kindergarten—and the more transitory students "from away" whose families were stationed at the nearby Air Force base.

The social boundaries were not exclusive or rigid, but they were there. The members of these groups often had different backgrounds. Their families were quite unalike and seldom knew one another. I never witnessed any overt or collective antagonism, but most kids' social bonds did follow a sense of connection and shared allegiance.

My classmate was right. I did have a penchant to associate with anyone. I enjoyed Saturday evenings at the air base "teen club" with friends from every corner of the world. I also loved to drive the tractor in haying season, and to fish and hunt with farm friends. Sports were a big part of high school life; I wore my varsity letter jacket with pride. The thrill of competition extended to go-karts, souped-up hot rods, and—to my parents' dismay—a brief episode of dirt-track, stock car racing. Despite my diversions, their college-bound expectations for me were never in doubt.

I had friends in all these circles. I enjoyed the mix of activities and individuals, with little thought of the disparities. Occasionally, a connection developed when my separate worlds touched. But more commonly I recall the spark of surprise between strangers in a dissonant triangle of mismatched poles. As I reflect on those events, I perceive an incipient curiosity about human relations that prefigures my interest in personality and social psychology—as well as, perhaps, the appeal of interdisciplinary collaboration.

Walls and Roads

A few years ago I came across a brief article in one of my monthly psychology journals. It began with this sentence: "The nature-nurture wars are over, and both sides won."[4] For more than a century, the human studies have straddled a battle line between genetic versus environmental explanations of individuality. It is a facile distinction, on the surface, that has stimulated countless attempts for an answer, one way or the other. But the debate has always seemed pointless to me. The answer had to be "both"; the real question was how? Nonetheless, the long-standing tradition within psychology—and many other fields—was to line up on one side or the other.

The perennial argument came to a heated climax in 1975 when E. O. Wilson published *Sociobiology: The New Synthesis*. Reactions to Wilson's mixing of genes and social theory inflamed academics—throughout biology, the humanities, and social sciences—and spread into public opinion. In his autobiography, *Naturalist,* Wilson recounts the student protests and the disdain he received from colleagues. The symbolic peak of the storm happened in February 1978 at a symposium of the American Association for the Advancement of Science in Washington, DC. As Wilson began his presentation, a group of protesters rushed onto the stage. One of them grabbed a pitcher of water and poured it over the biologist's head as the group chanted: "Wilson, you're all wet."[5]

"I believe," Wilson later commented, "I was the only scientist in modern times to be physically attacked for an idea."[6] His idea that certain mental structures are heritable was a form of scientific materialism that flew in the face of cherished beliefs. To further propose that religion itself might be "in our genes" was about as heretical a statement as could be conceived. It is not difficult to see why Descartes chose to keep these issues apart some four centuries ago. Even secular humanists—for whom free will and self-determination still remain sovereign—took it as a poisonous threat. As Wilson explains: "What made Sociobiology notorious then was its hybrid nature; ... the conjunction created a syllogism that proved unpalatable to many."[7]

I don't know if Wilson is as much a reductionist as he is made out to be. I doubt it. But the bifurcation with which he meddled was volatile. It is by no means the only fractious line through human thought. There are countless others. How we see the world, and how we organize our knowledge of it, reflects these fissures. They mark the boundaries of academic fields, where problems of thought have been solved with the placement of walls. Some of the walls are architectural; many are not.

It is always exciting to see a former student or colleague rise to distinction. So it was when John Cacioppo was elected president of the Association for Psychological Science a few years ago. John was a graduate student when I was at Ohio State, where we shared an interest in human psychophysiology. He is now a distinguished professor at the University of Chicago and director of the Center for Cognitive and Social Neuroscience. During his year at the helm of APS, I followed his presidential column in the monthly issues of the *APS Observer*. I was especially delighted when I read his report on the patterns of interdisciplinary influence within and across the sciences. It was a massive study of citation data from more than a million articles from 7,121 natural and social science journals. Using high-quality citation data, combined with sophisticated visualization techniques, a two-dimensional spatial map was constructed. The landscape of influence was depicted by each discipline's distance from all others. Disciplines that shared citations were in the same neighborhood; fields with many interdisciplinary links were near the center of the map; those with the least impact on others were on the periphery.[8]

John's message was the happy news that psychology had been identified as an interdisciplinary "hub." Its closest neighbors were biomedicine, neurological sciences, anthropology, education, statistics and public health. Six other hubs were identified: mathematics, chemistry, physics, medicine, social science and earth science—each surrounded by a cluster of affiliated subdisciplines. I was pleased to see ecology at the virtual center of the earth science cluster, which made good sense. A large portion of the map's outer edge (which resembled isolated coastal villages) was made up of specialty areas of medical research. Apparently, they pay little attention to each other (or anything else) and have little impact beyond their immediate domain. The isolated fields around the rim of the map's other side were a bit of a surprise. Among these were economics, law, international relations, political science and computer science. All were scattered around the outer most edge of the social sciences—quite separate from each other, and further still from everything else.

The closing point of John's paper drew a comparison between the traditional disciplinary boundaries by which universities are organized, and the actual exchange (or not) of cross-disciplinary knowledge disclosed by the citation analyses. My hunch is that he, a psychologist, recognized the play of other factors, i.e., the cultural qualities of academic subfields and the type of people they draw—along with the exigencies of professional status, research funds and the editorial standards of scholarly publications. Scientists and social scientists pay a lot of attention to citation data. It is one of their primary scorecards.

The mapped terrain of cross-disciplinary relations was curiously similar to the island where I live (also rather round—with mountains, clustered settlements and network of roads). Ecology and psychology were both nearer the center than the edge. So in the spirit of my "transect-and-plot" method, I drew a line between them. The path from ecology to psychology passed through zoology—and skirted the edges of meteorology, anthropology and finally neuroscience—on the way to its destination.

A more complete interdisciplinary study should include the humanities and arts as well. But they, most likely, would have been islands of their own. Herein lies COA's founding purpose. From the start, the college has held to a vision that the sciences, arts and human studies are equal partners in a human ecological education. This principle is exemplified in the requirement that all students choose at least two foundational courses from each of these "resource areas." This might be considered adequate grounding for self-directed, interdisciplinary study for some people. But we have maintained a further expectation. Every student also takes a human ecology "core course" in his or her first term. A faculty team, composed of seven or eight teachers drawn from across the resource areas, teaches the class. The teachers hold two small-group discussion sessions each week. These seminars introduce the complex nature of human ecological issues, as well as the reading, writing, and discussion skills necessary for interdisciplinary inquiry. Students also meet every week as a large group for a presentation from one of the core faculty. Each professor summarizes her academic background, and then, in her own way, expresses its relevance within the framework of human ecology. Immediately following each lecture, the faculty teaching team meets to explore ways to conduct the seminar discussion in the next day's small-group session with students. The readings chosen by the presenters constitute the course syllabus; their talks and supporting materials are the content of the weekly seminars.

All together, this is a demanding way to do education, especially as faculty membership on the teaching-teams rotates every year and thus necessitates a new course-plan and syllabus. During my years as dean, I took it as one of my duties to teach in the core. I frequently still do. It is challenging to handle the range of ever-changing ideas and course materials. No doubt it would be far easier to have a permanent core faculty and a "fixed" curriculum for students, rather than the open-ended model we use. On the other side of the coin, however, I have enjoyed an incomparable experience of "being-a-student" for three and a half decades—along with my students and faculty colleagues. Every cycle, like Whitehead's rhythms, still has its romance, rigors and enlargements of thought.

Returning for a moment, to the cross-disciplinary transect noted above, I have paused to contemplate the imaginary line between ecology and psychology. Many intriguing problems lie along the route. Some are ancient and intractable; others are on the cutting edge of contemporary knowledge. In many ways, they do not seem so far apart—and suggest an affirmation of long-held interests. I am sure they will meet and find commonalities; it is already happening. Their closeness, however, is only within the landscape of scientific considerations. Joining the "hubs" of environmental and social science, as intriguing as it may be, still leaves much of human ecology out of the picture. My intuition tells me to turn away from the peaks of citation indices. The air is too thin there. I need the company of philosophers, poets and artists—who bring an atmosphere of wider points of view.

Interaction: Process and Form

When my son Andrew was small he had a reversible hand-puppet that was two animals in one. In one form it was a rabbit. It could also be turned inside out, slipped over my other hand, and become a tortoise. I enjoyed inventing conversations and acting out story lines between the two characters—back and forth, over and over. For a while it was a favorite bedtime ritual (at least for me). One evening, as I fumbled with the handwork of turning the puppet inside out, my sense of reality also inverted. Instead of two separate entities exchanging words, I began to notice something unusually captivating. The two puppets were not just interacting. Each character was "ingesting" the other's words and "reforming" itself around them. In a Janusian involution, they became semiautonomous forms within a broader unifying experience.

I shared this story with my students. A few had owned one of the puppets. The anecdote made a useful metaphor for discussions about process, interaction and form. Everyone sees ways we are in continual interrelations with our environment. Every breath and morsel of food leaves us changed. The standard cliché holds that the molecules of our bodies are replaced every seven years. I don't know what truth there is to this notion; but I do know I am not the same person I was seven years ago. And yet, somehow, I am still me.

Our beingness arises, like a standing wave, amid the flow of life. The biologist Piaget found evidence of process and form in the growth lines of snail shells. Piaget, the psychologist, found still more in the epistemic layers of human cognition. For Whitehead—to see what is general in what is particular and what is permanent in what is transitory—was everywhere. (The puppets, incidentally, were also a way for me to generate an imaginary interaction between Bill and Joe.)

The aim of human ecology is to remind us that we are part of a complex and interactive living world. "Interaction affords a process bridge,"[9] as Gerald Young declares, that must be "brought out into the open, explicated and recognized for its significance." It is "the fundamental concept" of ecology and human ecology.[10] "It is easy to dismiss as tautological the fundamentality of interaction in human ecology: so obvious as to be of no theoretical importance, so obvious that it is accepted and each scholar in each discipline assumes it to be self-explanatory and therefore of little value."[11]

The academic world carves life into pieces. But that is not how things really are. "The unity of life," Theodosius Dobzhansky reminded us, "is no less remarkable than its diversity."[12] Humans are partners in this dance. The eternal processes that compose the unity and diversity of all things are also dancing within us. It is here, perhaps, where musicians may come closest to reality. The feeling of nature in Grofé's *Grand Canyon Suite* or Smetana's "Moldau" flow freely, unhindered by frozen abstractions. Aaron Copland's *Music for a Great City* and Duke Ellington's "Harlem" make real a "sense" of city life. The emotional pitch of war is tangible in Tchaikovsky's "1812 Overture"; Ken Burns's *The Civil War* is woven in a single story by the wistful strains of Jay Ungar's fiddle tune "Ashokan Farewell."

This unity of feeling, rhythm, and form is celebrated in other ways. Shakespeare put the words in King Lear's mouth: "How do you see the world?" he asked Glouster (who is blind). "I see it feelingly," he replied. Goethe said it like this: "I call architecture frozen music." Mozart may have possessed the rarest of talents for insight into process and form: "My subject enlarges itself, becomes methodized and defined, and the whole, though it be long, stands almost complete and finished in my mind, so that I can survey it, like a fine picture or a beautiful statue, at a glance. Nor do I hear in my imagination the parts successively, but I hear them, as it were, all at once."[13] This is how feeling and thinking really do meet. It is where aesthetics and science should meet, and when the prospects of human ecology will be self-evident. Life dangles on slender strands. The threads that tie to the future are also thin. May there always be the kinds of minds to weave the wider views that make life's wonders known.

CHAPTER 12

Insight

Insight is the first condition of Art.
—George Henry Lewes

The techniques of the arts provide the most valuable means of insight into the real direction of our own collective purposes.
—Marshall McLuhan

Most people are familiar with the plays of Anton Chekhov: *Uncle Vanya, Three Sisters,* or *The Cherry Orchard.* Tolstoy once compared Chekhov's magnificent storytelling and sensitive character development to impressionist painting. That Chekhov was a physician is less well known. By day he practiced medicine. At night he created literature. "Medicine," he once said, "is my lawful wife, literature my mistress." The creativity of fiction allowed Chekhov to go beyond the scientific rationalism of medicine. His psychological insights and nuanced portrayals are still admired as some of the best psychiatric descriptions of his time.

There is something in the openness of literature that invites a creative realignment of thought and feeling. Literary insights rearrange the inner workings of the psyche. They bring fresh meaning to everyday life—and sometimes to the universe as a whole. Arthur C. Clarke's short story "The Star" is a classic example.[1] The story takes place on board an intergalactic voyage four thousand years in the future. The narrative is told from the point of view of the chief astrophysicist, a Jesuit priest, facing a deep crisis of faith. The space explorers are returning to earth from an expedition to a remote white dwarf star created by a long-ago supernova explosion. When their spacecraft had entered the still-expanding clouds of glowing incandescence, they made an unexpected discovery. There, on the distant edge of the star system, was a planet. Amid the scorched mantle stood the fused remains of a mile-high monolith—evidence of intelligent life. They landed the craft to explore it more. Never expecting what they found, they were unprepared for an archaeological excavation. Eventually, with great effort, they were able to drill an opening through the thick stone walls by improvising their limited, onboard tools to the task. Inside the vault they found the elaborate archives of a civilization much like humans'. The doomed inhabitants had been aware of the forthcoming explosion of their sun. With no means to escape the inevitable end, they had spent their final generations preparing the monumental time capsule.

The earth explorers were deeply moved by the lost civilization's profound grace in its last bid for immortality. The artifacts and records were clearly meant to be a gift—on the thinnest of hopes of being found, in some distant future, by other living beings. The destruction of their culture, in the full flower of its achievement, was hardest for the Jesuit astrophysicist to reconcile. Were his fellow scientists right? Was the universe truly without purpose or divine justice? Where was the mercy of God? These troubling questions filled his head on the journey home. Sitting at his computer—beneath Ruben's engraving of St. Ignatius and his revered cross on the bulkhead wall—the story's final irony is given. The calculations he is working on from the rock records of the lost planet gave the exact date of the supernova explosion—and then—when its light was seen on earth. The blazing beacon in the winter sky is revealed: the Star of Bethlehem! Clarke's skillful writing holds us to the story. The ending brings reason and faith together in an unprepared mental collision, not with a single answer—but a wider point of view.

Ray Bradbury's classic bit of eco-fiction, "A Sound of Thunder," gives a more earthly rendering of literary insight.[2] The story is alleged to be the most widely read piece of science fiction—*ever*. Set in the mid-twenty-first century, the tale is the account of a group of men, three hunters and their two guides, who travel back by time machine to hunt a *Tyrannosaurus rex*. When the safari arrives at its destination sixty million years into the past, the hunters receive stern instructions to stay on an elevated path above the ground and cause no disturbance to the surroundings. The safari leaders on an earlier scouting trip have marked the prey animals with a patch of red paint. They have been carefully selected, based on knowledge of their imminent death from natural causes—like a tree falling on them or drowning in a tar pit. The safari is timed to arrive a few short minutes before their otherwise certain death. These precautions, as with the elevated path, are to protect the future. Even the smallest of changes, as the hunters are repeatedly told, have the potential to multiply dramatically in the sixty million years ahead.

As the *T. rex* lunges toward the group through the primeval mist, one of the hunters loses his nerve. The expedition leader orders him to return to the time machine. Meanwhile, the rest of the group completes their dangerous task of bringing down the enormous reptile. In a thunderous avalanche he crashes to the ground. Moments later another deafening sound marks the overhead breaking of a gigantic tree branch, which crashes upon the dead beast's body. The group returns to the time machine, where their overwhelmed companion lies shivering in fear. There is mud on his boots. In his frenzied return to the machine, he had accidentally stepped off the path. A heated altercation follows in which the irate expedition leader threatens to kill him and leave him behind. In the end, he is allowed to return to the present. When the group arrives, however, they notice some subtle and not so subtle changes. In the mud on the hunter's boot, they also discover the remains of a dead butterfly.

The intuitive understanding of "the butterfly effect," as it is commonly known, has probably conveyed the evolutionary significance of infinitesimally small changes across the vastness of time to more people than any biology textbook—maybe all. The idea has also been incorporated into nonlinear systems theory. In chaos theory, the notion is used to express the "sensitivity to initial conditions" of many complex phenomena. The difficulty in long-term prediction of weather systems is a familiar example. Edward Lorenz, a pioneer of chaos theory, was not entirely off base with his question "Does the flap of a butterfly's wings in Brazil set off a tornado in Texas?"[3] The "tipping point" concept, of how little things can make big differences, is another variation that has been applied across a multitude of settings.[4] Simple heuristic tools like these unlock our mind. The fresh light of insight arouses our feelings, reshapes our thoughts, and extends reality.

Insight is defined as a novel realization that occurs in an all-of-a-sudden manner. As a type of problem solving, it is usually considered to be the opposite of trial-and-error solutions. My appreciation of the mental processes of insight was enlarged by one of my favorite undergraduate courses. The class had a simple title: Thought. The professor was Clarke Burnham, who had just arrived at Texas from Stanford, where he had completed his doctoral studies under Leon Festinger. The course covered a broad range of topics from pre-Socratic philosophy to an up-to-date review of the emerging field of cognitive psychology. Among our reading materials was a fascinating book, *The Experimental Psychology of Original Thinking*.[5] It contained a theoretical overview of Gestalt psychology, along with many of the classic experiments on creative thought. Clarke followed up on these research studies with a collection of anecdotal accounts of insight by historically significant individuals. There was Henri Poincare's sudden solution to an intractable mathematical problem while stepping onto a bus. We read about Friedrich Kekule's discovery, during a fireside nap, of the circular structure of benzene from an image of a snake eating its tail. Einstein's epiphany about relativity may have come unexpectedly in a similar fashion. As his train pulled out of the Zurich station, according to one account, he glanced back at the tower clock. This set him to wondering: would a clock in his lap, as the train accelerated to the speed of light, still match the station clock? These famous "aha" events were often preceded by intensive concentration. But their occurrence came in moments of mental relaxation. The neuroscientist Eric Kandel, recipient of the 2000 Nobel Prize for Physiology or Medicine, makes a similar distinction in his autobiographical *In Search of Memory*. Kandel tells of his personal journey from early childhood in Austria, through his training as a Freudian therapist and subsequent career as a distinguished research scientist. There is a difference, as he describes, between "day science" and "night science." "Day science is rational, logical, pragmatic, carried forward by precisely designed experiments" on a clear scientific issue, using well-developed investigative methods. Night science, on the other hand, involves thinking far beyond established knowledge, "where hypotheses take the form of vague presentiments, of hazy sensations" and one "ultimately has to trust one's unconscious, one's instincts, one's creative urge."[6]

Kandel's account gives credence to both his psychoanalytic and scientific backgrounds. His understanding of this paradoxical pattern of problem solving, in which creativity happens spontaneously to a "prepared mind," validates the fruitfulness of psychological insight. Clarke Burnham brought this style of thinking to his students. By the end of the semester, the role of insight was one of my favorite psychological themes. His class opened my interests to psychology. It also prepared me for Joe Rychlak's dialectical version of consciousness and unconsciousness—wherein novel patterns spontaneously arise to reframe intentions, feelings, and meaning. But Joe's theory of mind is more than just a way of understanding scientific discoveries. Its relevance extends throughout human experience—from insights of memory, or the momentary revelations that lead to an apology, to the imaginative leaps of all forms of mental creativity.

One way to appreciate these processes comes from people who rely on them. The novelist and historian Arthur Koestler described his personal practice of creativity this way: "The moment of truth, the sudden emergence of a new insight, is an act of intuition. Such intuitions give the appearance of miraculous flushes, or short-circuits of reasoning. In fact they may be likened to an immersed chain, of which only the beginning and the end are visible above the surface of consciousness. The diver vanishes at one end of the chain and comes up at the other end, guided by invisible links."[7] The "chain reaction" of which Koestler spoke can happen anywhere along the line. Some authors need a clear end point before they can begin to write. The novelist John Irving is unable to start a novel until he has written the last sentence: "I always begin with the last sentence ...

the process is then writing toward that ending."[8] John Grisham does the same: "If I don't know the ending, I don't know the book."[9] The sparks of creativity for songwriter Suzanne Vega come as the first words. Once she had the opening line of "My Name Is Luka," "the song wrote itself."[10] For Annie Dillard, in contrast, writing "begins somewhere in the work's middle" ... "it is the beginning of a work that the writer throws away." "When you write, you lay out a line of words ... make the path boldly and follow it fearfully."[11] A sense of apprehension also guides Barry Lopez's writing: "I have to be frightened of what I am trying to do."[12] Other writers also describe emotions as crucial ingredients of their creative chains. "You start a novel," Peter Matthiessen once asserted, "with a feeling that you want to clarify"[13] or as Norman Mailer put it, "a feeling that doesn't coalesce."[14]

Paradigmatic shifts in science or in writing great literature are a combined result of sustained efforts and creative insights. The processes of insight are also a part of our basic psychological makeup and ongoing experience. We are constantly jumping from one thought to the next, or back and forth between subjective and objective self-awareness. Our mental capability to transcend unidimensional awareness—to both *be* ourself and reflectively see ourself *being ourself*—is a centerpiece of psychology. The dialectical nature of human consciousness is self-evident. Yet it remains one of the great mysteries, still far beyond our understanding or explanation.

Environmental Insights

Shortly after I arrived at COA, I was invited to join a small, informal group of environmental educators. The leader of the group was David Orr, who along with his brother Wilson had recently begun the Meadowcreek Project. The project was based in the Ozark region of northern Arkansas ninety-five miles from Little Rock near the small town of Fox. The project's 1,600 acres of rolling hills, farmland, and mixed forest follows a three-mile-long valley. The purpose of the venture was to create a model community based on principles of sustainable living, renewable energy, and social cooperation. In addition to its local community-building goals, Meadowcreek's founders also envisioned a center where college students, educators, and environmental professionals from across the country could meet and share ideas.

My first trip to Meadowcreek was in the fall of 1982. By then the project's staff and students had constructed the nucleus of their community. The buildings were fashioned from the site's timber and sawmill, including a spacious education and conference center. David's network brought together the academic leaders from newly created environmental studies programs as well as a broad cross section of the environmental policy and conservation leadership. The exchanges of these three- or four-day events were an invaluable collective learning for participants. They were a wonderful way to gather new curriculum ideas and explore the expanding career paths for environmental professions in government, business, and nonprofit sectors. Among the early visitors to Meadowcreek were: Amory and Hunter Lovins, Wendell Berry, Brock Evans, Paul Hawken, Hazel Henderson, Thomas Berry—as well as then-governor of Arkansas Bill Clinton and his wife Hillary.

Academic participants came from environmental programs springing up in existing colleges and universities. Their classes were overflowing. But the politics of departmental turf battles and administrative bureaucracy left them severely overworked and chronically underfunded. Gaining institutional recognition and support for the growing student demand for an environmental curriculum was a common problem everywhere. At COA we had no overarching structures. We were fully committed, as an institution, to an ecological mission. When I shared the college's new educational initiatives, people often voiced admiration for our capacity to experiment with classes and programmatic themes that could be bogged down for years in curriculum review committees at their institutions. Everyone seemed to enjoy hearing about COA and wanted to visit. Over the years, many have.

The friendships I developed among those early Meadowcreek participants have lasted a lifetime. Some of the closest connections, from the outset, were with my New England colleagues. So we made plans to coordinate our travel plans and share a rental van for the two-hour trips between Meadowcreek and Little Rock airport. Those conversations were a wonderful prelude and review for the larger get-togethers. They were especially enriching as a way to build institutional connections with my counterparts at Brown, Harvard, Yale, Dartmouth, Williams, University of Vermont, and other New England institutions. On one trip, we agreed to hold a smaller, regional equivalent of our autumn Meadowcreek gathering. The meeting was held at Williams College in the spring of 1985. It was an immediate success and quickly led to a commitment to meet annually on other campuses. Harold Ward, director of Brown's environmental studies program, agreed to host the next meeting of what became the New England Environmental Studies group—or NEES.

Only representatives from New England programs attended the Williams meeting. However, as word spread, subsequent events began to draw people from New York, Pennsylvania, and beyond. Thus it was decided to replace the initial New England designation with North East, while keeping the founding acronym. Since its founding, NEES has held its annual reunions on more than two dozen campuses, including COA's in the fall of 1993. In a recounting of NEES's history, Harold Ward characterized the group's unaltered informality as "a kind of extended academic unit" that "has steadfastly resisted adoption of membership procedures, debates over mission statements, election of officers, adoption of bylaws, and payment of dues," and quickly adds, "which may explain its longevity and the enthusiasm of those who attend the gatherings."[15] The group's members have been active in the Council of Environmental Deans and Directors (CEDD) and many other formally structured organizations, but they have never relinquished their Ozark roots at their annual spring get-togethers.

The relaxed traditions of NEES have always reminded me of COA's approach to education, where casual conversations can spark an unexpected fresh combination of ideas. During a dinner discussion at our 1987 Meadowcreek meeting, a group of us from northern New England were comparing our field-based approaches to education. It was fun to hear how real-world environmental problems in our respective locations were becoming part of each person's courses—and of students' continuing commitment to working on the issues thereafter. Suddenly, someone in the group suggested: "Why don't we do this together?"

That next fall, we did. The course was called the New England Environment. It was a coordinated effort among environmental programs across five states. On Friday afternoon a team of faculty and students from each college piled into a van and headed for one of their partners' campuses. Everyone arrived in time for an orientation to the place, introductory talks about the forthcoming activities, and a dinner party. Local students hosted visiting students, with similar arrangements among faculty participants. For the next two days everyone attended a rich series of presentations, which also included a field trip to the actual setting of the local environmental issue. The Brown University environmental studies program focused our attention on one of Rhode Island's most pressing problems: trash. The field trip visited the Johnston Landfill (the state's only waste facility and the largest in New England)—estimated to reach its capacity within the next twenty years. It was a staggering insight to the reality of waste management issues and the urgency of source reduction and recycling initiatives. In Vermont, we met at the statehouse in Montpelier. The UVM students and faculty met us there, along with a number of state legislators and environmental professionals. Together, they reenacted the debates that had led to the recent revision of the Vermont Municipal and Regional Planning and Development Act. "Act 200," as it is commonly known, was a landmark example of statewide collaboration of citizen participation at all levels of municipal, environmental, and regional planning. Our partners and host in Massachusetts were the faculty and students of the Williams College environmental center. Their theme was environmental history. Our field trip explored "changes in the land" through wonderfully executed illustrations of how to read landscape history in the field. At Dartmouth, our New Hampshire partner, we were guided through the on-site research of the Hubbard Brook Ecosystem Study. The project is one of the National Science Foundation's long-term ecological research (LTER) sites, famous for discoveries of acid precipitation, forest ecosystem functioning, and the biogeochemistry of watersheds. College of the Atlantic's weekend activities examined the coastal ecology of Maine. Mount Desert Island, as a gateway for Acadia National Park, had just fashioned an island-wide forum (MDI Tomorrow). We were deeply involved in a process of collaborative regional planning and decision making. The central issue was to find a balanced approach to growth management, environmental protection, economic sustainability, and development of low-impact ecotourism. The MDI Tomorrow coalition joined us for the workshop, after which everyone experienced one of Bar Harbor's fastest-growing ecotourism activities: an offshore whale-watching trip.

A month before the New England Environment course began, I received some unwelcome news. My mother had been diagnosed with cancer. The prognosis was not good. Her decline was rapid, and arrangements were made for her to stay in a hospital near my sister's home in New Jersey. I was able to spend time with her until classes began and on the weekends between my fall-term environmental road trips. The hospital's oncology ward had a guest room for family members. The staff gave her excellent care. She was without pain, clear-minded, and characteristically cheerful to the end. My mother's death was a heartrending loss. But in comparison to the sudden ending of my father's life, there was some relief in being able to share her experience of dying. Afterward, Joan and I began the task of sorting, selling, and dispensing of her belongings. Our mother was an avid collector of kitchenware, sewing fabric, furniture, and all sorts of household gadgets. My sister had little interest in any of them. It was harder for me to let go, especially of familiar things with childhood memories. And so, I ended up with a U-Haul truck full of "family treasures" with which I still happily live.

The long drive back to Maine—after all the sorting, clearing out, and cleanup—was grueling. I was exhausted. When I returned to work the next day, the first person I saw was Bill Drury. I had just parked my car. As I stepped through the back door of the arts and sciences building, which enters into the yawning stairwell, Bill was coming down the steps. He stopped instantly and in a wavering voice asked, "How are you doing?" Before I could reply, I saw tears fill his eyes. We were both speechless.

There was no need for words. Instead, we sat together on the stairs and cried openly. It was the first time I had been able to let my full grief come out. Bill was the adored son of a loving mother. He knew where I was. He didn't have to do what he did that day. Maybe he couldn't help it. Neither of us was able to speak. But those few minutes expressed "how I was doing" far beyond spoken words—and I am forever grateful that he asked.

The New England Environment course had an enormous impact on me. It was one of the most enriching educational experiences of my life. The topics we chose—and the thoughtful, in-depth exposure to them at each school—were a wealth of unforgettable insights, but like many life-changing experiences, it was also unrepeatable. It would not be long before many of the initial contributors moved on to tackle new and different environmental problems. Donald Worster returned to his home state and the University of Kansas, where he would write *The Wealth of Nature: Environmental History and the Ecological Imagination*, *A Passion for Nature: The Life of John Muir,* and other influential books of environmental history. Tom Jorling, director of Williams's Center for Environmental Studies, became Commissioner of the New York State Department of Environmental Conservation under Mario Cuomo. Later, as vice president for environmental affairs at International Paper, Tom helped to forge a 257,000-acre Adirondack forest conservation partnership among International Paper, the state of New York, and The Conservation Fund. His colleague at Williams, Bill Moomaw, moved on to the World Resources Institute (WRI) and thereafter became director of Tuft's Center for International Environment and Resource Policy. Bill was also lead author of the Intergovernmental Panel on Climate Change (IPCC), which shared the 2007 Nobel Peace Prize with Al Gore.

This was the last year of our Meadowcreek meetings as well. David Orr bid farewell to his Ozark dream project in 1989 to take a position at Oberlin College as director of environmental studies. Meadowcreek has continued, albeit with some variations of its founding vision. In 1996 it became an official wildlife preserve that continues to function as the region's prized nature and sustainable education center. Shortly after his move to Oberlin, David led a campaign to erect the first substantially green building on a U.S. college campus. The Adam Joseph Lewis Center—a living/learning laboratory for sustainable architecture—is the environmental centerpiece of the college's campus. Orr's commitment to ecological design also inspired a larger green community venture: The Oberlin Project. The project's aim is the creation of a thirteen-acre section of the city's downtown as a model LEED-Platinum neighborhood. The principles and realization of these ideals are conveyed in his books *The Nature of Design* and *Design on the Edge*. David has been a leader of ecological thinking at all levels. His *Ecological Literacy* and *Earth in Mind* have transformed educational curricula. The further goals of setting institution-wide practices that "teach by example" are behind a national movement toward carbon neutrality for college campuses. "The proper role of colleges and universities," in Orr's words, "is to lead the way by committing to climate neutrality, developing smart and farsighted plans to execute that goal, and equipping students for leadership in the challenges and opportunities ahead."[16] These far-reaching goals have stimulated numerous initiatives in which hundreds of colleges and universities have signed a pledge of sustainability—including the American College and University President's Climate Commitment (ACUPCC) and the former U.S. president's Clinton Climate Initiative.

It is perhaps noteworthy that College of the Atlantic was the first higher-education institution in the country to fully embrace these goals with campus-wide and trustee endorsement. The action was featured in *Grist* magazine, which named COA "The Greenest College in the World." In addition to acknowledging the college's commitment to carbon neutrality, the article concluded with these words: "Sustainability has been a hallmark for the college since its first year, in 1972, when COA students were instrumental in getting Maine's groundbreaking bottle bill into the legislature. Since then, the college has consistently incorporated sustainability into all its practices, from architecture to food systems to holding the first-known zero-waste graduation in 2007."[17] Leadership in sustainability practices brought additional recognition. The Sustainable Endowments Institute gave its first "Sustainability Innovator Award" to the college. Recognition also came from *The Chronicle of Higher*

Education: "When it comes to sustainability, the College of the Atlantic seems to be walking while the others are merely talking."[18] Tamar Lewin, from the *New York Times*, made a personal visit and went even further: "While sustainability and the physical environment are certainly major components," as she reported, "the concept of human ecology goes much further, encompassing almost anything."[19] These and other activities have brought COA's mission full circle. As the college's curricular goals and institutional operations merge toward a seamless integration, they have entered the forefront and broader aims of business and society. What once were considered alternative educational ideas are now in the mainstream of higher education.[20]

Significant Life Experiences

During my last two years at Texas, I had the good fortune to acquire a halftime staff position in the university library. My job was to operate the large camera system for microfilming dissertations and rare books (the rarest of which was a 1619 handwritten copy of Johannes Kepler's *Harmonices Mundi*). The position also provided a tuition waiver, retirement benefits, and a central-campus parking permit. My office was on the nineteenth floor of the UT Tower. It had a spectacular view of the campus and the surrounding hill country. There was seldom any other staff on the floor, which also gave me a quiet place to study when I wasn't working. One day, while waiting for the elevator, the sound of voices caught my attention. It was a conversation between two African American maintenance men sitting around the corner on their break, out of sight from where I stood. The sound of their voices suggested they were of different ages. Their exchange, before I arrived at the elevator, appeared to have been about some personal difficulties in the younger man's life. All I actually heard, in the minute or so I stood there, was the older man's counsel.

"Have you ever driven a nail into a tree?" he asked. "Yes," replied the other. "And when you come back years later, you know how the tree grows around the nail?" "Uh-huh." "If you want to remove the nail then, you need to cut out a lot of the tree." The older man paused—and gently added: "That's the way it is with hate."

The elevator opened. Their conversation continued as I stepped in and the doors closed. The unintended witnessing of their intimate exchange embarrassed me. I was also blown away by the elderly man's graceful wisdom. His example has stayed with me ever since. When I feel beset by bad temper, I often remind myself of his words.

Another unforgettable moment with lasting effects of this nature happened during a Meadowcreek meeting. A group of environmental studies students from a nearby college had produced a short documentary film. The screening was set as the closing event of our morning session. The film began with a cafeteria scene. A college student was moving along a lunch line, selecting food, and placing it on his tray. The camera zoomed in on the student's hamburger and then, farther in, to the beef patty. In a retrograde chain of events, the camera followed the burger back to the grill, to the walk-in refrigerator, and then the delivery truck. The filmmakers tracked the truck back to the distribution center—from there, to the loading dock at a slaughterhouse, through the processing plant, to the arriving cows. Along the way they did a brief interview with someone at each place. The final scene was on a farm—a feedlot really—where the camera approached a single cow, as if interviewing the animal. A similar sequence reviewed other items on the student's lunch tray: the tomatoes, strawberries, and onions. It was not a perfect reconstruction, and the production skills were a bit ragged. But the idea came through. It entirely changed my experience of the subsequent lunch—and many other meals, events, and moments since.

The branching chain that brings a hamburger to my plate has an absolute authenticity. If I could shake it, across the virtual expanse of space and time, the wriggling net would prove an ecological truth in every bite. The end of a fork is "an actual occasion" of human ecology. As Wendell Berry encapsulates it in *The Pleasures of Eating*, "How we eat determines, to a considerable extent, how the world is used."[21] My old friend Craig Greene was a masterful field ecologist and botanist who fully grasped the meaning of Berry's assertion. Craig's untimely death from pancreatic cancer was a sad event in the COA community. Yet I will never forget his carefully crafted public presentation when he was honored with the Elizabeth Battles Newlin Chair in Botany—the college's first endowed faculty chair. The title of his talk was "A Botanist at the Grocery Store." He began by holding up a selection of familiar produce items: a tomato, potato, melon, onion, and various other fruits, vegetables, and grains. Each one was the launching point for a taxonomic exploration of its geographic origins, species variations, and cultural history. Craig had an endless reservoir of ecological knowledge, as well as a magnificent slide collection to back up his story. By the end of his talk it was impossible to buy food without giving at least some thought to a larger picture of life. This was years before Michael Pollan's *The Botany of Desire* and *The Omnivore's Dilemma* or Mark Kurlansky's *Cod, The Big Oyster,* and *Salt*. These highly successful books have done a lot to bring ecological insights to the relationship between our mouth and the rest of the living world.

Insight and responsibility are closely related. "The science of ecology shows us that the scope of our intended actions is much wider than we may have imagined," as John Visvader maintains, "but once I learn that my action will be continuously attended by undesirable consequences, the significance of my action changes and the question of responsibility rises where it had not been raised before."[22] The customary meaning of "action" implies doing something on purpose—and carries the additional complexities of conscious intentionality. The path from insight, to responsibility, and then to action is problematic. We may *feel* responsible, but choose not to *act*—or not know *how to act*. Still, we make choices all the time. Our daily lives are filled with intentional actions that inevitably occur in a social and environmental context. Awareness of human actions and consequences has been the common core of conservation, environmental, and sustainability concerns for more than a century.

These relationships of mind and nature have been my hobbyhorse. I am constantly fascinated by the way people see the world and how they tell their stories. My Myers-Briggs profile suggests I have a tendency to be uncritical of alternative views, am somewhat obsessed with "the big picture," have a high need for closure, and spend too much time in my head. Well, on the whole, that's probably so. I also know how many times my own story has changed—usually by some unforeseen event. Intuition and insight are undeniable realities of human consciousness. In a different time, I might have been drawn to the varieties of religious experience like William James, America's first psychologist. But I was born in "the ecological century." An ecological worldview, in my mind, is no less varied—and equally wondrous. Life experience and intuition are as essential to ecological understanding as field studies, data sets, and multivariate algorithms. If Bill Drury was right—and I think he was—the living world is an endless unfolding of chance and change. To understand it we need to be likewise open-minded—which takes me back to where I began thirty-some years ago.

Thomas Tanner, from Iowa State University, was one of the first people to connect "significant life experiences" to environmental education. Tom and I met at a North American Association for Environmental Education conference in 1980. I had recently published a couple of articles on environmental beliefs and behavior in the *Journal of Environmental Education.* Tom's research on environmental insights had just appeared in the same journal. The centerpiece of his significant life experience approach was based on a dramatic anecdote in Aldo Leopold's essay "Thinking Like a Mountain." Having just shot an old female wolf, Leopold reached the animal "in time to watch a fierce green fire dying in her eyes." The moment changed his life. The wolf, as Leopold confessed in the essay, was not his to take; she belonged to the mountain. Tom discovered similar autobiographical and biographical accounts in the lives of many leading conservationists, including David Brower, Sigurd Olson, René Dubos, and others. In further research, on contemporary environmental activists, he showed that youthful experience of the outdoors in pristine natural settings was a dominant feature of their lives as well. A subsequent witnessing of the commercial development and eradication of these beloved places amplified these formative influences in many cases. Tom's findings had compelling implications for environmental education. Classroom instruction, by itself, was not enough. His conclusion was unambiguous: "Children must first learn to love the natural world before they can become profoundly concerned with maintaining its integrity."[23]

The environmental psychologist Louise Chawla has done years of work that affirms this view. The crucial childhood ingredients of dedicated environmental concern, as Chawla has shown, are many hours spent in "ecstatic" outdoor places and a supportive adult who taught respect for nature. The role of these keenly remembered places and relationships has inspired a new generation of psychologists and the emerging subfield of conservation psychology.[24] Richard Louv has raised public awareness about the complex negative consequences of the lack of significant environmental experiences among young people today. His books *Last Child in the Woods* and *The Nature Principle* make a strong case for what he calls "nature deficit disorder." Louv has stimulated an international Children and Nature Network for promoting individual creativity, mental health, and community planning through the restorative powers of the natural world. In the final section of his autobiography, E. O. Wilson put these ideas into words that express the significance of his own experiences: "The tributary sources extend far back in my memory, they still grip my imagination.... I am reluctant to throw away these precious images of my childhood ... I guard them carefully as the wellspring of my creative life, refining and overlaying their productions constantly."[25]

It has been my good fortune to work and live among people who appreciate this worldview. College of the Atlantic is a rookery for this uncommon strain. My initial study of COA—before I left Purdue—gathered examples of students' early life experiences. Their childhood memories were full of solitary explorations of nature, attentive mentors, and influential readings (e.g., *National Geographic, Scientific American*, etc.). I still collect accounts of personal ecological insights and significant life experiences. I have hundreds. Someday perhaps I will organize them in an orderly summary. Among them is one of particular significance.

After Bill Drury died, the college held a commemorative ceremony that brought together his family, former students, and friends from Harvard, Audubon, and College of the Atlantic. Bill, we discovered, had a long-standing bit of advice for his students—which has since become emblematic for many of us. It goes like this:

"When your views on the world and your intellect are being challenged and you begin to feel uncomfortable because of a contradiction you've detected that is threatening your current model of the world or some aspect of it—*pay attention*! You are about to learn something. This discomfort and intellectual conflict is when learning is taking place."

CHAPTER 13

Imagination

This world is but a canvas to our imaginations.
—Henry David Thoreau

Imagine.
—John Lennon

Imagination and insight are closely aligned. One might say they are two sides of the same coin. Whereas insights usually occur as a rapid reorganization of experience, imagination tends to be more of an ongoing and active mental process. The examples of literary insights explored in the preceding chapter are actually the outcome of sustained efforts of imagination by their authors. Conversely, the unity of each story is itself the creative product of multiple insights woven together.

According to the evolutionary psychologist Robert Arp, the conscious ability to segregate and integrate images into future scenarios was a crucial step in the emergence of *Homo sapiens*. This capacity to form and manipulate mental imagery—or *scenario visualization*, as he calls it—accounts for humankind's success as a species. It underlies our creative problem-solving abilities and makes possible the complexities of culture, language, technology, and art. Not everyone agrees with evolutionary psychologists on the origins of consciousness. But hardly anyone doubts the veracity of imagination as a significant feature of human experience.

Imagination is defined as "the act or power of forming a mental image of something not present to the senses or never before wholly perceived in reality."[1] Loren Eiseley called it a "second world" in which human thought and intentionality began to reshape the natural world. The powers of imagination have been a world-changing force, in Mikhail Gorbachev's words, "ever since humankind first conceived the morrow."*

Mental imagination takes perceptual reality beyond the mere physical stimulation of our sense organs. It allows consideration of memories and of future possibilities, and the weighing of alternatives. The ability to transform experience, through the creative powers of mind, is at the core of Rychlak's theory of mentality. To review it again, briefly: consciousness is the ongoing reaching-out and framing of intentions. In an ever-changing flow of affect and cognition, our minds "predicate" patterns of meaning by affirming, denying, or qualifying the future direction of thought and action. Imagination *is* this predication process; and willed, conscious action is the affirmation of our targeted mental extensions. Consciousness, thus, is not a passive "response" to the environment (as behavioral and cognitive scientists would have it)—but, rather, the subjective affirmation of a mental intention for the sake of which we actively "telospond." The Canadian psychologist Alan Paivio also endorses an active, dynamic process to account for imagery, perception, and memory. His research has led to a further discovery of two functionally dissimilar channels for the processing of visual and verbal information. Both means of mental imagery regularly interact, but each has its own quite specific forms of representation (cf. Ingmar Bergman's distinction between cinematic and literary imagination).

Jung's analytical psychology is another place where imagination plays a major role. His technique of "active imagination" was developed as a means of unconscious exploration and creative mentation. The method

---

*This phrase by Gorbachev was conveyed to me during the 1988 SHE conference in San Francisco by Ulrich Loening, former director of the Centre for Human Ecology at the University of Edinburgh. Ulrich had heard it in one of the early perestroika/glasnost speeches and was telling everyone about it. Unfortunately, he no longer recalls exactly when it was said, but he assures me that the words are correct (as translated).

relies on allowing a bit of edge-of-consciousness fantasy or dream imagery "to become active." The key to the practice is to exert as little conscious influence as possible on the material. Jung used active imagination as a therapeutic tool for helping his patients engage with their dream encounters and collective unconscious. Unlike Freud's formless free-association method, Jung's imaginal explorations called forth more evocative and numinous outcomes. As the popularity of his ideas grew, adaptations of the technique became widespread as a creative vehicle for artists, musicians, dancers, and writers. It was a significant aspect within his self-analysis as well. The recently published *Red Book* of Jung's elaborate illuminations and calligraphic text is a tour de force of its creative potential.

My COA colleague and friend Bill Carpenter uses dream journals and imaginal methods to teach creative writing; these inspire prodigious results from his students. Bill has a deep knowledge of Freudian and Jungian psychology. We have team-taught a course on Consciousness and had many lengthy conversations about psychological theory. Bill has a firsthand knowledge of Jungian psychology gained from his own analysis, which he was doing when I arrived at COA. It was a life-changing event that transformed him from a traditional literary scholar into a successful poet and novelist. My background in personality psychology included grounding in psychoanalytic theory, and I have always had a rich dream life. From time to time I dabble with recording and probing into them. But I never actively pursued the dreamworld, as Bill has, to enhance my teaching or personal creativity.

A few years ago I accompanied Patricia to a professional education course for her psychologist license renewal. The weeklong event was a fascinating gathering of analytical therapists and Jungian scholars. Our teacher on the final day was Claire Douglas, a training analyst with the Jung Institute of Los Angeles. Claire teaches on dreams and active imagination there and is author of several books on the history of analytical psychology. Her presentation was on "Shakti's Journey: Passion and the Divine Feminine" and, like all of the preceding days, was filled with mythic symbolism and imagery. The tantric feminine symbol for Shakti, as she explained, is a downward pointing triangle, representing the cervical yoni as the source of creative energy. Its masculine counterpart, Shiva, is an upward pointing triangle. Within her ascending journey through the chakras, she showed slides from Christiana Morgan's diary and visualizations of active imagination.*

The fourth (heart) chakra, Claire described, is where we learn to be vulnerable, as the masculine and feminine become linked and unite. From there she followed on through the fifth (throat), sixth (meditation), and final (crown) chakra of enlightenment. Every level, from beginning to end, was elaborated by visual, poetic, and living symbols—along with examples of famous individuals whose personality was characteristic of the typology at each stage.

Our week of presentations and group activities was coming to an end. But before it was over, Claire invited us to explore an exercise in active imagination as the finale. She encouraged everyone to look inward for an image, perhaps from a recent dream or whatever spontaneous source allowed its appearance, to use for our exercise. The most readily available image to my mind was the simple yoni triangle of the feminine pubis, which I had unthinkingly sketched in my notebook. As I darkened it in, a second, inverted male triangle embraced it. Next, a snakelike line passed through the interlocked figure and carried on across the page, where a flurry of contrasting triangular patterns erupted. Some were feminine with masculine interiors; others were reversed. As the combinations of Shakti and Shiva forms developed—black-in-white and white-in-black—the snake slid through that field too. It coiled back across the page, as if pulling them along. My pen was chasing a purely "felt" image, waiting to become itself. I drew whatever appeared, as if in a lucid dream. There was no thinking. A cross, within a circle, within a square leaped onto the page.

---

*Christiana Morgan was analyzed by Jung and became a powerful source of inspiration for his archetypal theory of unconscious masculine (animus) and feminine (anima) conflict. She also maintained a lengthy professional and extramarital relationship with the distinguished Harvard psychologist Henry Murray—who, many maintain, used her ideas without acknowledgment. Her evocative charcoal drawings led to the widely used, projective Thematic Apperception Test (TAT).

The snake passed underneath—deposited another collection of images—whereupon it emerged headfirst beyond, as I hurriedly filled out the image.

I know. It sounds a bit nutty. The whole event, from initial triangle to what turned into a closing mandala, took perhaps twenty minutes. But the actual experience was profoundly compelling. I really was submerged in the depths of my psyche, completely unaware of my surroundings, and grippingly pursuant of importunate closure. The final result, though only a crude approximation, was the kind of image one might put on a coat of arms or use as the symbolic icon for a flag.

In the final moments of the workshop, before we departed, Claire asked us to share our images. So I showed my drawing to the person sitting beside me. Without pause, she handed me her piece, which was in the form of a poem—to the earth. I read it slowly and thanked her for sharing it. "Please keep it," she said affectionately. "It is part of what you have done."

I have taken other workshops with Patricia. But that week of scholarship and contemplation was uniquely powerful. Reflecting on the depths of mind released an exceptional level of intimacy and authenticity among the participants. It was refreshing to share vulnerable moments in group activities and personal exchanges. Unlike the guarded interactions of many get-togethers, the atmosphere of openness was a delight. I learned something else: trust inspires active imagination.

The Artful Mind

The first human ecologists, in my opinion, were not scientists or scholars. They were storytellers. It is unlikely we will ever know how the art of telling stories began. Perhaps the primal roots, as some suggest, lie in imitative dance or rudimentary drawing. But one thing is certain. At some point, our forebearers began to develop an aptitude to symbolically encode remembered and imagined events. These mental representations also became shaped into vocalizations, capable of reproduction and meaningful exchange. Oral communication was a world-changing palette for binding human experience, memory, and imagination.

When or how human language abilities developed is a major debate. Anatomical evidence suggests the larynx in the vocal tract—one prerequisite for complex sound production—was in its place in the early Pleistocene. Thus *Homo ergaster* may have possessed some ability for speechlike vocalization well before the appearance of the anatomically modern *Homo sapiens*. Other anatomical changes, such as the enlargement of the hypoglossal canal, through which the nerves pass for intricate tongue movements, point to a much later date. The fossil record furnishes few hard clues as to when the brain regions for speech production and comprehension appeared. Even if they were sufficiently developed for complex cognitive processing, how linguistic syntax and grammar actually unfolded remains speculative. My hunch is that language was very much shaped by human affairs. Unfortunately, the most valuable evidence—the actual sounds of it—disappeared into thin air as soon as they were voiced.

Those traces of imagination from prehistoric language are forever lost. But the human urge for creativity has left its mark in countless other modes along the way. When the prehistoric cave paintings were discovered at Altamira in northern Spain in the mid-nineteenth century, they were at first considered forgeries. No one could believe that such skillful images were not the work of modern artists. As more examples were encountered elsewhere—in the caves of Chauvet, Pech Merle, and Lascaux—archaeologists gradually revised their opinions. Many other examples of Paleolithic engravings, sculptured figurines, decorative pottery, and ornamental beads, dating from ten thousand to forty thousand years ago, have been found worldwide. Some archaeologists believe that signs of symbolic representation appear in artifacts far older, from perhaps as much as a half million years ago.

Wherever one draws the line, the prehistoric signature of humankind's image-making aptitude is remarkable. As the U.S. poet laureate William Stanley Merwin succinctly put it: "What distinguishes us is not language … it is imagination."[2] As he well knows, imagination is a requisite of good poetry. But words are by no means the sole vehicle of creative expression. The artfulness of mind is found everywhere in our world-shaping inheritance. The Cambridge art historian Nigel Spivey has traced the record of humanity's artistic endeavors. His book *How Art Changed the World*—and the BBC documentary of the same name—gives a compelling account of how humans made art, and how art made us human.

Art is a tricky term. It is sometimes used in the restrictive sense of a "work of art," as might be found in a museum. Art is also a *process*—common throughout human experience—that is not restricted to only artists' creation. Adam Weinberg, Director of the Whitney Museum of American Art, makes a helpful clarification: "Art is an appetite."[3] Some people possess exceptional creative talents and the desire to fashion fine art. Appreciation of their work fulfills our appetites in many ways. In accord with Weinberg's meaning, however, everyone has artistic sensitivities and practices aesthetic values. We do so in infinite ways. Our thoughts and feelings combine in novel patterns every time we "frame a new intention" (to use Rychlak's terms) and move forward in life. This is the imaginative mind.

George Lucas describes the imaginative process in his account of making *Star Wars*. His struggles to unfold and advance the story line disclose the progress of sustained creativity. "Art," as Lucas describes it, "is a way of communicating emotions." The final product, in his case, was a movie of mythic proportions. It was an enormously complex production that required multiple takes, from myriad angles, and countless revisions. Miles of unused film were left on the editing room floor.[4] His dialogue with Charlie Rose is an insightful explication of the complex, iterative processes of art. Filmmaking is not efficient. The same may be said about all artistic endeavors. Every artist's studio holds a river of detritus that never finds the light of day. If death is part of life, it is a major part of art as well.

The difference between art-as-object and art-as-process was vividly brought to my attention, during my first venture to Europe in search of human ecology, in the summer of 1984. While visiting Torsten Malmberg at the University of Lund, Torsten took me to the university's magnificent Skissernas Museum (Museum of Sketches). The museum's aim is to show the actual creative process of the artist, from initial idea through its stages to the final product. Many of the exhibits are arranged in displays reminiscent of the artist's cluttered studio. The archive of more than thirty thousand items is the world's largest collection of sketches by leading Swedish and international artists—including Matisse, Orozco, and Rivera. The museum, still unique in its mission, continues to add to the collection from all over the world. The interplay of fresh ideas and subtle judgments leading to a completed work of art is alluring. To a casual observer the discarded models and drawings might appear quite acceptable. Yet they were somehow insufficient for the artist. Then, inexplicably, the final (and often familiar) piece does indeed seem to be the fitting conclusion.

Judy Russell, one of Patricia's best friends, reminded me of my Skissernas experience a couple of years ago. Judy is a landscape artist who takes painting classes every summer to improve her skills. During a class break one day, her favorite teacher told the following parable (from my recollection of Judy's account):

> One time, long ago, the emperor of a distant land was making arrangements for the wedding of his beloved daughter. The young princess had a great fondness for ducks. Her favorite childhood toy was a velvet duck. Her affection for ducks continued, as she grew older. She often spent long hours beside a nearby pond feeding and talking to the ducks, to whom she had given each a name. So the emperor—wishing to please his daughter with a special wedding gift—made plans to acquire the most exquisite drawing of a duck ever made. He summoned his envoy to find the finest artist in the land. The emperor's messenger combed the kingdom from end to end and, at long last, located the one man considered to be the greatest of artists. The royal envoy, upon arriving at the artist's studio, knocked on the door. He knocked again. After a long pause, the door slowly opened. Half-hidden in the shadowed portal stood an aged man. "What do you want?" he asked in a scarcely audible voice. "I am here at the behest of the emperor," the visitor said, "to commission a drawing of a duck for his daughter's wedding." "Come back tomorrow," the old man grumbled as he slowly shut the door. The next day the emperor's representative returned. "I am here for the drawing," he declared. But the old artist, as on

the previous day, told him to return the next day. The routine would be repeated—over and over. By now the wedding was very near. The emperor was enraged by the artist's insubordination. So too was his envoy, whose many fruitless trips had yet to collect the long-awaited artwork. Finally, on the day before the wedding, the emperor himself rode out to confront the feckless artist—accompanied by a troop of armored horsemen. He pounded on the studio door. As before, it slowly opened. "Where is my daughter's wedding picture?" the emperor thundered. "If I do not have it now, my guards will bind you and drag you to my dungeon." "Wait here," the old man replied. A few moments later he shuffled forth from the shadows—an ink stick in one hand, a blank canvas in the other. In a single, unbroken gesture, his pen flashed across the canvas. When his hand lifted, he presented the emperor with the most magnificent piece of art the emperor had ever seen. The emperor, delighted with the drawing, thanked the old man. His agent was less sanguine. "Why," he demanded, "did you make me return again and again, incur the wrath of my sovereign, and then in a few brief moments produce the drawing for which we waited so long?" "Follow me," said the aged artist. The emperor and his associate entered the shadowy building, whereupon the old man circled the room opening cupboards and drawers. All of them, every nook and cranny, were filled with sketches of ducks.

Marvelous achievements often seem effortless. But the grace that makes them appear easy is gotten by hard work. Doing something well takes enduring intentions to constantly improve. Genuine mastery is always demanding. The old way of saying this comes from Thomas Edison: "Genius is one percent inspiration and ninety-nine percent perspiration." The new way, popularized by Malcolm Gladwell, is the "10,000-Hour Rule," i.e., the amount of practice required to reach world-class standing in a variety of specific domains—including science, medicine, art, music, and sports. The magic number behind Gladwell's achievement-is-talent-plus-preparation hypothesis comes from several sources.

One is K. Anders Ericsson, a research psychologist and authority on the attributes and achievements of highly experienced professionals. An editor of the *Cambridge Handbook of Expertise and Expert Performance* and other books, Ericsson has also conducted numerous studies of professional development, expert performance, and superior memory. Another is Daniel Levitin, an interdisciplinary scholar who skillfully draws on anthropology, evolutionary biology, neuroscience, and music. The story of Levitin's dual-career life as a professional musician and a professor of cognitive science is told in his books *This Is Your Brain on Music: The Science of a Human Obsession* and *The World in Six Songs: How the Musical Brain Created Human Nature*.

The 10,000-Hour Rule seems a bit fanciful. But it does hold up in many cases. Achieving professional expertise as a musician or a brain surgeon apparently requires dedicated practice of this order. It works out to be about the same to complete an undergraduate and graduate education. The 720 days of sea-time to qualify for my 100-ton Coast Guard captain's license was about half. In the decade and a half since then, I have logged the rest and can surely feel the difference in competence as an ocean sailor. It took me about a decade to develop proficiency at teaching psychology, another to coalesce the intricacies of academic administration, and at least as much to get my head around human ecology.

Ecological Imagination

This last one—human ecology—poses a curious problem. On the one hand, my years of exploring the origins and development of human ecology have affirmed the impediments to interdisciplinarity. Opportunities to study it or to find a professional home to practice it, as I have, are rare. Wish as I might that it was otherwise—the truth is human ecology remains far from the mainstream. On the other hand, I also know the ingredients of a human ecological perspective present themselves endlessly in daily life. We are surrounded by opportunities to enlarge our experience into wider views. Every moment is an occasion to actively imagine and to reframe our perception and appreciation.

It is easy to overlook how chance moments can be poignant events. A stranger's smile, a memorable scent, or the springtime sound of peepers can send us into reverie. Even the tiresome lull of a checkout line can bring surprises. That is where I saw the tabloid picture of Francis Johnson, who set my mind churning over his obsession with string. It is also where George Bilgere was inspired to write this poem:

Desire

The slim, suntanned legs
of the woman in front of me in the checkout line
fill me with yearning
to provide her with health insurance
and a sporty little car with personalized plates.

The way her dark hair
falls straight to her slender waist
makes me ache
to pay for a washer/dryer combo
and yearly ski trips to Aspen, not to mention
her weekly visits to the spa
and nail salon.

And the delicate rise of her breasts
under her thin blouse
kindles my desire
to purchase a blue minivan with a car seat,
and soon another car seat, and eventually
piano lessons and braces
for two teenage girls who will hate me.

Finally, her full, pouting lips
make me long to take out a second mortgage
in order to put both kids through college
at first- or second-tier institutions,

> then cover their wedding expenses
> and help out financially with the grandchildren
> as generously as possible before I die
> and leave them everything.
>
> But now the cashier rings her up
> and she walks out of my life forever,
> leaving me alone
> with my beer and toilet paper and frozen pizzas.[5]

This is not an ecological poem. But Bilgere does bring forth the rapture of imagination. Who has not been touched by fantasies of a stranger? Our imagination is stirred in never-ending ways. It happens when we make our choice of college, plan our next vacation, hear a ringing phone, or shop for a dinner party with friends. It happens all the time. That is my point. My other point is that our lives can be even richer.

Former *Time* magazine journalist, and author of *A Passion for This Earth,* Valerie Andrews puts it simply. "Perhaps the most important thing we can do," she writes, "is to open ourselves to receive the living world."[6] Siegfried Fischbacher (of Siegfried and Roy fame) expressed a comparable thought. The week after his partner's near-fatal attack by a white tiger, he gave his advice to a nationwide *Good Morning America* audience: "Look for the magic around you and let it enlighten your life and your heart."[7] The novelist Ruth Ozeki gives a matching view: "Without the power of imagination we lack the power to alter outcomes, so if we can't imagine better outcomes in a better world, we cannot act to achieve these"—to which she adds a finer point: "You can't make something you can't imagine."[8]

These calls to use imagination to intensify life go beyond old-school environmentalism. They are not legal arguments, policy recommendations, or activist agendas. The focus is both inward and outward. My way of holding this position is with the banner of human ecology. But other terms can work as well. Bonnie Tai, COA's Director of Education Studies, reverses the words. In her faculty human ecology essay, she introduced the term "ecological humanism" to guide her approach to cultural and educational studies. It is a minor adjustment, but not without purpose. I appreciate Bonnie's humanistic inclination and subtle counterbalancing to bring "the ecological" more fully into "the human." Andrew Light, Director of George Mason's Center for Global Ethics, offers another fine-tuning: "I actually prefer the term 'ecological citizen' over environmentalist."[9] This is Light's way to shed some of the antiurban bias of traditional environmentalism and move into a larger sense of ecology and community. Words really do matter. They help us to reposition our views and to notice things in new ways. But words alone do not change minds.

Awakening our aesthetic senses and our compassion will be indispensable for a livable future. The future calls for imagination—and the very best of it. This is not to suggest the answers lay hidden somewhere in art, or in the minds of artists. We must look elsewhere, perhaps everywhere, to find the way. Mihaly Csikszentmihalyi, an expert on quality of experience and the creative process, believes "Change often comes from the periphery."[10] His studies of creativity find that it often begins at the edges of experience. The advocate of mind/body medicine and mental imagery Gerald Epstein concurs: "Imagination is the vehicle that allows penetration from outside to inside."[11] Epstein, a psychiatrist at Mount Sinai Medical Center, Director of the American Institute for Mental Imagery, and a successful author, has studied and employed a combination of Western and Eastern techniques in his psychiatric practice.

The Jungian analyst Thomas Moore also combines the traditions of Western and Eastern philosophy. His *Care of the Soul* was a *New York Times* best seller, which has allowed him to become an independent scholar and writer. Patricia and I spent a week at one of his Cape Cod Institute summer seminars a few years ago. Moore is an excellent lecturer, and I gained a lot from his presentations. His discussion of desire made some useful distinctions: between desire "to do," desire "to understand," and the desire "to desire." The latter, though he didn't put it this way, is very much akin to Maslow's higher levels of "being" motivation to experience beauty, joy, and love (which Maslow drew from Hindu philosophy). Seeing the world (human and natural) in nonjudgmental observation, without the need to understand or manipulate, is "mindfulness." As the Sri

Lankan monk Henepola Gunaratana explains, "Mindfulness is to observe without criticism and without surprise. It is a balanced interest in things as they are. Mindfulness is not thinking—it is perceiving; it is attention."[12]

The meditative attention of mindfulness is an intuitive art. It is where insight and imagination meet. This is also where experience and ecology combine in the fullest sense of "mind in nature." Intuition, in the term's literal sense, means "without tuition." But our understanding of tuition has become clouded. Most people think of it as a monetary expression about the cost of instruction. The actual root meaning of tuition, however, is about the teaching itself (i.e., *tutored* knowledge). The magic of insight is when our (taught) knowledge of tuition and (untaught) processes of intuition conjoin. This is the alchemy of human creativity—and why the arts and sciences must be partners in an ecological future. As Bill Carpenter contends, "The requirements of a Human Ecologist and a creative artist are much the same, the same openness toward experience, the same ability to tolerate paradox and ambiguity and to perceive the order in disorder, and the willingness to recognize that the enemy is yourself wearing a different mask." Human ecology is not just a subject matter that is taught. It is also a creative process—of ecological insight and imagination—in which we are authors, actors, and partners in all of life's drama. "What Human Ecology has to do," in Carpenter's view, "is to reconstruct a worldview in which the mental and physical are reunited … The reunification of mind and nature is our main philosophical goal."[13] The keys to this challenge lie in integrating the best of our knowledge *and* our powers of imagination.

CHAPTER 14

Keyholes

Who looks outside, dreams. Who looks inside, awakens.
—Carl Jung

To thine own self be true.
—William Shakespeare

The dean of American broadcasting, Edward R. Murrow, introduced his audience to an innovative approach to radio listening in 1951. The program was called *This I Believe.* For the next five years, his listeners were treated to a diverse collection of personal essays. Famous people—like Eleanor Roosevelt, Albert Einstein, Carl Sandberg, Helen Keller, and Arnold Toynbee—wrote some of them. Others came from regular daily listeners. Murrow's invitation was based on a straightforward though demanding request. The challenge for each individual was to express, in a few hundred words, the core principles that guided his or her life. The resulting personal credos became one of the most popular programs of its time.

National Public Radio renewed the idea fifty years later. In the midst of the news programs *All Things Considered* and *Morning Edition,* radio audiences heard a fresh round of self-reflections and personal philosophies from a diverse collection of new contributors. NPR published eighty samples of these masterful thought pieces, from Murrow's original show and the revival edition, in a special-edition book, *This I Believe*. The personal essay is a highly adaptable and creative literary device. The term comes from the Old French *essai* ("to try or attempt"), which is akin to the English *assay* ("to test or weigh in"). Essays usually render a speculative and brief personal view. They give us insight to the author's private world of meaning and beliefs on a topic. Reading them, or hearing them read, is often inspiring and evocative. The invitation extended by Murrow and National Public Radio, for example, stimulated many thousands of individual submissions.

Aldous Huxley once compared the essay to looking at the world through a keyhole. Its flexible form may be extended to musical, cinematic, and photographic compositions. Irrespective of its domain, the essay relies on an economy of expression. The approaches of contemporary filmmakers, like Ken Burns and Michael Moore, rely on a basic essay style to combine historical, current, and anecdotal materials within a personal narrative. Murrow, himself, relied on these devices throughout his influential radio/television career. His pioneering *Harvest of Shame* gave television audiences a vivid introduction to the new media's potential to teach using essays. They continue as a significant feature of investigative and interpretive journalism.

Woody Guthrie's "This Land Is Your Land"—and his many labor songs and dustbowl ballads—were legendary musical essays. So was his son Arlo's "American Pie," as well as many of the politically oriented '60s and '70s folk songs. Environmental essays were also put to song in Gordon Lightfoot's "Canadian Railroad Trilogy," Patty Larkin's "Metal Drums," and Joni Mitchell's "Big Yellow Taxi."

In recent years the essay has moved beyond its persuasive and entertainment status. It is now a nearly universal entrance requirement for competitive college admissions, with which many high school seniors struggle to find "their story." At College of the Atlantic this initial entry hurdle has been raised further. In their final year, all COA students must complete another "human ecology essay" as a part of their graduation requirements. Ever since the college opened in 1972, each student's completed essay has been part of their permanent academic record and official transcript.

As might be expected, students often struggle with this task. But over the years we have discovered that an early deadline for first drafts, frequent meetings with academic advisers, and an open-door program of tutors in the writing center ease the pain. The challenge is rendered somewhat less daunting by encouraging students to read essays by former graduates, which are published annually in a special collection. Most faculty have written their own versions, and these too are shared with the students. Some teachers have written several. My friend and colleague John Visvader has produced more than a dozen—all of them from diverse approaches and superbly crafted.

The social psychologist Leon Festinger, author of cognitive dissonance theory, once made a counterintuitive observation about attitude change. In advance of a challenging and ego-involving test, most people hold a negative opinion about what lies ahead. Once the task is completed, however, their attitude shifts in a positive direction. In short, as he once put it, "We come to love the things for which we suffer." Description of the psychological processes of dissonance reduction is beyond the present context. But Festinger's précis gives a good accounting of COA students' opinions about their essay degree requirement. Anxiety, procrastination, and even disdain for the requirement can be widespread beforehand. Afterward, the negativity is washed away, as students enthusiastically share their finished products—in anticipation of the final printed collection.

Dozens of students have worked with me over the years as they developed and revised their thoughts. I have read countless other students' attempts to grapple, each in their own ways, with the meaning of human ecology. It is a valuable pedagogical exercise to pause in the midst of a college education to reflect on and identify core beliefs. I believe that coalescing our thoughts, from time to time throughout life, and putting them into words, is a worthwhile activity.

Actually, reflective narratives have become an increasingly important component of the professional workplace. Their use in the context of personnel selection, executive assessment, and career development is spreading. At the organizational level, it is now common practice to have a clear and concise statement of mission and values. How these values are put into action as goals and objectives are the fundamentals of strategic planning. In many instances, these institutional "essays" are authored collectively in collaborative visioning and planning sessions.

No one wishes to reach the end of life in regret and despair. Some people are content to drift along. Others adopt "packaged" solutions for their identity questions, opt to follow whatever path is "given" to them, or see life in terms of fate. For most of us, however, the issues of self-identity are deeply challenging. The psychological process of planting one's feet in grounded beliefs, as Erik Erikson maintained, is a crucial stage of personality development. The freedom—and responsibility—to choose our values is a prerequisite of personal fidelity in the life we live. The artful phrasemaker René Dubos gave it a term: meaningful livelihood. There is no common definition, no universal solution, no grand theory. We are not born with a common operating manual; we are individuals. Each of us must grapple with the private discovery and construction of personal meaning. The answer lies in the fullness of experience—in principles—as Benjamin Franklin* proclaimed in the Declaration of Independence, which are *self*-evident. This is what Edward R. Murrow invited his listeners to consider. The multitude of thoughtful and soul-searching responses is evidence of their personal importance. Our assessments do not need to be exhaustive. They can be quite brief, as in a five-minute essay. Hearing one, honestly executed, is a potent stimulus to craft our own.

The one-hundredth anniversary of Rachel Carson's birthday was in 2007. On my birthday that year I received a telephone call from David Hales, COA's president, and Ken Hill, my successor as academic dean. I had been selected to receive the college's newest endowed chair: The Rachel Carson Chair in Human Ecology. What a birthday surprise! I was overwhelmed—and delighted. A few weeks later I was invited to speak at a special event, in part to honor me, but also to meet the donors to the chair—and other potential donors to future endowed chairs. In

---

*Thomas Jefferson is rightly given credit as author of the document. As I understand it, however, when Benjamin Franklin was given the chance to review it, he scratched out Jefferson's words "sacred and undeniable," replacing them with "self-evident."

preparation for my talk, I threw myself into the task of becoming more familiar with Carson's life and work. My presentation was a review of Carson's life, which included a number of one-degree-of-separation links between her life and the lives of various founders of COA. It ended with a posthumous welcoming of her to the college—as would surely have happened, had her life not been cut off as early as it was. The talk was warmly received by the group and later published as an invited essay in an academic journal.

My association with Rachel Carson, through a named chair in her honor, led to other things. One of them, the following summer, was the Fifth Annual Environmental Writers' Conference. These meetings are actually more like workshops than conferences, where up to a hundred nature writers, from across the country, convene to share their interests and talents. The thought of addressing an audience of writers, who likely knew more about Carson than I, was somewhat daunting. Nonetheless, I took it as a chance to explore a "This I Believe" opportunity, as well as fashion a keyhole to what was becoming the skeleton for this book. My invitation had apparently been sparked by one of the conference organizers having read my essay from the summer before—which he had sent to all of the attendees in advance of the workshop. The workshop was in Boothbay Harbor that year, not far from where Carson's island home was located. As many of the participants were from elsewhere around the country, I also took it as an opportunity to welcome them to Maine. The title of my greeting was: A Welcome to Rachel Carson's Worlds: Ecology, Experience, Language—and Maine.

> In your packets Joe Doll has included a short essay I wrote last year on the occasion of Rachel Carson's one-hundredth birthday. I had just received an endowed chair in her name at College of the Atlantic, so it seemed fitting to welcome her back to Maine—to College of the Atlantic really. Although the college wasn't founded until after Carson's death, I am sure she would have become a part of it, as did many of her friends.
>
> This year, the table is turned a bit. I have been asked to welcome you—Rachel Carson's friends and followers—to her world here in

Maine. Many of you are visiting from out of state, some for the first time. If you drove here, you saw the sign, just after the Kittery Bridge, which proclaims: "Maine—The Way Life Should Be." That might appear a crass ploy of tourism. But for many of us who live here, those words are a source of re-inspiration each time we return home.

These feelings have been captured in many other ways. Some of my favorite images come from the words of the Maine native singer-songwriter, David Mallett, who grew up in the Dover-Foxcroft area. Dave has a wonderful sense of what life is like in the Maine countryside. His "Garden Song"—"inch by inch, row by row, gonna make this garden grow. All it takes is a rake and a hoe, and a piece of fertile ground"—is included among the fifty most famous folk songs of all time, recorded by Paul Stookey, Pete Seeger, Arlo Guthrie, John Denver, and even the Muppets. Perhaps my personal favorite of Dave's songs is: "I Knew This Place"—which recaptures my own childhood experiences in the rich textures and unforgettable images of growing up in the country. And then there is the moving story of his childhood farm, struck by lightning from a summer storm, and burning to the ground. The words paint a powerful picture of rural New England—main house, middle house, back house, barn. All one—and all gone at once.

Anyone who has experienced loss by fire knows the anguish of trying to retrieve what you can, and then coming to the point when it is no longer possible to save any more. We had that experience twenty-five years ago this summer, when the main building at College of the Atlantic burned to the ground. The fire was discovered and reported early on the morning news before anyone had arrived on campus. But word got around quickly. Everyone rushed to the scene and immediately began to retrieve whatever furniture, lab equipment, or office belongings we could pull through side doors and windows. As the fire spread beyond the administrative offices and into the dining hall, all efforts focused on the library—first to whatever books and journals we could carry—and finally to the student senior projects. Many things were saved, but the entire building complex was a total loss.

As I recall that day, I am reminded of how such events clarify what is really important to us. But instead of clutching the *objects* of our lives, what if we were pressed to choose the *ideas* we most cherish?—that handful of foundational beliefs at the core of our worldviews. For me—life is grounded in three fundamental ideas on which I rely, a triad of essential truths at the core of existence. It is a conviction that we live in three convergent worlds.

The first is the living world itself. By whatever cosmogony one may choose—whether by Brahma, by Genesis, or by Darwin—it is the oldest. The earth and life upon it, I am confident, really does exist—in ever-changing and unfolding intricacies.

Next is what Loren Eiseley called the "second world"—which emerged from the natural world. It is the world of the mind and of humanity. Though the moment of its origins is lost in the mists of time, it has been here, as Mikhail Gorbachev once put it, "ever since humankind first conceived the morrow."

And finally, we live in a third world—of words—a further creation of the second, human world. This is the realm which bridges us back to our origins. In words we name the objects and experiences of life, and through words we imagine and create the worlds of the future.

Language is more than merely communication between humans. It lies at the center of all experience. It guides perception, structures memory, and propels our imagination. The understanding of life expands on all sides through our *wording* of the world. Those of us who sit before the blank page, awaiting the appearance of words, know the rapture that can arise from this third world too. Rachel Carson lived and was at home in all three of these domains. She was at home in the limpid tide pool at dawn, a careful and curious observer of the living world. Yet her experience went well beyond the inquiring mind of a scientist. She not only *knew* about nature— she *felt* it. And with the restless pen of a poet, she wove the ecological and experiential together.

Like Carson, we hover in midstream between the lands of nature and the mind. Oftentimes it is nature that inspires us. Other times the sources of creation are in the imagination. Fresh insights endow new perceptions. They lead to unforeseen places and open new horizons of caring and responsibility. Here is where all things meet. Here is where humans take back the past, feel the present, and touch the future.

Words complete the circle of life. They span the gulf between fact and feeling and fix the images of life's unfolding, moment by moment, into a seamless flow. Like strands of DNA they fasten life to life in ever-changing code.

But words are but a part of this larger whole. Their magic works best when unnoticed. I can still recall my first experiences of reading, and the joy of passing through their veil. The words, the page, the book itself disappeared. Through the spectrum of language I was transported elsewhere.

The psychologist Mihaly Csikszentmihalyi calls the experience "flow." It is when we lose the sense of our self as an object, and consciousness becomes a subjective, continuous process. This integration is what Abraham Maslow meant by peak experiences—a unifying perception of being-in-becoming. For Rachel Carson it was the "sense of wonder." Her writing was tied to breathing—written and revised through reading aloud. She unified nature and consciousness, like yogic stretching, slipping deeper with each breath into the feeling of life. The place she loved to do that most was here. Here on the Maine coast, where we are now.

And so, it is with great pleasure that I welcome you. In the memory of Rachel Carson, may we all discover the words to tell our stories of the way life should be.

For the Love of Life

Huxley's keyhole metaphor for the essay is a robust comparison. It is a reminder, like the frame around Bill Carpenter's father's painting canvas, of the role of values and creativity in human perception.[1] Conservationists have a long tradition of using metaphors to frame their ideas and subject matter. Their keyholes for combining scientific knowledge and value-based claims are the familiar webs and pyramids and niches of ecological theory. Ecologists know what will happen if a pine forest is destroyed. But ecologists "can shed no light," as Paul Shepard stressed, on the question of whether humans "actually will or will not cut down the pine forest."[1] For this answer, we must reverse our view and look back through the keyhole in the opposite direction.

This is the orientation of "conservation psychology"—a new and exciting field focused on the human dimensions of ecology. Gene Myers, a former COA student who subsequently completed his PhD in psychology under Mihaly Csikszentmihalyi at Chicago, has become a leader of this approach. Along the way, Gene invited me to contribute to a special issue of *Human Ecology Review* that he and Carol Saunders were editing on conservation psychology. The publication included theory and research articles from the field's pioneers, along with essays and commentaries from Mihaly Csikszentmihalyi, Louise Chawla, and others.

Gene brought many of us together at SHE's 20th Anniversary Conference in Salt Lake City the following year. His daylong symposium, and follow-up forum with conservation biologists, was an immersion into the interdisciplinary issues of conservation. Amid the meeting's many forward-looking contributions, there was a sobering report by Britain Scott and Sue Koger on the status of psychology in environmental curricula. Scott and Koger had surveyed some seven hundred undergraduate environmental programs nationwide. Only 5 percent of environmental studies programs, they discovered, required a psychology course—in environmental science programs, it was zero!

The equation has improved since then, largely due to the dedicated efforts by those symposium participants. The group has organized the research literature and developed much-needed education materials. Gene's *Conservation Psychology* (coauthored with Susan Clayton), Sue Koger's *The Psychology of Environmental Problems*, and Peter Kahn's *Ecopsychology* are among the most influential examples—along with important contributions by other members of the Salt Lake meeting.

For my part in Gene's symposium, I wanted to explore the keyhole notion in a different way. Huxley's metaphor is a compelling frame that highlights the essay's integrative literary utility. The extended version of a keyhole, as a two-way window, gives an additionally useful opening to weave the interdisciplinary strands of psychology and biology. Ecologists have historically relied on metaphors to communicate the complex processes of nature. In the waning light of ecosystem and balance-of-nature conceptions, many biologists have shifted their focus toward species-level views. A new ecological language was emerging—of keystones, flagships, umbrellas, and so on. This reframing of ecology altered both the guiding principles of conservation practice, as well as the means of communicating them publicly. Conservation ecologists had the further responsibility, in the midst of this paradigm shift, of reeducating their colleagues in other academic and applied fields. John Anderson chaired the panel of biologists at the Salt Lake meeting who met with the conservation psychology group. His account of the transitions within ecological science and explanation of their implications was a timely updating on the status of the field. It was also a special opportunity to consider ecology and psychology in a new light.

The biologists at the table were there to learn some psychology as well. My thinking, in advance of the meeting, was to start at the core of contemporary psychology—with something that combined theoretical significance and empirical grounding. One of the most comprehensive frameworks of this type is the "Big Five" model of personality. The model is based on decades of factor-analytic research that shows a coherent structure of five personality traits: Openness, Conscientiousness, Extraversion, Agreeableness, and Neuroticism. These domains have been shown to have considerable validity and utility throughout psychology. It was not difficult to imagine extending them in the direction of ecological concepts or conservation behavior. Another possibility was to look toward the research studies on values and attitudes associated with environmental sensitivity and responsibility—of which there are many. This was where I began years ago. Most of the psychologists on the forthcoming meeting agenda were active researchers in this domain. Their knowledge was more current and likely deeper than mine. Moreover, to be honest, I really wasn't much interested in data-driven social science anymore. Gene's invitation was a chance to try something a bit more open-ended and speculative.

The upcoming Salt Lake City meeting that fall was the first SHE conference in the United States since before the World Trade Center disaster. The uncertainties surrounding air travel after 9/11, and the impending decision to invade Iraq, forced cancellation of SHE's plans for an April 2002 conference at Michigan State. The added difficulties of obtaining visas had a cooling effect on international conferences for several years. SHE was able to convene a successful meeting, hosted by the University of Quintana Roo, in Cozumel, Mexico, during February 2004. As executive director through these years, I was excited to see things come together again.

The summer of 2005 was my first without college administrative duties in more than two decades. Patricia and I were free to enjoy the Maine coast on our sailboat, and we did. Andrew was a year out of college. He was living in New York City and happily working for the A&E television network. It was also the summer of my sixtieth birthday. That same week, *The Chronicle of Higher Education* published an essay I had written on my years as COA's academic dean, entitled "The Art of Deanship." The paper received a number of positive reactions. It was selected by the Council of Independent Colleges for their New Chief Academic Officers Workshop Program and was reprinted in several places. I enjoyed the informal and reflective distilling of those remembrances. The remaining issues on my mind, about conservation psychology, seemed to call for a similar introspective attitude. I began by reviewing my seminal interests in human/environmental issues—and the chronology of their development; I perused the hundreds of ecological insights and life-experience statements collected from students; I reflected on decades of interactions with ecologists and environmentalists; I reread the autobiographical summaries contributed to human ecology directories over the years; and I scanned the senior project titles of COA graduates. My aim was to enter a familiar arena and, with an ethnographer's eye perhaps, discern unnoticed attributes in well-known territory. I was looking for new keyholes and—in a Batesonian abduction (i.e., reverse-engineering) kind of way—a different set of keys.

My return to full-time teaching required new classes. During that summer, I was also preparing an upper-level, interdisciplinary course called Ecology and Experience—the possible seedbed, I hoped, for an eponymous manuscript. The seminar was built around a diverse collection of primary source materials from evolutionary biology, ecology, and psychology. Much of the material was new to me. The class enrolled a group of hardworking students, and we had a great deal of fun in lively discussions. The course materials and my introspective self-study had produced dozens of pages of notes, but no coherent outline for the approaching conference.

As Gene's former teacher, and a presumptive elder of environmental psychology, I had been given broad latitude. Nonetheless, I still had no real notion of what to say, or even a title, for my presentation as "cross-disciplinary discussant" at the closing session on conservation biology/conservation psychology. My mind was full of ideas. I had just read David Keller and Frank Golley's *The Philosophy of Ecology*, Ernst Mayr's *What Makes Biology Unique?*, and Sam Glucksberg's *Understanding Figurative Language* with my class. We were also reading a selection of Loren Eiseley's essays, portions of Anthony Stevens's writings on the natural history of the mind, as well as Rollo May, Viktor Frankl, and other humanistic psychologists. These were amazing materials—full of rich ingredients. But my churning had yet to harden into an outline for my thoughts. I needed a sounding board.

Our COA faculty retreat that fall was held at the Acadia National Park lodge on Schoodic Point two weeks before the SHE meeting. As usual, it was an overnight event that allowed for casual discussions after the day's agenda. During the happy hour, before dinner was served, I asked Steve Ressel to join me for a beer. I described the SHE symposium and posed the question of interviewing him—as a personal portrait for my talk. He readily agreed.

Steve is a biologist whose background is in herpetology, ecology, and conservation. He came to COA in 1993 in the dual role of professor and director of the college's natural history museum. Steve grew up in the Amish region of Pennsylvania and spent a lot of time outdoors as a child. He had, in his words, "a self-identification" with animals. He liked to hold them, and was the kind of boy who often had a box turtle or a snake in his pocket. On his college application, his father suggested he check the box for biology as his area of interest. He started out in marine biology for a while, but was taken under the wing of one of his professors, who was a field ecologist and herpetologist. He became further immersed in herpetology at the University of Vermont, where he completed a master's degree. From there, he went to the University of Connecticut for doctoral studies and field research in Panama. His knowledge of ecological science found new direction at the university's Center for Conservation and Biodiversity and the Connecticut State Museum of Natural History—where his interests in early education and informal education took shape.

Steve calls himself "a pragmatic conservationist." He used to be strongly antihunting, mostly because of how hunters "take over the woods." His opinions on conservation biology are mixed. "Frogs," he declared, "are not mysterious." Conservationists' emphasis on emblematic species, as he rightly pointed out, has yet to dispel the negative attitudes toward reptiles and amphibians. The goal of conservation education should be "to bring them into consciousness," to put "meaning in action," and to begin early in life.

When Steve arrived at the college, we had a tiny two-room museum and no curriculum in museum studies. A few years later the Town of Bar Harbor began plans for a new YMCA. The site for the new facility was at the southern edge of town, beside the local ball fields, within easy walking distance for community children and residents. Unfortunately, there was a historic building in the middle of the property. The structure was the original headquarters building of Acadia National Park. The National Park Service had relocated its main offices inside Acadia's boundaries, but the distinctive board-and-batten building was still a beloved, local landmark. Moreover, it had been the office of George B. Dorr—ANP's first superintendent and a heroic figure in Mount Desert Island history. It was Dorr who helped to conceive the idea of a national park and dedicated his life to convincing Congress to protect the island's beauty. No one wished the building to be razed.

The solution was to give it to the college. But getting it to the other side of town would be a formidable feat. Late in the fall of 1996, after all of Bar Harbor's tourists were gone, it was moved across town in the middle of the night—slowly dropping telephone and power lines all the way—during the first snowstorm of the season. Over the next few years, funds were raised to renovate the original building and erect a substantial addition. The George B. Dorr Museum of Natural History officially opened on May 19, 2000. George Page, creator and narrator of PBS's *Nature*, was the dedication speaker. The multifunction facility—comprising a public museum, offices, teaching classrooms, and exhibit-preparation spaces—is the welcoming sight to all who enter through COA's main entrance.

Since then, Steve and his colleagues have fashioned an outstanding center for natural history and conservation education. All of the museum's exhibits are designed and constructed through student and faculty collaborations. Many are interactive—like the saltwater "touch tank," with living coastal organisms. Others are superb taxidermy exhibits of local species displayed in carefully crafted ecological context. The museum also offers outreach education programs for area schools, a summer field studies program for children, guided nature tours, and college-level classes in museum preparation and management. All the things Steve did as a child, and has done with his own children, are now shared with other children who visit or take part in the museum's programs. Nearly ten thousand visitors—local residents, seasonal tourists, and cruise ship passengers—enjoy themselves there. In addition to his teaching and museum activities, Steve is also an active member of the North Atlantic Amphibian Monitoring Program for indicator species.

Hearing Steve's story was a treat. The openness with which he revealed his sentiments and expressed his recollections was just what I needed. He was the genuine article: a conservation ecologist with a heart. I had the structure and title for my presentation: "Starthrowing: Delight, Authenticity, and Meaning in Conservation Education." With a single slide, and no notes, I gave a four-part sketch on the psychology of conservation. It was really a reflection of what Steve had given me—in a different voice. Here are some of the key elements.

Starthrowing: This term comes from an essay by Loren Eiseley. The setting is the beach of Costabel, littered with shells, sponges, and starfish thrown up after a storm. The narrator, having a sleepless night, takes a walk on the beach, where he encounters the waving flashlights of professional collectors, who boil the specimens and sell them to tourists. Farther up the beach he sees a distant figure stooping and flinging his arm. It is a different sort of collector—throwing starfish back to the sea. When he catches up with the star thrower, he asks him, "Do you collect?" "Only like this," he replies. "Only for the living." The next night, again with trouble sleeping, the man's mind is filled with dreamlike memories of returning home after his parents were gone. Other images come: of childhood treasures collected on his solitary walks in the fields and woods, an old photograph of his mother as a child, a lock of her hair. In his reverie he remembers her face, these things, the love he once had for "the world" and "its small ones." He rises and sets forth to find the star thrower. When they meet it is raining and morning has come. He joins him in silence and picks and throws as well. "I understand," he says. "Call me a thrower too." He feels his compassion once again, as a thread of life returns to the sea unbroken, not to die on the beach. His actions here, however small, seem to make a difference.

Eiseley's vision is larger than a single organism. The threads stretch back to the beginning of life. The strands may go as long perhaps into an unknown future. The conversion of the man's attitude, and his return to join the thrower on the beach, is a special kind of insight. There is a bit of it in all who know the love of life. The future is the gift. I felt it in Steve's pain for the condemned creatures he knows so well. It is often in the vegetarian's choice, a window opened for a wasp, a tangled whale released, the planting of a seed.

Delight: The compassion of Eiseley's character has many layers. The depths of pleasure rekindled by his trance of childhood memories is what makes the essay work. I settled on "delight" to make this bridge. Steve's delight was fully evident in his description of chasing crayfish and frogs as a boy. It was no less present when he talked of taking his winter ecology class to find hibernating bears. The vicarious pleasure he gets from them is still the same enchantment. The word "delight" itself, "to take great pleasure," is a pleasing one—as a noun or a verb. It comes from *de* ("away") and *lacere* ("to lure or entice"). It combines a sense of the numinous, of illumination, and personally compelling passion and compassion. I see it as akin to the psychoanalytic idea of "cathexis" (i.e., an object filled by desire)—but in a more purely appreciative way, united in a relationship of identification and identity. In this sense it resembles the Buddhist notion of "opening the heart." As an expression of intersubjectivity—and "a way of holding another's experience"—delight can be shared with all living things.

Authenticity: This is very much a psychological term. It comes primarily from existential and humanistic psychology, where "self" is a core notion. There is some debate about whether authenticity should be treated as a concept—or encountered at the experiential level. The word comes from the Greek *auto* or *auth* ("self") and *ento* ("inside"). Carl Rogers saw authenticity as the honest experiencing of the self. For James Bugental it involves self-respect and self-enactment as well. Sartre went further: "There is no doubt that authenticity demands much courage."[2] I believe most people are on a path of self-discovery—to find their intrinsic interests, discover their talents, and realize their potential. The sleepless man in Costabel experienced the resurrection of his authentic self. His return to the beach, to join the star thrower, was its self-enactment. As Eiseley's essay suggests, childhood may be a critical period for authenticating a delight in nature. Steve Ressel surely thought so—as did Rachel Carson, Bill Drury, and every other joyous naturalist I have known. Their reenactment, as teachers, is a torch that lights the world—and all its little ones.

Meaning: I believe, like Viktor Frankl, we are most fulfilled when we feel helpful, useful, and wanted. Meaning in life "is not something vague, but something very real and concrete"; it comes from commitment and action beyond oneself.[3] It is not about what one needs, but that one is needed. A meaningful life is doing what we love, where we are necessary in the world. The living world needs advocates—as Steve is for snakes and turtles and frogs. Conservation education should raise awareness and teach about less-popular organisms. If not, who will be guardians of their needs? Without star throwers who delight in and care for them, the future is a gamble. Meaning comes in many ways. Most often it is framed by human needs. But all of life is worthy of caring for, and its needs should not be denied. We may find our meaning in a lifelong attitude that frames a professional life. It may come, as well, in more circumscribed occasions. Every moment is there to endow our experience with meaningfulness.

What I said seemed to resonate with both groups. The terms were familiar enough to work as a structure for everyone. Their added depth, as established psychological concepts, gave further grounding for the dialogue. Steve's portrait was a statement of their common experiences too. The conversation that followed was an uninhibited exchange of ideas, personal events, and recollections. I had found a keyhole for nature and mind to meet. It was an opening for myself—as well—to try a newfound course.

CHAPTER 15

Ecology and Identity

I do not want to get to the end of my life and find that I just lived the length of it. I want to have lived the width of it as well.

—Dianne Ackerman

Criticism is easy; empathy is hard.

—Keira Knightley

Oliver Wendell Holmes Sr. made a distinction about three kinds of minds in his 1872 *The Poet at the Breakfast Table*.[1] "One-story intellects," as he described, are the "fact-collectors ... who have no aim beyond their facts." Two-story intellects "compare, reason, generalize, using the labors of the fact-collectors as well as their own." Beyond them, in the attic, are the third-story intellects who "idealize, imagine, predict; their best illumination comes from above, through the skylight." Each, as a rule, tends to excel at their respective level. But—sometimes—there are minds that move freely across all stories. These are the intellects, as the word suggests, who see between the lines and gather from all levels—e.g., *inter + legere*.

Rachel Carson was one of them. Her combination of scientific evidence, theoretical understanding, and poetic vision was a rare talent. By now, you have probably figured out most of the others who have inspired my interests. Bill Drury and Joe Rychlak were surely the most directly influential three-story personalities. Bill's worldview was grounded in rock-solid knowledge of geology, which seamlessly extended to botany, animal behavior, and human ecology. Bill did not doubt the existence of consciousness. As he once told Bob Trivers, "Bob, once you've learned to think of a herring gull as an equal, the rest is easy."[2] Joe, in contrast, began with human imagination—yet never repudiated science as a valid way to explore it. Both men appreciated the multilayered complexity of physical, biological, and experiential perspectives without the need to privilege one over the others.

Their kind of open-mindedness did not fit comfortably into academic structures. As Nicholas Wade reminds us, "specialists tend to resent the generalist who shows how their little patch relates to a larger order."[3] E. O. Wilson likewise faced such prejudices. He stated the problem this way: "The greatest enterprise of mind has always been and always will be the attempted linkage of the sciences and humanities. The ongoing fragmentation of knowledge and resulting chaos in philosophy are not reflections of the real world but artifacts of scholarship."[4] This is where second-story minds battle one another and—worst of all—collectively conspire to diminish all third-floor views. Michael Pollan decries the tyranny of such thinking as "the scientific method at its reductionist worst." When applied to the intricacies of biology,

> Complex qualities are reduced to simple quantities; biology gives way to chemistry.... The problem is that once science has reduced a complex phenomenon to a couple of variables, however important they may be, the natural tendency is to overlook everything else, to assume that what you can measure is all there is, or at least all that really matters. When we mistake what we can know for all there is to know, a healthy appreciation of one's ignorance in the face of a mystery ... gives way to the hubris that we can treat nature as a machine.[5]

On the other end of the spectrum from scientism, we encounter the "incredulity toward meta-narratives" of postmodernism. The full impact of postmodernism on science, religion, humanism, language, and the arts is difficult to assess. The movement's emphasis on uncertainty, doubt, ambiguity—and rejection of the doctrine of reason—has permeated all academic fields. Its (deliberately elusive) stance revolves around a contention that there is no ultimate foundation for anything. Truth is all relative.

Postmodern approaches to meaning are useful interpretive tools, and the deconstruction of totalizing explanations has been a liberating influence on thinking, language, and social relations. But there is a difference, as even the most prominent of American postmodernist philosophers Richard Rorty cautions, between being open-minded and having minds so open that our brains fall out.

When the theory is to have no theory—as sometimes appears to be the case in postmodern philosophy—the peril is solipsism and nihilism. Michael Werner, past president of the American Humanist Association, states it clearly: "We cannot give up the powers of our minds to those who would tell us they have *the* truth or to those, just as absolute, who say there is none."[6] Werner prefers the search for a dynamic middle ground. So do I. My observation of postmodernist attitudes brings me to a further conclusion: Those who start in criticism—usually end in criticism. It might be fun for a while. Over the long run, however, such a life would feel like an empty shell.

Human ecology requires critical thinking and careful attention to language. It also holds a place for natural realities, actual events, and conscious human beings. Paul Shepard offered his thoughts on postmodernism in one of his final essays, shortly before he died: "Paradoxically, the postmodern rejection of Enlightenment positivism has about it a grander sweep of presumption than the metaphysics of being and truth that it rejects. There is an armchair or coffeehouse smell about it … no glimmer of earth, of leaves or soil." Its supposition "that the words for things are more real than the things they stand for … is a continuation of an old, anti-natural position that David Ehrenfeld has called the arrogance of humanism." For Shepard, postmodern deconstruction of reality to a world of human language webs, semiotics, and simulacra (that refer only to other such constructions) contradicts the testimony of life itself. It is a view "engaged in demonstrating the inaccessibility of reality," where "nothing can be traced further than the semiotic in which everything is trapped." Connections to the world, beyond words, are meaningless. The result, as Shepard concludes, is that "No one cares about authenticity ... or the undiluted joy of nature ... and the cognitive processes of identification."[7]

Michael Soulé, a founding member of the Society for Conservation Biology, shares these concerns. Soulé was coeditor of *Reinventing Nature?: Responses to Postmodern Deconstruction*, in which Shepard's essay appeared. Like Shepard (and most ecologists), Soulé "assumes that the world, including its living components, really does exist apart from humanity's perceptions and beliefs about it."[8]

There is an old problem here—between two basic paradigms of Western thought. The philosopher Wallace Matson calls them *inside-out* versus *outside-in* philosophizing. If you begin from the inside, with human consciousness as the starting point, there is the problem of how to escape to the external realities of the world. The danger is to be trapped inside the labyrinths of phenomenology. (French deconstructionist epistemology arose in the inside-out tradition of continental phenomenology. In its extreme forms, this includes denial of a real world and everything else historically prior to humans.) The other approach, *outside-in*, begins in the external world and explains mind and knowledge in terms of that account. Scientific cosmology and evolutionary biology follow this view. It is, in a sense, like playing Aristotle's material, efficient, formal, and final causes one way—or the other. In one case, consciousness constructs reality; in the other, matter becomes mind. Descartes, of course, filleted them down the middle. Rychlak and Drury move toward recombining them—albeit from their own respective backgrounds.

Minding the World

I will grant the postmodern position that we live in a world of words. It is equally evident—to me—that we also inhabit a real and knowable world of rocks and water and living things. The third leg of my stool comes from psychology. As William James pronounced, "The universal conscious fact is not 'feelings and thoughts exist,' but 'I think' and 'I feel.' No psychology ... can question the *existence* of personal selves."[9] John Dewey said it this way: "The self not only exists, but may know that it exists; psychical phenomena are not only facts, but they are facts of consciousness."[10] A more current statement of the same variety comes from G. W. Farthing: "Consciousness is the subjective state of being currently aware of something, either within oneself or outside of oneself."[11]

There have always been psychologists who have difficulties with this position. But it was Joe Rychlak who dispelled these doubts for me. Joe was a forthright "identity advocate." "The personality theorist," as he declared, "takes it as given that identity *is* something."[12] His goal was to show how this subjective entity—the identity—*acts* within and upon the world. The self, by means of conscious (and sometimes unconscious) intentions, moves forward in mental meaning-making and "identification." Michael Polanyi made the same claim in an influential 1968 paper, "Life's Irreducible Structure," in *Science* magazine: "There is no reason for suspending recognition of the obvious fact that consciousness is a principle that fundamentally transcends not only physics and chemistry but also the mechanistic principles of living beings."[13] This approach is akin to Alfred Korzybski's multilayered system of conceptual mapping. Ian McHarg's method for human ecological planning—fashioned around overlay maps of geology, hydrology, soils, organisms, and human features—was a more literal version. The final layers were really maps of human values and the projection of conscious intentions into landscape design. There have been many times when I have come across a survey team or discovered their pins while walking. They are the first signs "that something is about to happen here." I will wager that most people have an unsettling feeling whenever they happen upon these first markers in their favorite woodland or lakeside retreat. What it will be, however, is still elsewhere—in the imagination of the landowner or locked up in some developer's office.

Mountains

I am reminded here of John Muir. Muir's family moved from Scotland to Wisconsin in 1849 when John was still a young boy. Later, at the University of Wisconsin, he studied geology and botany. In his twenties, while working in an Indianapolis factory, he had an accident that nearly left him blinded. After a slow recovery of his sight, Muir vowed to "be true to myself" and become a dedicated naturalist. His new life began with a hike from Indiana to Florida, later recounted in his *A Thousand-Mile Walk to the Gulf*. From Florida he sailed to San Francisco and then walked to the Sierra Nevada. Muir fell in love with Yosemite, where he worked as a sheepherder and roamed the region doing geology and botany. He became convinced that glaciers had formed the valley, rather than catastrophic earthquakes—as was the popular theory of the time. When the renowned geologist Louis Agassiz visited Yosemite in 1872, he affirmed Muir's interpretation. Agassiz also offered Muir a position at Harvard; Muir turned it down—preferring, as he said, to stay with his "university of the wilderness."

That same year, Congress and President Grant created Yellowstone as America's first National Park. Muir held similar hopes for preservation of Yosemite. After much effort, the National Park bill was passed in 1890 establishing the Yosemite and Sequoia National Parks—based largely on Muir's vision and persuasive writing. To his dismay, however, they were left under state control. Other visitors to Muir's Yosemite during these years included Ralph Waldo Emerson, the botanists Asa Gray (from Harvard) and Sir Joseph Hooker (from Kew Gardens), as well as the noted British evolutionist Alfred Russel Wallace. Muir also traveled extensively. He explored—and wrote compellingly about—the beauties of nature in North and South America, Europe, Africa, Asia, Australia, and elsewhere in the world.

In 1892, Muir helped to found the Sierra Club, serving as its president for more than two decades, until the time of his death. The organization vigorously opposed efforts to reduce the park's size and was influential in creating the Sierra Forest Reserve in 1893 and later the Sierra National

Forest. John Muir was a prolific nature writer. His keen perception and love of nature inspired many. But the Sierra and its preservation were his central passion. In May 1903, President Theodore Roosevelt visited Muir for three days, during which they camped alone and explored Yosemite. Muir described the unbridled exploitation of the valley's resources and urged the president to bring the park under federal management. Roosevelt agreed. Three years later, Roosevelt signed a resolution of recession, withdrawing state control and putting Yosemite under federal protection. That was also the year of the great San Francisco earthquake and fire, which quickened the Sierra Club's fight to protect the Hetch Hetchy Valley. The city had petitioned the U.S. Department of the Interior to gain water rights to the Tuolumne River. Because the valley was inside the national park, an act of Congress was needed. Muir and the Sierra Club led the opposition in what became one of the country's most heated environmental debates. But in 1913, Woodrow Wilson signed the bill authorizing the dam.

John Muir died the following year. It would take another decade to complete O'Shaughnessy Dam and flood Muir's beloved glacial valley. He had seen the human "intentions" placed upon the land—and knew what was to come. Muir's identification with nature also shaped the future and continues in the Sierra Club's vision and plans. In 1962 they gave their John Muir Award to Olaus Murie. Murie and his wife Margaret had begun a campaign in the 1950s to protect what is now the Arctic National Wildlife Refuge (ANWR). Eight million acres became a designated "federal protected area" in 1960 under President Dwight Eisenhower. Olaus and Margaret were also instrumental in enlarging the boundaries of Glacier, Olympia, and Grand Teton National Parks. Following Olaus's death in 1963, Margaret returned to Alaska to continue her research and make presentations at wilderness conservation hearings on behalf of the National Park Service. Under President Carter, in 1980, the ANWR was doubled in size to nineteen million acres. The Sierra Club awarded the John Muir Award to Margaret in 1983. Olaus's younger brother Adolph, also a wildlife biologist, was a pioneer in the scientific study of wolves, bears, and coyotes in their natural habitat. His careful field research and classic books *The Wolves of Mt. McKinley* and *Ecology of the Coyote in Yellowstone* transformed ecological management practices—putting an end to predator elimination programs in both parks. Adolph Murie's words were celebrated in Ken Burns's six-part PBS series *The National Parks: America's Best Idea*. "In our thinking of McKinley, let us not have puny ideas," Murie said. "Let us think on a greater scale. Let us not have those of the future decry our smallness of concept and lack of foresight."[14]

Cities

Foresight and grand ideas come in many varieties. I will never forget my trip to Florence, Italy, in 1998. It was for a meeting of the International Congress of Ecology (INTECOL), at which I had been invited to prepare a session on human ecology. Firenze (as Italians know it) is the capital of Tuscany and birthplace of the Renaissance. At the heart of the historic district sits Cattedrale Santa Maria del Fiore or, as it is commonly called, Duomo di Firenze, i.e., the dome of Florence. The cathedral was built between 1296 and 1436 (we don't do things this way now). When it was conceived, no one knew how the dome would be constructed. In 1419, the clever architect Filippo Brunelleschi finally figured out a way to do it—without any use of internal scaffolding. It was an extraordinary achievement and remains the largest masonry dome ever built.

On March 20, 2011, the *New York Times* featured the two-hundredth birthday of Manhattan's two-thousand-block plan of eleven avenues and 155 crosstown streets.[15] The population at the time was about sixty thousand inhabitants. Today there are more inhabitants than that on every one of the island's twenty-two square miles. No one knew, or could even imagine, the city of their dreams would *grow up*. Nineteenth-century buildings were seldom more than four or five stories tall. But invention of the world's first safety elevator by Elisha Otis, and the engineering developments of steel beam construction, changed everything. With completion of the Brooklyn Bridge in 1883, and the subway system in 1904, New York City grew out as well. The city's developers competed among themselves (and with Chicago) for claims of the "world's tallest building." The Empire State Building, completed in 1931, took the record for the next forty years—until the first tower of the World Trade Center surpassed it in 1972.

Another of Manhattan's striking features, in stark contrast to its skyscrapers and bustling streets, is the tranquillity of Central Park. The 843-acre rectangular slot of trees, lakes, and pathways—amid the center of the island—was America's first "urban park." Designed by Calvert Vaux and Frederick Law Olmstead, it remains the most visited city park in the country. Olmstead's talents would later become widespread. His landscape designs were utilized in innumerable other cities and towns, as well as for dozens of universities and colleges. Where Muir strived to keep urban tentacles out of the wilderness, Olmstead championed ways to bring nature into city life.

New York City has the highest population density of any major American city. It stands as a marvel of engineering and long-range planning. The city's water system of gravity-fed aqueducts, stretching to the Catskill Mountains, supplies 1.2 billion gallons of pure, fresh water daily to eight million citizens. Its wastewater treatment system, with more than 6,500 miles of sewer lines, handles the same amount every day. New Yorkers consume 33.5 million tons of food each year.[16] The supply chain is a huge and multilayered system, by which 95 percent of all food movement is by truck. Because of its density, the city is one of the most energy efficient in the country, with the highest rate of public transportation and the lowest carbon footprint per person.

Love it or hate it, New York City is an object lesson in human ecology. I have some ambivalence too. When my father completed college, he went directly to the city. His years with the New York Dock Company, on the waterfront of Brooklyn, must have been a heady experience for a young engineer. Later, with the Port Authority, he contributed to some of the city's major construction projects, including the second deck of the George Washington Bridge and Idlewild (later JFK International) Airport.

I never had a desire for urban life. New York, in my opinion, was a rather dirty, noisy, and unfriendly place. The city has changed for the better over the years, and I have grown to enjoy visiting it. I find it curious that Andrew, like his grandfather, was drawn there too after college. He currently lives on the top floor of an old Brooklyn warehouse, beside the East River, which overlooks the very waterfront where my father began his career. The docks and railways are no longer in operation. But many of the old buildings have become popular hot spots for young urbanites—and the DUMBO (Down Under the Manhattan Bridge Overpass) region is now a lovely waterfront public park with spectacular views of Manhattan. Andrew never knew my father, who died six years before he was born. But I have a warm and happy feeling knowing how each of them has identified with the same place—as if somehow they share an invisible connection.

New York was a leader of modern development. Its gridlike hub of high-rise skyscrapers is the signature model of urban America. Many American cities have pioneered another significant feature of metropolitan design: sprawl. One of the panelists at the 2012 Frankfurt Global Economic Forum (to explore a European college of human ecology) was Ernst Weizsäcker. Weizsäcker is cochair of the U.N. International Panel for Sustainable Resource Management and a member of the Club of Rome. On the topic of U.S. urban sprawl, he noted that Atlanta occupies twenty-five times the land area of Barcelona, but has a lower population. The environmental impact of his comparison is not insignificant.

A century ago, only 10 percent of the world lived in urban areas. Today, most people live in cities. By 2050, the United Nations projects that 75 percent of the world's population will be urban. The majority of this growth is centered in developing countries. China is perhaps the most dramatic example. The country was less than 20 percent urban in 1980; it is expected to reach the three-quarters mark by 2030—all in just fifty years! Beijing's first skyscraper was built in 1959. Nearly a thousand high-rise buildings now define the city's skyline. Seven out of ten of the world's tallest buildings are Chinese. The acceleration of urbanization is occurring at a staggering pace. On my first visit to China in 1994, Beijing was still a rambling web of hutong districts filled with rivers of bicycles. When I returned in 2007, for the Fourth International EcoSummit, the city was a transformed world of high-rise complexes, superhighways, and automobiles.

After the convention, I joined Rusong Wang and an evaluation team of ecologists and city planners to visit ten ecological restoration sites in the Mentougou district. It is a remote, rural region that has been heavily mined for coal and limestone for nearly a thousand years. The district's 230,000 inhabitants had been actively restoring the blight for five years—turning old mines and pits into parks, reconstructing rivers, and redesigning an attractive and habitable landscape. The outcome was impressive. The project was part of a much larger Ecopolis movement, whose leaders include Rusong and Ian Douglas, UNESCO's chairman of the Scientific Committee on Problems of the Environment (SCOPE) Expert Group on Urban Futures (and a past president of the Society for Human Ecology). They have been tireless champions of sustainable city design. Their International Eco-City Conferences, begun in 1990, have gathered a substantial following of urban planners.

One of the most exciting results is the coastal Tianjin Eco-City project, about an hour from Beijing. Tianjin is a model of sustainable development. Instead of using arable land or an existing urban footprint, it is being built from scratch on reclaimed industrial dumping grounds. The city will have 350,000 inhabitants in a land area half the size of Manhattan. They will live in state-of-the-art sustainable buildings, with resource-efficient transportation and integrated food systems. The first inhabitants have already begun to move in. The eco-city model is being adapted to other cities in China—and elsewhere around the world. If it catches on, urban life could be much different than before. This is human ecology on a grand scale. Through its keyhole a hopeful future may be seen.

Inside Stories

Connection with place is one side of an ecological identity. The inner world of selfhood is the other. This is where the sense of authenticity and delight, which we touched on in Chapter 14, gives us meaning. I have recently come across another candid "identity advocate": Brené Brown.

Her clear-minded TED (Technology, Entertainment, Design) Talk was sent to me by one of my students. Brown has a doctorate in social work and is a licensed therapist and research professor. Her work looks at issues of vulnerability, courage, and authenticity. The center of her thinking is tied to "connection"—from which we derive our sense of purpose and meaning. But it is the fear of disconnection and being "unworthy" that destroys our connection to life. Her research is based on thousands of personal stories of how shame limits experience. The inability to allow ourselves to be vulnerable makes us numb—to the pain of our imperfections—but also to joy, love, empathy, and belonging. The courage to accept imperfection in the world and ourselves expands our perception and our practice of gratitude. "Shame," as Brown asserts, "prevents us from presenting our real selves to the people around us—it sabotages our efforts to be authentic."[17]

Self-Truth

Brené Brown doesn't dance around authenticity; she dives into it. In addition to her scholarly and academic writing, she also writes popular articles. Her piece "We Should All Take 'Voice Lessons' from Dixie Chicks"—written shortly after the 2007 Grammy Awards show—is a good example.[18] If you don't know the backstory, it goes like this. The all-girl band, which formed in the early 1990s, remained under the radar until their single "Wide Open Spaces" (and album of the same name) broke through to the top of the country music charts. In 1998, the Dixie Chicks sold more CDs than all other country performers combined. The group's next album, *Fly*, continued the momentum, with the top awards of Billboard, the American Music Association, and the Academy of Country Music. At their March 2003 concert in London, in the run-up to the Iraq War, the group's lead singer, Natalie Maines, spoke her mind: "We do not want this war, this violence, and we're ashamed that the president of the United States is from Texas." The band members are all from Texas, where George W. Bush had been governor prior to becoming president. In the uproar that followed, many radio stations stopped playing their music, former fans refused to attend their concerts, some burned their CDs, concerts were canceled, sponsors dropped them, and Maines was the target of multiple death threats. Things remained difficult for the next few years. In March 2006 the group released a single, "Not Ready to Make Nice," and later an album, *Taking the Long Way*. At the Grammy Awards the next February, they were voted the best single and best album, with the group winning all five categories for which they were nominated. Public support for their advocacy of free speech has continued to grow. Deep down, I am a Dixie Chicks kind of guy. Maybe it's the driving harmonies, the cowboy boots, the ragged-but-right fiddling, or their unflinching convictions—probably all of them. They spoke their truth, took the hit, and made it back. They were, in Brown's account, vulnerable—but not shamed into "making nice." They were authentic.

Gene Robinson is another instance of personal truth in the face of vulnerability. Robinson grew up on a tobacco farm in rural Kentucky. After graduating from the University of the South (Sewanee), he moved to New York and completed divinity studies at the General Theological Seminary. In 1972 he married Isabella Martin. They moved to New Hampshire, where he was an Episcopal priest, and the couple had two daughters. The Robinsons separated in 1986 after thirteen years of marriage. Gene had experienced doubts about his sexuality since he was a boy, but had kept them buried. Now—the truth was undeniable. He chose not to hide his sexual identity. Soon thereafter he met Mark Andrew, who would become his life partner. Eventually, he rose to the position of Canon to the Ordinary (executive assistant to the bishop of New Hampshire). In a highly controversial decision, Robinson was elected as the ninth bishop of the Diocese of New Hampshire in 2003—in the first-ever bishopric nomination of an openly gay, noncelibate Christian priest. A storm of controversy followed throughout the Episcopal Church and the Anglican Convention. Conservative leaders and members threatened to leave the church. His ordination was delayed by a flurry of accusations of impropriety—all of which were investigated and deemed without substance. Then came the death threats. At the final consecration, Robinson and other members of the ceremony had to wear bulletproof vests. Gene and

Mark maintain strong connections with Gene's former wife, his children, and his grandchildren. The couple was married in a civil ceremony on June 7, 2008. The following January, Barack Obama invited Robinson to deliver the invocation at the opening inaugural ceremonies on the steps of the Lincoln Memorial. Gene, now retired, recounts these events in his recent book, *God Believes in Love.* They are also told in the 2012 Sundance film "Love Free or Die" and an earlier, feature-length documentary, "For the Bible Tells Me So." Gene Robinson is a living symbol of personal truth. When he tells of the internal and public challenges he has faced, it is impossible to not admire his authenticity and courage.

Food and Love

If the story of human life could be told in one giant volume it would be interesting, perhaps, to look at the first and the last chapters—for it is often the boundaries that teach us the most. I suspect it might begin with the minimal conditions of survival, the essential material of staying alive: food. Life is intimately, and ultimately, tied to consuming other life. This is the most basic lesson of ecological food chains. Food is a daily necessity that binds life together.

If food is the common denominator of material living, love is another story. Love is the epitome of humans' immaterial endowments. The capacity to express caring beyond individual self-interest is often linked to spiritualism and higher powers. In humanistic traditions it is tied to ego transcendence and self-actualization. What exactly love is and where it comes from has intrigued philosophers and poets from time immemorial. In contemporary science the "problem of altruism" remains one of the most intriguing issues for evolutionary philosophers. Whatever it is tied to—or however it is defined—love is a profound and creative force.

Despite all differences, love and food are conjoined in human affairs. There are few places where the hearth was not the center of daily life. Every culture fashions its own connections. All of us have tasted love at the end of a fork. Time and again I have thumbed through my mother's handwritten recipe cards. Her peach cobbler, with "special" sauce, is a heartwarming return to the childhood comforts of a doting mother. Laura Esquivel's *Like Water for Chocolate* is a stirring example of these complex interactions.

I lately encountered a mixing of food and love of another sort. It comes from Natalie Barnett, a recent COA graduate. Natalie grew up in northern New York State. During college her interests turned to the history of agriculture. In the spring of 2010, Natalie went to the Organic Research Centre in Hampstead Marshall, England, to study the growth of organic food markets. The center is in rural Berkshire County, without easy access to a train station, and has only one nearby pub. When she and her fellow students went there, Natalie tried the local (hard) cider. "Cider hits your tongue decisively," she later wrote. "I couldn't avoid the bubbles and bite ... it was pleasantly dry and emanated the tart aroma of apples."[19] She had never tasted anything like it before, and she began to wonder why. Natalie threw herself into "the cider question" for the next year. The answer turned out to be a long and interesting one, in which Natalie would uncover deep historical roots to Maine—and many other things about apples. The final product of her efforts is a wonderfully crafted one-hundred-page senior thesis. Here are a few of the highlights.

In the mid-1800s apple orchards became a significant part of Maine farms. Maine apples were highly prized for their quality and distinctive flavors. They were especially popular in England, where they were shipped in barrels, and auctioned to eager buyers on Liverpool's docks. For the people of Maine, apples were a major cash crop, which came to be known as "mortgage busters." The U.S. Census of 1870 showed the average value of a Maine farm to be around $1,700. A one-acre apple orchard could net $400 in a year; five acres of trees were enough to pay for an entire farm. As railroads began to connect inland farms and coastal shipping ports, the boon spread statewide. In the mid-1880s Liverpool was receiving more than a hundred thousand barrels of Maine apples a week during late fall. The Maine apple industry, thereafter, began to run into problems. Some came from changes in British import policies, others from several years of devastating killing frosts, still more from heat waves, droughts, and the Great Depression.

But that is only part of Natalie's story. Her thesis also contains chapters on the distinctive heterozygosity and cross-pollination characteristics of apple trees; the staggering range of resulting varieties—and their numerous culinary and animal food stock uses; a treatise on scions, rootstocks, and the art of asexual grafting; a history of pomology and the growth and influence of professional pomological organizations in the United States and the United Kingdom; as well as biographical summaries of influential figures in apple history. Natalie's passion for apples took her to the docks of Liverpool and the Merseyside Maritime Museum, to Maine libraries and historical societies, to agricultural meetings, and across the state's landscape. Along the way she met an untold number of apple growers and connoisseurs. One of them was a man who can identify more than a hundred apple varieties by taste alone. When Natalie bites into an apple now, her experience is vastly different from when she took her first sip of English cider. Every backyard orchard or lonesome roadside tree is part of a chronicle that traces back to the fruit's early Asian ancestral roots. It is a human ecological story.

Natalie's passion for apples—and all she learned through her delight in them—highlights another set of "keyholes." One is the notion of *terroir*. The word comes from the French for "soil." It is traditionally applied to the unique qualities of wine, which result from local soil type, water drainage, and other geographic and microclimate factors. Serious wine tasters are able to detect these qualities—from region to region and from year to year. Similar skills are found in coffee tasters and, as Natalie found, among pomological experts. I once saw a demonstration of a man who identified the water of each of the Great Lakes in a blind taste test. These are true talents based on real chemical qualities. I think that terroirlike perception is possible with other senses too—as in seeing family resemblances, hearing hints of accents, smelling past experiences, or intuiting hidden motives. If I am right, terroir may be a place where mind and nature meet.

Another keyhole feature of Natalie's apples is the concept of *provenance*, also a French word—meaning "to come from." Unlike terroir, which suggests something of a molecular connection, provenance refers to connections "by association." I enjoy PBS's *Antiques Road Show* and can't resist making a guess at the dollar value of each featured item. The "rest of the story"—with which an antique, artwork, or craft object is associated—often enhances its value. A baseball is a baseball. But if it was signed by Babe Ruth, or was from the last home run he hit, it is more than merely a baseball. This is what Natalie did to apples. She gave them more story. Provenance enlarges the experience of objects by surrounding them with meaningful context. It enriches experience—not only of human things—but any thing.

It is customary, in many households, to say grace before a meal. Most dinner blessings give thanks for the food about to be received. A different, less common, practice involves giving thanks *to the food*. Here, what is about to become part of our bodies is encountered more directly. Here, food and love are fastened by *identification*—in an ecological experience of knowledge, sensation, anticipation, and appreciation.

Yes and ...

One more keyhole still remains. It comes, as well, from a student—Sean Fitzgerald—who taught me (his adviser) something really important. Sean began his studies at COA in biology. In time, his interests grew larger—into the human studies, to art, and then theater. During his junior year, Sean took a course in comedic improvisation. It was a bit of a whimsy. But he learned an invaluable lesson from the class. Improvisational comedy is built on two simple principles: The first is "active listening" to the other performers—which is often affirmed by repeating the previous performer's line. The second is that you *always* add to their contribution (this is the "yes and" part). "In improvised comedy," as Sean told me, "agreement is the only rule you never want to break." When the time came later that year to write his human ecology essay, he put this insight to good use. Sean's essay expressed a variety of ways an attitude of "yes and" has changed his life. He wrote of how it helps him remain open while receiving feedback, of its usefulness in personal conversations and group discussions, and even within his own thinking.

The closing section of Sean's essay applied the principle to human ecology, which … "requires connections between different disciplines and different groups to come together to create a common perspective."[20] He's right. Instead of the typical "yes but" of academic discourse, this simple rule would surely be a game changer. Adding to the contributions of others (rather than seeking to refute them) is where interdisciplinarity begins. This is when creative collaboration, intellectual symbiosis, and true "team-teaching" happens. It is in additive engagement, where validation of everyone may yield an unforeseen greater good. This is not a denial of the usefulness of critical methods, or an argument that cooperation is better than competition and debate. My point, simply, is of the value of "yes and" approaches, *in addition to* adversarial techniques, for developing an integration of knowledge.

A more prosaic version goes like this. My son Andrew has surpassed me on the tennis court. So instead of head-to-head competition, we sometimes try to hit the ball "to each other." The aim of the game then becomes seeing how long we can maintain a volley. If either of us fails to return the ball into the other's hitting zone, we often utter a spontaneous "I'm sorry." It's a different kind of game—for sure. But I also know it has done more to improve my backhand than a day of useless lunges at balls beyond my reach.

Beyond Words

The Maine coast is a lovely place. The curves and coves of its jagged coastline are mirrored by some five thousand islands (the actual number depends upon the level of twice-daily, twelve- to fifteen-foot tides). Mount Desert Island (MDI) is the highest elevation along the North Atlantic coast. The island is composed of ten major rock types. On the whole, the mixture gives a primeval appearance. That is because the geology really is ancient. As you drive over the bridge onto the island's north end, the first rock you see is the Ellsworth schist. This is the oldest exposed rock on the Maine coast. It was formed from silt, clay, and volcanic ash beds, deposited in the midlatitudes on the edge of the supercontinent Rodinia. The beds were metamorphosed into schist around the time of the Precambrian-Cambrian transition, six hundred million years ago, before any life had appeared on land. At the time, the beds were near the South Pole in a subduction zone at the edge of the opening Iapetus Ocean.

The island's most prominent topographic feature is Cadillac Mountain. All of MDI's mountains have been eroded from 420-million-year-old igneous intrusions as the Avalonian plate (and what eventually would become Maine) approached the North American plate. North America was still located south of the equator, and much of it was beneath the ocean. This was the late Silurian, when the first primitive fish were evolving. Mosses and bryophytes were beginning to appear along the water's edge, as insects moved onto the land. The distinctive pink granite of Cadillac was formed then. Our home, which borders Acadia National Park, is pinned to this pink granite. Its exposed surface defines the edge of our garden patio.

The igneous intrusions of granite and dark-gray gabbro were caused by explosive volcanism. After the eruptions, a ten-mile-wide caldera formed and filled with water. Other volcanoes followed around 360 million years ago, as Avalonia and other terranes completed their collision with North America. Between 300 and 275 million years ago, Africa collided with North America to form the Appalachian Mountains and the supercontinent Pangaea. This was the "age of reptiles." By now, the first angiosperms and gymnosperms had split. Their heirs are the mixed woodland of spruce, fir, maples, and birch that cover the island. In the Triassic, fifty million years or so later, Pangaea broke up and left Avalonia with North America as the Atlantic Ocean opened. It was about here the first birds appeared. Unlike most of their reptilian relatives, they were able to fly through the massive Cretaceous-Tertiary (K-T) extinction. Their descendants visit our feeder in winter; others are eaten on Thanksgiving in *Mayflower* celebrations.

From 420 million years ago to now, MDI has undergone continuous erosion by water, and in the last million or so years by glaciation. During that interval, two vertical miles of rock have been removed to form the present landscape, carved in the depths of the original magma chamber.

At the peak of the last North American glacier, twenty-five thousand years ago, MDI was covered with a mile of ice. The ice border extended two hundred miles farther south. The ice scoured the landscape, rounded mountaintops, and carved the island's current geomorphology. Between seventeen thousand and sixteen thousand years ago, it slowly melted across the island. As the glacier paused in retreat, it left several distinctive moraines. One of the most prominent is where the Acadia National Park's Jordan Pond House is now located. Visitors have enjoyed the view northward from atop it for more than a century, as they are served popovers and lobster bisque.

I recently attended a presentation at the college's Geographic Information System (GIS) lab. The lab had just acquired a LiDAR topographic data set (LiDAR stands for Light Detection And Ranging). It is an optical remote-sensing technology using laser pulses to penetrate the vegetation to reveal surficial patterns not noticeable even when you are standing right on top of them. One of the striking features of its high-resolution map was a series of bands running east and west across the island. The lines, about 150 meters apart, are remnants of annual "push moraines." They mark the summer retreat, and winter pushback, of the glacier as it receded from its stabilized position south of Jordan Pond. I have since found several of these bands not far from our house. No one ever noticed them before. Now, I can't help seeing their rhythmic waves across the island.

The island's shoreline was far higher than today when the ice first retreated. Relief from the enormous weight of the glacier, however, caused substantial rebounding of the land. The land rose much faster than sea levels were increasing. By eleven thousand years ago, the island's shoreline was two hundred feet lower than its current level—and as much as ten miles farther seaward. The first human inhabitants arrived about then. They were probably following caribou and other game animals through the coastal tundra. Between then and now, sea level continued to rise. Finding archaeological evidence of the first Paleo-Indian sites from those depths is virtually impossible. A lot more is known about later periods, after Samuel de Champlain arrived in 1604 and laid claim to the island as French territories.

Near the end of our driveway stands the case-hardened skeleton of a dead white pine. The milky-gray trunk and stubbed branches are reminiscent of old whalebones. It is a stalwart vestige of the 1947 fire that swept across the eastern half of the island. Like a schooner's keel-line, from which everything arises, it stands as a proud statue of the phoenix. We cannot cut it down. The landscape around our home is quite unlike what was before the fire. All of the grand old pines are gone. Pioneer trees that struggle to grow on the exposed ledges and eroded soil have slowly replaced them. From the top of Cadillac, the imprint of the blaze is readily observable—especially in the fall. This is when the brightly colored yellow and red leaves of postfire birches, beech, and maples stand in blazing contrast to the uniform green of the island's older conifers. The river of fire, driven by gale-force winds, rolled across the island from west to east. Half of Bar Harbor was consumed. In town, it is not difficult to find the fire line. On one side, buildings seem timeless; on the other, the feeling of urgency to rebuild is observable, in a distinctive post–World War style. My first Bar Harbor home was one of them. Though hastily constructed with limited resources, the Yankee pride of craftsmanship was still there. On the other side of town, the fire stopped just short of where COA now is. Everything inland of the coastal road to Bar Harbor was lost. On the ocean side, protected from the howling west winds, a slender band of the shoreline estates was preserved.

It takes ten minutes to drive from the Ellsworth schist, at the head of the island, to the tourist shops of Bar Harbor. Between them lies half a billion years—of drifting continents, evolving life, volcanoes, glaciers, and human history. I wish people would pause, even briefly, to ponder this gap. I do not mean only on the roadway of this island, but wherever they may be. We are surrounded by the deep experience of life everywhere we go. If we can discover ways to be in touch with it, and allow it to touch us, this world will be a better place.

CHAPTER 16

The Unfinished Course

> Follow your heart ... everything else is secondary.
> —Steve Jobs

I have a recurrent dream. In the dream I am still in college. The semester is about to end. I am enrolled in a course, but have not attended classes. It is time for the final exam. I am unprepared. The drama plays out in various ways. Sometimes I am trying to persuade my professor to allow an extension or grant a late withdrawal. Other times I am frantically attempting to borrow class notes, to find the textbook, or to cram for the exam. The dream's original version was about a history course. Later on, for a while, it took the form of a noncredit degree requirement to pass a swimming test. I am running around campus, on the day before graduation, but cannot find the gymnasium, or if I do, the doors are locked and no one is around. In recent years, I am the professor—who has forgotten to show up to class, sometimes for the entire term. The dream does not correlate with the events of my daily life. It simply returns from time to time. Despite changing details, what stands out most is the consistent pattern of disbelief, mixed emotions, and desperate challenges.

A few years ago, I raised the topic during a lull at an evening dinner party. I was scarcely through my introduction when one guest blurted out his own version, followed quickly by someone else, and then another. What I thought was a personal quirk revealed itself as a widespread occurrence. The particulars varied from person to person. But the basic theme was the same: an unattended class, a final exam, total unpreparedness, no time, no way out. Everyone at the table had had the dream. Our sharing of them led to a spirited conversation.

It was a bit of a relief to discover I was not an anomalous case with a rare symptom. The dinner group that evening was composed of colleagues, like myself, who had spent many years as students and teachers. A straightforward explanation of the phenomenon would treat it as a residual of life experience—an academic hybrid, perhaps, of otherwise common dream motifs such as falling or flying or being lost and unable to find the way home. Still, I wondered why it was so common and how, or when, it developed.

As COA's academic dean, I often had to speak publicly about the institution's educational goals and curriculum. One of the most important events was our spring tour for high school seniors in the final stage of choosing the college they would attend. Parents accompany their daughters and sons to these occasions, where they also attend classes and explore the campus. The visit culminates with a group session in the college auditorium. Family members usually sit together for the final faculty panel discussion about specific courses, degree requirements, and questions about college life. At the close of one of these events, I asked the audience an impromptu question: "How many of you have ever had a dream of an unfinished course?" Hands went up across the room. It was the parents' arms in the air. Their daughters and sons seemed surprised by the spontaneous participation of their parents. Several volunteered their stories. The prospective students witnessed their mothers' and fathers' contributions with a look of curious intrigue and befuddlement. After a sample of disclosures, I concluded the meeting with a tongue-in-cheek remark that one more thing we get from a college education is our dreams (even if they are sometimes fictional). Several parents came up afterward to share accounts of our common, dreamworld bond. On several occasions thereafter I conducted informal polls with my students. First-year students seldom report having the dream; by their senior year, many have vivid versions, which they eagerly relate and compare.

The sequelae of unresolved life events and the need for mental closure have long been a subject matter of psychology. Bluma Zeigarnik revealed their commonplace occurrence with her doctoral dissertation research at the University of Berlin under Kurt Lewin in the 1920s. Her experimental demonstration that uncompleted tasks remain more active in memory than completed tasks was one of the pioneering studies in social psychology. Later, after Lewin came to America, the "Zeigarnik Effect" would be a cornerstone of cognitive dissonance theory and of further discoveries of subtle unconscious processes in memory, perception, and attitude change. Our inclinations for cognitive resolution, even in anticipatory ways, have been celebrated in the recent National Public Radio *Driveway Moments* series. These highly popular stories, as the name implies, make you stay in the car to hear the end, often while you sit in your own driveway. Like Paul Harvey's and-now-for-the-rest-of-the-story radio motif of years ago, they hold our attention in the dynamic anticipation of completion.

My unfinished-course dream became less enigmatic in this light. Rather than a personal idiosyncrasy, it seemed to fit into the general category of an acquired anxiety reaction. Like other psychological responses at the boundary of life's demands and fears of failure, my built-in need for mental closure was doing its job—even as I slept. This interpretation brought my mind to rest for a while, but did not erase the dream's midnight reappearance. Fragments of the motif lingered at the edge of my waking curiosity. Like a small beach stone slipped into my pocket and carried for years, it was sometimes revived as a conversation topic. The reveries also surfaced in daydreams or streamed together as elusive symbols and intuitions. Through these tiny portals I met an urge to probe the imaginal world.

Hidden Dimensions

Psychotherapists delve into their clients' lingering wounds, broken relationships, and ungrieved losses. They pursue these buried encounters amid the hidden levels of the psyche. Healing the tattered fabric of this inner world, and restoring the creative whole of one's personality, is the essence of psychological counseling. Talking therapy and dream analysis were Freud's gateway to the personal unconscious and the repressed conflicts of early childhood. These mysteries—through careful analysis and interpretation—could be unveiled and transformed, and peace of mind restored. Dramas of the unconscious and dreams held even greater significance for Jung. The quest of analytical psychology follows the soul's encounters into the deepest realms of a transpersonal world.

The Australian psychologist Benjamin Bradley offers another way to consider the depths of mind. Bradley begins with a distinction between two "senses" of experience. One type of experience refers to past events that accumulate over time, which Bradley calls the *formative* or *diachronic* (i.e., through time) sense of experience. This dimension of experience, set in the past, is the basis of the learning and memories that pattern our current responses to the world. Bradley's second "sense" of experience refers to what is happening in "the here and now," which he states, "is often very hard to pin down in words precisely." Formative experience must be processed first in terms of present experiences—and constructed from them: "Hence immediate experience is the primary sense, so far as psychology is concerned."[1] Here-and-now experience, according to Bradley, is synchronic, ephemeral, and atemporal. "Its form does not depend primarily on (then→now) causal relations but on the 'simultaneity' of meanings within which it and we are situated." Moreover, "These simultaneities are collectively maintained ... shared between people ... [and thus are] ... supra-individual or '*intersubjective*.'" Bradley's highlighting of these two dimensions is an attempt to redress the long-standing tendency in psychology to overlook synchronic processes that structure experience independently of time. His goal (much like Joe Rychlak's) is to heal the disjunction of psychology's scientific-objective and empathic-intersubjective orientations. It was this prospect that drew me to psychology in the first place. These questions still fascinate me.

Long before Google and the internet, I had a highly effective and reliable search engine. It was my mother. After visits home or phone conversations, a thick envelope filled with excerpts from newspapers and magazines soon followed. Many items from my mother's "clipping service" are still in my research files. I am holding one now. It is a tiny fragment, browned with age, barely two square inches in size. The text is an anecdotal account of Henry James taking care in the instruction of his nephew Willie—son of William James, the eminent pioneer of American psychology—as to the three most important things in life: "to be kind, and then to be kind, and then to be kind." I can recall receiving it, nearly forty years ago, shortly after I arrived at Purdue. Its poignant message stands out now—as it did then. My mother sent it when my interests were just beginning to turn toward issues of ecological concern. I can't say it was a singular catalyst, but I do know it affirmed my developing sense that "caring" had to be a central aspect of human/environmental relationships. The synchrony of James's caring for his nephew, my mother's for me, and mine for all of life was not lost.

Love and vulnerability are alloyed. Parenthood, as someone once put it plainly, is to forever live with your heart outside your body. The courage to live with an open heart—to have the fear and do it anyway—is the hallmark of love. The ability to love and the need for love are central to human experience. According to the Israeli psychologist Ada Lampert, "Love is an evolutionary product, born in the mammalian relationship between mother and infant ... [without which] ... the human species could not have been able to evolve." Lampert, in her book *The Evolution of Love*, outlines the processes that selected these abilities and shaped the human species over many generations. As she concludes, "Maternal love is both the first love created by evolution and the first love that everyone experiences ... [as well as] ... the prototype of all subsequent loves we will know in the course of our life span."[2] Lampert is not the only evolutionary psychologist to consider the origins of love, and not everyone concurs on the details. Nevertheless, her basic position strikes me as fundamentally sound. In short, evolution invented love. It is engraved in our DNA. The capacities to render and receive love were world-changing features in human evolution. Extension of the self in empathic sensitivity to others lies at the core of our social consciousness. Fuller understanding of the origins of human compassion will surely bring further insights. But retrospective knowledge of the evolutionary past, interesting as it is in its own right, is only part of the story.

I am shifting now to the here-and-now "experience" of love. Love, in this sense, refers to the actual expression of a living being in present time. Human caring takes many forms in the context of life. As Erich Fromm lamented, however, the most common forms of love tend to be narrow, sentimental, and selfish. True love requires courage, humility, and discipline. "The art of loving," to use Fromm's words, must be cultivated through diligence and be practiced with faith. Like our inherent linguistic talents, perhaps, we are born with the basic capabilities for love, but their elaboration demands concerted effort. When genuine love surrounds experience, the ordinary presents itself as extraordinary. "Like flashes of the 'erotic' or the 'holy,' we never forget these moments," affirms the Jungian scholar Ann Ulanov. "We need a durable container [of love] in which we can enlarge and transform ourselves; these psychic realities connect us to the whole of life.... The 'liquid flame of love' is everywhere in life," she declares, "from our relationships and favorite music to our daily food; its numinous energy ... can land anywhere." *The Pulitzer Prize–winning author and anthropologist Ernest Becker gave this analysis: "Love is the problem of an animal who must find life, [and] create a dialogue with nature in order to experience his own being.... When we understand man is the only animal who must create meaning, who must open a wedge into neutral nature, we already understand the essence of love."[4]

For the last episode of PBS's *Bill Moyers Journal*, the former presidential press secretary invited Barry Lopez as his final guest. Their conversation explored the sources of Lopez's inspiration and his views on faith, nature, and the human condition. "To live fully," Lopez explained, "means

---

*Ulanov places an interesting historical frame around the psychology of the self. The basic question of the twentieth century, she suggests, was: "How to assert 'being' in the face of non-being"—and related existential issues of death, authenticity, and meaning. The twenty-first-century question, as she posits, is now: "How to be committed to one's path in the face of contextual truth and post-modern relativism." Her answer is refreshing: "But that doesn't mean that reality is not real!"

allowing yourself to experience ... even those things that break your heart." His words were not only about human relations. He was speaking of the greater whole, where "nature is the full expression of life" and, through our senses, we come to this awareness.[5] These thoughts bring us back to Bradley's two "senses" of experience. Here-and-now experiences are momentary, atemporal, and synchronic. Bradley's other—formative or diachronic—"sense" of experience refers to the enduring residue of prior here-and-now experiences. The reader may recall an earlier diachronic/synchronic distinction from back in Chapter 2. Aldo Leopold used it as a way to highlight the difference between ecological and evolutionary questions. Ecology, as he noted, tends to focus on short-term (synchronic) interactions. Evolutionary questions emphasize long-term (diachronic) features. It is important to not conflate the comparisons. Leopold's is a strictly biological distinction between relations among living organisms versus patterns of evolutionary change and longevity. Bradley's is a psychological assertion about momentary awareness and memorability. There is a common recognition, in both cases, that "the now" can endure, and when it does, it holds a chance in the future. Throughout most of evolutionary time, life happened biologically in accordance with the "blind" mechanisms of natural selection. When humans arrived on the scene, "artificial" (i.e., intentional) selection began to creep into the story. Natural and human ecology have been mixed together ever since. This is where both types of synchrony/diachrony do meet—and there is plenty of confusion about how.

To the psychologically minded reader, a hint of Orwellian angst may be sensed in Bradley's comparison, e.g., "who controls the present controls the past; who controls the past controls the future."[6] This bit of mental gymnastics has not gone unnoticed by Anthony Greenwald, a social psychologist well versed in research on human cognition. The ego (or self), according to Greenwald, "is characterized by cognitive biases strikingly analogous to totalitarian information-control strategies." They include: seeing one's self as more central to events than it is; selective self-perception of responsibility for desired, but not undesired, outcomes; a disposition to preserve existing knowledge structures; and the rewriting of personal history to fit with a self-image of infallibility. These intrapsychic biases, Greenwald stresses, are "pervasive in and characteristic of normal personalities." In addition to being widespread in normal human cognition, they "are found in actively functioning, higher level organizations of knowledge, perhaps best exemplified by theoretical paradigms in science."[7] It may seem paradoxical that a person can deceive him- or herself. Yet there is ample evidence from psychological research, and even casual observation, that people do maintain unrealistic positive self-images, erase unwanted memories, and hold false beliefs and biased "facts" about their own past.

Looking Back and Looking Forward

The evolutionary theorist Bob Trivers maintains that a predisposition to actively (and unconsciously) misrepresent reality is built into the permanent architecture of our mind. Hiding our true intentions by means of covert "self-deception," according to Trivers, had adaptive advantages. The ability to keep one's motives outside of awareness, in the act of misleading others, is still a beneficial strategy. The best liar, in other words, is the one who buries a lie in unconsciousness—and thereby masks the cues of dishonest intent. Trivers's views of human mentality go beyond the classical Freudian model of unconscious/conscious relations. The origins of psychic individuality, for Freud, lay in the splitting of consciousness and unconsciousness (his topological model). The further sculpting of the ego and superego (his structural model) came later. Innate (primal) repression was the fundamental mechanism. Trivers's evolutionary account adds a major twist to the story. As self-interested individuals encountered each other in social competition, the stage was set for a primordial version of "mind games." The player who was more effective at detecting deception had the upper hand. The best protection against that, Trivers argues, was to erase one's real motives—via self-deception. Insofar as these skills were heritable, they continue to be permanent features of our psyche. Our unconscious mind, in other words, was itself shaped by social evolution to receive the contents of awareness being pushed back into the shadows.

This turning around of mental operations redefines the notion of repression. Moreover, the power to fool ourselves carries an added danger—of believing we are immune to it.

This is where Trivers's evolution of an adaptive mind meets Greenwald's revision of contemporary psychology. Both theorists make a compelling case for biased and self-serving unconscious processes throughout individual psychology. Trivers gives the evolutionary (diachronic) account of why cognitive distortions are common, whereas Greenwald shows how these elaborate (synchronic) processes function in everyday thought and social interactions. They likewise see these features permeating all levels of human organizational, political, and group psychology as well. Their views are controversial and unsettling to many, but they are firmly grounded in careful research.

My preoccupation with ecology and psychology is a long one. But they were tied together mainly in terms of situational or short-term historical thinking. Bill Drury's evolutionary logic deepened my understanding of ecology. But my views of the mind were still very much rooted in contemporary psychological concepts. Evolutionary themes seldom appeared in the psychological literature. I am sure I would have come upon these ideas sooner or later. But the truth is I have known Tony Greenwald and Bob Trivers for decades. Tony's office was just around the corner from mine at Ohio State. At the time, he was an editor of *The Journal of Personality and Social Psychology*—one of the leading journals in psychology research. Tony was familiar not only with every published report, but he also read countless unpublished manuscripts that were rejected. He knew more about ongoing research than anyone else I knew—and gladly shared it whenever we talked.

I was already at COA when Tony's article on the fabrication and revision of personal history appeared in *American Psychologist*. The area of psychology he covered was familiar to me. Tony's article even incorporated some of my own research on group identification and "basking in reflected glory." But his reinterpretation of unconscious cognition was a significant departure from the standard social science model common to psychological theory and research. I read it carefully in an effort to comprehend his shift in orientation. In a footnote, thanking people who had given helpful comments on the manuscript, I noticed Bob Trivers's name.

Bob was a graduate student at Harvard, working with Ernst Mayr and Bill Drury, when he came up with the evolutionary concepts of reciprocal altruism and parental investment. His ideas about self-deception appeared a few years later, at about the time Bill came to COA. When Greenwald's totalitarian ego article was published, Bob was an up-and-coming theorist on social evolution. I got to know Bob during his occasional trips to Maine to see Bill and Mary. During one of those visits, I asked him to join me in my psychology class, hoping he would share his thoughts on evolution and the unconscious. The class that day was on Freud. To my surprise, Bob never ventured a word. Instead, he sat there tugging at his beard in taciturn reserve for an hour and a half. It was a most disturbing experience. As we walked back to the dining hall after class for a cup of coffee, disappointed and unnerved by his reticence, I asked him for his thoughts. "Your understanding of psychoanalysis is very good," he said, "but it is all wrong!" I was baffled, stunned really, but somehow found the words to ask what he meant. My unguarded request somehow eased his stiffness. In the conversation that followed, Bob flooded me with an alternative vision of psychology—most of which escaped my comprehension. But his advice on whose work was interesting, and how to find them, was not wasted.

Evolutionary thinking about human consciousness was controversial at the time. The political-correctness movement was at its height on campuses everywhere. Several books on race and intelligence had blemished the ideas on genetic heritance; and E. O. Wilson's sociobiology was the favorite whipping boy of humanists. Nonetheless, I set out to read the growing literature on evolutionary psychology. The following summer I attended my first Human Behavior and Evolution Society (HBES) meeting. The program was full of meticulous research studies. Every topic was framed in evolutionary theory: from medicine, parenting, and social relations, to ethics, religion, and literary motifs. These were serious evolutionists. They knew their Darwin well and were spinning it out in countless directions. I loved it. But I was also somewhat concerned my new interests might be troubling to some of my colleagues and students. (I was, after all, dean of a very liberal-minded college.) So I kept these ventures private for a while. My incipient paranoia peaked during one of the HBES meetings, when I discovered the person across the table from me at lunch was from *The New Republic*. "Uh-ho," I thought to myself, "here comes another scathing exposé on Darwin and human affairs." I could not have been more mistaken. My dining partner that day was Robert Wright, who later authored a best-selling evolutionary account of unconscious processes: *The Moral Animal*. I did not make the connection, of course, until after the book appeared. But when it did, I felt a fresh measure of resolve: "Relax, Rich—it's okay; follow your intuitions—trust yourself."

There is an intimate relationship between one's worldview and one's experience. As Patricia often reminds me, based on her practice of psychotherapy, "The stories we tell ourselves really matter." As in the Gallup Poll conducted on the two-hundredth anniversary of Darwin's birthday showed, only four out of ten Americans said they believe in evolution. It was half that for people with an education of high school level or less. There is a strong relationship with further education; however, nearly three-fourths of respondents with postgraduate degrees reported believing in a Darwinian view. A significant relationship exists for religious beliefs as well; those who attend church most often are the least likely to say they believe in evolution. But religious practice and Darwin are not incompatible. A third of weekly churchgoers do consider evolution to be an accurate account of life.

The vast majority of members of the National Academy of Sciences report being atheists or agnostics. Biologists are the least religious of the academy's science disciplines, with only about 5 percent believing in God. Even so, I have several good friends who are evolutionary biologists who fall into this category. I also know many who don't. They are more like Pearl S. Buck, who put it this way: "I am so absorbed in the wonder of earth and the life upon it that I cannot think of heaven and angels."[8] One of them declares her atheism with delight. She is a resolute evolutionist whose view of life is full of beauty, wonder, and joy. "I have these feelings too," she proclaims—and clearly she does. "There is grandeur in this view of life"—as Darwin penned in the final words of *On the Origin of Species*—"from so simple a beginning endless forms most beautiful and most wonderful have been, and are being, evolved."[9] That nature was not divinely planned did not make it less beautiful for him. But for most of his contemporaries it was an unbearable thought. It still is for many people.

The Course Ahead

I often listen to *The Writer's Almanac* on PBS radio. Garrison Keillor always starts the program with "Today is the birthday of" ... so-and-so ... and ... so-and-so ... and closes with "a poem for the day." I was struck, one morning, by a line in *"The Hugeness of That Which Is Missing"* from Forrest Gander: "I have lost the consolation of faith, though not the ambition to worship."[10]

The thought kept rolling around in my mind for the rest of the day. The more I puzzled over it, the more I realized I probably would have said it the other way around. I grew up with a religious background. Worship services and prayer were a regular part of life. As I drifted away from religion, praying also faded from my life. I surely have no "ambition" to worship—and am uneasy during public prayers. My sense of faith, on the other hand, has remained active.

But what is faith? Commonly defined, faith refers to a commitment to things beyond explanation or without proof. As a religious term, the meaning pertains expressly to faith (i.e., belief) in God. In other contexts, faith may be used as a substitute for trust, hope, or conviction. I am reminded here of something a friend said many years ago: "Trust is as essential to human relationships as breath is to life." Faith—like trust—is defined by experience. "Faith brings us back to life," as Barry Lopez says: "We have to have faith in humanity to have faith in life ... and ... the natural world brings us fully to life." Lopez's conclusion fits my own: "I am perfectly comfortable being in a state of ignorance before something incomprehensible."[11] But to have faith we must be prepared to be vulnerable—like we must to have love. The first act of love is listening. "The great problem for humans," Alan Watts opined, "is to come back to their senses ... to listen to nature without thoughts or words ... and aware of the huge past within us."[12] As the Native American poet Linda Hogan has stated, "There is a way that nature speaks ... [but] ... most of the time we are simply not patient enough, quiet enough, to pay attention to the story."[13]

The earth turns and we turn with it. Time creeps onward. Here is where we are, midway between a star-filled universe and clouds of oscillating quanta. Here is where we come from. We are the earth—coming to know itself—gradually, incompletely, and persistently. For three billion years life didn't need us. The processes of evolution created and maintained its diversity through five massive extinctions. But now—as the former editor of *What Is Enlightenment?*, Craig Hamilton, declares: "Evolution needs our participation."[14] So does E. O. Wilson. Wilson is the leading advocate for conservation of the critical "hotspots" of biodiversity around the world. These areas represent the most threatened reservoirs of plant and animal life and contain 70 percent of all known species. Saving the species in these areas from extinction is a readily solvable and affordable problem. The total, onetime cost—including support for the people who live in and around them to manage them sustainably—is on the order of $50 billion. As Wilson puts it in perspective: this is equivalent to one-tenth of 1 percent of the annual world domestic product (i.e., the total of all national GDPs). The payments, spread over a decade, would be one ten-thousandth of annual global economic activity. Five billion dollars a year is a small price to pay.[15] The 2012 revenues of the National Football League (NFL) were more than twice that amount (and will double again in the coming decade); global expenditures on video games were $100 billion; and Americans threw away some $165 billion of food during that same year.[16] Surely we can find a way.

It was not so long ago when a city's prestige was measured by the grandeur of its cathedral. Nowadays a domed stadium is the more-revered symbol. We spend our time rushing from place to place, in air-conditioned automobiles, talking on cell phones, shopping at the mall. The ethos of growth and progress predominates because it is easy to quantify.

We count things that do not count. Hence the scorecards have no meaning, except to try for more. A line from Rodgers and Hammerstein rings true on this: "If you don't have a dream, how you gonna have a dream come true?"[17] To save the living world is a dream worth having and one I hope comes true. The world is calling us—to revise our understanding of and place in it. "Whatever a sustainable society may be," as David Orr proclaims, "it must be built on the most realistic view of the human condition possible."[18]

The failure to see humanity as "a part of it all"—and not the "purpose of it all"—is perhaps our greatest obstacle. The experience of wonder and eternity is everywhere. Life is ever coming into being—as are we. Joseph Campbell believed we must find the beauty in our scientific knowing. But, as he also counseled, "You don't worship nature; we *are* nature!"[19] E. O. Wilson's opinion—that the evolutionary epic is the best myth we have—comes close to the mark here. But our imagery has to keep up with what is known. We must cultivate our imagination to intensify life. When the mind and the world meet, we see with depth. Wonder fills the senses with receptivity, in what Keats termed "negative capability." Science feeds our minds; empiricism is a sharing of experience. But experience also speaks for itself.

This chapter opened with a dream. It was a dream about closure—and might be considered a "small" dream. Some dreams go the other way. They ask questions and open us to mystery. Those are the "big" dreams. They may happen just once, but are never forgotten. There is wisdom in such dreams that transforms our lives. Sometimes they can change the world. If we do find the bona fide faith to bring us back to nature, it will surely show up in our dreams. On this question, the words of Anthony Stevens are prophetic: "Our ecological circumstances reflect our spiritual condition, and in the course of the next century our thinking about ourselves as a species will have to undergo a revolution so profound as to make all previous revolutions seem like minor reorganizations of a parish fete … [T]hat is precisely what dreams evolved to provide."[20]

PART IV
CODA*

The best thing about the future is that it comes one day at a time.
—Abraham Lincoln

Only that day dawns to which we are awake.
—Henry David Thoreau

I AM SITTING IN ONE OF MY FAVORITE SPOTS, on the northern end of Eagle Lake in Acadia National Park, a mile or so from our house. It is a brilliant midwinter afternoon. The sunshine of a January thaw warms the day with a misleading hint of spring. The ice around the lakeshore has opened in a band of sparkling water. For the moment at least, the gap is too wide to reach the colorful ice shacks where local residents huddle over narrow holes, waiting for trout and landlocked salmon to trip their baited lines. A faint smell of detritus from last summer's ferns and leaves

---

*A coda in musical terminology is a brief "look back"—and closing repetition of a composition's main themes. In this case, it is also an opportunity to step back from the complexity of life and recount the splendor of its unity.

rises through a patch of bare ground in the melting snow. If I sit quietly, the sound of winter wildlife filters through the trees. A chorus of chirps and trills from chickadees, juncos, and grosbeaks fills the air. Farther off in the distance I hear a raven's croak, the chatter of a red squirrel, and the drumming of a pileated woodpecker. The nighttime tracks of snowshoe hare, whitetail deer, and coyotes crisscross through the snow and trees beyond the water's edge.

Things will stay this way in the weeks and months ahead, until late April when the ice is out. Spring in Maine comes with fits and starts. Yet each day brings something new. As the ground thaws, tree buds start to swell. Clusters of arbutus and shadbush flowers erupt throughout the woods. Horsetails and pussy willows push their way into the warm sunshine. The fiddleheads of ancient ferns unfurl, as if to greet their primeval dragonfly and water strider cousins. Loons begin their mating season on fresh water and join returning grebes, mergansers, and ducks. The trees begin to leaf—every day in different shades of green. The long migration of warblers from Central and South America and the evening uproar of tree frogs affirm the coming summer.

The granite bowl surrounding the lake is a timeless vista of trees and sky. To the south lies Pemetic Mountain. On my right is the eastern slope of Sargent Mountain; to the left, the west face of Cadillac. These are the prominent landscape features that drew Samuel de Champlain to land on these shores in September of 1604. Champlain named the island Île des Monts Déserts for its barren mountain peaks. He also laid claim to it—along with much of the North Atlantic coast—as New France.

Nine years later, at the invitation of the local Penobscot chief Asticou, a small group of French missionaries was welcomed and aided in starting a colony. The cultural history of the island dates back six thousand years as a summer encampment for Native Americans. The rich natural resources of berries, game animals, finfish, and shellfish were sun-dried or smoked to sustain them during the long winter months in their mainland communities. The new French settlement of Saint Sauveur was located on the island's southern shore, known today as Fernald Point, at the mouth of Somes Sound. The mission's leader was Pierre Biard, a Jesuit priest and former professor of theology at the University of Lyons. The settlers erected a fort, planted crops, and set about baptizing the natives. Their initiative was cut short, however, when Captain Samuel Argall from the British colony of Virginia arrived on his ship, *Treasurer*. Argall and his crew plundered the settlement, killed several inhabitants, and took the remaining men, including Biard, as prisoners. The boundary dispute between British New England and French Acadia remained a heated one for the next 150 years. No other European colonies were attempted on Mount Desert Island during that time. The sole exception came in the summer of 1688, when Antoine de la Mothe Cadillac and his bride resided here briefly to explore his land grant of MDI and surrounding coastal areas. But Cadillac soon moved on westward to found the city of Detroit and later serve as governor of French Louisiana.

Following defeat of the French at Quebec in 1759, the Acadia region was finally open for British settlers. Abraham Somes, James Richardson, and their families founded the first permanent European settlement in 1761—at the urging of and offer of free land from Sir Francis Bernard, governor of the Massachusetts Bay Colony. The village of Somesville was established at the northern tip of Somes Sound, the only fjord on the U.S. Atlantic coast. The sound's five-mile-long arm of sea divides the island into an eastern lobe and a western lobe.

After American independence in 1776, new communities sprang up in other sheltered harbors around the island. Final determination of the border between the United States and maritime Canada, along the St. Croix River, however, would not be resolved until 1783. When Maine separated from Massachusetts in 1820, as the twenty-third U.S. state, the island's population had grown to a thousand inhabitants. Principal occupations were farming, lumbering, fishing, and shipbuilding, which were often combined in the annual activities of residents.

One of the first summer visitors to Mount Desert Island was Thomas Cole, founder of the Hudson River School of landscape painting. Cole's trip was in 1844. He boarded at the Schooner Head farm of William and Crosha Lynam. Captivated by the island's beauty, he returned several more times with other artists, including Fitz Hugh Lane, William Hart, and Frederic Church. It was Church who named Eagle Lake, where I am now sitting, in a glorious oil painting from atop Cadillac Mountain. The stunning portrayals by the Hudson River artists captured the interest of wealthy collectors in Philadelphia, Boston, and New York. On Church's fourth trip to the island, in the summer of 1855, he brought along a party of twenty-six people. This pattern continued as other "rusticators" from eastern cities followed and found accommodations in the households of local residents. As the influx of visitors grew, a new era of larger and progressively fancier hotels began.

The island's gilded age was severely threatened in August 1873 by an outbreak of typhoid and a few weeks later by scarlet fever. Several hotels were forced to close. Tourists fled the town. The problem was traced to septic infiltration into wells caused by rapid overbuilding. National news of the outbreaks spread. Newspaper articles warned that the island's name, "Mount Desert," might be its fateful prophecy. Without the earnest action of residents and hotel owners, it may have come true. The proposed solution was to build a system of aqueducts and pipelines to connect the waters of Eagle Lake and the town. Construction began the following May at a frantic pace. By July a newly laid system was providing safe water to the hotels and dwellings of Bar Harbor. With the help of well-placed newspaper articles and publicity, disaster was averted. The resort reopened to a successful 1874 season.

By 1880 Bar Harbor had thirty hotels. Tourism became its major industry. Rodick House, in the center of town, was the nation's largest summer hotel of the time—with four hundred rooms and a dining hall that served a thousand guests. The island's emergence as a leading resort attracted the wealthiest and most prominent Americans. Many of them, including the Rockefeller, Vanderbilt, Ford, Astor, Carnegie, and Pulitzer families, began to build "cottages" of their own. Despite the unpretentious name, they were actually magnificent mansions with as many as fifty rooms each.

Amid this rapid development, a group of prominent summer residents initiated a movement to protect significant portions of the island. Under leadership from Harvard College's president Charles W. Eliot, they set out to establish a nature reserve for future generations. George B. Dorr, also a Boston summer resident and a friend of Eliot, accepted the task of directing the effort. With help from George Vanderbilt and other supporters, the acquisition of mountaintops, woodlands, and other spectacular and fragile land parcels began in 1901. When Congress established the National Park Service in August 1916, Dorr and his friends foresaw an opportunity to join the new park system. Dorr pushed untiringly to achieve the goal. On February 26, 1919, President Wilson signed the legislation for Lafayette National Park. It was the first national park east of the Mississippi, and the only one created entirely by gift of lands. The name was changed to Acadia in 1929.

The park continued to grow. More than eleven thousand acres were added through the generosity of John D. Rockefeller Jr. Between 1913 and 1940, Rockefeller created fifty-seven miles of graveled carriage roads that meander through the forest, around lakes, and over sixteen beautifully designed granite bridges. It is ironic, perhaps, that a family that made its wealth in oil would go to such lengths to preserve a horse-drawn tradition. The beauty of "Rockefeller's Roads" became an unrivaled refuge for summer hikers, horseback riders, and open carriages—as well as a spectacular winter network of peaceful ski trails.

The Great Depression and World War II put a damper on MDI's opulent lifestyles. The devastating fire of 1947 delivered the coup de grâce. The blaze consumed seventeen thousand acres, nearly half of it parkland. Five major hotels, sixty-seven palatial summer estates, and two hundred year-round homes were destroyed. The natural beauty of Bar Harbor that had drawn people from all over the world was erased. Most of the lavish estates destroyed by the fire were not rebuilt. Many others were abandoned and fell into disrepair. The town struggled to rebuild in the charred and barren landscape left behind in the fire's wake. Without the summer allure, on which it financially depended, the island's future was bleak.

As the natural ecology recovered, a new legion of summer visitors gradually arrived. But the permanent and summer residents who had not abandoned the island wanted a more balanced economy. The notion of a college seemed an ideal counterpart to the seasonal cycle of tourism.

Leslie Brewer, a Bar Harbor businessman, and Fr. James Gower, parish priest of the town's Catholic church, led the initiative. Brewer and Gower were childhood friends. They graduated from Bar Harbor High School in 1940 at the top of their class and were cocaptains of the football team. After college and service in World War II, both men returned to their home. They knew many of the academic and affluent summer residents who might offer assistance to re-create the town's future.

College of the Atlantic was chartered in 1969 and opened for classes in 1972. Its educational focus of human ecology—the interdisciplinary study of the relations of humans and the environment—is credited to James Gower. The idea of human ecology is what brought me here. It has shaped my life ever since. Fr. Jim died while I was working on this final coda. The opportunity to write a tribute to his life was given to me. He is very much on my mind as I sit here looking out across Eagle Lake. The foregoing island-in-time portrait is entwined by these feelings. So are many themes from the preceding pages—of space and time, death and life, ecology, imagination, beauty, and love.

Back in the middle of the book, I equated the biorhythm of a heartbeat to earth's yearly revolution around the sun. I would like to revisit the analogy. Instead of heartbeats-to-years, the algorithm will use the second hand of my watch—the ratio being roughly the same. A minute of time through this lens corresponds to sixty years. Adding a few more seconds covers the duration of my life. It also frames the landscape surrounding me. Evidence of the '47 fire that roared across the island clearly remains. Off to my right a few acres of old forest were somehow spared, as the blaze swept down the entire western shore of the lake. Only half the shoreline on the other side burned, when the October winds shifted and pushed the inferno over Cadillac Mountain and down onto Bar Harbor. The fire line defines two unmistakable patterns of forest ecology. The arching hemlock and white pine, with annual rings dating back hundreds of years, stand in stark contrast to the other side—all of which has regrown in my lifetime. We are linked in time, and I feel the difference.

Three minutes, by my watch, mark Cole's first trip to MDI and Church's painting of this lake. Champlain's landing and naming of the island come four minutes earlier. I must wait at least two hours to sense the arrival time of the first indigenous people—a half dozen millennia ago—and the true origins of human ecology in this place. In another two hours, a mile-high glacier covers everything. Ice sculpted the island's geology over thousands of years—carving the central fjord, rounding mountaintops, and chiseling lakes a hundred feet deep, like the one before me. This time tomorrow, the sweep of my second hand will find the island still covered by ice. The seconds-to-years conversion will also show *Homo sapiens* not yet out of Africa. Still thousands of years lie ahead before they begin the venture around the world. This is one of the clearest demarcations, perhaps, to an ecology of humans.

The solitude of this winter day is ideal for contemplating the synchrony of Pleistocene Africa and North American ice sheets. In summer, millions of visitors come to Acadia. The carriage road and trails around the lake will swarm with hikers. Today no signs of humanity can be seen. A handful of fish shacks dot the ice of one cove, but they are hidden from view behind a stand of trees. This reverie of seclusion is unexpectedly arrested, however, when high above in the clear blue sky my eye catches the silvery reflection of an airplane. Before it slips past the crest of Cadillac, another takes its place. The line of jets crisscrossing the Atlantic is ceaseless. I am not alone. A continuous stream of humanity passes overhead, thousands every hour, day and night. The woolly contrail of each aircraft is a telltale warning of atmospheric residue. I am reminded of other human impacts to the air and to the environment. Some are the sulfurous by-products of inland coal-fueled power plants and industry, blown downwind across New England. Others come in the form of nitrate compounds released by petroleum usage. At one point, in the summer of 1984, the acid level of fog measured in Acadia National Park reached a pH value equivalent to commercial vinegar. Things have improved since the 1990 amendments to the Clean Air Act, but chronically high levels of acidity still remain in the island's air and water.

Two hundred years ago, a galloping horse was the fastest form of communication. Today we travel near the speed of sound and communicate with the speed of light. These changes have happened with astonishing rapidity. They are accompanied by an equally amazing degree of unconsciousness, not only of society's energy dependence—but also about the fossil fuels that make it possible, and what they really are. A return to our wristwatch analogy, one last time, illustrates the point. Petroleum (oil and natural gas) comes from tiny marine zooplankton and phytoplankton that died, accumulated on the bottom of large bodies of water, and became trapped beneath layers of inorganic sediment. The organic material was then converted to complex hydrocarbons by the enormous forces and heat of sedimentary compression. Coal is made of much larger nonmarine organisms, primarily ferns and trees, also laid down and compressed beneath layers of rock. Petroleum and coal are hundreds of millions of years old. Both are the residual accumulation of past life-forms and solar energy that required hundreds of millions of years to form. To experience that range of time I must sit here, counting the passing seconds, for decades!

Worldwide, a hundred million barrels of oil and twenty million tons of coal are consumed every day. This gorging on the past is given little thought. The accelerating dependence on fossil fuels, like the exponential growth of the human population, seems to escape comprehension. We have heard these warnings for decades. The point here, however, is not about environment risks; my concern is the limits of experience. It really is difficult to bring these gaps into mind. Before throwing a birch log into our woodstove, I can count its fifty-odd annual rings since the 1947 fire cleared the landscape of my backyard. The stored energy in each layer of wood and the sunlight streaming through the window are fairly easy to connect. The context that links the use of my car key, our kitchen range, or a light switch is much less easily recounted. Yet all of these daily actions are ecological facts of life. We live in a human ecological world. It stretches beyond our individual lives—much further, even, than our existence as a species on this planet.

Human ecology is a way of looking at the world. As a philosophical perspective, it seeks an understanding of how the world really is, how it was, how it never will be again, and how it could be. I have had the opportunity to work and live in an educational community that shares these aims. These ideals are by no means limited to higher education. If I had my way, every schoolgirl and -boy would begin the life of learning in personal discoveries of their ecological context. There is nothing special in the brief snapshot of Downeast Maine portrayed earlier. Every place holds a story of natural, cultural, and personal ecology from which to begin. My years of contemplation along the trails of this island are merely a continuation of self-taught lessons and practices of childhood. Had schools back then offered such a curriculum, this book would have been easier to write. It pains me to realize how little early education has changed in the interim. Some strides have been made here and there. Yet I am often reminded by alumni, with high hopes of applying their interdisciplinary education as teachers, who discover the inflexibility of traditional structures. Irrespective of these impediments, I remain hopeful. The intuitive impulse behind questions of sustainability is growing. Climate change and other anthropogenic issues have begun to pass the threshold of economic and political concern. Discussion of these broad-scale themes and their future directions lies beyond the scope of this book.

The focus across these pages has been at a more psychological level. The central question was this: "How to experience life?" The answer, in short, is *identification*. The act of enfolding subjective experience and external reality is deeply personal. Its representation defies abstract formulas, written words, or coded rules. Nature and mind are too fleeting to be seized. A story's flowing stream or the timeless repose of meditation are perhaps the closest we come. My mandala for the contemplation of life is life itself—in the ever-changing patterns of ecology. Everyone can find a private spot to know some place this way, around the seasons and across the depths of time. The experience of being alive in this evolving world will flow from there—to other places—and all events. Ownership and assets do not measure the quality of life. Life is measured in the quality of our experience. All the world is open to experience. The richness of the living world, conversely, may well depend on our caring enough to do so.

I expressed an aim in the preface to keep this book's narrative near the surface. It was not without the hope that some insights and intuitive connections might arise along the way. My outline was unconventional.

The contents were a combination of academic fragments, bits of popular culture, personal recollections, and self-reflections. On the whole the pieces have wound together as a story of life—wrapped in a life story. The exercise has been satisfying and, by and large, I am where I hoped to find myself. We all have a ball of string. This was mine. I enjoyed the opportunity to prepare it and share it. My personal advice on this is clear: gather your memories; find the story; weave them together.

A number of topics were left on the sidelines. I have made little mention of several large ones—most notably, questions of a higher power, spirituality, and the human soul. It is not that I don't have such concerns or appreciate their significance in the light of human affairs. But rather, it signifies an unknowing of where I stand in the welter of sacred interpretations. The fringe around the tapestry of creation escapes my cognizance and capability of expression. This world by itself is a wonder. The experience of being here, in celebration of the whole of life, is to make the most of it. When the time comes, as Patricia paints it, "to go back into the soup," I am prepared to meet it as a homecoming. Everything else is mystery.

Bibliography

Allison, Jay, and Dan Gediman, eds. *This I Believe: The Personal Philosophies of Remarkable Men and Women.* New York: Henry Holt and Company, 2007.

Amory, Cleveland. *The Last Resorts.* New York: Harper, 1952.

Anderson, John G. T., and Catherin M. Devlin. "Conservation Biology and Human Ecology: Umbrellas, Flagships and Keystones." *Human Ecology Review* 3, no. 2 (1996/97): 238–47.

Andrews, Valerie. *A Passion for the Earth.* New York: HarperCollins, 1990.

Bateson, Gregory. *Mind and Nature: A Necessary Unity.* New York: Hampton Press, 1979.

———. *Steps to an Ecology of Mind.* Chicago: University of Chicago Press, 1972.

Bews, J. W. *Human Ecology.* London: Oxford University Press, 1935.

Birx, H. James, ed. *Encyclopedia of Time: Science, Philosophy, Theology, & Culture.* Thousand Oaks, CA: Sage, 2009.

Borden, Richard J. "The Art of Deanship." *Chronicle of Higher Education,* July 8, 2005.

———. "A Brief History of SHE: Reflections on the First Twenty Five Years of the Society for Human Ecology." *Human Ecology Review* 15, no. 1 (2008): 95–108.

———. "Ecology and Identity." In *Ecosystems and New Energetics,* edited by J. F. G. Grosser and F. Schmeidler, 25–42. Munich: Man and Space, 1986.

———. "The Future of Human Ecology." *Human Ecology: Journal of the Commonwealth Human Ecology Council,* no. 23 (2011): 47–49.

———. "An International Overview of the Origins of Human Ecology and the Restructuring of Higher Education: On Defining and Evolving Process." In *Integration of Environmental Education into General University Teaching in Europe,* edited by C. Susanne, L. Hens, and D. Devuyst, 297–309. Brussels: VUB Press, 1989.

---. "Looking Back and Looking Ahead: A View from the Crossroads of Evolution, Human Ecology and Environmental Policy." *Human Ecology Review* 1 (1994): 24–33.

---. "Psychology and Ecology: Beliefs in Technology and the Diffusion of Ecological Responsibility." *Journal of Environmental Education* 16 (1984–85): 14–19.

---. "Redrawing the Campus Map: Interdisciplinary Studies." *CONNECTION: New England's Journal of Higher Education and Economic Development* 6 (1991): 39–41.

---. "Technology, Education and the Human Ecological Perspective." *Journal of Environmental Education* 16 (1985): 1–5.

---. "Welcoming Rachel Carson to College of the Atlantic: A Centenary Celebration of Life." *Journal of Mediterranean Ecology* 9 (2008): 31–34.

Borden, Richard J., William A. Fisher, and Linda J. Doyle. "Ecology and Changing Lifestyles: Environmental Concern as a Determinant of Household Items and Activities." *Housing Educators' Journal* 4 (1977): 29–34.

Borden, Richard J., and Janice F. Francis. "Who Cares about Ecology?: Personality and Sex Differences in Environmental Concern." *Journal of Personality* 46 (1978): 190–203.

Borden, Richard J., Jamien Jacobs, and Gerald L. Young, eds. *Human Ecology: A Gathering of Perspectives.* College Park, MD: Society for Human Ecology, 1986.

---. *Human Ecology: Research and Applications.* College Park, MD: Society for Human Ecology, 1988.

Borden, Richard J., and P. R. Powell. "Androgyny and Environmental Orientation: Individual Differences in Concern and Commitment." In *Current Issues in Environmental Education and Environmental Studies* VIII, edited by Arthur B. Sacks, Louis A. Iozzi, and Richard J. Wilke, 261–75. 1982.

Borden, Richard J., and Andrew P. Schettino. "Determinants of Environmentally Responsible Behavior: Facts or Feelings?" *Journal of Environmental Education* 10 (1979): 35–39.

Botkin, Daniel B. *Discordant Harmonies: A New Ecology for the 21st Century.* New York: Oxford University Press, 1990.

Boyden, Stephen. "An Integrative Approach to the Study of Human Ecology." In *Human Ecology: A Gathering of Perspectives*. Edited by Richard J. Borden, Jamien Jacobs, and Gerald L. Young, 3–25. College Park, MD: Society for Human Ecology, 1986.

Boyden, Stephen, Sheelagh Millar, Ken Newcombe, and Beverley O'Neill. *The Ecology of a City and Its People: The Case of Hong Kong*. Canberra: Australian National University Press, 1981.

Bresler, Jack B., ed. *Human Ecology*. Reading, MA: Addison-Wesley, 1966.

Caras, Roger. *Death as a Way of Life*. Boston: Little, Brown and Company, 1970.

Carson, Rachel. *The Sea Around Us*. New York: Oxford University Press, 1961.

———. *The Sense of Wonder*. New York: Harper & Row, 1965.

———. *Silent Spring*. Boston: Houghton Mifflin, 1962.

Chawla, Louise. *In the First Country of Places: Nature, Poetry and Childhood Memory*. Albany, NY: State University of New York Press, 1994.

———. "Significant Life Experiences Revisited: A Review of Research on Sources of Environmental Sensitivity." *Journal of Environmental Education* 29, no. 3 (1998): 1–21.

Cialdini, Robert B., Richard J. Borden, Avril Thorne, Marcus R. Walker, Stephen Freeman, and Lloyd R. Sloan. "Basking in Reflected Glory: Three (Football) Field Studies." *Journal of Personality and Social Psychology* 34, no. 3 (1976): 366–75.

Clayton, Susan, and Gene Myers. *Conservation Psychology: Understanding and Promoting Human Care for Nature*. Hoboken, NJ: Wiley-Blackwell, 2009.

Coffin, Charles C. *Winning His Way*. Boston: Dana Estes and Co., 1893.

Colinvaux, Paul. *Ecology*. New York: Wiley, 1993.

Cronbach, Lee J. "Beyond the Two Disciplines of Scientific Psychology." *American Psychologist* 30 (1975): 671–84.

Csikszentmihalyi, Mihaly. *Flow: The Psychology of Optimal Experience*. New York: Harper and Row, 1990.

Darwin, Charles. *On the Origin of Species by Means of Natural Selection*. London: Watts, 1859.

Dorr, George B. *The Story of Acadia National Park.* Bar Harbor, ME: Acadia Publishing, 1997.

Drury, William H., Jr. *Chance and Change: Ecology for Conservationists.* Berkeley, CA: University of California Press, 1998.

Drury, William H., Jr., and Ian C. T. Nisbet. "Succession." *Journal of the Arnold Arboretum* 54 (July 1973): 331–68.

Dubos, René. *So Human an Animal: How We Are Shaped by Surroundings and Events.* New York: Scribner, 1968.

Dubos, René, and Barbara Ward. *Only One Earth: The Care and Maintenance of a Small Planet.* New York: Norton, 1972.

Dyball, Robert, Richard J. Borden, and Wolfgang Serbser. "New Directions in Human Ecology Education." In *Current Trends in Human Ecology.* Edited by Priscila Lopes and Alpina Begossi, 250–72. Newcastle, UK: Cambridge Scholars, 2009.

Ehrlich, Paul R., and Anne H. Ehrlich. *Population, Resources, Environments: Issues in Human Ecology.* San Francisco: W. H. Freeman, 1972.

Eiseley, Loren. *The Immense Journey.* New York: Random House, 1957.

———. *The Star Thrower.* New York: Random House, 1978.

Ekehorn, Eva. "International Directory of Organizations in Human Ecology." *Humanekologi* 4 (1992): 5–15.

Ericsson, K. Anders. *The Cambridge Handbook of Expertise and Expert Performance.* Cambridge: Cambridge University Press, 2006.

Erikson, Erik H. *Identity: Youth and Crisis.* New York: Norton, 1968.

Erikson, Erik H., and Joan Erikson. *The Life Cycle Completed.* New York: Norton, 1987.

Esquivel, Laura. *Like Water for Chocolate.* New York: Doubleday, 1992.

Everett, Daniel L. *Language: The Cultural Tool.* New York: Pantheon, 2012.

Fischer, David Hackett. *Liberty and Freedom: A Visual History of America's Founding Ideas.* New York: Oxford University Press, 2005.

Fischer, Joern, Robert Dyball, Ioan Fazey, Catherine Gross, Stephen Dovers, Paul Ehrlich, Robert J. Brulle, Carleton Christensen, and Richard J. Borden. "Human Behavior and Sustainability." *Frontiers in Ecology and the Environment* 10, no. 3 (2012): 153–60.

Frankl, Viktor E. *Man's Search for Meaning.* New York: W. W. Norton, 1960.

Freud, Sigmund. *The Ego and the Id.* New York: Norton, 1960.

Freud, Sigmund. *The Standard Edition of the Complete Psychological Works of Sigmund Freud.* Edited by J. Strachey. London: Hogarth, 1955.

Friedan, Betty. *The Feminine Mystique.* New York: W. W. Norton, 1963.

Glaeser, Bernhard, ed. *Humanökologie.* Opladen, Germany: Westdeutscher Verlag, 1989.

Goethe, Johann W. "Die Metamorphose der Pflanze." *British Journal of Botany.* 1863. English translation by Anne E. Marshall and Heinz Grotze. Wyoming, RI: Biodynamic Literature, 1978.

Golley, Frank. *A History of the Ecosystem Concept.* New Haven, CT: Yale University Press, 1993.

Gould, Stephen Jay. *Wonderful Life: The Burgess Shale and the Nature of History.* New York: W. W. Norton, 1989.

Gray, David, Richard J. Borden, and Russel Weigel. *Ecological Beliefs and Behaviors: Assessment and Change.* Westport, CT: Greenwood, 1985.

Haeckel, Ernst. *Generelle Morphologie der Organismen.* Berlin: George Reimer, 1866.

———. *The History of Creation.* New York: D. Appleton and Co., 1914.

Hall, Calvin S., and Gardner Lindzey. *Theories of Personality.* New York: Wiley, 1978.

Hansson, Lars O., and Britta Jungen, eds. *Human Responsibility and Global Change.* Göteborg, Sweden: University of Göteborg, 1992.

Hawking, Stephen. *A Brief History of Time.* New York: Bantam, 1988.

Hayakawa, S. I. *Language in Thought and Action.* New York: Harcourt, Brace and World, 1964.

Hens, Luc, Richard J. Borden, Shosuke Suzuki, and Gianumberto Caravello, eds. *Research in Human Ecology: An Interdisciplinary Overview.* Brussels: Vrije Universiteit Press, 1998.

Hübendick, Bengt. *Människoekologi.* Malmö, Sweden: Gidlunds, 1985. In Swedish.

Huib, E., ed. *Pathways to Human Ecology: From Observations to Commitment.* Bern, Switzerland: P. Lang, 1994.

James, William. *The Principles of Psychology.* Chicago: Encyclopedia Britannica, 1953. Originally published in 1890.

James, William. *The Varieties of Religious Experience: A Study in Human Nature.* New York: New American Library, 1958. Originally published in 1902.

Jung, C. G. *The Red Book (Liber Novus).* New York: Norton, 2009.

Jung, C. G., G. Adler, R. F. C. Hull, eds. *The Collected Works of C. G. Jung.* Princeton, NJ: Princeton University Press, 1977.

Kahn, Peter, and Patricia H. Hasback, eds. *Ecopsychology: Science, Totems and the Technological Species.* Cambridge, MA: MIT Press, 2012.

Keller, David R., and Frank B. Golley. *The Philosophy of Ecology: From Science to Synthesis.* Athens: University of Georgia Press, 2000.

Kendler, Howard H. "Psychology and Phenomenology: A Clarification." *American Psychologist* 60, no. 4 (2005): 318–24.

Kingsland, Sharon E. *The Evolution of American Ecology: 1890–2000.* Baltimore, MD: Johns Hopkins University Press, 2005.

Koffka, Kurt. *Principles of Gestalt Psychology.* New York: Harcourt, Brace, 1935.

Koger, Susan M., and Deborah Du Nann Winter. *The Psychology of Environmental Problems: Psychology for Sustainability.* New York: Taylor and Francis, 2010.

Köhler, Wolfgang. *Gestalt Psychology.* New York: Mentor, 1947.

Kübler-Ross, Elisabeth. *On Death and Dying.* New York: Routledge, 1969.

Kurlansky, Mark. *The Big Oyster: History on the Half Shell.* New York: Random House, 2006.

———. *Cod: A Biography of the Fish That Changed the World.* New York: Penguin, 1998.

———. *Salt: A History of the World.* New York: Penguin, 2002.

Latané, Bibb, and John M. Darley. *The Unresponsive Bystander: Why Doesn't He Help?* New York: Appleton Century-Crofts, 1970.

Levi-Montalcini, Rita. *In Praise of Imperfection: My Life and Work.* New York: Basic Books, 1989.

Levintin, Daniel. *This Is Your Brain on Music: The Science of a Human Obsession.* New York: Penguin, 2007.

———. *The World in Six Songs: How the Musical Brain Created Human Nature.* New York: Dutton, 2009.

Light, Andrew, and Jonathan M. Smith, eds. *The Aesthetics of Everyday Life.* New York: Columbia University Press, 2005.

Lynch, Kevin. *What Time Is This Place?* Cambridge, MA: MIT Press, 1972.

Lytle, Mark H. *The Gentle Subversive: Rachel Carson, Silent Spring, and the Rise of the Environmental Movement.* New York: Oxford University Press, 2007.

Machado, Paulo A. *Ecologia Humana.* São Paulo, Brazil: Cortez, 1985. In Portuguese.

Malmberg, Torsten. "House as Territory." Research project no. 84-0120-4. Stockholm: Swedish Council for Building Research, 1986.

———. *Human Territoriality.* New York: Mouton, 1980.

Marten, Gerald G. *Human Ecology: Basic Concepts for Sustainable Development.* Sterling, VA: Earthscan, 2001.

May, Rollo, Ernest Angel, and Henri F. Ellenberger, eds. *Existence: A New Dimension in Psychiatry and Psychology.* New York: Simon and Schuster, 1958.

Mayr, Ernst. *What Makes Biology Unique?* New York: Cambridge University Press, 2004.

McHarg, Ian L. *Design with Nature.* New York: Natural History Press, 1969.

McIntosh, Robert P. *The Background of Ecology.* New York: Cambridge University Press, 1985.

Milgram, Stanley. "The Small World Problem." *Psychology Today* 1 (May 1967): 61–67.

Milgram, Stanley, Leonard Bickman, and Lawrence Berkowitz. "Note on the Drawing Power of Crowds of Different Size." *Journal of Personality and Social Psychology* 13, no. 2 (1969): 79–82.

Moore, Thomas. *Care of the Soul: A Guide for Cultivating Depth and Sacredness in Everyday Life.* New York: HarperCollins, 1992.

Morrison, Philip, and Phylis Morrison. *Powers of Ten.* New York: Scientific American Books, 1982.

Murie, Adolph. *Ecology of the Coyote in Yellowstone.* (Conservation Bulletin no. 4.) Washington, DC: U.S. Government Printing Office, 1940.

———. *The Wolves of Mount McKinley.* Seattle: University of Washington Press, 1985.

Nathawat, G. S., Z. Daysh, and G. J. Unnithan, eds. *Human Ecology: An Indian Perspective.* Jaipur, India: Indian Human Ecology Council, 1985.

Nearing, Helen, and Scott Nearing. *Living the Good Life.* New York: Schocken, 1954.

Neisser, Ulrich. *Cognitive Psychology.* New York: Appleton-Century-Crofts, 1967.

Odum, Eugene. *Fundamentals of Ecology,* 3rd ed. Philadelphia: W. B. Saunders, 1971. 1st ed. published in 1953.

Ophuls, William. *Ecology and the Politics of Scarcity.* San Francisco: Freeman, 1977.

Park, Robert E., and Ernest W. Burgess. *Introduction to the Science of Sociology.* Chicago: University of Chicago Press, 1921.

Perls, Friedrich S. *Ego, Hunger and Aggression.* London: G. Allen and Unwin, 1947.

Perls, Friedrich S., Ralph Hefferline, and Paul Goodman. *Gestalt Therapy: Excitement and Growth in the Human Personality.* New York: Delta, 1951.

Piaget, Jean. *Genetic Epistemology.* New York: Columbia University Press, 1968.

Pickett, Steward T. A. *The Ecology of Natural Disturbance and Patch Dynamics.* New York: Academic Press, 1985.

Pinker, Steven. *The Language Instinct.* New York: HarperCollins, 1994.

———. *The Stuff of Thought.* New York: Viking, 2007.

Quinn, James A. *Human Ecology.* New York: Prentice Hall, 1950.

Rabineau, Louis, and Richard J. Borden. "Human Ecology and Education: The Founding, Growth and Influence of College of the Atlantic." In *Human Ecology, Environmental Education and Sustainable Development,* edited by Z. Daysh et al., 137–41. London: Commonwealth Human Ecology Council, 1991.

Rogers, Carl R. *On Becoming a Person: A Therapist's View of Psychotherapy.* Boston: Houghton Mifflin, 1961.

Rogers, Carl R., and B. F. Skinner. "Some Issues Concerning the Control of Human Behavior." (The Rogers/Skinner debate.) *Science* 124 (1956): 1057–66.

Rychlak, Joseph F. *The Human Image in Postmodern America*. Washington, DC: American Psychological Association, 2003.

———. *In Defense of Human Consciousness*. Washington, DC: American Psychological Association, 1997.

———. *Introduction to Personality and Psychotherapy*. Boston: Houghton Mifflin, 1981.

———. *A Philosophy of Science for Personality Theory*. Boston: Houghton Mifflin, 1968.

———. *The Psychology of Rigorous Humanism*. New York: NYU Press, 1988.

Sargent, Frederick, II, ed. "Human Ecology." Special issue, *BioScience* (August 1965): 509–35.

Sargent, Frederick, II. *Human Ecology*. New York: American Elsevier, 1974.

Saunders, Carol D., and Olin Eugene Myers, Jr., eds. "Conservation Psychology." Special issue, *Human Ecology Review* 10, no. 2 (2003): 87–186.

Skinner, Burrhus F. *Walden Two*. New York: Macmillan, 1948.

Sloane, Eric. *A Reverence for Wood*. New York: Funk and Wagnalls, 1965.

Spivey, Nigel. *How Art Made the World*. New York: Basic Books, 2005.

Steiner, Dieter, and Marcus Nauser, eds. *Human Ecology: Fragments of Antifragmentary Views of the World*. London and New York: Routledge, 1993.

Suzuki, Shosuke, Richard J. Borden, and Luc Hens, eds. *Human Ecology— Coming of Age: An International Overview*. Brussels: Vrije Universiteit Press, 1991.

Tanner, Thomas. "On the Origins of SLE Research, Questions, Outstanding, and Other Research Traditions." *Environmental Education Research* 4, no. 4 (1998): 419–24.

Taylor, Stuart P., Richard Shuntich, Patrick McGovern, and Robert Genthner. *Violence at Kent State: The Students' Perspective*. New York: College Notes and Texts, 1971.

Theodorson, George A. *Studies in Human Ecology*. Evanston, IL: Row, Peterson and Co., 1961.

U.S. Government. *The Report of the President's Commission on Campus Unrest.* (The Scranton Commission Report.) Washington, DC: U.S. Government Printing Office, 1970.

Wang, Rusong. *Human Ecology in China.* Beijing: China Science and Technology Press, 1990.

Wells, H. G. *The Outline of History.* New York: Doubleday, 1949.

Wells, H. G., Julian S. Huxley, and George P. Wells. *The Science of Life.* New York: Literary Guild, 1934.

Whitehead, Alfred North. *Modes of Thought.* New York: Free Press, 1968. Originally published in 1938.

———. *Process and Reality.* New York: Free Press, 1978. Originally published in 1929.

———. *Science and the Modern World.* New York: Free Press, 1967. Originally published in 1925.

Williams, Lewis, Rose Roberts, and Alastair McIntosh. *Radical Human Ecology: Intercultural and Indigenous Approaches.* London: Ashgate, 2012.

Worthington, E. Barton. *The Ecological Century: A Personal Appraisal.* Oxford, UK: Oxford University Press, 1983.

Wright, Robert. *The Moral Animal: Why We Are the Way We Are: The New Science of Evolutionary Psychology.* New York: Vintage, 1994.

Yalom, Irvin. *Existential Psychotherapy.* New York: Basic Books, 1980.

Notes

Preface

1. G. K. Chesterton, *Tremendous Trifles* (New York: Dodd, Mead, 1909), 7.
2. Daniel Dennett, College of the Atlantic—Champlain Society, "Coffee and Conversation," August 28, 2012.
3. Rollo May, *The Cry for Myth* (New York: Delta, 1991), 20, 15, 31.
4. Ibid., 9.
5. Joseph Campbell, *The Power of Myth*, 1988.
6. Campbell, *Mythos*, 1996.
7. Ibid.
8. Campbell, *Transformations of Myth Through Time* (New York: Perennial Library, 1990), 101.
9. Henry Murray, *Myth and Mythmaking* (New York: Braziller, 1960), 114.
10. Campbell, *Mythos*, 1996.
11. May, *The Cry for Myth*, 25.
12. Campbell, *The Power of Myth*, 1988.
13. E. O. Wilson, *On Human Nature* (Cambridge, MA: Harvard University Press, 1979), 201.
14. May, *The Cry for Myth*, 246.
15. Betty Sue Flowers, "Practicing Politics in the Economic Myth," in *The Vision Thing: Myth, Politics and Psyche in the World*, ed. Thomas Singer (New York: Routledge, 2000), 207–12. Also reprinted in *SALT Journal* 2, no. 6 (Fall 2000).
16. Ludwig Wittgenstein, *Tractatus Logico-Philosophicus* (New York: Harcourt, Brace & Company, 1922), 189.

Chapter 1. The Arc of Life

1. Ralph Waldo Emerson, "Experience," in *Selected Writings of Emerson*, ed. Donald McQuade (New York: Modern Library, 1981), 329.

2. Edith Cobb, "The Ecology of Imagination in Childhood," *Daedalus* 88, no. 3 (1959): 537.
3. "America's Sewage System and the Price of Optimism," *Time* magazine 94, no. 5 (August 1, 1969): 41.
4. Emerson, "Experience," 329.

Chapter 2. Ecology

1. See Vladimir Dimitrov, "Synergy of Ecology of Learning and Health Ecology," www.zulenet.com/vladimirdimitrov/pages/SynergyEcologyLearning.html.
2. Gunnar Broberg, *Carl Linnaeus* (Stockholm: Swedish Institute, 2006), 22.
3. F. Darwin and A. C. Seward, eds., *More Letters of Charles Darwin* (London: John Murray, 1903), 117.
4. Charles Darwin, *Autobiography of Charles Darwin* (London: Thinkers Library, 1929), 58.
5. "Letter from Adam Sedgwick to Charles Darwin, November 24, 1859," in *The Life and Letters of the Reverend Adam Sedgwick*, eds. John Willis Clark and Thomas McKenny Hughes (Cambridge: The University Press, 1890), 2:356.
6. Charles Lyell, *The Student's Elements of Geology* (London: John Murray, 1874), 138.
7. Thomas Malthus, "An Essay on the Principle of Population" (1798), in *Oxford World Classics*, reprint xxix, 61.
8. W. C. Allee, Alfred E. Emerson, Orlando Park, and Karl P. Schmidt, *Principles of Animal Ecology* (Philadelphia: W. B. Saunders, 1949).
9. Aldo Leopold, *A Sand County Almanac: With Essays on Conservation from Round River* (New York: Ballantine, 1972), 188.
10. Ibid., 290.
11. Eugene Cittadino, "Ecology and the Professionalization of Botany in America, 1890–1905," *Studies in the History of Biology* 4 (1980): 180.
12. Ibid., 181.
13. Ibid., 188.
14. Peder Anker, *Imperial Ecology: Environmental Order in the British Empire* (Cambridge, MA: Harvard University Press, 2001), 24.

15. A. G. Tansley, "The Use and Abuse of Vegetational Concepts and Terms," *Ecology* 16 (1935): 284–85.
16. Ibid., 299.
17. Frank Golley, *A History of the Ecosystem Concept* (New Haven, CT: Yale, 1993), 16.
18. Leopold, *A Sand County Almanac*, 262.
19. Aldous Huxley, "The Politics of Ecology," November 30, 1962, Lecture: Center for the Study of Democratic Institutions, http://digital.library.ucsb.edu/items/show/4898. Also reprinted in *Center Magazine*, 1963.
20. Hugh Raup, "Some Problems in Ecological Theory and Their Relation to Conservation," *Journal of Animal Ecology* 33 (1964): 21.
21. See Edward Goldsmith, "Whatever Happened to Ecology?" (July 1, 2002), 7, www.edwardgoldsmith.com/page21.html. This article is an extended and updated version of the article "Whatever Happened to Ecology?" first published in *The Ecologist* 15, no. 3 (March–April 1985).
22. James R. Karr and Kathryn E. Freemark, "Disturbance and Vertebrates: An Integrative Perspective," in *The Ecology of Natural Disturbance and Patch Dynamics*, eds. S. T. A. Pickett and P. S. White (Orlando, FL: Academic Press, 1985), 154.
23. Donald Worster, *The Wealth of Nature: Environmental History and the Ecological Imagination* (New York: Oxford University Press, 1993), 163.

Chapter 3. Experience

1. Quentin Lauer, *Phenomenology: Its Genesis and Prospect* (New York: Harper and Row, 1958), 5.
2. Bernard J. Baars, "There Is Already a Field of Systematic Phenomenology, and It's Called 'Psychology,'" in *The View from Within: First-Person Approaches to the Study of Consciousness*, eds. Francisco Varela and Jonathan Spear (Bowling Green, OH: Imprint Academic, 2000), 219.
3. Robert Trivers, *Natural Selection and Social Theory* (New York: Oxford University Press, 2002), 257.

4. Hermann Ebbinghaus, *Psychology: An Elementary Textbook* (Boston: D. C. Heath, 1908), 3.
5. May, *The Cry for Myth*, 74.
6. C. J. Ducasse, *A Critical Examination of the Belief in a Life After Death* (Springfield, IL: C. C. Thomas, 2006), 212.
7. Solomon Diamond, *The Roots of Psychology* (New York: Basic Books, 1974), 55.
8. William Sahakian, *History and Systems of Psychology* (New York: John Wiley & Sons, 1975), 37.
9. Ibid., 43.
10. Ibid., 29.
11. John B. Watson, "Psychology as a Behaviorist Views It," *Psychological Review* 20 (1913): 158.
12. Fritz Perls, "A Life Chronology" (unpublished manuscript). Perls wrote this piece as an introduction to his 1969 revision of *Ego, Hunger and Aggression*, but it somehow did not appear in the final publication. A copy of the original can be found at www.gestalt.org/fritz.htm.
13. William James, "Experiments in Memory," *Science* 6 (1885): 198–99.
14. Amy Cynkar, "The Changing Gender Composition of Psychology," *APA Monitor* 38, no. 6 (2007): 46.
15. Joseph F. Rychlak, *In Defense of Human Consciousness* (Washington, DC: American Psychological Association, 1997), 231.
16. Ibid., 272.

Chapter 4. Human Ecology

1. Paul Shepard, "Whatever Happened to Human Ecology?" *BioScience* 17 (1967): 891–94.
2. Gerald L. Young, ed., *Origins of Human Ecology* (Stroudsburg, PA: Hutchinson-Ross, 1983), 1.
3. John Visvader, "Philosophy and Human Ecology," in *Human Ecology: A Gathering of Perspectives*, eds. R. J. Borden, J. Jacobs, and G. L. Young (Bar Harbor, ME: Society for Human Ecology, 1986), 125.

4. Roy A. Rappaport, "Adaptation and Maladaptation in the Evolution of Culture, Technology, and Society," in *Crossroads: Society and Technology*, ed. John H. Baldwin (Troy, OH: NAEE, 1983), 3. Proceedings of the Twelfth Annual Conference of the National Association for Environmental Education.
5. Frank Fenner, "Professor Stephen Boyden: Human Ecologist." Interviews with Australian Scientists, Australian Academy of Sciences, 2003, http://science.org.au/scientists/interviews/b/sb.html.
6. Ian McHarg, "Human Ecological Planning at Pennsylvania," *Landscape Planning* 18, no. 2 (1981): 110.
7. Carol L. Moberg and Zanvil A. Cohn, "René Jules Dubos," *Scientific American* (May 1991): 74.
8. Paul B. Sears, "Human Ecology: A Problem of Synthesis," *Science* 120 (December 1954): 959–63.
9. Paul R. Ehrlich and Anne H. Ehrlich, *Population, Resources, Environment: Issues in Human Ecology*, 2nd ed. (San Francisco: W. H. Freeman, 1972), preface.
10. Gunnar Myrdal, *Against the Stream: Critical Essays on Economics* (London: Macmillan, 1973), 142.
11. CHEC Mission Statement. From "What Is Human Ecology?" *Commonwealth Human Ecology Council Membership Brochure* (2000): 1.
12. Prince Philip, Duke of Edinburgh, "Prefatory Remarks: First Commonwealth Conference on Development and Human Ecology," Malta, October 18–24, 1970. Reprinted in H. Bowen-Jones, ed., *Human Ecology in the Commonwealth* (London: Charles Knight, 1972), preface.
13. A. H. Maloney and M. P. Ward, "Ecology: Let's Hear from the People: An Objective Scale for the Measurement of Ecological Attitudes and Knowledge," *American Psychologist* 28 (1973): 583–86. A. H. Maloney, M. P. Ward, and G. N. Bracht, "A Revised Scale for the Measurement of Ecological Attitudes and Knowledge," *American Psychologist* 30 (1975): 787–90.
14. "New Science. Mrs. Richards Names It Oekology," *Boston Globe*, December 1, 1892, 1.

15. Harlan H. Barrows, "Geography as Human Ecology," *Annals of the Association of American Geographers* 13, no. 1 (1923): 14.
16. Gerald L. Young, "Human Ecology as an Interdisciplinary Concept: A Critical Inquiry," *Advances in Ecological Research* 8 (1974): 58.
17. H. G. Wells, *Experiment in Autobiography* (Philadelphia: J. H. Lippincott, 1934), 552–53, 617.
18. Wolfgang F. E. Preiser, "Letter from the President," *Human Ecology Bulletin* 3 (1986): 1–4.
19. Emin Tengström, "Human Ecology: A New Discipline?" *Humanekologiska Skrifter* 4, Gothenburg University (1985): 28–29.
20. Manfred A. Max-Neef, "Foundations of Transdisciplinarity," *Ecological Economics* 53 (2005): 8.

Chapter 5. Education

1. G. K. Chesterton, *Illustrated London News*, July 5, 1924.
2. Bill Ellis, response letter to "Four Scenarios for the Future of Education," *The Futurist* (March/April 2005): 4.
3. Jean Piaget, Invited Lectures—Conference on Cognitive Studies and Curriculum Development, Cornell University, March 11–13, 1964. Translated and reprinted in Eleanor Duckworth, "Piaget Rediscovered," *Journal of Research in Science* 2 (1964), 175.
4. Alfred North Whitehead, *The Aims of Education* (New York: Macmillan, 1929), 1–4.
5. "A Conversation with Ossie Davis and Ruby Dee," *Charlie Rose*, PBS, November 24, 1998.
6. Anthony Stevens, *Archetypes Revisited: An Updated Natural History of the Self* (Toronto: Inner City Books, 2003), 2.
7. Chögyam Trungpa, *Cutting Through Spiritual Materialism* (Boston: Shambhala, 1973), 39–40.
8. Reprinted with permission of the author, September 4, 2012.
9. Charles Homer Haskins, *The Rise of Universities* (Ithaca, NY: Cornell University Press, 1957), 21.
10. H. G. Good, *A History of American Education* (New York: Macmillan, 1962), 60.

11. For the preceding, see: H. G. Good, 1962; *The American College in the Nineteenth Century,* ed. Roger L. Geiger (Nashville, TN: Vanderbilt University Press, 2000); *The Founding of American Colleges and Universities Before the Civil War,* ed. Donald G. Tewksbury (Hamden, CT: Archon Books, 1965); *The Emergence of the American University,* ed. Laurence R. Vesey (Chicago: University of Chicago Press, 1965).
12. *Report on the Course of Instruction in Yale College* (New Haven, CT: printed by Hezekiah Howe, 1828), 9.
13. Henry D. Thoreau, *Walden: A Story of Life in the Woods* (New York: A. L. Burt Company, 1902), 55.
14. Daniel Fallon, *The German University* (Boulder: Colorado Associated University Press, 1980), 2.
15. Frederick Jackson Turner, *The Frontier in American History* (New York: Holt, Rinehart and Winston, 1962), 284.
16. Fallon, 1980, 52; see also Daniel Fallon, "German Influences on American Education," in *The German-American Encounter,* eds. F. Trommler and E. Shore (New York: Berghahn, 2001), 77–87.
17. Roger L. Geiger, ed., *The American College in the Nineteenth Century* (Nashville, TN: Vanderbilt University Press, 2000), 35.
18. "Environmental Response: Edward Larrabee Barnes," *Progressive Architecture* 55 (1974): 62–63.
19. Jonah Lehrer, "Groupthink," *The New Yorker* (January 30, 2012): 27.
20. Ibid., 25.
21. Vartan Gregorian, "Education and Our Divided Knowledge," *Proceedings of the American Philosophical Society* 137, no. 4 (1993): 609.
22. Judith Rodin and Nancy MacPherson, "Shared Outcomes: How the Rockefeller Foundation Is Approaching Evaluation with Developing Country Partners," *Stanford Social Innovation Review* 10, no. 3 (Summer 2012).
23. Amy Gutmann, "What Would They Do?" *Newsweek* (September 11, 2011).
24. Mark C. Taylor, "End of the University as We Know It," *New York Times,* April 27, 2009.

PART II. FACETS OF LIFE

1. Edward O. Wilson, *Consilience* (New York: Vantage, 1998), 8.
2. Peter Matthiessen, *Charlie Rose*, PBS, May 27, 2008.
3. Ingo F. Walther, *Pablo Picasso* (Cologne: Taschen, 2000), 20.

Chapter 6. Time and Space

1. Torsten Malmberg, "Time and Space in Human Ecology," in *Human Ecology: Research and Applications*, eds. R. J. Borden, J. Jacobs, and G. L. Young (College Park, MD: Society for Human Ecology, 1988), 44.
2. Ernst Mayr, *What Makes Biology Unique?* (New York: Cambridge University Press, 2004), 84.
3. Malmberg, 44.
4. Loren Eiseley, "How Natural Is Natural?" *The Star Thrower* (New York: Harcourt, Brace, 1978), 288.
5. Rollo May, Ernest Angel, and Henri F. Ellenberger, eds., *Existence* (New York: Simon and Schuster, 1967), 67.
6. St. Augustine quoted by Paul Ricoeur, *Time and Narrative* (Chicago: University of Chicago Press, 1984), I:7.
7. *New York Herald*, November 18, 1883.
8. Nick Herbert, *Elemental Mind: Human Consciousness and the New Physics* (New York: Dutton, 1993), 50.
9. Verlyn Klinkenborg, "Grasping the Depth of Time as a First Step in Understanding Evolution," *New York Times*, August 23, 2005.
10. "Space," *Encyclopedia Britannica* online, www.britannica.com/EBchecked/topic/557313/space.
11. Carl Sagan, *Cosmos* (New York: Random House, 1983), 179.
12. Nina Munteanu, "The Subversive Biology of Lynn Margulis," *The Alien Next Door*, June 16, 2007, http://sfgirl-thealiennextdoor.blogspot.com.
13. Kevin Lynch, *What Time Is This Place?* (Cambridge, MA: MIT Press, 1972), 147.

Chapter 7. Death in Life

1. Carl Zimmer, "How Many Species on Earth? It's Tricky," *New York Times*, August 30, 2011.

2. W. D. Hamilton, *Narrow Roads to Gene Land: Evolution of Sex* (New York: Oxford University Press, 1999), 2:419.
3. David Braun, "White-eyed Birds Are on Evolution Fast Track," *National Geographic News Watch,* January 26, 2009; Janice Britton-Davidian et al., "Environmental Genetics: Rapid Chromosomal Evolution in Island Mice," *Nature* 403 (2000): 158.
4. Amanda Leigh Haag, "Patented Harpoon Pins Down Whale Age," www.nature.com/news/2007/070619/full/news070618-6.html; John Roach, "Rare Whales Can Live to Nearly 200, Eye Tissue Reveals," *National Geographic News,* July 13, 2006, http://news.nationalgeographic.com/news/2006/07/060713-whale-eyes.html; Andrew D. Foote, Kristin Kaschner, Sebastian E. Schultze, Cristina Garilao, Simon Y. W. Ho, Klaas Post, Thomas F. G. Higham, Catherine Stokowska, Henry van der Es, Clare B. Embling, Kristian Gregersen, Friederike Johansson, Eske Willerslev, and M. Thomas P. Gilbert, "Ancient DNA Reveals That Bowhead Whale Lineages Survived Late Pleistocene Climate Change and Habitat Shifts," *Nature Communications* 4, article no. 1677 (2013).
5. *World Mortality Report 2011,* United Nations, Department of Economic and Social Affairs, Population Division, 2012, www.un.org/en/development/desa/population.
6. *World Fertility Data 2012,* United Nations, Department of Economic and Social Affairs, Population Division, Fertility and Family Planning Section, www.un.org/en/development/desa/population.
7. *Four Screenplays of Ingmar Bergman,* trans. from Swedish by Lars Malmstrom and David Kushner (New York: Simon and Schuster, 1960), xv–xvii.
8. George Lucas, *Charlie Rose,* PBS, September 9, 2004.
9. Bergman, 1960, xxi.
10. Larry King, *Charlie Rose,* PBS, June 20, 2006.
11. Edward C. Hegeler, "The Problem of Good and Evil," *Monist* 6, no. 1 (1895): 580; see also "The Philosophical Problem of Good and Evil," in *The History of the Devil,* ed. Paul Carus (Charleston, SC: Forgotten Books, 2008), originally published in 1900.
12. Media Education Foundation, "Media Violence: Facts and Statistics," 2005, www.mediaed.org/Handouts/ChildrenMedia.pdf; American

Psychological Association, "Violence in the Media," February 19, 2004, www.apa.org/research/action/protect.aspx.

13. State of Maine Department of Health and Human Services, Maine Suicide Prevention Program, www.maine.gov/suicide/about/faq.htm.

14. Sigmund Freud, *Beyond the Pleasure Principle (1920)*, in *The Standard Edition of the Complete Psychological Works of Sigmund Freud*, ed. J. Strachey (London: Hogarth, 1955), XVIII:38.

15. Sheldon Solomon, Jeff Greenberg, and Tom Pyszczynski, "A Terror Management Theory of Social Behavior: The Psychological Functions of Self-Esteem and Cultural Worldviews," in *Advances in Experimental Social Psychology*, ed. Mark P. Zanna (San Diego, CA: Academic Press, 1991), 93–160; "Fear, Death and Politics: What Your Mortality Has to Do with the Upcoming Election," interview with Sheldon Solomon by *Mind Matters* ed. Jonah Lehrer, *Scientific American*, October 23, 2008, www.scientificamerican.com/article.cfm?id=fear-death-and-politics&print=true; Nathan Heflick, "How We Cope with Death: A Theory of Terror Management," June 10, 2012, www.psychologytoday.com/blog/the-big-questions/201206/how-we-cope-death.

16. Leopold, *A Sand County Almanac*, 197.

17. Edward O. Wilson, *Lord of the Ants*, NOVA, PBS, May 20, 2008.

Chapter 8. Personal Ecology

1. Peter Gay, ed., *The Freud Reader* (New York: W. W. Norton, 1989), 32.

2. Peter Gay, *Freud: A Life in Our Time* (New York: Doubleday, 1988), 19; The Wolf Man, "How I Came into Analysis with Freud," *Journal of the American Psychoanalytic Association* 6 (1958): 348–52.

3. See Muriel Gardiner, ed., *The Wolf Man by the Wolf Man* (New York: Basic Books, 1971); Sandra Bowdler, "Freudian Archeology," *Anthropology Forum* 7 (1996): 419–38; Gerald Schoenewolf, *Turning Points in Analytic Therapy: The Classic Cases* (Northvale, NJ: Jason Aronson, 1990).

4. William McGuire, *The Freud/Jung Letters* (Princeton, NJ: Princeton University Press, 1994), 82.

5. Freud, "Totem and Taboo and other works," in *The Standard Edition of the Complete Psychological Works of Sigmund Freud*, ed. J. Strachey (London: Hogarth, 1955), XIII:15.
6. Freud, "The History of an Infantile Neurosis," in *The Standard Edition of the Complete Psychological Works of Sigmund Freud*, ed. J. Strachey (London: Hogarth, 1955), XVII:97.
7. Freud, "Introductory Lectures on Psychoanalysis," in *The Standard Edition of the Complete Psychological Works of Sigmund Freud*, ed. J. Strachey (London: Hogarth, 1955), XV:199; or Freud, Lecture 13, ILP, *Pelican Freud Library* 1:234.
8. Anthony Stevens, *Private Myths* (Cambridge, MA: Harvard University Press, 1996), 135–36.
9. Meredith Sabini, ed., *The Nature Writings of C. G. Jung* (Berkeley, CA: North Atlantic Books, 2002), 100.
10. Anthony Stevens, *Evolutionary Psychiatry* (London: Routledge, 2000), 19.
11. S. Conway-Morris and H. B. Whittington, "Animals of the Burgess Shale," *Scientific American* 241 (1979): 122–33; H. B. Whittington, *The Burgess Shale* (New Haven, CT: Yale University Press, 1985); Stephen Jay Gould, *Wonderful Life: The Burgess Shale and the Nature of History* (New York: Norton Press, 1989); D. E. G. Briggs, "Extraordinary Fossils," *American Scientist* 79 (1991): 130–41.
12. Colin Tudge, *The Time Before History* (New York: Simon and Schuster, 1996); Andrew Knoll, *Life on a Young Planet: The First Three Billion Years of Evolution on Earth* (Princeton, NJ: Princeton University Press, 2003); Michael Marshall, "Timeline: The Evolution of Life," *New Scientist* 11, no. 6 (July 14, 2009); Carl Zimmer, *The Tangled Bank: An Introduction to Evolution* (Greenwood Village, CO: Roberts and Company, 2009).
13. *Faces of America with Henry Louis Gates, Jr.*, Episode 3, PBS, March 3, 2010.
14. I want to thank Helen Hess, my colleague in invertebrate and evolutionary biology, for helpful comments on this section. See also Henry Gee, *Before the Backbone: Views on the Origin of the Vertebrates* (New York: Thompson Science, 1996); Eddy M. De Robertis and Yoshiki Sasai, "A Common Plan for Dorsoventral

Patterning in Bilateria," *Nature* 380 (March 1996): 37–40; D. Arendt and K. Nübler-Jung, "Comparison of Early Nerve Cord Development in Insects and Vertebrates," *Development* 126 (1999): 2309–25; Niles Eldredge, "Species, Speciation and the Environment," American Institute of Biological Sciences (AIBS), October 2000, www.actionbioscience.org/evolution/eldredge.html.

15. Jeffrey Gordon et al., *Extending Our View of Self,* National Human Genome Research Institute (NHGI) white paper, 2005; Gary Huffnagle, *The Probiotics Revolution* (London: Vermillion, 2007); Asher Mullard, "The Inside Story," *Nature* 453 (May 2008): 578–80; Apoorva Mandavilli, "Straight from the Gut," *Nature* 453 (May 2008): 581–82; David Relman et al., eds., *Microbial Evolution and Coadaptation* (Washington, DC: National Academies Press, 2009); I also want to thank Peter Fuerst of Jackson Laboratories for a personal tutorial on microbial ecology and meta-genomics.

16. Alexander Tsiaras, *Charlie Rose,* PBS, May 17, 2005.

17. The preceding was composed from years of scattered notes, web surfing, and late-night public television. Most of the details, however, can be traced to Alexander Tsiaras's books, *Charlie Rose* interviews, the BBC "Science and Nature" online library (www.bbc.co.uk/sn), and Mitchell Charity's "A View from the Back of the Envelope" website (www.vendian.org/envelope), which is full of useful resources and interesting facts.

18. Samuel Ellison and Joseph Jones, *Walking the Forty Acres: Building Stones—Precambrian to Pleistocene* (Retired Faculty-Staff Association: University of Texas, 1984).

19. P. Cram, A. M. Fendrick, J. Inadomi, M. E. Cowen, D. Carpenter, and S. Vijan, "The Impact of a Celebrity Promotional Campaign on the use of Colon Cancer Screening: The Katie Couric Effect," Archives of Internal Medicine 163, no. 13 (2003): 1601–5. See also "The Courage of Couric" (Featured Interview), *Prevention* 64, no. 4 (2012): 56–63.

Chapter 9. Context

1. Anthony G. Greenwald, "The Totalitarian Ego: Fabrication and Revision of Personal History," *American Psychologist* 33, no. 7 (1980): 604.

2. Emily Dickinson, *The Complete Poems of Emily Dickinson* (Boston: Little, Brown, 1924), Part Two: Nature #24.
3. Thoreau, *Walden*, 108.

Chapter 10. Metaphor and Meaning
1. Sam Glucksberg, *Understanding Figurative Language* (New York: Oxford University Press, 2001), 68.
2. Glucksberg, "The Psycholinguistics of Metaphor," *Trends in Cognitive Sciences* 7, no. 2 (2003): 92.
3. Glucksberg, 2001, 16.
4. Walt Whitman, *Leaves of Grass* (New York: Simon and Schuster, 2006), 105.
5. Gregory Bateson, *Mind and Nature: A Necessary Unity* (New York: Hampton Press, 1979), 158.
6. Charlotte Brontë, *Jane Eyre* (New York: W. W. Norton, 2000), 147.
7. Joseph Grinnell, "Presence and Absence of Animals," *University of California Chronicles* 30 (1928): 435.
8. Announcement of the 96th ESA Annual Meeting, Earth Stewardship: Preserving and Enhancing Earth's Life-Support Systems, August 7–12, 2011, Austin, TX, www.esa.org/austin.
9. Ibid.
10. Ecological Society of America, "ESA History," www.esa.org/history.
11. Richard A. Underwood, "Towards a Poetics of Ecology: A Science in Search of Radical Metaphors," in *Ecology: Crisis and New Vision*, ed. Richard E. Sherrel (Richmond, VA: John Knox Press, 1971), 144–54.
12. Paul Shepard, "Whatever Happened to Human Ecology?" *BioScience* 17 (1967): 894.
13. Marshall McLuhan, "At the Moment of Sputnik the Planet Becomes a Global Theater in Which There Are No Spectators but Only Actors," in *Marshall McLuhan: The Man and His Message*, eds. George Sanderson and Frank Macdonald (Golden, CO: Fulcrum, 1989), 71.
14. Neil Postman, *Technopoly: The Surrender of Culture to Technology* (New York: Vintage, 1993), 18.

15. Robert Hoffman, "Recent Research on Metaphor," *Semiotic Inquiry* 3 (1983): 35–62.
16. George Lakoff and Mark Johnson, *Metaphors We Live By* (Chicago: University of Chicago Press, 1980), 158.
17. Rafaela von Bredow, "Brazil's Pirahã Tribe: Living without Numbers or Time," *Spiegel Online International,* May 3, 2006, http://tinyurl.com/mgqgz2c.
18. Alfred North Whitehead, quoted by Maurice Merleau-Ponty, *Nature: Course Notes from the Collège de France* (Evanston, IL: Northwestern University Press, 2003), 118, English translation.
19. Rachel Carson, *The Sense of Wonder* (New York: HarperCollins, 1999), 56.
20. Philip J. Stewart, "Eddies in the Flow: Towards a Universal Ecology," in *Where Next? Reflections on the Human Future,* ed. M. E. D. Poore (Kew, UK: Royal Botanic Gardens, 2000).

PART III. WIDER POINTS OF VIEW

1. Ann Ulanov, "The Erotic and the Holy," Eleventh Annual Jung on the Hudson Seminar Series, Presented by The New York Center for Jungian Studies, July 18–23, 2004.
2. Robert Frost, "Mending Wall," in *North of Boston* (New York: Henry Holt, 1914), 11.

Chapter 11. Kinds of Minds

1. Alfred North Whitehead, "The Philosopher's Summary," in *The Philosophy of Alfred North Whitehead,* ed. P. A. Schilpp (New York: Tudor, 1941), preface.
2. Alfred North Whitehead, *Science and the Modern World* (Cambridge: Cambridge University Press, 1926), 90.
3. Mark Lytle, *The Gentle Subversive* (New York: Oxford University Press, 2007), 88.
4. Richard Herbert, "Genes and Behavior Focus on King's College Center," *APS Observer* 16, no. 6 (2003): 1.
5. Edward O. Wilson, *Naturalist* (New York: Warner Books, 1994), 349.
6. "Lord of the Ants," NOVA documentary, PBS (WGBH), May 20, 2008.

7. Wilson, *Naturalist*, 335–36.
8. John Cacioppo, "Psychology Is a Hub Science," *APS Observer* 20, no. 8 (2007): 1. Original research by K. W. Boyack, R. Klavans, and K. Börner, "Mapping the Backbone of Science," *Scientometrics* 64 (2005): 351–74.
9. Gerald L. Young, "A Conceptual Framework for an Interdisciplinary Human Ecology," *Acta Oecologiae Hominis: International Monographs in Human Ecology*, no. 1 (Lund, Sweden: University of Lund, 1989), 74.
10. Ibid., 12.
11. Ibid., 15.
12. Theodosius Dobzhansky, "Nothing in Biology Makes Sense Except in the Light of Evolution," *The American Biology Teacher* (March 1973): 12.
13. Stevens, *Private Myths*, 1996, 285.

Chapter 12. Insight

1. Arthur C. Clarke, "The Star," in *The Nine Billion Names of God: The Best Short Stories of Arthur C. Clarke* (New York: Signet, 1974), 235–40.
2. Ray Bradbury, "A Sound of Thunder," in *R Is for Rocket* (New York: Doubleday, 1952).
3. Edward N. Lorenz, "Predictability: Does the Flap of a Butterfly's Wings in Brazil Set Off a Tornado in Texas?" 139th Annual Meeting of the American Association for the Advancement of Science, December 29, 1972.
4. Malcolm Gladwell, *The Tipping Point: How Little Things Can Make a Big Difference* (Boston: Little, Brown, 2000).
5. Wilbert S. Ray, *The Experimental Psychology of Original Thinking* (New York: Macmillan, 1967).
6. Eric R. Kandel, *In Search of Memory* (New York: W. W. Norton, 2006), 240.
7. Margaret A. Boden, *The Creative Mind: Myths and Mechanism* (New York: Routledge, 2004), 15.

8. John Irving, *New York Times* writers' blog interview by Sam Tanenhaus, June 5, 2009, http://graphics8.nytimes.com/podcasts/2009/06/05/05bookreview.mp3.
9. John Grisham, *Charlie Rose*, PBS, January 29, 2008.
10. Suzanne Vega, *Charlie Rose*, PBS, October 10, 1997.
11. Annie Dillard, *The Writing Life* (New York: Harper and Row, 1989), 3–5.
12. Barry Lopez, *Bill Moyers Journal*, PBS, April 30, 2010.
13. Peter Matthiessen, "No Boundaries," PBS documentary, WQED, April 24, 2009.
14. Norman Mailer, *Charlie Rose*, PBS, January 29, 2003.
15. Harold Ward, "Capsule History of the NEES Gathering," www.nees-group.org/pages/History.html.
16. David Orr, from American College & University Presidents' Climate Commitment (ACUPCC) website, www.presidentsclimatecommitment.org/about/mission-history.
17. Scott Carlson, "World's Greenest College," *Chronicle of Higher Education*, August 14, 2007, http://chronicle.com/blogs/buildings/worlds-greenest-college-at-least-according-to-grist/4750.
18. Richard Monastersky, "Colleges Strain to Reach Climate-Friendly Future," *Chronicle of Higher Education*, http://chronicle.com/free/v54/i16/16a00101.htm.
19. Tamar Lewin, "Eco-Education," *New York Times*, November 4, 2007, http://tinyurl.com/lyeqrj4.
20. See also Kiera Butler, "Earning a Degree in Green," *Plenty* magazine (December 11, 2007), www.plentymag.com/features/2007/12/college_of_the_atlantic.php.
21. Wendell Berry, "The Pleasures of Eating," *What Are People For?* (Berkeley, CA: Counterpoint, 2010), 148.
22. John Visvader, "Philosophy and Human Ecology," in *Human Ecology: A Gathering of Perspectives*, eds. R. J. Borden, J. Jacobs, and G. L. Young (College Park, MD: Society for Human Ecology, 1986), 121.
23. Thomas Tanner, "Significant Life Experiences: A New Research Area in Environmental Education," *Journal of Environmental Education* 1, no. 4 (1980): 20–24.

24. Louise Chawla, "Ecstatic Places," *Children's Environments Quarterly* 7, no. 4 (1990): 18–23; *In the First Country of Places: Nature, Poetry and Childhood Memory* (Albany, NY: State University of New York, 1994); "Significant Life Experiences Revisited: A Review of Research on Sources of Environmental Sensitivity," *Journal of Environmental Education* 29, no. 3 (1998): 11–21.
25. Edward O. Wilson, *Naturalist*, 1995, 363.

Chapter 13. Imagination

1. "Imagination," *Merriam-Webster* online, www.merriam-webster.com/dictionary/imagination.
2. W. S. Merwin, PBS Newshour, October 27, 2010.
3. Adam D. Weinberg, "Farnsworth Forum," Farnsworth Art Museum, Rockland, ME, July 7, 2011.
4. George Lucas, *Charlie Rose*, PBS, September 9, 2004.
5. George Bilgere, "Desire," *The Writer's Almanac*, NPR, April 2, 2012.
6. Valerie Andrews, "Rekindling a Sense of Place," *Common Boundary* (November/December 1990).
7. *Good Morning America*, ABC-TV, October 9, 2003.
8. "A Conversation with Ruth Ozeki," in Ruth Ozeki, *My Year of Meats* (New York: Penguin, 1999), 12.
9. Andrew Light, "Trip the Light Fantastic: Andrew Light, an Enviro-Academic, Answers Grist's Questions," *Grist magazine* (July 26, 2004), http://grist.org/article/light4/full/.
10. Mihaly Csikszentmihalyi (with Jeffrey Mishlove), "Flow, Creativity and the Evolving Self," *Thinking Allowed*, 1996 (DVDs).
11. Gerald Epstein, "The Imaginal, the Right Hemisphere of the Brain, and the Waking Dream," www.biomindsuperpowers.com/Pages/Imaginal.html.
12. Henepola Gunaratana, "Conscious Notes," *Lotus: Journal for Personal Transformation* (Autumn 1995): 16.
13. William Carpenter, "Creative Ecology," address at the Eleventh College of the Atlantic Commencement. Reprinted in the *Ellsworth American*, section II (June 9, 1983): 12.

Chapter 14. Keyholes

1. "Human Ecology: The Possibility of an Aesthetic Science" in *Human Ecology: Research and Applications*, eds. R. J. Borden, J. Jacobs, and G. L. Young (College Park, MD: Society for Human Ecology, 1988), 1–8.
2. Paul Shepard, "Whatever Happened to Human Ecology?" *BioScience* 17 (1967): 892.
3. Jean-Paul Sartre, *Existentialism and Humanism* (London: Methuen, 1948), 90.
4. Viktor Frankl, *Man's Search for Meaning* (New York: Simon and Schuster, 1959), 123.

Chapter 15. Ecology and Identity

1. Oliver Wendell Holmes, *The Poet at the Breakfast Table* (Boston: J. R. Osgood, 1872), 50.
2. Robert Trivers, *Natural Selection and Social Theory* (New York: Oxford University Press, 2002), 57.
3. Nicholas Wade, *Before the Dawn* (New York: Penguin, 2006), 222.
4. Wilson, *Consilience*, 8.
5. Michael Pollan, *The Omnivore's Dilemma* (New York: Penguin, 2006), 148.
6. Michael Werner, "Postmodernism and the Future of Humanism," *Humanism Today* 8 (1993): 29.
7. Paul Shepard, "Virtually Hunting Reality in the Forests of Simulacra," in *Reinventing Nature?: Responses to Postmodern Deconstruction*, eds. Michael E. Soulé and Gary Lease (Washington, DC: Island Press, 1995), 17–29.
8. *Reinventing Nature?*, preface, xv.
9. William James, "The Principles of Psychology," in *Great Books of the Western World*, ed. R. M. Hutchinson (Chicago: Encyclopedia Britannica, 1952), 53:147. Originally published in 1890.
10. John Dewey, quoted in Joseph F. Rychlak, *In Defense of Human Consciousness* (Washington, DC: American Psychological Association, 1997), 8.
11. G. William Farthing, *The Psychology of Consciousness* (New York: Basic Books, 1992), 6.

12. Joseph F. Rychlak, "Personality Theory: Its Nature, Past, Present and—Future?" *Personality and Social Psychology Bulletin* 2, no. 3 (1976): 210.
13. Michael Polanyi, "Life's Irreducible Structure," *Science* 160 (1968): 1308–12.
14. Adolph Murie, in Dayton Duncan, *The National Parks: America's Best Idea* (New York: Knopf, 2009), 358.
15. Sam Roberts, "200th Birthday for the Map That Made New York," *New York Times,* March 20, 2011.
16. *Understanding New York City's Food Supply,* Workshop on Applied Earth Systems Policy Analysis completed on behalf of the New York City Mayor's Office of Long-Term Planning and Sustainability by Columbia University, http://mpaenvironment.ei.columbia.edu/news/documents/UnderstandingNYCsFoodSupply_May2010.pdf.
17. Brené Brown, "The Power of Vulnerability," www.ted.com/talks/brene_brown_on_vulnerability.html; "Listening to Shame," www.ted.com/talks/brene_brown_listening_to_shame.html.
18. Brené Brown, "We Should All Take 'Voice Lessons' from Dixie Chicks," *Houston Chronicle,* February 17, 2007, www.chron.com/opinion/outlook/article/We-should-all-take-voice-lessons-from-Dixie-1808725.php.
19. Natalie Barnett, "The Great Apple Growing State of Our Country: The Nineteenth Century Apple Industry in Maine," unpublished senior project, College of the Atlantic, 2011.
20. Sean Fitzgerald, "Yes and the World Goes On," unpublished human ecology essay, College of the Atlantic, 2009.

Chapter 16. The Unfinished Course

1. Benjamin Bradley, *Psychology and Experience* (Cambridge: Cambridge University Press, 2005), 7–8.
2. Ada Lampert, *The Evolution of Love* (Westport, CT: Praeger, 1997), 17, 23, 39.
3. Ann Ulanov, "Jung on the Hudson," July 23, 2004.
4. Ernest Becker, *The Structure of Evil* (New York: G. Braziller, 1968), 177.

5. Barry Lopez, *Bill Moyers Journal*, PBS, April 2, 2010.
6. George Orwell, *Nineteen Eighty-Four* (New York: Harcourt, Brace, 1949), 32.
7. Anthony G. Greenwald, "The Totalitarian Ego: Fabrication and Revision of Personal History," *American Psychologist* 33, no. 7 (1980): 603–18.
8. Pearl S. Buck, in *The Book of Green Quotations*, ed. James Daley (Mineola, NY: Dover Publishing, 2009), 20.
9. Charles Darwin, *On the Origin of Species by Means of Natural Selection* (London: Watts, 1859).
10. Forrest Gander, "The Hugeness of That Which Is Missing," *Torn Awake* (New York: New Directions Publishing, 2001), 8.
11. Barry Lopez, *Bill Moyers Journal*, PBS, April 2, 2010.
12. Alan Watts, *The Best of Alan Watts*, Wellspring Media, 1994 (video).
13. Linda Hogan, in *Listening to the Land: Conversations about Nature, Culture and Eros*, ed. Derrick Jensen (White River Junction, VT: Chelsea Green Publishing, 2004), 124.
14. Craig Hamilton, "Craig Hamilton on Sri Aurobindo," *What Is Enlightenment?* (Spring/Summer 2002): 160.
15. E. O. Wilson, *The Low Cost of Protecting Biodiversity Hotspots*, Palo Alto lecture, May 10, 2009 (video).
16. Daniel Kaplan, "Can the NFL Get to $25 Billion?" *Sports Business Journal* (January 28, 2013), www.sportsbusinessdaily.com/Journal/Issues/2013/01/28/In-Depth/NFL-revenue.aspx; Liana B. Baker, "Factbox: A Look at the $65 Billion Video Games Industry," June 6, 2011, http://uk.reuters.com/article/2011/06/06/us-videogames-factbox-idUKTRE75552I20110606; Ira Flatow, "The Ugly Truth about Food Waste in America," *Talk of the Nation*, NPR, November 23, 2012, www.npr.org/2012/11/23/165774988/npr-the-ugly-truth-about-food-waste-in-america.
17. Rodgers and Hammerstein, *South Pacific*.
18. David W. Orr, *Ecological Literacy* (Albany, NY: State University of New York Press, 1992), 1.
19. Campbell, *Mythos*, 1996.
20. Stevens, *Private Myths*, 1995, 353.

Index

A

Abduction, 277
Abelard, Peter, 168
Abraham, 76
Abstraction, levels of, 6
Academic freedom, 172, 176
Academy of Natural Sciences, 42
Acadia National Park, 313, 347–49, 371–72, 389–90, 393, 395
Accommodation, 105, 158
Ackerman, Dianne, 353
Adler, Alfred, 94
Agassiz, Louis, 42, 358
Agriculture, U.S. Department of, 50, 174
Ainsworth, Mary, 157
Al-Asma'i, 38
Al-Biruni, Abu Rayhan, 38
Alden, John and Priscilla, 12
Al-Dinawari, 38
Alexander the Great, 83–84, 190
Alexandria, Library of, 38
Al-Jahiz, 38
Al-Nabati, Abu al-Abbas, 39
American Association for the Advancement of Science (AAAS), 51, 140, 298
American Association of Family and Consumer Sciences, 130
American College and University President's Climate Commitment (ACUPCC), 315
American Home Economics Association (AHEA), 129–30
American Museum of Natural History, 43, 247
American Philosophical Association, 104
American Psychological Association (APA), 4, 22, 75, 90, 98, 104, 106–7
Analogies, 271, 273
Anaximander, 37
Anaximenes, 37
Anderson, John, 67–68, 143, 345
Andrew, Mark, 365–66
Andrews, Valerie, 333
Angell, James, 91, 96
Ani, Papyrus of, 222
Animals
    evolution of, 238–40
    oldest-living, 218
Animism, 75
Animus and anima, 325
Anker, Peder, 55
Anthropology, 132
Antioch College, 173–74
Anxiety, 100, 102, 103, 221, 225, 227
Apoptosis, 228, 295
Apuleius, 79, 80
Archetypes, 157, 236
Architecture, 177–80
Arctic National Wildlife Refuge (ANWR), 359
Argall, Samuel, 391
Aristotle, 37, 43, 82–83, 91, 110, 150, 270, 272, 356

Arp, Robert, 322
Art
  impact of, 328
  mastery of, 329–31
  meaning of, 328
  as object vs. as process, 328
  prehistoric, 327
  science and, 272
Asclepius, 81
Assimilation, 105
Association for Humanistic Psychology (AHP), 107
Association for Psychological Science (APS), 107, 299
Association of American Geographers, 132
Asticou, 390
Atomic Energy Commission, 59
Attachment theory, 157–58
Attitudes
  changes in, 338
  concept of, 257–58
  rapid spreading of, 260
Augustine, St., 83, 198, 199
Australian National University (ANU), 116, 147–48
Authenticity, 351, 363–65
Autonomic nervous system (ANS), 244–45
Averroes, 82
Avicenna, 82

B

Baars, Bernard J., 73
Bacon, Francis, 86
Bacon, Kevin, 252
Bacon, Roger, 39

Baldwin, James Mark, 91, 96
Banks, Joseph, 42
Baraka (film), 203
Barker, Roger, 132
Barnes, Edward Larrabee, 180
Barnett, Natalie, 367–68
Baron, Seymour, 28–29
Barrows, Harlan, 132
Bartlett, Frederic, 104–5
Bateson, Gregory, 212, 247, 270, 274–78, 283, 294
Bateson, Mary Catherine, 272
Becker, Ernest, 227, 379
Beethoven, Ludwig van, 102
Behaviorism, 95–98, 102, 106
Beneffectance, 256
Bergman, Ingmar, 219–20, 221, 323
Berkeley, George, 86
Berlin, University of, 42, 171–72
Bernard, Francis, 391
Berra, Yogi, 112–13
Berry, Thomas, 310
Berry, Wendell, 196, 310, 317
Bessey, Charles, 52–53
Bews, J. W., 132
Biard, Pierre, 390
Bilgere, George, 332–33
Binet, Alfred, 105
Binswanger, Ludwig, 101, 227
Biology
  origins of, 40
  psychology and, 345–46
  splitters vs. lumpers in, 194
  uniqueness of, 111
Biomes, 49
Bion, Wilfred, 227
Birx, H. James, 198

Black United Students (BUS), 26
Blank, Judith, 154
Bonding, 157–58
Book of the Dead, 75, 222
Borden, Amy Moore (mother), 10–12, 14, 16–17, 266–67, 313, 377–78
Borden, Andrew (son), 302, 346, 362, 370
Borden, George (father), 10–12, 15, 16, 20, 263–67, 361, 362
Borden, Hiram (great-grandfather), 161
Borden, Jay Ross (grandfather), 160–62, 206
Borden, Joan (ancestor), 12, 205
Borden, Joan (sister), 12, 14, 16, 17, 20, 205, 267, 268–69, 313
Borden, Richard
  advent of human ecology for, 8–9, 120–26
  birth of, 12
  childhood of, 9, 13–19, 160–65, 224–26, 247, 263–64
  at College of the Atlantic, 4, 61, 126–28, 137, 152–53, 155, 301, 309, 339–40, 346–47, 375
  environmental movement and, 24–25
  father's death and, 264–67
  first car of, 20
  in high school, 20, 296–97
  in Iceland, 123–26, 268
  influences on, 34–35, 109
  in junior high school, 19–20
  at Kent State, 22–31
  on mother's death, 313–14
  at Ohio State, 31–32, 255, 299
  at Purdue University, 32–33, 120
  research of, 5, 33, 255, 320
  in Society for Human Ecology, 4–5, 134, 136, 138, 141, 143, 346
  at University of Texas, 21–22, 154, 156, 248, 307, 316
Borden, Richard (ancestor), 12, 205
Borges, Jorge, 190
Bosch, Hieronymus, 87–88
Bose, Amar, 184
Boss, Medard, 101, 227
Botkin, Daniel, 69
Bowlby, John, 157
Boyden, Stephen, 115–16, 138
Bradbury, Ray, 305–6
Bradley, Benjamin, 377, 380
Brain development, 295
Brentano, Franz, 98, 100
Brewer, Leslie, 394
The Bridge (film), 223
Bridgeman, Percy W., 273
British Ecological Society (BES), 4, 54
British empiricism, 86, 88, 97
British Museum, 42
Brontë, Charlotte, 278
Brower, David, 319
Brown, Brené, 363–64
Brown University, 169
Brunelleschi, Filippo, 360
Bruner, Jerome, 107
Buchanan, James, 174
Buck, Pearl S., 384
Buddhism, 76, 222, 351
Buffon, Georges, 40, 41, 42

Bugental, James, 351
Burdach, Karl Friedrich, 40
Burgess, Ernest W., 132
Burgess Shale, 237–38, 247
Burnham, Clarke, 307, 308
Burns, Ken, 303, 337, 360
Bush, Benjamin and Bertha, 164–65
Bush, George W., 364
Butterfly effect, 306–7
Bystander inhibition, 30–31, 254–55

C

Cacioppo, John, 299
Cadillac, Antoine de la Mothe, 391
Caivano, Roc, 127, 154
Calkins, Mary Whiton, 104, 107
Calment, Jeanne, 218
Cambodia, U.S. invasion of, 26
Cambridge University, 169, 178
Campbell, Joseph, 77, 88, 221, 237, 387
Caras, Roger, 223
Carbon neutrality, 315
Carpenter, JoAnne, 152–53
Carpenter, William, 138, 152–53, 289, 324, 335, 343
Carson, Rachel, 20, 59, 63, 165, 230, 248, 252, 253, 289, 294, 339–43, 351, 353
Carter, Jimmy, 128, 359
Carus, Paul, 222
Catastrophism, 41–42, 44
Cattell, James McKeen, 90
Cave paintings, 327
Central nervous system (CNS), 244–45

Central Park, 361
CERN (European Organization for Nuclear Research), 208
Champlain, Samuel de, 373, 390, 394
Chance and Change (Drury), 68
Chaos theory, 306–7
Chapin, Stuart, 144, 281
Charcot, Jean-Martin, 89, 92
Chase, Chevy, 188
Chavez, Cesar, 25
Chawla, Louise, 9, 320, 344
Chekhov, Anton, 6, 304
Chesterton, G. K., 149
Cheyney University, 173
Chicago, University of, 132, 175–76, 294
Children
   cognitive development in, 105–6
   death and, 224–26
   family resemblances in, 246–47
   language acquisition skills of, 286
   nature and, 19, 66, 319–20
China
   human ecology in, 141–42
   urbanization in, 362–63
Chloroplasts, 214
Chomsky, Noam, 106, 184, 285–87
Christianity, 76, 222
Church, Frederic, 392, 394
Churchill, Winston, 177
Cialdini, Bob, 255
Circadian rhythm, 202–3
Cities. *See* Urbanization
Civil rights movement, 8
Clarke, Arthur C., 304–5

Clark University, 175, 233–34
Clayton, Susan, 344
Clean Air Act, 395
Clean Water Act, 24
Clements, Frederic, 52–53, 54, 55–56, 62, 66
Climate change, 4, 314, 397
Clinton, Bill, 310, 315
Clinton, Hillary, 310
Clinton Climate Initiative, 315
Clocks, 199–202
Closure, need for, 376
Club of Rome, 33, 117, 362
Cobb, Edith, 19, 288
Coffin, Charles Carleton, 162–63
Cognitive psychology, 98, 104–5, 107
Cognitive styles, 105, 194, 272
Cohen, Joel, 287
Cold War, 13
Cole, Thomas, 391, 394
Colinvaux, Paul, 69
Collective unconscious, 94, 236
College of the Atlantic (COA)
   campus of, 180–81
   colors of, 182
   courses at, 300–301
   faculty of, 152–55
   fire at, 136, 181, 341
   founding of, 64, 394
   graduation requirements for, 337
   as host of SHE conferences, 138, 143
   human ecology essay at, 337–38
   informality of, 150–51
   mission of, 180, 293, 300, 316
   nondepartmentalized structure of, 127, 310
   philosophy of education at, 150–52
   seal of, 182
   students of, 30, 33, 122–23, 127
   sustainability and, 315–16
Colon, 244, 250
Columbia University, 169
Commoner, Barry, 60
Commonwealth Human Ecology Council (CHEC), 119–20, 135, 140, 141
Comte, Auguste, 89, 273
Confucius, 76
Connell, Joseph, 69
Consciousness
   beginning of, 295, 322
   being and, 101
   dialectical nature of, 309
   evolution and, 91, 383
   identity and, 357
   neurophysiology of, 295
   reality and, 71
   rejection of, by behaviorism, 96
   telic nature of, 110
   unifying aspects of, in Gestalt psychology, 98
Conservation psychology, 344–45, 346, 349–52
Context
   concept of, 251
   decision making and, 260–63
   demonstrations of, 252, 261–62
   groups and, 259–60
   holism and, 253–58
   social, 254–55

Cook, James, 42
Cooper, John, 291–92
Copernicus, Nicolaus, 39, 84, 85, 209
Copland, Aaron, 303
Coulter, John M., 53
Council of Environmental Deans and Directors (CEDD), 311
Couric, Katie, 250
Covich, Alan, 144
Cowles, Henry Chandler, 53, 54
Creation stories, 87–88
Creativity, 308–9, 327, 334, 335
Crockett, Davy, 14
Cronbach, Lee, 75, 106, 288
Crutzen, Paul, 70
Csikszentmihalyi, Mihaly, 9, 165, 334, 343, 344
Cuomo, Mario, 314
Cuvier, Georges, 40, 41–42, 44
Cuyahoga River, 24
Cyanobacteria, 213, 215

D

Darland, Dallas, 256
Dartmouth College, 169
Darwin, Charles, 44–47, 48, 52, 74–75, 194, 234, 235, 237, 252, 273, 385
Da Vinci, Leonardo, 82
Davis, Ossie, 155–56
Davis, Richard, 152, 154, 155
Daysh, Zena, 119, 138
DDT, 253
Death
  acceptance of, as natural process, 229
  anxiety and, 221, 225, 227
  attitudes toward, 229
  awareness of, 219–26
  children and, 224–26
  drive, 226–27
  ecology of, 230
  programmed cell, 228
  religion and, 222
  rituals, 222
  sexual reproduction and, 216
  of species, 216–17
  suicide, 223
Death by Design (film), 228
Deaux, Kay, 288
Declaration of Independence, 339
Defense mechanisms, 7, 221
Delight, 350–51, 363
Denial, 7, 103
Denver, John, 341
Depth psychology, 92–95
Derfel, Ari, 188–89
Descartes, René, 84–85, 88, 298, 356
Deutsch, Helene, 95
Deutsche Gesellschaft für Humanökologie (DGH). *See* German Society for Human Ecology
Dewey, John, 91, 96, 107, 357
Dewey, Melvil, 189
Diamond, Solomon, 85
Dickinson, Emily, 6, 221, 261–62
Dillard, Annie, 309
Dimitrov, Vladimir, 36
Displacement, 7
District of Columbia, University of, 128–29

Dixie Chicks, 364–65
Dobzhansky, Theodosius, 303
Doll, Joe, 340
Dollard, John, 97
Dorr, George B., 348–49, 393
Douglas, Claire, 88, 324–26
Douglas, Ian, 363
Dreams, 88, 93, 235, 236, 247, 324, 374–75, 377, 387
Drude, Oscar, 49–50, 52–53
Drury, Mary, 68, 383
Drury, William H., Jr., 34–35, 61–69, 73, 142, 154, 227, 230–31, 277–78, 285, 288, 313–14, 319–21, 351, 353–54, 356, 382, 383
Dual-reference theory, 272, 288
Dubos, René, 116, 117, 133, 319, 339
Duckworth, Eleanor, 106
Duke University, 176
Duomo di Firenze, 360

E

Eames, Ray and Charles, 210–11
Ears, 246
Earth
    age of, 43, 44
    biological diversity of, 36
    as symbol, 24
Earth Day, 24, 26
Ebbinghaus, Hermann, 74, 77, 104, 108
Eco-city model, 363
Ecological Society of America (ESA), 4, 54, 70, 144, 281
Ecological Society of China, 143

Ecology. *See also* Human ecology
    behavioral, 132–33
    chasm between biological and human, 283
    compounding effects in, 253
    of death, 230
    definition of, 48
    early history of, 4, 47–56
    equilibrium paradigm of, 56–59, 68
    ethical dimensions of, 59, 318
    etymology of, 47, 274, 278
    evolution and, 48–49, 380
    "four laws" of, 60
    identity and, 357, 363–64
    imagination and, 331–35
    impact of, 283
    interdisciplinary nature of, 145, 274, 299
    metaphors in, 278–84
    mind and, 272–78
    nonequilibrium paradigm of, 61–70
    personal, 241, 247
    popularization of, 59
    psychology and, 54–55, 132–33, 301
    roots of, in natural history, 37–43
    social, 133
    subversiveness of, 60, 118
    tensions within field of, 282
Ecosystems
    concept of, 55–56
    environmentalism and, 60–61
    equilibrium within, 56–59
    succession and, 59

Eden, Oscar, 163–64
Edison, Thomas, 330
Education. *See also* Higher education; Teachers
   as art, 150
   environmental, 319–20
   etymology of, 149
   goals of, 149, 150
   role of feeling in, 294
   self-directed, 295
   threats to, 150
Edwards, Cecile, 129
Ego
   -centric bias, 256, 380–81
   concept of, 93–94
   defense mechanisms, 7
Egyptians, ancient, 75–76, 222
Ehrenfeld, David, 355
Ehrlich, Anne, 118
Ehrlich, Paul, 60, 118
Einstein, Albert, 102, 197, 226, 273, 307, 336
Eiseley, Loren, 20, 149, 197, 247, 294, 323, 342, 347, 350, 351
Eisenhower, Dwight, 359
Ekehorn, Eva, 143
Eliot, Charles, 155, 174, 392
Eliot, Mary Kay, 182
Eliot, Sam, 155
Eliot, T. S., 3
Ellington, Duke, 303
Ellis, Bill, 149
Ellison, Samuel P., 248
Elton, Charles, 57, 279
Emerson, Ralph Waldo, 9, 33, 358
Empedocles, 37, 81
Endangered Species Act, 60

Environmental Design Research Association (EDRA), 141
Environmental history, 119
Environmental movement
   beginning of, 24
   central question of, 4
   ecosystems and, 60–61
Environmental Protection Agency (EPA), 24, 165
Episcopal Church, 365–66
Epstein, Gerald, 334
Erdrich, Louise, 241
Ericsson, K. Anders, 331
Erikson, Erik, 95, 159, 339
Eros, legend of Psyche and, 79–80
Esquivel, Laura, 367
Essays, 336–45
Eukaryotes, 214–15
European Association for Human Ecology (EAHE), 140, 141, 142
European Organization for Nuclear Research (CERN), 208
Evans, Brock, 310
Everett, Dan, 286
Everett, Edward, 173
Evolution
   of animals, 238–40
   consciousness and, 91, 383
   Darwinian, 44–47
   early concepts of, 38, 40, 43–44
   ecology and, 48–49, 380
   embryo development and, 235
   of humans, 240–41
   Lamarckian, 44
   love and, 378
   poll on belief in, 204, 384
   tree image for, 74–75, 273

Evolutionary psychology, 107, 383–84
Eward, Ann, 134
Existentialism, 101–2
Experience. *See also* Psychology
   border between personal and transpersonal, 249
   definition of, 72–73
   etymology of, 72
   identification and, 397
   language at center of, 342–43
   mythic, 77
   past vs. current and future, 73
   tabula rasa conception of mind and, 86
   two senses of, 377, 380
   worldview and, 76–77, 384
Expertise, developing, 330–31
Eyes, 245

F

Fabian social movement, 54
Faces of America (television series), 241
Faith, 385–86
Fallon, Daniel, 175, 176
Farming
   decline of, 268
   introduction of, 115
Fechner, Gustav, 90
Fertility rates, 219
Festinger, Leon, 307, 338
Field Museum of Natural History, 43
Fischbacher, Siegfried, 333
Fischer, David Hackett, 7, 251
Fitzgerald, Sean, 369–70

Flagship species, 279
Flow, concept of, 9, 166, 343
Food
   love and, 366–68, 369
   provenance, 368–69
   rituals, 369
   terroir, 368
Forbes, Stephen A., 53
Fossil fuels, dependence on, 396
Francescato, Guido, 134, 137, 146
Frank, Glenn, 28
Frankl, Viktor, 88, 102, 258, 347, 351
Franklin, Benjamin, 339
Frazer, James George, 234
Frederick William III (king of Prussia), 171
Freud, Anna, 95
Freud, Sigmund, 7, 54–55, 88, 92–94, 97, 102, 226, 233–36, 247, 249, 279, 295, 377, 381
Friedan, Betty, 7–8
Friedlaender, Salomo, 100
Fromm, Erich, 379
Frost, Robert, 262, 292
Fuller, Buckminster, 33, 124
Fundamentals of Ecology (Odum), 57–58, 60, 118

G

Gaia hypothesis, 61
Galen, 38, 82
Galileo, 39, 84, 86, 200, 207, 209
Galvani, Luigi, 40, 88
Gander, Forrest, 385
Gastrulation, 242–43
Gates, Henry Louis, Jr., 241

Gay, Peter, 234
Geiger, Roger, 176
Genetic epistemology, 105
Genovese, Kitty, 254
Geography, 132
Georgia, University of, 170
German Society for Human Ecology, 146, 182–83
Gestalt psychology, 98–101, 254
Gettysburg Address, 7
GI Bill, 176
Gilman, Charlotte Perkins, 251
Gladwell, Malcolm, 260, 330
Gleason, Henry, 62, 64
Glucksberg, Sam, 272, 288, 347
Goethe, Johann Wolfgang von, 272, 275, 284–85, 303
Goldsmith, Edward, 68
Golley, Frank, 49, 55, 59, 347
Good, H. G., 170
Goodman, Paul, 100
Gorbachev, Mikhail, 323, 342
Gordian knot, 83–84, 190
Gore, Al, 314
Gould, Stephen Jay, 237
Gower, James, 394
Grant, Ulysses, 358
Gray, Asa, 42, 52, 53, 358
Great Pyramid of Giza, 205
Greeks, ancient, 37, 78–84, 199, 222–23
Greene, Craig, 232, 317–18
Greenwald, Anthony, 256, 380–83
Gregorian, Vartan, 185
Grinnell, Joseph, 278
Grisham, John, 309
Grofé, Ferde, 303

Groups, effects of, 259–60
Guare, John, 252
Guessing, 260–61
Guilt, 102
Gunaratana, Henepola, 335
Guthrie, Arlo, 337, 341
Guthrie, Woody, 337
Gutmann, Amy, 185

H

Habermas, Jürgen, 106
Haeckel, Ernst, 47–48, 49, 130, 235, 274, 278
Hales, David, 339
Hall, G. Stanley, 90, 233
Hamilton, Craig, 386
Hamilton, W. D., 216
Hamlet (Shakespeare), 284
Hardin, Garrett, 60, 138
Harlow, Harry, 102, 157
Harrison, John, 200
Harrison, William Henry, 267
Hart, William, 391
Harvard Museum of Natural History, 42
Harvard University, 169, 170, 173, 174, 178
Harvey, Paul, 376
Harvey, William, 82
Hawken, Paul, 310
Hawking, Stephen, 198
Hawley, Amos, 132
Hayakawa, S. I., 6
Hayden, Tom, 26
Hayes, Woody, 255
Hearing, sense of, 245–46
Hebb, Donald, 107

Hefferline, Ralph, 100
Hegel, Georg Wilhelm Friedrich, 295
Hegeler, Edward C., 222
Heidegger, Martin, 100–101
Helmholtz, Hermann von, 40
Henderson, Hazel, 310
Henry II (king of England), 168
Hens, Luc, 67
Heraclitus, 82
Hesiod, 199
Hesse, Hermann, 6
Hetch Hetchy Valley, 359
Higher education
  architecture and, 177–80
  concern of, 294
  growth of, 176–77
  history of, 167–77
  interdisciplinary learning within, 185–86
  power of, 166–67
Hill, Ken, 182, 339
Hinduism, 76, 87, 198, 219, 222, 289, 334
Hippocrates, 81–82
Hiranyagarbha, 87
Hitchcock, A. S., 51
Hobbes, Thomas, 86
Hogan, Linda, 386
Holism, 253–58
Holmes, Oliver Wendell, Sr., 353
Home economics, 129–30
Homer, 82, 289
Homestead Act, 174
Hong Kong Human Ecology Programme, 116
Hooke, Robert, 40, 207

Hooker, J. D., 194
Hooker, Joseph, 358
Horney, Karen, 100
Hudson, Henry, 67
Hudson River School, 11, 391–92
Hull, Clark, 97
Human Behavior and Evolution Society (HBES), 107, 383–84
Human ecology
  aim of, 113, 302, 396
  anthropology and, 132
  central problem of, 114, 118, 189
  chasm between biological ecology and, 283
  "Chicago School" of, 132
  cities and, 360–63
  as creative process, 335
  definitions of, 119, 135, 144
  early proponents of, 115–19
  geography and, 132
  history of, 131–33, 147
  home economics and, 129–30
  interaction and, 302–3
  interdisciplinary mandate of, 146–47
  origins of, 114
  scope of, 8, 113, 115
  sociology and, 132
  transdisciplinary perspectives of, 147–48
  varied approaches to, 145–46
Human Ecology in China (Wang), 141
Human Ecology Review, 143, 344
Humanistic psychology, 102–4, 107
Humans
  as builders, 296

evolution of, 240–41
fertility rate for, 219
life expectancy of, 218–19
longest-living, 218
microorganisms and, 243
migration of, 114
organs of, 243–45
senses of, 245–46
Humboldt, Alexander von, 41, 46, 171, 176
Humboldt, Wilhelm von, 171–72
Humboldt Museum für Naturkunde, 42
Hume, David, 86
Hunter-gatherers, 115
Husserl, Edmund, 100
Hutchinson, G. Evelyn, 57, 279
Huxley, Aldous, 337, 343, 344
Huxley, Thomas H., 45, 235
Huygens, Christiaan, 200
Hyman, Harris, 154

I

Ibn al-Baitar, 39
Iceland, 123–26, 258, 268
Id, 93–94
Identity
    consciousness and, 357
    crisis, 95
    ecology and, 357, 363–64
Idioms, 271
Imageability, 211–12
Imagination
    active, 323–26
    definition of, 323
    ecological, 331–35
    insight and, 322
    significance of, 322, 327, 333–34

The Immense Journey (Eiseley), 247
Indian Society for Human Ecology, 140
Indicator species, 280
Individuality, 295–96, 381
Inferiority complex, 94
Insight
    definition of, 307
    examples of, 307–9
    imagination and, 322
    literary, 304–6, 308–9
    responsibility and, 318
Institute of Ecosystem Studies (IES), 141
Intentionality, 100, 111
Interaction, fundamentality of, 302–3
Interdisciplinarity
    of ecology, 145, 274, 299
    expansion of, 185–86
    of human ecology, 146–47
    of psychology, 299
    within the sciences, 299–300
    "yes and" approaches and, 369–70
Intergovernmental Panel on Climate Change (IPCC), 314
International Association for Impact Assessment (IAIA), 140
International Biological Programme (IBP), 59
International Congress of Ecology (INTECOL), 360
International Council of Scientific Unions, 59
International Organization for Human Ecology (IOHE), 135, 141, 145–46

International Paper, 314
International Union for
 Conservation of Nature
 (IUCN), 33, 123
International Union of
 Anthropological and
 Ethnological Sciences (IUAES),
 141, 145
Intuition, 335
Invasive species, 57
Irving, John, 308–9
Islam, 76, 222

J

Jacobs, Jamien, 140
James, Henry, 378
James, William, 78, 90, 104, 222,
 249, 295, 319, 357, 378
Japanese Society of Health and
 Human Ecology, 140, 142
Jardin des Plantes, 42
Jastrow, Joseph, 90
Jefferson, Thomas, 170–71, 178,
 179, 339
Jesus Christ, 76
Jobs, Steve, 184, 213, 374
Johns Hopkins University, 175
Johnson, Francis, 187–88, 189,
 190–91, 194, 332
Jones, Joseph M., 248
Jorling, Tom, 314
Judaism, 76
Juet, Robert, 67
Jung, Carl, 6, 78, 88, 94–95, 102,
 157, 221, 233–34, 236–37, 247,
 249, 285, 293, 323–25, 336, 377
Jungen, Britta, 138

K

Kaelber, Ed, 64, 68, 128, 131, 150–
 55, 182, 186
Kaelber, Pat, 64
Kahn, Peter, 344
Kaila, Eino, 221
Kandel, Eric, 307–8
Kane, Daniel, 152, 154, 155
Kant, Immanuel, 76, 86–87, 88
Katona, Steve, 122, 153, 154
Keats, John, 387
Keillor, Garrison, 385
Kekule, Friedrich, 307
Keller, David, 347
Keller, Helen, 336
Kendeigh, Charles, 58
Kendler, Howard, 288
Kennedy, John, 63
Kennedy, Robert, 25
Kent State University, 22, 24, 26–31
Kepler, Johannes, 39, 273, 316
Keppel, Francis, 151–52, 155, 186
Ketchum, Carl, 154
Keyhole, metaphor of, 337, 343–44,
 345
Keystone species, 279–80
Kierkegaard, Søren, 71, 101
King, Larry, 222
King, Martin Luther, Jr., 25
Kingsland, Sharon, 69
Klein, Melanie, 95, 227, 295
Klinkenborg, Verlyn, 204
Knapp, David, 130
Knightley, Keira, 353
Knötig, Helmut, 146
Koch, Robert, 88
Koestler, Arthur, 308

Koffka, Kurt, 99
Koger, Sue, 344
Kohane, Isaac, 184
Kohlberg, Lawrence, 106
Köhler, Wolfgang, 99, 107
Korzybski, Alfred, 6, 212, 357
Koyaanisqatsi (film), 203
Kraepelin, Emil, 90
Kroeber, Alfred, 132
Krummel, John, 134
Kübler-Ross, Elisabeth, 228–29
Kurlansky, Mark, 318

L
Lacan, Jacques, 227
Lakoff, George, 285, 286
Lamarck, Jean-Baptiste, 40, 41, 42
Lampert, Ada, 378
Land og Synir (film), 268
Lane, Fitz Hugh, 391
Language. *See also* Metaphors
    acquisition of, 158, 286–87
    anatomical changes and, 327
    at center of experience, 342–43
    commonalities within, 114–15
    comprehension of, 272
    denotative vs. connotative, 270
    dual-reference theory of, 272, 288
    figurative, 271, 273, 285
    fluency in, 270
    human capacity for, 7
    human nature and, 287
    levels of abstraction and, 6
    perception and, 286
    structure of, 106
Language: A Cultural Tool (Everett), 286

Language in Thought and Action (Hayakawa), 6
Lao-tze, 76
Large intestine, 244
Larkin, Patty, 337
Latané, Bibb, 30–32, 254–55
Lauer, Quentin, 71
Lavoisier, Antoine, 273
Learning, stages of, 294
Leeuwenhoek, Anton van, 40, 207
Lehrer, Jonah, 184
Leibniz, Gottfried, 85
Lennon, John, 322
Leopold, Aldo, 48, 59, 230, 319, 380
Levi-Montalcini, Rita, 227–28
Lévi-Strauss, Claude, 49
Levitin, Daniel, 331
Lewes, George Henry, 304
Lewin, Kurt, 99, 132, 376
Lewin, Tamar, 316
Liberty and Freedom (Fischer), 7
Life
    classification system for, 215–16
    as drama, 219
    experiencing, 397
    imagination and, 333–34
    meaning in, 351–52
    origins of, 213
    primary purpose of, 219
Life expectancy, 218–19
Life span
    of individual organisms, 217–18
    of species, 217
Light, Andrew, 334
Lightfoot, Gordon, 337
Lincoln, Abraham, 7, 102, 174, 389
Lincoln University, 173
Lindeman, Raymond, 57

Linnaeus, Carl, 39, 284
Living the Good Life (Nearing and Nearing), 25
Locke, John, 86, 88, 97
Loeb, Jacques, 96
Loening, Ulrich, 323
Loftus, Elizabeth, 106
Lopez, Barry, 309, 379–80, 385
Lorenz, Edward, 307
Lorenz, Konrad, 157–58
Loring, Bill, 134
Lotka, Alfred, 57
Louis XIII (king of France), 42
Louv, Richard, 320
Love
    as creative force, 366
    evolution and, 378
    expressing, 379
    food and, 366–68, 369
    need for, 366, 378
    parenthood and, 378
    vulnerability and, 378
Lovelock, James, 61
Lovins, Amory and Hunter, 310
Lucas, George, 220–21, 328
Lucretius, 38
Ludwig, Carl, 88
Lungs, 243, 244
Lyell, Charles, 44, 46
Lynam, William and Crosha, 391
Lynch, Kevin, 211–12
Lytle, Mark, 294

M

Ma, Yo-Yo, 241
MacArthur, Robert, 57
Machado, Paulo, 138
Machiavelli, Niccolò, 89
MacMillan, Conway, 51–52, 53
Mailer, Norman, 309
Maines, Natalie, 364–65
Malcolm X, 25
Mallett, David, 341
Malmberg, Torsten, 138, 196–97, 211, 212, 328
Malthus, Thomas, 46
Mammals
    evolution of, 240
    longest-living, 218
Mann, Horace, 173
Marcuse, Herbert, 291
Margulis, Lynn, 61, 209
Martin, Isabella, 365
Marx, Karl, 89
Maslow, Abraham, 9, 78, 102–3, 107, 187, 249, 334, 343
Massachusetts Audubon Society, 62
Massachusetts Institute of Technology (MIT), 184
Mass extinctions, 216–17, 239, 240, 371, 386
Matisse, Henri, 329
Matson, Wallace, 356
Matthiessen, Peter, 191, 309
Max-Neef, Manfred, 147–48
May, Rollo, 77, 88, 101, 197–98, 227, 347
Maya, 199
Mayr, Ernst, 47, 62, 68, 111, 197, 347, 383
McCarter, Katherine, 144
McHarg, Ian, 116–17, 357
McIntosh, Robert, 49
McKenzie, R. D., 132

McLuhan, Marshall, 23, 283, 304
McNamara, Robert, 285
MDI Tomorrow, 313
Meadowcreek Project, 309–11, 314, 317
Meadows, Donella and Dennis, 33, 124
Meaning, 351–52
Medicine, history of, 81–82
Mehrtens, Sue, 153
Meiklejohn, Donald, 152
Meiosis, 216
Mendeleev, Dmitri, 88
Merleau-Ponty, Maurice, 288
Merwin, William Stanley, 327
Metaphors
  as abduction, 277
  complexity of, 270
  comprehension of, 272
  definition of, 270
  ecological, 278–84
  frequency of usage of, 285
  misplaced, 285
  similes vs., 271
  universality of, 277
Metera Babies' Center, 156–57
Michigan, University of, 173, 174
Microscope, invention of, 40, 207
Milgram, Stanley, 251–52, 259
Miller, Neal, 97
Million Dollar Password (television show), 260
Mills College, 173
Mind
  -body dualism, 85, 88
  depth model of, 92–94
  ecology and, 272–78

intentionality and, 100
philosophical approaches to, 86–87, 88
tabula rasa conception of, 86
Mind and Nature (Bateson), 274
Mindfulness, 334–35
Mirror neurons, 158
MIT (Massachusetts Institute of Technology), 184
Mitchell, Joni, 337
Mitochondria, 214
Mitosis, 216
Moberg, Carol, 117
Molière, 79
Monahan, Jay, 250
Monotheism, 76
Montgomery, George, 14
Moomaw, Bill, 314
Moon, formation of, 203
Moore, Michael, 337
Moore, Thomas, 334
Morgan, Christiana, 325
Morrill, Justin, 174
Morrill Act of 1862, 50, 128, 174
Moses, 76
Mount Desert Island, 202, 231, 288, 313, 348–49, 370–73, 389–95
Mount Holyoke College, 173
Moyers, Bill, 379
Mozart, Wolfgang Amadeus, 303
Muhammad, 38, 76
Muir, John, 358–59
Mumford, Lewis, 133
Murie, Adolph, 359–60
Murie, Olaus and Margaret, 359
Murray, Henry, 325
Murrow, Edward R., 336–37, 339

Muséum National d'Histoire Naturelle (Paris), 42
Museums, creation of, 42–43
Mussolini, Benito, 227
Myers, Gene, 344–45, 347
Myrdal, Gunnar, 118
Myths, 77

N

Nagy, Maria, 224
National Academy of Sciences, 384
National Museum of Natural History, 43
National parks, 358, 360, 393
National Public Radio, 336–37, 376
National Science Foundation, 59, 312
Natural history, 37–43, 48
Nature
    children's exposure to, 19, 66, 319–20
    deficit disorder, 320
    early views of, 37
    vs. nurture, 298
Nature Conservancy, 58
Nearing, Helen and Scott, 25
Neisser, Ulric, 104, 106
Nelson, Steve, 122
Nervous system, 244–45
Neurosis, 92–93, 95, 96, 102, 234
Neville, Anthony, 134
New England Environment course, 312–13, 314
Newman, John Henry, 169
Newman, Randy, 24
Newton, Isaac, 39, 273, 293
New York City, 13, 15, 360–62

Niche, concept of, 57, 278–79
Nietzche, Friedrich, 101
Nisbet, Ian, 63, 69
Nixon, Richard, 26, 63
Nordic Society for Human Ecology, 141, 143, 146
North Carolina, University of, 170
North East Environmental Studies (NEES), 311
Notre Dame, 168
Nuland, Sherwin, 229
Nuttman, Christopher, 138

O

Obama, Barack, 366
Obeng, Letitia, 123
Oberlin College, 173, 314–15
Oberlin Project, 315
Odum, Eugene, 33, 57–59, 60, 62, 63, 64, 118, 124, 279
Odum, Howard, 57, 58–59, 64, 279
Oedipus complex, 94, 234–35
Ohio State University, 30, 31–32, 177, 255
Olivier, Fernande, 192
Olmstead, Frederick Law, 361
Olson, Sigurt, 319
On Death and Dying (Kübler-Ross), 228
On Human Nature (Wilson), 64
On the Origin of Species (Darwin), 45–46, 47, 52, 75, 385
Open-mindedness, 354, 355
Operational definition, 273
Ophuls, William, 118
Origins of Human Ecology (Young), 133

Orozco, José Clemente, 329
Orr, David, 309–10, 314–15, 387
Orr, Wilson, 309
O'Shaughnessy Dam, 359
Ostrom, Elinor, 144
Otis, Elisha, 360
Oxford University, 168–69, 178
Ozeki, Ruth, 333

P

Page, George, 349
Paivio, Alan, 323
Paley, William, 40
Pammel, Louis H., 49
Pangu, 87
Pankejeff, Sergei, 234
Park, Robert E., 132
Parmenides, 37, 81
Password (television show), 260–61
Pasteur, Louis, 88
Pauling, Linus, 33, 123
Pavlov, Ivan, 95–96
Peak experiences, 9, 103, 249, 343
Peirce, C. S., 222, 277
Pennsylvania, University of, 169, 185
Perception
  Gestalt laws of, 98–99
  language and, 286
Perls, Frederick (Fritz), 100
Personality, "Big Five" model of, 345
Pesticides, 252–53
Petrarch, 39
Phanes, 87
"Phenomena," etymology of, 87
Phenomenology, 100–101, 356

Philbin, Regis, 260
Philip, Prince, 119
Phillips, Duane, 183
Piaget, Jean, 105–6, 110, 149, 158, 295, 302
Picasso, Pablo, 192–93, 194
Pickett, Steward, 69
Pinker, Steven, 106, 285–86, 287
Pirahã, 286, 287
Pixar Animation Studios, 184
Plants, oldest-living, 218
Plato, 82, 83
Pliny the Elder, 38, 207
Plotinus, 83
Plutarch, 149
Poetry, 273, 277, 327
Poincare, Henri, 307
Polanyi, Michael, 357
Pollan, Michael, 318, 354
Polunin, Nicholas, 123
Population growth, 3, 46–47, 115
Postman, Neil, 284
Postmodernism, 98, 107, 110, 354–56
Pound, Roscoe, 52–53
Powers of Ten (film), 210–11
Preiser, Wolfgang, 134, 135, 136, 146
Princeton University, 169
Priority species, 280
Process and form, 302–3
Programmed cell death (PCD), 228
Projection, 7
Prokaryotes, 214
Protogonos, 87
Provenance, 368–69
Psyche and Eros, legend of, 79–80

Psychoanalysis, 7, 54, 94–95, 101, 102, 103, 106, 233–36
Psychological contagion, 260
Psychology
American, 90–92, 99–100
behaviorism, 95–98
biology and, 345–46
cognitive, 98, 104–5, 107
conservation, 344–45, 346, 349–52
depth, 92–95
diversity of approaches within, 22, 73, 74, 75, 106–7
Eastern vs. Western, 77–78
ecology and, 54–55, 132–33, 301
etymology of, 78
evolutionary, 107, 383–84
existential, 101, 102
functionalist/structuralist controversy within, 91–92
Gestalt, 98–101, 254
growth of, 108
humanistic, 102–4, 107
interdisciplinary nature of, 299
long past of, 75–89
philosophy and, 84–87, 88, 89, 100
scientific, 89–90
social, 254
as study of human conscious experience, 73
today, 106–9
training in, 107, 108
Psychonomic Society, 107
Purdue University, 32–33
Pythagoras, 81, 199

Q
Quinn, James, 132

R
Rabineau, Lou, 137, 140, 141, 186
Ramsey, Henry, 166–67
Rapoport, Amos, 138
Rappaport, Roy, 114, 132
Rationalization, 7
Raup, Hugh, 62, 67
Reality
consciousness and, 71
predisposition to misrepresent, 381
Reich, Wilhelm, 95, 100
Reiter, Hanns, 49
Religion
death and, 222
faith and, 385–86
genes and, 298
mind/body dualism and, 85
psychological aspects of, 75–77
science and, 384–85
Renaissance, 39, 84, 360
Responsibility, 318
Ressel, Steve, 347–49, 350–52
A Reverence for Wood (Sloane), 25
Reykjavik, Iceland, 123–26, 258, 268
Rhodes, Jim, 26
Rice, Grantland, 162
Richards, Ellen Swallow, 129
Richardson, James, 391
Rivera, Diego, 329
Robinson, Gene, 365–66
Rockefeller, John D., Jr., 393
Rodin, Judith, 185

Rogers, Carl, 102, 103–4, 107, 351
Rogerson, Donald, 262–63
Romans, ancient, 38, 223
Roosevelt, Eleanor, 102, 336
Roosevelt, Theodore, 359
Rorty, Richard, 355
Rose, Charlie, 328
Rose, Dan, 134
Royal Observatory (Greenwich), 200, 201
Rubin, Jerry, 26
The Rural School (film), 13–14
Russell, Bertrand, 6
Russell, Judy, 329
Rutgers University, 169
Rychlak, Joseph, 34–35, 109–11, 120, 277, 288, 308, 323, 328, 353–54, 356, 357, 377

S

Sagan, Carl, 209
Salisbury Cathedral, 199
Sandberg, Carl, 336
Sapir, Edward, 286
Sargent, Frederick, 117, 134, 135
Sartre, Jean-Paul, 101, 351
Saunders, Carol, 344
Scenario visualization, 322
Schizocoely, 242
Schumacher, Ernst, 33, 124
Science
    analogies in, 273
    art and, 272
    day vs. night, 308
    operational definition in, 273
    paradigm shifts in, 227, 309
    religion and, 384–85

Science and the Modern World (Whitehead), 152
Scientific theory, origins of, 39
Scott, Britain, 344
The Sea Around Us (Carson), 59, 248
Sears, Paul, 60, 118
Sedgwick, Adam, 46
Seeger, Pete, 341
Self-deception, 381, 383
Self-realization, 159
Seneca, 207
Sequoia National Park, 358
Serbser, Wolfgang, 183
Serendipity, 190
The Seventh Seal (film), 219–20
Sex
    death and, 216
    Freudian view of, 236
Shakespeare, William, 79, 284, 303, 336
Shakti, 324–25
Shame, 364
Shelford, Victor, 54, 58, 282
Shepard, Paul, 60, 113, 283, 344, 355
Shiva, 325
Sierra Club, 358, 359
Sierra National Forest, 358–59
Significant life experiences, 9, 316–21
Silent Spring (Carson), 59–60, 63, 230, 252
Similes, 271
Simplicity, voluntary, 25
Six degrees of separation, 252
Skidmore, Owings and Merrill, 179

Skin, 245
Skinner, B. F., 97, 104, 106, 286–87
Skissernas Museum, 328–29
Slatyer, Ralph, 69
Sloane, Eric, 25
Sloane, Hans, 42
Small intestine, 243–44
Smell, sense of, 246
Smetana, Bed ich, 303
Smith, Adam, 89, 273
Smithsonian Institution, 43, 237
Snow, C. P., 272, 274
Social psychology, 254
Society for Human Ecology (SHE), 4–5, 117, 133–44, 146, 148, 344, 346
Sociology, 132, 273
Socrates, 150
Somes, Abraham, 391
Soulé, Michael, 356
Space
   definition of, 206
   dimensions of, 196–97, 207
   interconnection of time and, 196–97
   personal, 249
   sense of, 209–12
Species
   classification of, 39–40, 41, 43
   competition between, 57
   endangered, 60, 386
   extinct, 216–17, 386
   flagship, 279
   indicator, 280
   invasive, 57
   keystone, 279–80
   life span of, 217
   number of, 36
   oldest extant, 217
   priority, 280
   trigger, 280
   umbrella, 280
Spence, Kenneth, 97
Spinoza, Benedict, 85
Spivey, Nigel, 327–28
Springer, Hugh, 119
Stanford University, 176
Stanton, Elizabeth Cady, 222
Starthrowing, 350
Star Wars trilogy, 220–21, 328
Steel, Eric, 223
Steinberg, Volker, 183, 184
Steps to an Ecology of Mind (Bateson), 274, 294
Stevens, Anthony, 156–57, 236, 347, 387
Steward, Julian, 132
Stewardship, 280–81
Stewart, Philip, 138, 289
Still Life (film), 204, 218
Stoermer, Eugene, 70
Stonehenge, 199, 205
Stookey, Paul, 341
Storytelling, 326
Straus, Donald B., 139
Streep, Meryl, 241
Strong, Maurice, 124
Students for a Democratic Society (SDS), 26
Stumpf, Carl, 98, 100
Suburbia, growth of, 12–13
Succession, 53–54, 59, 63
Suicide, 223
Superego, 93–94

Superorganicism, 55–56
Surowiecki, James, 260
Suzuki, D. T., 222
Suzuki, Shosuke, 67
Swazey, Judith, 131, 137
Sykes, Kathy, 165
Syllogisms, 276–77
Symbiosis, 278

T

Tai, Bonnie, 333
Tanner, Thomas, 9, 319
Tansley, Arthur George, 54–56, 58, 62, 279
Taoism, 76
Tappan, Henry Philip, 173
Taste, sense of, 246
Taylor, Mark, 185
Taylor, Stuart, 29, 30
Taylor-Wood, Sam, 204, 218
Tchaikovsky, Pyotr, 303
Teachers
    dead, 165–66
    influence of, 155–56
    search for, 159
Technology, 284
Telescope, invention of, 207–8
Tengström, Emin, 147, 148, 182
Tennyson, Alfred, 233
10,000 Hour Rule, 330–31
Terroir, 368
Texas, University of, 21, 248
Thales of Miletus, 37
Thematic Apperception Test (TAT), 325
Theodorson, George, 132
Theophrastus, 37
"Thing," etymology of, 258

This I Believe (radio show and book), 336–37
Thomas, Lewis, 36
Thoreau, Henry David, 102, 173, 264, 322, 389
Thorndike, Edward, 91, 96, 99
Tianjin Eco-City project, 363
Tillich, Paul, 77
Time
    concept of, 198
    interconnection of space and, 196–97
    local, 200–201, 202
    measuring, 198–202, 394–95
    sense of, 202–6
    standard, 201
    transcending, 197–98
    zones, 201
Tipping behavior, 255
Tipping point, 307
Titchener, Edward B., 78, 90, 91
Tocqueville, Alexis de, 89
Tolba, Mostafa, 123
Tolstoy, Leo, 222, 304
Totalization, 285
Toynbee, Arnold, 336
Treviranus, Gottfried Reinhold, 40
Trigger species, 280
Trivers, Robert, 73–74, 75, 354, 381–83
Trungpa, Chögyam, 159
Truth
    personal, 364–66
    postmodern view of, 355
Tulane University, 176
Turner, Frederick Jackson, 175
Twine Ball Museum, 187–88

U

UDC. *See* District of Columbia, University of
Ulanov, Ann, 88, 292, 379
Umbrella species, 280
Unconscious
    collective, 94, 236
    role of, 7, 92–93
Understanding Figurative Language (Glucksberg), 288
Underwood, Richard, 283
UNESCO, 116, 141, 363
Ungar, Jay, 303
United Farm Workers, 25
United Nations, 177–78
United States Air Force Academy, 179–80
United States Military Academy (West Point), 172, 179
Universities. *See* Higher education
Urbanization
    beginning of, 115
    growth of, 362–63
    human ecology and, 360–63

V

Valadez, Joseph, 134
Vanderbilt University, 176, 393
Vann, Anthony, 138
Vasalius, Andreas, 82
Vaux, Calvert, 361
Vayda, Andrew, 132, 138
Vega, Suzanne, 309
Vermont Municipal and Regional Planning and Development Act (Act 200), 312
Vietnam War, 26, 30, 285
Virginia, University of, 170–71, 173, 179
Vision, 245
Visvader, John, 84, 114, 142, 143, 318, 338
Volta, Alessandro, 40
Volterra, Vito, 57
Vulnerability, 364, 365, 378

W

Waddington, Conrad, 117
Wade, Nicholas, 354
Walcott, Charles, 237
Wallace, Alfred Russel, 45, 46, 358
Walls, effects of, 296–99
Walpole, Horace, 190
Walter, Marie-Therese, 192
Wang, Rusong, 141–42, 143, 363
Ward, Barbara, 117
Ward, Harold, 311
Warming, Eugenius, 49–50, 52–53
Warren, Robert Penn, 221
Washburn, Margaret, 107
Washington, George, 162
Watson, John Broadus, 96, 107
Watts, Alan, 386
Wayne, Peter, 131
Weber-Fechner law, 90
Weinberg, Adam, 328
Weizsäcker, Ernst, 362
Wells, H. G., 112, 133
Wells Cathedral, 199
Werner, Michael, 355
Wertheimer, Max, 78, 98
West Point, 172, 179
Wheeler, John Archibald, 196
White, Lynn, Jr., 119

Whitehead, Alfred North, 133, 150, 151, 285, 287, 291–92, 293–95
Whitman, Walt, 277
Whorf, Benjamin Lee, 286
Wilberforce University, 173
Wilderness Act of 1964, 60
William and Mary, College of, 169
William of Ockham, 39, 86
Williams, John, 220
Wilson, E. O., 64, 189, 208, 232, 289, 298–99, 320, 354, 383, 386, 387
Wilson, Woodrow, 359
Winning His Way (Coffin), 162–63
Wolanski, Napoleon, 145
Women's movement, 7–8
Wonder, 387
Wood, Karen, 262–63
World War II, 12, 14, 176, 177, 393
World Wildlife Fund (WWF), 280
Worster, Donald, 69, 112, 314
Worthington, E. Barton, 59, 119
Wright, Herbert, 132

Wright, Robert, 384
Wundt, Wilhelm, 78, 89–90, 98

Y

Yale University, 169, 172–73, 174
Yalom, Irvin, 102
Yankovic, Weird Al, 188
Yellowstone National Park, 358
"Yes and" approaches, 369–70
Yoga, 193, 194
Yosemite National Park, 358–59
Young, Gerald, 114, 131, 133–34, 302
Young, Robert K., 156

Z

Zacharias, Jerrold, 184
Zeigarnik, Bluma, 99, 376
Zeigarnik Effect, 376
Zeno, 81
Zoroastrianism, 76

About the Author

Courtesy of College of the Atlantic

RICHARD J. BORDEN holds the Rachel Carson Chair in Human Ecology at College of the Atlantic in Bar Harbor, Maine—where he teaches psychology, community planning, and the history and philosophy of human ecology. Borden served as COA's academic dean for twenty years. Before COA, he was on the faculty at Purdue University and The Ohio State University. He is past president and former executive director of the Society for Human Ecology, as well as a founding member of the human ecology section of the Ecological Society of America. His educational background includes a BA from the University of Texas; an MA and a PhD in psychology from Kent State University; and a University Postdoctoral Fellowship in animal behavior and ecology at Ohio State. He has coauthored and edited several books and published more than seventy research reports, journal articles, and essays. He has served as a USIA academic specialist in the area of human ecology and an interdisciplinary program consultant in China, Russia, Europe, and North and South America. In addition to his passion for networking human ecology worldwide, Borden also enjoys the domestic pleasures of cooking, carpentry, traditional music, and sailing.

North Atlantic Books
Berkeley, California

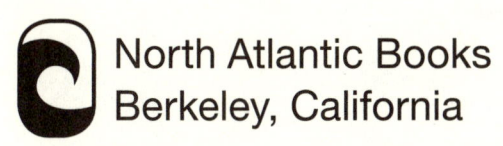

Personal, spiritual, and planetary transformation

North Atlantic Books, a nonprofit publisher established in 1974, is dedicated to fostering community, education, and constructive dialogue. NABCommunities.com is a meeting place for an ever-growing membership of readers and authors to engage in the discussion of books and topics from North Atlantic's core publishing categories.

NAB Communities offer interactive social networks in these genres:
- **NOURISH:** Raw Foods, Healthy Eating and Nutrition, All-Natural Recipes
- **WELLNESS:** Holistic Health, Bodywork, Healing Therapies
- **WISDOM:** New Consciousness, Spirituality, Self-Improvement
- **CULTURE:** Literary Arts, Social Sciences, Lifestyle
- **BLUE SNAKE:** Martial Arts History, Fighting Philosophy, Technique

Your free membership gives you access to:
- Advance notice about new titles and exclusive giveaways
- Podcasts, webinars, and events
- Discussion forums
- Polls, quizzes, and more!

Go to www.NABCommunities.com and join today.